SURRY COUNTY, VIRGINIA, WILLS, ESTATE ACCOUNTS AND INVENTORIES 1730-1800

by

Lyndon H. Hart, III

Please direct all correspondence and orders to:

www.southernhistoricalpress.com
or
SOUTHERN HISTORICAL PRESS, Inc.
PO BOX 1267
375 West Broad Street
Greenville, SC   29601
southernhistoricalpress@gmail.com

ISBN #0-89308-325-9

Printed in the United States of America

SURRY COUNTY

Surry County was formed in 1652 from the portion of James City County south of James River. It ran from the river to the North Carolina border and was bounded on the southeast by Isle of Wight County and on the northwest by Charles City County (after 1703 Prince George). In 1723 the southern portion was cut off to form a part of Brunswick County (for which new courts were not set up at the time) and additional Surry land was added to Brunswick in 1732 when the courts of that county began operation. The middle portion of original Surry County was formed into Sussex County in 1753 and Surry then attained its present boundaries.

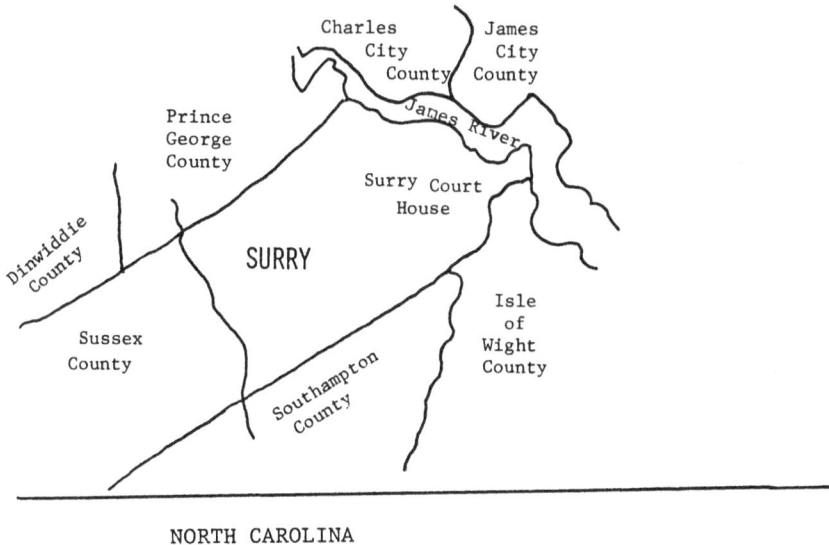

NORTH CAROLINA

Page 1005: JOHN WHITE. Will. Date: 8 Dec. 1729. Rec.: 18 Feb. 1729. Thomas Lawrence, Executor. Son-in-law: Thomas Lawrence. Cousin: Sarah Heys. Grandsons: William Morris and John Lawrence. Granddaughter: Elizabeath Lawrence. Witnesses: Lawrence House, William Renn and Edward Wingfield.

Page 1008: HOWELL EDMUNDS. Inventory. Date: ---. Rec.: 18 Feb. 1729. Thomas Edmunds, Executor. Legacies to: Howell, Nicholas, Elizabeth, Anne Edmunds and Sarah Jones.

Page 1015: CURTIS LAND of Surry. Will. Date: 15 Dec. 1729. Rec.: 18 Mar. 1729. Mary Land, Executrix. Sons: Curtis, Thomas, William, John and Robert. Daughter: Rebeckah. Wife: Mary. Witnesses: Richard Avery and Richard Parker.

Page 1020: THOMAS THROWER. Will. Date: 14 Nov. 1729. Rec.: 15 Apr. 1730. Mary and Thomas Thrower, Executors. Son: Thomas. Daughters: Elizabeth, Hester and Mary. Wife: Mary. Witnesses: John Curtis, William Harper and John Freeman, Jr. Mentions: land in Prince George County.

Page 1024: NICHOLAS BREWER. Inventory. Date: 15 Mar. 1729/30. Rec.: 15 Apr. 1730. John Davis, Administrator. Richard Pace, Charles and Isaac House, Appraisers.

Page 6:   MATHEW STURDIVANT. Account Current. Date Ordered: 18 Mar.
           1729. Rec.: 15 Apr. 1730. Hollum Sturdivant returned.
           Richard Blunt and Christopher Tatum, Auditors.

Page 6:   ROBERT KATE. Inventory. Date Ordered: 18 Feb. 1729. Rec.:
           15 Apr. 1730. Returned by Ann Kate. Christopher Tatum,
           William Tomlosson and Edward Davis, Appraisers.

Page 7:   ANN FLOOD. Inventory. Date: 10 Apr. 1730. Rec.: 15 Apr.
           1730. Thomas Colyer, Executor.

Page 14:   CHARLES BRIGGS. Will. Date: _ July 1729. Rec.: 20 May
           1730. Howell Briggs, Executor. Sons: George and Howell.
           Daughters: Sarah Nicholson, wife of Joshua Nicholson; and
           Frances Rose. Grandchildren: Henry Vaughn (not 21), Eliza-
           beth Vaughn (not 18), Elizabeth Nicholson. Mentions: land
           in Isle of Wight County. (page torn). Witnesses: --- Del-
           oney, Thomas and Howell Edmunds. Codicil: Date: 20 Nov.
           1729. Witnesses: Joel Barker, William Thomas and W. Rose.

Page 20:   THOMAS THROWER. Inventory. Date: (page torn). Rec.: 19 Aug.
           1730.

Page 21:   CURTIS LAND. Inventory. Date: 12 June 1730. Rec.: 19
           Aug. 1730. Mary Land, Executrix.

Page 40:   ISAAC HALL of Southwark Parish, Surry. Will. Date: 2 Dec.
           1728. Rec.: 19 Aug. 1730. Judith Hall, Executrix. Sons:
           Lewis, George and William. Wife: Judith. Mentions: child-
           ren. (page torn). Witnesses: John Spaine, William -----,
           and Peter Green.

Page 41:   NICHOLAS DAVICE. Will. Date: 1728/9. Rec.: (torn). Son:
           William. Daughters: Mary and Elizabeth. Wife: Elizabeth.
           Mentions: John Davice, no relation stated, to receive an
           equal share with daughters. Witnesses: Edward Bailey and
           John Simmons, Jr.

Page 51:   ISAAC HALL. Inventory. Date: -----. Rec.: - Sept. 1730.
           Judith Hall, Executrix. (torn). Henry Freeman and William
           Richesson, Appraisers.

Page 52:   JOHN THROWER. Inventory. Date: 7 Sept. 1730. Rec.: 16
           Sept. 1730. Returned by Ann Thrower. William Parham, John
           Jackson and William Parham, Jr., Appraisers.

Page 53:   NICHOLAS DAVIS. Inventory. Date: 11 Sept. 1730. Rec.:
           16 Sept. 1730. Elizabeth Davis, Executrix. Jos'a Nichol-
           son, John Collyer and Richard Lewis, Appraisers.

Page 58:   CHARLES BRIGGS. Inventory. Date: -----. Rec.: 21 Oct'r.
           1730. Howell Briggs, Executor.

Page 60:   ELIZABETH WARREN. Will. Date: 21 Aug. 1724. Rec.: 21
           Oct. 1730. Robert Warren, Executor. Sons: John, Robert,
           William and Joseph. Grandchildren: Mary and Thomas Warren,
           and James Davis. Witnesses: Michael Harris, Allen Warren
           and Catherine Harris.

Page 63:   ROBERT LITTLEBOY of Surry. Will. Date: 6 Feb. 1720/21.
           Rec.: 21 Oct. 1730. Elizabeth Littleboy, Executrix. God-
           son: Edward Matthews. Wife: Elizabeth.

Page 67:   ROBERT LITTLEBOY. Inventory. Date: -----. Rec.: 18 Nov.
           1730. Elizabeth Littleboy, Executrix.

Page 67:   JOHN THROWER. A/C. Date: --. Rec: 18 Nov. 1730. (torn).

Page 69:   ELIZABETH WARREN. Inventory. Date: 9 Jan. 1730. Rec.:
             30 Jan. 1730. Returned by Robert Warren, Executor. (torn).

Page 70:   ------ FLOOD. Account Current. Date: ----. Rec.: 20 Jan.
             1730. Returned by ---- Blackburn. (torn). Gregory Rawlings
             and Thomas Edmunds, Auditors.

Page 70:   GEORGE EZEL of Southwark Parish, Surry. Will. Date: 8 Aug.
             1730. Rec.: 20 Jan. 1730. Rebeccah Ezel and William ---,
             Executors. Sons: George, William, John and Edmond. Daugh-
             ter: Mary Ezell. Wife: Rebeccah. Mentions: rest of the
             children. (torn). Witnesses: Thomas Cock, Jeremiah Ellis,
             Jr. and William Tharp.

Page 74:   SAMUELL FRENCH. Inventory. Date: 27 Oct. 1730. Rec.: 20
             Jan. 1730. Richard Lewis, Administrator. Jos'a Nicholson,
             Harry Floyd and Charles Lucas, Appraisers.

Page 75:   ROBERT MAGEE. Inventory. Date: 1730. Rec.: 20 Jan.1730.
             Henry Harrison, Administrator. Richard Parker, Thomas Pet-
             ers and Amos Tims, Appraisers. (torn).

Page 75:   JOHN WHITE. Inventory. Date: ----. Rec.: ----. Returned
             by Thomas ----. (torn).

Page 85:   GEORGE EZELL. Inventory. Date: ----. Rec.: 17 Mar. 1730.
             Rebecka Ezell and William ----, Executors. (torn). William
             Short, William Harris and Richard Bullo--.

Page 86:   THOMAS HOLT. Will. Date: 1 Nov. ---. Rec.: 17 Mar. 1730.
             Mary Holt, Executrix. Daughters: Elizabeth Cock, wife of
             Mr. Nicholas Cock; Mary, wife of William Hansford; Kather-
             ine, wife of Mr. Thomas Cock; Martha, wife of Mr. John New-
             som; Lucy Holt. Sons: Thomas, Henry and James. Grand-
             daughter: Martha Hansford. Wife: Mary. Witnesses: Timo-
             thy Tharp, Charles Barham and Samson Wilson.

Page 89:   HENRY GALLER. Inventory. Date: ----. Rec.: ----. (torn).
             William Richardson and Henry Freeman, Appraisers.

Page 92:   WILLIAM JONES. Inventory. Date: 13 Apr. 1731. Rec.: --
             Apr. ---. Elizabeth Jones, Administratrix. (torn). Jos'a
             Nicolson, Richard Lewis and Charles ----, Appraisers.

Page 92:   ROBERT WHITEHEAD. Inventory. Date: ----. Rec.: 21 April
             1731. Elizabeth Whitehead, Administratrix. John Threeweet,
             Sloman Wynne and Jollum Sturdivant, Appraisers.

Page 105:   THOMAS SISSON of Surry. Will. Date: 18 Dec. 1730. Rec.:
             16 June 1731. -----, Ex. Sons: Thomas and Stephen. Daugh-
             ters: Elizabeth, Ann, Isabel and Mary Sisson. Friends:
             John Reigns, John Denton and Peter Simmons. Son: William.
             Mentions: land in Brunswick County. (torn). Witnesses:
             John Raines, John Denton and Peter Simmons.

Page 108:   ROBERT WHITEHEAD. Account Current. Date: ----. Rec.: 16
             June 1731. Elizabeth Whitehead, Administratrix. William
             Rookings and John Chapman, Auditors.

Page 112:   ELIZABETH HEATH of Surry. Will. Date: 10 May 1729. Rec.:
             16 June 1731. Benjamin Jones, Executor. (torn). Legatees:
             Thomas Jones of Surry; Elizabeth ----, widow; John Avery.
             Daughter: Dinah Heath. Cousin: Benjamin Jones. Mentions:
             Prince George County. Witnesses: John Hammersley, Richard
             Jones and John Jones.

Page 119:   NATHANELL MUNGER. Will. Date: 26 May 1731. Rec.: 21 Jul.
             1731. Will Drew, Executor. Legatees: Mary Benitt, Mary
             Roberson and Will Drew. Godchildren: Children (2) of Will

3

(Page 119-MUNGER cont'd.): Cogings, child of Newitt Edwards, and child
of Will Stanley. Mentions: Prissilla Harrison, daughter
of Will Drew. Witness: William Coging.

Page 122:   WILLIAM FLAKE. Account Current. Date: ----. Rec.: (torn)
              --- ----ms, Adm. Jos'a Nicolson and Howell Briggs, Auditors.

Page 123:   THOMAS SISSON. Inventory. Date: 14 Aug. 1731. Rec.:---
              (torn). Thomas Sisson, Executor. William Martin, Adam
              Tapley and ---- Raines, Appraisers.

Page 128:   JOHN BAMER of Surry. Will. Date: 31 Mar. 1731. Rec.: --
              (torn). Wife: Anne. Sons: William, John (not 21).
              Daughters: Hannah, Mary Bamer (not 20). Friend: John Chap-
              man. Witnesses: George peta---, Tho---.

Page 134:   ELIZABETH HEATH. Inventory. Date: ----. Rec.: 20 Oct'r.
              1731. Benjamin Jones, Executor. William Short, Mr. Will-
              iam Short, Jr. and Mr. William Harris, Appraisers.

Page 135:   JOHN BAMER. Inventory. Date: 18 Aug. 1731, ordered.Rec.:
              20 Oct. 1731. Ann Bamer returns. William Edwards, Samuel
              Thompson and William Marriott, Appraisers.

Page 135:   THOMAS GOODWYN of Southwark Parish, Surry. Will. Date: 7
              Feb. 1730. Rec.: 20 Oct. 1731. John Goodwin, Executor.
              Sons: Francis, William (not 19); John. Wife: Mary.
              Daughter: Pennellopy Taylor. Witnesses: William Shands,
              Charles Gee and Mazareth Shands.

Page 137:   SAMUEL CORNWELL ye Elder. Account Current. Date: ----.
              Rec.: 20 Oct. 1731. Executor of Samuel Cornwell, Jr. Jo-
              seph Allen and ---- Delony, Auditors.

Page 137:   SAMUEL CORNWELL the Younger. Account Current. Date: 1731.
              Rec.: 20 Oct. 1731. Samuel Sebrell and Jacob Cornwell,
              Executors.

Page 138:   WILLIAM RAY. Will. Date: 1 June 1731. Rec.: 20 Oct'r.
              1731. William Ray, Executor. (torn). Eldest son: William.
              Wife: ----. Brother-in-law: William Pittman. Witnesses:
              Howell Briggs, William Clary and Richard Parker.

Page 138:   RICHARD SHOCKYE. Inventory. Date ordered: 18 Aug. 1731.
              Rec.: 20 Oct. 1731. Alice Shockey, Administratrix. Thomas
              Washington, Sampson Lanier and John Justice, Appraisers.

Page 139:   Capt. THOMAS HOLT. Inventory. Date: 6 Apr. 1731. Rec.:
              20 Oct. 1731. Mary Holt, Executrix. William Gray, Chris-
              topher Clinch and Thomas Taylor, Appraisers.

Page 144:   NATHANIEL MUNGER. Inventory. Date: 1731. Rec.: 17 Nov.
              1731. William Drew, Executor. Francis Little, John Tooke
              and William Coging, Appraisers.

Page 144:   NATHANIEL MUNGER. Account Current. Date: 1730. Rec.: 17
              Nov. 1731. Howell Briggs and Richard Blow, Auditors.

Page 145:   THOMAS SISSON. Add. Inventory. Date: ----. Rec.: 17 Nov.
              1731. Thomas Sisson, Executor. William Maclin, Adam Tap-
              ley and John Denton, Appraisers.

Page 149:   WILLIAM THARP. Account Current. Date: 1731. Rec.: 17
              Nov. 1731. Thomas and Mary Thornton, Administrators.
              Jos'a Nicholson and Robert Jones, Auditors.

Page 150:   WILLIAM (W)RAY. Inventory. Date ordered: 20 Oct. 1731. Rec:
              19 Jan. 1731. William Wray, Executor. John Deberry, Nich-
              olas Proter and Roge Williams, Appraisers.

4

Page 151: JOHN RAINES of Surry. Will. Date: 18 Aug. 1731. Rec.: 19 Jan. 1731. Hannah Raines, Executrix. Wife: Hannah. Child in Esse. Legacies: Richard Raines, son of Nathaniel. Mentions: land in Brunswick County. Witnesses: James Maclin, John Denton, Edmond Denton and John Maclin.

Page 151: THOMAS GOODWYNE. Inventory. Date: 20 Nov. 1731. Rec.: 19 Jan. 1731. John Goodwyn, Executor. Thomas Taylor, Charles Gee and Thomas Tomlinson, Appraisers.

Page 161: JAMES VAUGHAN of Surry. Will. Date: 8 Dec. 1730. Rec.: 16 Feb. 1731. William Seward, Executor. Legatee: Mrs. Hannah Clinch. Daughter-in-law: Lucy Morland. Friends: James Ransom, Mrs. Mary Holt, widow of Capt. Thomas Holt, and Mr. William Seward. Witnesses: John Glover and Arthur Taylor.

Page 164: WILLIAM WYCH. Account Current. Date: ----. Rec.: 16 Feb. 1731. Richard Parker, Jr., surviving husband of Judith Parker, Executor. James Washington and James Gee, Auditors.

Page 168: JOHN WARREN. Inventory. Date: 9 Mar. 1731. Rec.: 15 Mar. 1731. Sarah Warren, Administratrix. Michael Harris, William Smith and Robert Gray, Appraisers.

Page 172: JOHN RAINES. Inventory. Date: ----. Rec.: 15 Mar. 1731. Hannah Raines, Executrix.

Page 172: THOMAS GOODIN. Inventory. Date: ----. Rec.: 15 March 1731. William Jones, Administrator. Richard Woodroof, John Hally and Philip Bayley, Appraisers.

Page 179: JAMES VAUGHAN. Inventory. Date: 18 Mar. 1731/32. Rec.: 19 Apr. 1732. William Seward, Executor. Roger Delk, Thomas Taylor and Thomas Edwards, Appraisers.

Page 183: JOHN CARGILL of Southwark Parish, Surry. Will. Date: Jan. 4, 1731/32. Rec.: 19 Apr. 1732. John Cargill, Executor. Wife: (not named). Son: John. Brother: David. Sister: 7 (not named). Witnesses: William Phillips, Robert Wager and John Jarrat.

Page 191: JOHN HANCOCK of Lawnes Creek Parish, Surry. Will. 24 Nov. 1731. Rec.: 17 May 1732. Jean Hancock, Executrix. Wife: Jane (ex.). Sons: Joseph, and John. Daughters: Duejates, Elizabeth and Martha Hancock. Witnesses: John Bittle, John Taillor and John Price.

Page 195: WILLIAM HOWELL of Surry. Will. Date: 28 Mar. 1732. Rec.: 17 May 1732. Mary Howell, Executrix. Children: Joannah, Elizabeth (not of age). Child in esse. Witnesses: William Browne, Jr., Edmund Howell, Eavan Thomas and John Barnes.

Page 196: JOHN WILLIAMSON of Southwark Parish, Surry. Will. Date: 30 Jan. 1731. Rec.: 17 May 1732. Cuthbert Williamson, and Robert Green, Executors. Daughters: Elizabeth, wife of Hollum Sturdivant; Susanna Rottenbury, wife of John; Edith Williamson; Hannah, wife of Richard Fox. Son: Cuthbert (not 21). Grand-daughter: Sarah. Brother: Cuthbert. Witnesses: Judith Harper and Edward Farrington.

Page 203: POLLARD DENTON of Surry. Will. Date: 10 Apr. 1727. Rec.: 19 July 1732. Elizabeth Denton, Executrix. Wife: Elizabeth. Daughters: Elizabeth, Francis. Witnesses: William Hulme, Christopher Tatum and Henry Tatum.

Page 203: JOHN CARGILL. Inventory. Date: 21 June 1732. Rec.: 19 July 1732. John Cargill, Executor.

5

Page 205:   THOMAS JUDKINS. Will. Date: 26 Jan. 1731/32. Rec.: July 19, 1732. Charles Judkins, Executor. Brothers: William, James and Charles. Witnesses: Howell Briggs, John Owen & Thomas Alsobrook.

Page 206:   THOMAS KING. Will. Date: 23 Aug. 1731. Rec.: 19 July 1732. Deborah King, Executrix. Sons: John, Joseph, William, James and Benjamin; Thomas (not 20). Daughters: Elizabeth, Mary and Jane. Wife: Deborah. Witnesses: William Baldwin, William Newsom and Phil(1)is Newsom.

Page 212:   JAMES VAUGHN. Account Current. Date: ----. Rec.: 16 Aug. 1732. William Seward, Executor. Mentions: legacies to executor, Lucy Morland and Hannah Clinch. Henry Browne and William Edwards, Auditors.

Page 219:   THOMAS KING. Inventory. Date: 9 Aug. 1732. Rec.: 16 Aug. 1732. Deborah King, Executrix.

Page 222:   JOHN HANCOCK. Inventory. Date: 9 Aug. 1732. Rec.: 16 Aug. 1732. Jean Hancock, Executrix.

Page 230:   POLLARD DENTON. Inventory. Date: ----. Rec.: -----. Elizabeth Denton, Executrix.

Page 230:   THOMAS JUDKINS. Inventory. Date: ----. Rec.: 20 Sept. 1732. Charles Judkins, Executor. Mentions: legacies to James, William and Charles Judkins.

Page 230:   ELIZABETH LITTELLBOY of Lyons (Lawnes) Creek Parish, Surry. Will. Date: 2 Dec. 1731. Rec.: (torn). 1732. Edward Maithes, Executor. Legatee: Edward Maithes, son of ----. Witnesses: ---- Little and Henry Atkerson.

Page 232:   Mr. WILLIAM COCKE. Inventory. Date: 18 Sept. 1732. Rec.: 20 Sept. 1732.

Page 233:   ELIZABETH LITTELLBOY. Inventory. Date: 10 Oct. 1732. Rec.: ----. Edward Mathis, Executor.

Page 234:   WILLIAM HOWELL. Inventory. Date: ----. Rec.: 18 Oct. 1732. Mary Howell, Executrix. Robert Watkins, Henry Watkins and Charles White, Appraisers.

Page 239:   JOSEPH HOLLIMAN. Account Current. Date: ----. Rec.: 18 Oct. 1732. Robert Wesson and Unity Wesson, formerly Holliman, Administrators. James Washington and Edward Bailey, Auditors.

Page 240:   WILLIAM THOMPSON of Surry. Will. Date: 20 Dec. 1731. Rec.: 18 Oct. 1732. Sons: James and John. Daughters: (illegible), Hannah Thompson. Wife: Martha. Witnesses: Jane Riggan, Mary Regan and Mary Martin.

Page 241:   EDWARD BROWN(E). Will. Date: (none). Rec.: 15 Nov. 1732. Mary Brown, Executrix. Wife: Mary. Witnesses: Thomas Goltne (Gwaltney), and Robert Lancaster.

Page 246:   JOHN COLLIER of Surry. Will. Date: 3 July 1732. Rec.: 15 Nov. 1732. Moses Jo(h)nson and Thomas Collier, Executors. Daughters: Mary and Grace. Sons: John, Thomas, Benjamin, Henery; William and Charles (not 20). Witnesses: William Hux, Solomon Hawkins and Charles Lucas.

Page 247:   JOHN HICKS. Will. Date: 25 Mar. 1721. Rec.: 15 Nov.'r. 1732. Isodenias Christian Hicks, Executrix. Grandson: William Hicks, son of William. Son: Joseph. Daughter: Cristiana. Wife: Isodenias Christian. Witnesses: William Cruse, James Massingell and Thomas Burgiss.

Page 248:   JOHN COLLIER. Inventory. Date: (none). Rec.: 20 Dec.
            1732. Moses Johnson and Thomas Collier, Executors.

Page 249:   ---- PENNINGTON. Account Current. Date: ----. Rec.: 20
            Dec. 1732. John New and Tabitha New, Executors.

Page 249:   WILLIAM TOMLINSON. Will. Date: - Dec. 1730. Rec : 20 Dec.
            1732 Richard Tomlinson, Executor. Mentions: Mary Oliver,
            William Burnwell, John Tomlinson, Petter Brooks (mulatto,
            not 21). Brother: Richard. Witnesses: Nicholas Part-
            ridge, Christopher Tatem and John Mason.

Page 253:   JOHN HIX. Inventory Date: 19 Dec. 1732. Rec.: 17 Jan.
            1732. Isodenia Christian Hix, Executrix.

Page 257:   WILLIAM GWALTNEY. Will. Date: - Mar. 1728. Rec.: 21 Mar.
            1732. Mar--(torn) Gwaltney, Ex. Daughters: Ruth, wife
            of Robert Petaway: Mary and Marthew. Son: John. Grandson:
            Thomas; Edward Boykin. Witnesses: Thomas Halleman, John
            Brown and -----.

Page 262:   WILLIAM THOMPSON. Inventory. Date: 15 Nov. 1732.   Rec.:
            21 Mar. 1732. Martha Thompson, Executrix.

Page 263:   MARY HARRISSON of Surry. Will. Date: 25 Feb. 1732. Rec.:
            21 Mar. 1732. Armistead Churchill and John Cargill, Exe-
            cutors. Daughters: Hannah Churchill, Elizabeth Cargill,
            Sarah Bradby; Jane and Mary Harrison. Son: Benjamin Har-
            rison, Gent. Friends: James Bradby and Nathaniel Harrison.
            Witnesses: Lewis Delony and Thomas Brown and ----.

Page 264:   JAMES PORCH of Southwark Parish, Surry. Will. Date: Feb.
            6, 1732/33. Rec.: 21 Mar. 1732. Henry Porch, Executor.
            Sons: Henry and James. Wife: Margery. Grandson: Alexan-
            der Hay. Mentions: William Scoggen. Witnesses: John Payn-
            ter, William Bridgers and Alexander Hay.

Page 267:   WILLIAM BLACKBURN of Surry. Will. Date: 5 Jan.1732. Rec:
            21 Mar. 1732. Joseph Blackburn, Executor. (torn) Legatees;
            ---'s son, Wm. Brother: Joseph. Sister: Mary Brown.
            Witnesses: William Saunders, William Drudge and Francis
            Smith.

Page 268:   NATHANIEL MALLONE of Southwark Parish, Surry. Will. Date:
            17 Feb. ---. Rec.: 21 Mar. 1732. Sons: Nathaniel, Dru-
            ry, Thomas and Daniell. Son-in-law: Joseph Harper. Dau.:
            Amey. Mentions: land in Prince George County. Witnesses:
            Robert Wynne, William Harper and John Gillion, Jr. Nath-
            aniel Mallone, Executor.

Page 270:   JOHN WILLIAMSON. Inventory. Date: ----. Rec.: 21 Mar.
            1732. Robert Green and Curthburth Williamson, Executors.

Page 282:   MARY FLOOD of Southwark Parish, Surry. Will. Date: 20
            Feb. 1724/25. Rec.: 18 Apr. 1733. Anne Cocke, surviving
            Executrix. Brother: William. Sister: Anne Cocke. Both
            legatees named as Executors. Witnesses: Richard Price
            and William Saunders.

Page 283:   PRISCILLA THOMAS of Surry. Will. Date: 15 Mar. 1732.
            Rec.: 18 Apr. 1733. William Blunt, Executor. Sons: Will-
            iam, Henry, Benjamin Blunt; Henry Thomas. Witnesses:
            Thomas Edmunds and Evin Thomas.

Page 284:   WILLIAM GEORGE. Account Current. Date: ----. Rec.: 18
            Apr. 1733. William Batts, who married Sarah George, Admin-
            istrator presents.

Page 284:   ELIZABETH PARTIN. Inventory. Date: 22 Jan. 1732/33.Rec.:

7

(Page 284 - PARTIN cont'd.): 18 Apr. 1733. Robert Partin, Administrator. William Rookings, Solomon Harrison and Thomas Allstin, Appraisers.

Page 285: THOMAS SIMMONS of Lyons (Lawnes) Creek Parish, Surry. Will. Date: 7 Feb. 1725/26. Rec.: 18 Apr. 1733. Joseph Simmons, Executor. Sons: Thomas, Joseph and Edward. Wife: Sarah. Daughter: Elizabeth Simmons. Witnesses: Bernard Sykes, Edward Prince and Edward Prince, Jr.

Page 288: JAMES POR(T)CH. Inventory. Date ordered: 21 Mar. 1732. Rec.: 16 May 1733. Henry Porch, Executor. Christopher Tatum, Henry Mechum and John Weaver, Appraisers.

Page 291: WILLIAM GAULTNEY. Inventory. Date: 5 May 1733. Rec.: 16 May 1733. Martha Gualtney, Executrix.

Page 296: THOMAS SIMMONS. Inventory. Date: 8 May 1733. Rec.: 16 May 1733. Joseph Simmons, Executor. James Jones, William Moss and John Moss, Appraisers.

Page 302: WILLIAM SIMMONS of Surry, Schoolmaster. Will. Date: 22 Sept. 1732. Rec.: 20 June 1733. Wife: Elizabeth. Daughter: Hannah Chapman Simmons. Son: Stephen. Kinsman: Augustin Hargrave. Witnesses: John Drew, John -------, Alice Drew and -------.

Page 303: NATHANIEL MALONE. Inventory. Date: 15 June 1733. Rec.: 20 June 1733. Nathaniel Mallone, Executor. John Freeman, John Jackson and William Harper, Appraisers.

Page 310: WILLIAM LONGBOTTOM of Lines (Lawnes) Creek Parish, Surry. Will. Date: 20 Feb. 1733. Rec.: 18 July 1733. Jean Longbottom, Executrix. Sons: James, William, Samuel, John and Tommos. Wife: Jean. Child in esse. Witnesses: Robert Webb, Jr., Gregory Rawlings and John -assell.

Page 311: JOSEPH BELL of Liens (Lawnes) Creek Parish, Surry. Will. Date: 5 Jan. 1731/32. Rec.: 18 July 1733. John Bell, Executor. Cousin: Borrel. Brother: John. Witnesses: Gregory Rawlings and John Clark.

Page 311: JOSEPH BELL. Inventory. Date: ----. Rec.: 18 July 1733. John Bell, Executor.

Page 312: NICHOLAS DAVIS. Account Current. Date: ----. Rec.: July 18, 1733. Edward Bayley and James Gee, Auditors.

Page 313: WILLIAM PARHAM. Inventory. Date: 25 July 1733. Rec.: 15 Aug. 1733. William Parham, and Matthew Parham, Administrators. Thomas Wynn, John Freeman and John Jackson, Appraisers.

Page 313: MARY FLOOD. Inventory. Date: 12 Aug. 1733. Rec.: 15 Aug. 1733. Ann Cocke, Executrix.

Page 314: JOSEPH BLACKBURN. Inventory. Date: 8 Aug. 1733. Rec.: 15 Aug. 1733. Faith Blackburn, Administratrix. Benjamin Chap. Donaldson, Nicholas Maggett and Joseph Witherington, Appraisers.

Page 315: JOHN EVINS. Account Current. Date: ----. Rec.: 15 Aug. 1733. Returned by Thomas Gwaltney and Mary Gwaltney, als. Evens. Mentions: legacies to the widow and son John. William Edwards and Charles Lucas, Auditors.

Page 318: Mrs. MARY HARRISON. Inventory. Date: ----. Rec.: Aug. 15, 1733. Armistead Churchill, Executor. Mentions: debts due decedent appearing on the books of Col. Nathaniel Harrison.

Page 322:   PRISCILLA THOMAS. Inventory. Date ordered: June 1733.
             Rec.: 15 Aug. 1733. William Blunt, Executor. Samuel
             Briggs, Samuel Maget and Bartholomew Figuers, Appraisers.

Page 323:   WILLIAM WINKEL(L)S of Surry. Will. Date: 30 Apr. 1733.
             Rec.: (illegible). Sons: Isack, John and James. Daugh-
             ters: Frances, Elizabeth, Amy and Mary Winkells. Wife:
             Easter. Witnesses: James Chappell, William Burges and
             James Turner.

Page 324:   WILLIAM SIMMONS. Inventory. Date: ----. Rec.: 15 Aug.
             1733. Elizabeth Simmons, Executrix. Carter Crafford, Aug-
             ustin Hunnicutt and John Newsom, Appraisers.

Page 325:   ALLEN WARREN, JR. of Lawnes Creek Parish, Surry. Will.
             Date: 16 Dec. 1732. Rec.: 15 Aug. 1733. Ann Warren, Ex-
             ecutrix. Daughters: Sarah, Lucy, Elizabeth and Mary.
             Sons: Allen; Robert (not 20). Mentions: land in Prince
             George County. Witnesses: Charles Binns, ---- Sands and
             Thomas Foster.

Page 326:   WILLIAM THOMAS. Account Current. Date: ----. Rec.: 19
             Sept. 1733. William Blunt, Executor of Prissala Thomas,
             Executrix of decedent. James Washington and Mo. Johnson,
             Auditors.

Page 329:   WILLIAM TOMLINSON. Inventory. Date: ----. Rec.: Sept.
             19, 1733. Richard Tomlinson, Executor.

Page 330:   WILLIAM LONGBOTTOM. Inventory. Date ordered: 18 July
             1733. Rec.: 19 Sept. 1733. Jean Longbottom, Executrix.
             Gregory Rawlings, Robert Webb and Charles Judkins, Apprais-
             ers.

Page 330:   BURRELL GREEN. Inventory. Date: ----. Rec.: 19 Sept.
             1733. Ann Green, Administratrix. Henry Mitchell, John
             Weaver and Christopher Tatem, Appraisers.

Page 331:   EDWARD BROWNE. Inventory. Date: ----. Rec.: 19 Sept.
             1733. Mary Browne, Executrix.

Page 337:   WILLIAM WINKILLS. Inventory. Date: ----. Rec.: 17 Oct.
             1733. Easter Winkills, Executrix.

Page 338:   THOMAS GOODWYN. Account Current. Date: ----. Rec.: 17
             Oct. 1733. (illegible), Adm. J. Edmunds and Charles Binns,
             Auditors.

Page 344:   NICHOLAS JARRAD (JARRATT). Inventory. Date: 9 Jan. 1733.
             Rec.: 16 Jan. 1733. Sarah Jarratt presents. Robert Jones,
             Samuel Chappell and James Chappell, Appraisers.

Page 345:   ALLEN WARREN, JR. Inventory. Date: ----. Rec.: 16 Jan.
             1733. Anne Warren, Executrix. Samuel Taylor, Nicholas
             Thompson and William Batte, Appraisers.

Page 353:   THOMAS ALLEN of Southwark Parish, Surry. Will. Date: 30
             Mar. 1733. Rec.: 20 Feb. 1733. Elizabeth Allin, Execu-
             trix. Wife: Elizabeth. Witnesses: William Rookings and
             John Collins.

Page 354:   THOMAS ALLEN. Inventory. Date: ----. Rec.: 20 Feb'y
             1733. Elizabeth Allin, Executrix.

Page 358:   DANIEL EPPES, JR. Inventory. Date ordered: 16 Jan. 1733.
             Rec.: 20 Mar. 1733. Mary Eppes, Administratrix. William
             Shands, Thomas Hood and Robert Doby, Appraisers.

Page 359:   ANTHONY BURTON. Inventory. Date ordered: 17 Oct. 1733.
             Rec.: 20 Mar. 1733. William Atkeison, Administrator. John
             Weaver, Daniel Epes and Henry Mitchell, Appraisers.

Page 361:   RICHARD WASHINGTON. Account Current. Date: ----. Rec.:
             20 Mar. 1733. George and Thomas Washington, Executors.
             Mentions: legacies to Robert Hart's wife; Jos'h Barker's
             wife; Josiah Barker, Jr. and Richard Barker. Benjamin Ed-
             wards and John Ruffin, Auditors.

Page 366:   ABRAHAM HEATH, JR. Inventory. Date ordered: 20 Feb. 1733.
             Rec.: 17 Apr. 1734. Ursula Heath, Administratrix. Will-
             iam Shands, John Tomlinson and Christopher Tatum, Appraisers

Page 382:   BENJAMIN HARDIN of Surry. Will. Date: 6 Feb. 1732. Rec:
             19 June 1734. Benjamin Hardin, Executor. Daughter: Martha
             Hardin. Wife: Sarah. Son: Benjamin. Mentions: Eliza-
             beth Mason. (illegible). Witnesses: James Baker, William
             Stanly and Henry Gray.

Page 383:   BENJAMIN HARDIN. Inventory. Date: ----. Rec.: 19 June
             1734. Benjamin Hardin, Executor.

Page 391:   THOMAS EMERY of Southwark Parish, Surry. Will. Date: 6
             May 1734. Rec.: 17 July 1734. Susannah Emery, Executrix.
             Sons: Benjamin, Green; Thomas, John (not 21). Wife: Su-
             sannah. Witnesses: Thomas Eppes, Jeremiah Ellis and Re-
             becher Ezell.

Page 397:   Mr. WILLIAM SIMMONS. Account Current. Date: ----. Rec.:
             17 July 1734. Elizabeth Simmons, Executrix.

Page 398:   ABRAHAM HEATH, JR. Account Current. Date: ----. Rec.: 17
             July 1734. Ursula Heath, Administratrix. Thomas Edmunds
             and William Simmons, Auditors.

Page 411:   ADAM SKOOT (SCOTT). Inventory. Date: 23 July 1734. Rec.:
             21 Aug. 1734. Comfort Scott, Administratrix. James Chapp-
             ell, Thomas Peters and William Hindes, Appraisers.

Page 411:   WILLIAM CLARK. Account Current. Date: ----. Rec.: 21 Aug.
             1734. Nicholas Cocke, presents.

Page 412:   ELIZABETH PARTIN. Account Current. Date: ----. Rec.: 18
             Sept. 1734. Robert Partin, Administrator.

Page 415:   Capt. JOHN DILL. Account Current. Date: ----. Rec.: 20
             Sept. 1734. Thomas Avent, Sheriff, presents.

Page 425:   JAMES COOPER of Southwark Parish, Surry. Will. Date: 28
             Feb. 1729/30. Rec.: 20 Nov. 1734. Elizabeth Cooper, Ex-
             ecutrix. Wife: Elizabeth. Sons: John, William and Thomas
             (none 21). Daughters: Martha Cooper (not 21); Johana Gil-
             bert. Witnesses: William Saunders, Richard Steward. Codi-
             cil: Date: 9 Oct. 1734.

Page 428:   THOMAS LANE, late of Surry, but now of Isle of Wight Co.
             Will. Date: 8 Oct. 1733. Rec.: 20 Nov. 1734. Mary Hart,
             Executrix. Grandsons: Thomas Lane (land his father lived
             on); John and Joseph Lane. Daughter: Mary Hart. Mentions:
             Rebekah White, cattle at Roanoak. Witnesses: Robert Ricks,
             Thomas Lanier and William Barten.

Page 431:   THOMAS DREW, SR. of Lawnes Creek Parish, Surry. Will. Date:
             17 Mar. 1733/34. Rec.: 20 Nov. 1734. William Drew, Exe-
             cutor. Sons: John, Thomas and William. Grandchildren:
             William, Martha and Elizabeth Drew. Wife: Faith. Friend:
             James Ransom. Witnesses: John Wills, Francis Litle (also
             Little), Robert Little. Proven by 1 wit'n. Mar. 19, 1734.

Page 432:   HINSHEA GILLIAM of Lower Parish, Surry. Will. Date: 13
            Jan. 1733. Rec.: 20 Nov. 1734. Thomas Gilliam, Executor.
            Sons: Hinshea, Walter, Thomas and Charles. Grandson:
            Charles Gilliam, son of Charles. Wife: Fortain (Fortane).
            Daughters: Priscilla, Lydea Gilliam. Witnesses: Benjamin
            Clements, John Gilliam and Edward Clanton.

Page 437:   Capt. JOHN DILL. Account Current. Date: ----. Rec.: 17
            Dec. 1734. Thomas Avent, Sheriff presents.

Page 437:   WILLIAM PHIL(L)IPS of Surry. Will. Date: 5 Dec. 1734.
            Rec.: 15 Jan. 1734. Mary and John Phillips, Executors.
            Daughters: Mary; Sarah, Faith (not 18). Son: John. Men-
            tions: Mrs. Ann Hamlin to care for daughter Sarah. Wit-
            nesses: Nicholas Mag(g)et(t), Thomas Reekes and Jane Reekes

Page 443:   NICHOLAS WEBB. Inventory. Date: 20 July 1734. Rec.: 15
            Jan. 1734. --- Delony, Adm. W. Rookings, Thomas Allstin
            and Joseph Witherington, Appraisers.

Page 443:   JANE HANCOCK of Lawns Creek Parish, Surry. Will. Date: 21
            May 1733. Rec.: 15 Jan. 1734. Joseph Hancock, Executor.
            Sons: William, John and Joseph. Daughters: Elizabeth Og-
            burn; Mary, wife of Thomas Clary; Duejates, wife of Will-
            iam Rain; Martha Hancock. Witnesses: Charles Holt and
            William Carrell.

Page 456:   JAMES COOPER. Inventory. Date: 21 Jan. 1734. Rec.: 19
            Feb. 1734. Elizabeth Cooper, Executrix. Thomas Allstin,
            John Griffith and Joseph Witherington, Appraisers.

Page 457:   WILLIAM PHILLIPS. Inventory. Date: 18 Feb. 1734. Rec.:
            19 Feb. 1734. Mary Phillips, Executrix. John Jarrat, John
            Moring and Joseph Witherington, Appraisers.

Page 458:   THOMAS EMRY. Inventory. Date: 19 Feb. 1734. Rec.: Feb.
            19, 1734. Susanna Emery, Executrix.

Page 458:   HENRY BROWNE of Southwark Parish, Surry. Will. Date: 23
            Sept. 1734. Rec.: 19 Feb. 1734. William Browne, Jr., Ex-
            ecutor. Wife: Elizabeth. Son: Henry. Daughters: Jane,
            Elizabeth and Ann Browne. Child in esse. Brother: William.
            Brother: Henry Edloe. Sister: Ann Browne. Wife's child-
            ren: Jane, Ann, Alexander, and John Boling. Legacies to:
            William Rogers, Edward Harris, Mr. William Simmons and wife
            and children, Mr. John Simmons and wife, Mr. Howell Briggs
            and wife, Mr. Richard Cocke and wife and son Hartwell, Rev.
            Eelbeck and wife, Rebecca Edloe, John Andrews and wife and
            children. Father: William. Mentions: land in Brunswick
            County; wife to pay legacies due from Stith Bolling's Es-
            tate; forgives debts of John Bynum, Edward Harris, Richard
            Bennit, Sr., John Bell, Thomas Bell, John Andrews; his
            children not of age. Witnesses: Henry Eelbeck, Christo-
            pher Clinch, Charles White and Richard Cocke.

Page 462:   RICHARD BELL of Surry. Will. Date: 8 Nov. 1734. Rec.:
            19 Feb. 1734. Sarah Bell, Executrix. Sons: William, Rich-
            ard, Joseph and Benjamin. Daughters: Mary, Sarah, Eliza-
            beth and Amy Bell. Wife: Sarah. Witnesses: Thomas Ed-
            munds and Bartholmew Figures.

Page 463:   JOHN MOSS of Southwark Parish, Surry. Will. Date: 11 Oct.
            1734. Rec.: 19 Feb. 1734. Martha Moss, Executrix. Wife:
            Martha. Sons: John, Henry and Thomas. Witnesses: John
            Mason, William Moss and John Moss.

Page 468:   THOMAS TYUS. Account Current. Date: ----. Rec.: 19 Feb.
            1734. Returned by John Tyus. Mentions: part received of
            executors of my father's (John Tyus) estate. John Chapman

11

Page 469:   ISAAC CORNWELL. Account Current. Date: 1727. Rec.: 19
            Feb. 1734. Elizabeth Taylor, Executrix. John Chapman and
            Thomas Edmunds, Auditors.

Page 469:   RICHARD BELL. Inventory. Date: 17 Mar. 1734/35. Rec.:
            19 Mar. 1734. Sarah Bell, Executrix. Samuel Maget, Bar-
            tholomew Figuers and William Owen, Appraisers.

Page 470:   JAMES PORCH. Account Current. Date: ----. Rec.: 19 Mar.
            1734. Henry Porch, Executor. Thomas Wynne and John Wills,
            Auditors.

Page 474:   Capt. HENSHAW GILLAM. Inventory. Date: ----. Rec.: 19
            Mar. 1734. Thomas Guillam, Executor.

Page 475:   JOHN MOSE (MOSS). Inventory. Date: 18 Mar. 1734/35. Rec:
            19 Mar. 1734. Martha Moss, Executrix. James Chappell, Sam-
            uel Chappell and Robert Jones, Appraisers.

Page 476:   WILLIAM LONGBOTTOM. Account Current. Date: ----. Rec.:
            16 Apr. 1735. Francis Hutchins and Jane Hutchins, Execu-
            trix. Mentions: legacy to John Longbottom. Robert Gray
            and Howell Briggs, Auditors.

Page 481:   JANE HANCOCK. Inventory. Date: 17 Nov. 1734. Rec.: 16
            Apr. 1735. Joseph Hancock, Executor.

Page 495:   THOMAS ADAMS of Surry. Will. Date: 1 Feb. 1734. Rec.:
            21 May 1735. Ann Adams, Executrix. Sons: William; and
            Peter (not 21). Wife: Ann. Witnesses: William Marriott
            and Miles Lewis.

Page 496:   ELIZABETH WASHINGTON, Relict of RICHARD WASHINGTON of South-
            wark Parish, Surry. Will. Date: (none). Rec.: 21 May 1735.
            Thomas Washington, Executor. Sons: George, Richard, John,
            Thomas, William, James and Arther. Daughters: Elizabeth
            Lanier, Prissilah Lanier, Faith Barker, Mary Hart and Ann
            Washington. Witnesses: Benjamin Reeks, Thomas Drinkard &
            Robert Clary.

Page 498:   JOHN WARREN. Account Current. Date: ----. Rec.: 21 May
            1735. Returned by Stevenson Buxton. John Simmons, Jr. and
            Thomas Eldridge, Jr., Auditors.

Page 503:   THOMAS ADAMS. Inventory. Date: 11 June 1735. Rec.: 18
            June 1735. Ann Adams, Executrix. Robert Gray, William
            Warren and Joseph Warren, Appraisers.

Page 504:   JAMES EWART. Account Current. Date: 4 July 1735. Rec.:
            (none). Thomas Avent, Sheriff.

Page 509:   Capt. HENRY BROWNE. Inventory. Date: ----. Rec.: July
            16, 1735. William Browne, Jr., Executor. Mentions: lega-
            cies to Henry, Jane, Elizabeth, Ann, Rebecca. Property at
            Brunswick Qtr., Spring Swamp Qtr., Blackwater Qtr., Swans
            Pt. Nicholas Maget, Richard Cocke and Charles White, Ap-
            praisers.

Page 511:   JAMES EWART. Account Current. Date: 24 July 1735. Rec.:
            (none). Thomas Avent, Sheriff.

Page 512:   RICHARD LEWIS of Surry. Will. Date: 18 Mar. 1732/33.
            Rec.: 17 Sept. 1735. William Simmons and Thomas Edmunds,
            Executors. Legatees: Sarah Tyas, daughter of John and
            Anne Tyas; William Simmons; Capt. Thomas Edmunds. Wit-
            nesses: Charles Lucas, Samuel Sorsby and George Branch.

Page 513: EDWARD DAVIS. Will. Date: 3 June 1735. Rec.: 17 Sept. 1735. Elizabeth Davis, Executrix. Friend: Richard Curby. Wife: Elizabeth. Witnesses: Robert Nicolson and Richard Curby.

Page 514: BENJAMIN CHAMPION of Lawnes Creek Parish, Surry. Will. Date: 6 Apr. 1735. Rec.: 17 Sept. 1735. Elizabeth Champion, Executrix. Sons: John, Charles and Benjamin. Daughters: Elizabeth, Anne, Mary. Wife: Elizabeth. Witnesses: Charles Binns, Samuel Lancaster, Jr. and John Wall.

Page 520: JONATHAN CHAMBERS. Inventory. Date ordered: 21 May 1735. Rec.: 17 Sept. 1735. Israel Pickins, Administrator. John Wilbourn, William Green and Henry Freeman, Appraisers.

Page 521: JONATHAN CHAMBERS. Account Current. Date: ----. Rec.: 17 Sept. 1735. Israel Pickins, Administrator.

Page 526: WILLIAM ATKISSON. Inventory. Date ordered: 12 Jul. 1735. Rec.: 15 Oct. 1735. Elizabeth Atkisson, Administratrix. James Washington, Augustine Hargrave and John Hancock, Appraisers.

Page 527: NATHANELL ROBERTSON of Surry. Will. Date: 27 Jan. 1734. Rec.: 15 Oct. 1735. Elizabeth Robertson, Executrix. Wife: Elizabeth. Son: Drury (not 21). Child in esse. Witnesses: Henry Freeman, Christopher Robbertson and Peter Green.

Page 529: ELIZABETH WASHINGTON. Inventory. Date: 10 Oct. 1735. Rec: 15 Oct. 1735. Thomas Washington, Executor. Legacies to: George, Richard, John, Thomas, and William Washington, Arther Washington and wife; daughter: Elizabeth Lanier; dau.: Faith Barker; daughter: Mary Heart; daughter: Ann Steavens; Thomas Steavans, son of John; Thomas Lanier, son of Robert.

Page 530: DANIELL TURNER of Surry. Will. Date: 18 Feb. 1734/35. Rec: 15 Oct. 1735. Sarah Turner, Executrix. Sons: John, Jeames, and David. Wife: Sarah. Legatee: John Clarke. Mentions: 5 children. Witnesses: William Rose, Wallis Jones and John Clark.

Page 531: NATHANIEL ROBERTSON. Inventory. Date: ----. Rec.: 15 Oct. 1735. Elizabeth Robertson, Executrix.

Page 536: BENJAMIN CHAMPION. Inventory. Date: ----. Rec.: 19 Nov. 1735. Elizabeth Champion, Executrix.

Page 537: ROBERT CRAFFORD. Will. Date: 9 Oct. 1735. Rec.: 19 Nov. 1735. Carter Crafford, Jr., Executor. Cousin: Carter Crafford, Jr. Brother: Carter. Cousin: Marry Crafford, daughter of Carter. Witnesses: Henry Mcdonnae, James Worden and John Brown.

Page 537: ANNE FATHERBE of Lawnes Creek Parish, Surry. Will. Date: 17 May 1734. Rec.: 19 Nov. 1735. William Evans, Executor. Sons: William and Anthony Evans. Grandson: John Evans. Daughters: Mary, Elizabeth, Martha and Anne ---(no surname given). Witnesses: Charles Binns and Samuel Warren.

Page 546: ANN FEREBE (FERREBY). Inventory. Date: ----. Rec.: 17 Dec. 1735. William Evans, Executor.

Page 547: PETER BAGLEY of Southwark Parish, Surry. Will. Date: 15 Nov. 1735. Rec.: 17 Dec. 1735. George Bagley, Executor. Sons: George and John. Daughter: Sarah Tucker. Cousin: John Bagley. Servant: Simon Rowland (to be free at age 28). Witnesses: William Short, Richard Bullock and William Short, Jr.

Page 554:   JOHN FIELDS of Surry. Will. Date: 20 Oct. 1735. Rec.: 21
Jan. 1735. Jean Fields, Executrix. Wife: Jean. Witnesses:
Thomas Edmunds and Anne Edmunds.

Page 559:   ROBERT CRAFFORD. Inventory. Date: 12 Oct. 1735. Rec.:
21 Jan. 1735. Carter Crafford, Executor.

Page 560:   ELEANOR MAYBURY of Surry, widow. Inventory. Date: 5 Nov.
1735. Rec.: 21 Jan. 1735. Francis Mabrey, Administrator.
Christopher Tatum, Robert Doby and Henry Mitchell, Appraisers.

Page 564:   JOHN FI(E)LDS. Inventory. Date: 13 Feb. 1735/36. Rec.:
18 Feb. 1735. Jane Fields, Executrix.

Page 564:   BENJAMIN CLARY. Inventory. Date: 23 Jan. 1735. Rec.: 18
Feb. 1735. Lewis Delony, Administrator. Harry Floyd, Solomon Harrison and Thomas Hamlin, Appraisers.

Page 565:   ROBERT TAYLOR. Inventory. Date: 23 Jan. 1735. Rec.: 18
Feb. 1735. Lewis Delony, Administrator. Harry Floyd, Solomon Harrison and Thomas Hamlin, Appraisers.

Page 565:   ELIZABETH ALLIN. Will. Date: 2 Feb. 1735/36. Rec.: 18
Feb. 1735. Thomas Allstin, Executor. Friend: Thomas Al-
stin. Legatees: Hannah Steward, Ann Collins, Mary Pening-
ton, Mary Knot, Sarah Grimmer and Thomas Hawkins. Goddaughter: Elizabeth Evens. Witnesses: James Rookings and
Tabitha Niblit.

Page 568:   Mr. RICHARD PRICE. Inventory. Date: 13 June 1735. Rec.:
18 Feb. 1735. Mr. William Drummond, Administrator. William
Edwards, John Newsum and Thomas Edwards, Appraisers.

Page 569:   RICHARD BENNETT. Inventory. Date ordered: 21 Jan. 1735.
Rec.: 18 Feb. 1735. Benjamin Bennett, Administrator. James
Washington, William Evans and Thomas Bell, Appraisers.

Page 570:   RICHARD LEWIS. Inventory. Date: ----. Rec.: 18 Feb. 1735.
Thomas Edmunds and William Simmons, Executors.

Page 573:   JAMES BRUTON of Lawnes Creek Parish, Surry. Will. Date: 5
Feb. 1734/35. Rec.: 17 Mar. 1735. William Bruton, surviv-
ing Executor (wife deceased). Daughters: Elizabeth, Mary
Kae; and Ann Jurdin. Grandsons: Bruton and John Kae;
James Bruton. Son: William. Wife: (not named). Wit-
nesses: Charles Binns and Benjamin Bell.

Page 574:   PETER ADAMS of Southwark Parish, Surry. Will. Date: 21 Mar.
1734. Rec.: 17 Mar. 1735. Ann Adams, Executrix. Sons:
Thomas and William. Daughters: Mary, Elizabeth and Susannah. (None of children are 16 years of age). Wife: Ann.
Witnesses: William Edwards and Samuel Judkin.

Page 576:   PETER BAGBY. Inventory. Date: 3 Feb. 1735. Rec.: 17 Mar.
1735. George Bagby, Executor. William Harriss, Richard
Jones and Richard Bullock, Appraisers.

Page 577:   JOHN TURNER. Inventory. Date: 17 Feb. 1735/36. Rec.: 17
Mar. 1735. Thomas Burgiss, Administrator. James Chappell,
James Jones and Robert Jones, Appraisers.

Page 579:   JAMES BRUTON. Inventory. Date: ---. Rec.: 21 Apr. 1736.
William Bruton, Executor.

Page 580:   AUGUSTIN BERRYMAN of Surry. Will. Date: 23 Oct. 1735.
Rec.: 21 Apr. 1736. Ann Berryman, Executrix. Wife: Anne.
Sons: John, Joseph and William. Daughters: 3 (not named)
Witnesses: William Drew, John Thompson and Henry Mcdonnae.

Page 581: RICHARD BELL. Account Current. Date: ----. Rec.: 21 Apr. 1736. Sarah Bell, Executrix. Mentions: payment for the burying of Ann Bell. Benjamin Cocke and Henry King, Auditors.

Page 581: BENJAMIN COLLIER. Inventory. Date: 6 Mar. 1735. Rec.: 21 Apr. 1736. Elizabeth Collier, Administratrix. Jos. Nicholson, Charles Lucas and Marmaduk Cheatham, Appraisers.

Page 585: CORNELUS LOFTIN of Southwark Parish, Surry. Will. Date: 5 Apr. 1735. Rec.: 21 Apr. 1736. Cornelus Loftin, next of kin, granted administration. Sons: William and Cornelus. Daughters: Rebeckcah, Clee, Mary, Elizabeth and Sarah. Wife: Mary. Witnesses: John Bell, Silvanus Stokes, Jr. and Jones Stokes.

Page 589: MARY TYUSS. Inventory. Date: 4 Mar. 1735/36. Rec.: 21 Apr. 1736. John Tyus, Administrator. Joshua Nicolson, Charles Lucas, and John Collier, Appraisers.

Page 597: PETER ADAMS. Inventory. Date: ----. Rec.: 19 May 1736. Anne Adams, Executor. Samuel Judkin, Edward Pettway and George Piland, Appraisers.

Page 597: AUGUSTINE BERRYMAN. Inventory. Date: 10 May 1736. Rec.: 19 May 1736. Ann Berryman, Executrix. William Drew, Joseph Hancock and John Thompson, Appraisers.

Page 598: EDWARD DAVIS. Inventory. Date: 19 May 1736. Rec.: May 19, 1736. Elizabeth Davis, Executrix.

Page 599: WILLIAM TAYLOR of Surry. Will. Date: 8 Mar. 1735. Rec: 19 May 1736. Etheldred Taylor, Executor. Brothers: Samuel, Henry and Etheldred. Legatee: Martha, wife of John Ruffin. Witnesses: John Ruffin, Peter Robins and Thomas Hall.

Page 600: GEORGE GINN. Account Current. Date: ----. Rec.: 19 May 1736. Thomas Avent, Sheriff.

Page 600: ELIZABETH CHAMPION. Inventory. Date: ----. Rec.: 16 Jun. 1736. Charles Champion, Adminstrator. Robert and Samuel Lancaster, and Thomas Bell, Appraisers.

Page 604: WILLIAM GRAY of Lawnes Creek Parish, Surry. Will. Date: 10 Mar. 1730/31. Rec.: 16 June 1736. William, Robert, Joseph and Thomas Gray, Executors. Sons: William, Robert, Joseph, Thomas, James; Edmund (not 21). Brother: Gilbert. Daughter: Lucy Brigs, wife of Howell Brigs (Briggs). Wife: (not named). Mentions: land in Isle of Wight County. Witnesses: Timothy Thorpe, Joseph Thorpe, Sampson Wilson and Nathaniel Gibbs.

Page 610: CORNELIUS LOFTIN. Inventory. Date: 15 June 1736. Rec.: 16 June 1736. Cornelius Loftin, Administrator.

Page 613: WILLIAM RAY. Will. Date: 9 Dec. 1735. Rec.: 21 Jul. 1736. Martha Ray, Executrix. Wife: marthay. Son: Lenard. Witnesses: Henry Sowerby and Benjamin Sowerby.

Page 617: SAMUEL SANDS. Inventory. Date: 22 June 1736. Rec.: 21 July 1736. Leonard Oney, Administrator. George Piland, William Hott, and Joseph Hart, Appraisers.

Page 627: ELIZABETH ALLEN. Inventory. Date: ----. Rec.: 18 Aug. 1736. Thomas Allstin, Executor.

Page 627: THOMAS ADAMS. Account Current. Date: ----. Rec.: 20 Oct. 1736. John Pully, who married Ann Adams, Executor. Mentions

(Page 627 - ADAMS cont'd.): legacy to Peter Adams. John Simmons, Jr. and Benjamin Cocke, Auditors.

Page 632: WILLIAM TAYLOR. Inventory. Date: ----. Rec.: 20 October 1736. Etheldred Taylor, Executor.

Page 633: Capt. THOMAS HOLT. Account Current. Date: ----. Rec.: 20 Oct. 1736. Mary Holt, Executor. Mentions: legacies to Nicholas Cocke, William Hansford, Thomas Cocke, John Newsum, Martha Hansford, Lucy Holt, Thomas Holt, Lucy Holt by Mrs. Mason. John Simmons, Jr. and Benjamin Cocke.

Page 634: JOHN HALLEMAN of Surry. Will. Date: 18 Sept. 1736. Rec: 20 Oct. 1736. Josias John Halleman, next of kin, granted administration. Sons: Henery, Robert, John and Matthew (youngest). Daughter: Martha Halleman. Wife: Mary. Witnesses: Absalom Atkinson, William Pittman and Benjamin Pittman.

Page 635: MARY HALLEMAN of Surry. Will. Date: 7 Oct. 1736. Rec.: 20 Oct. 1736. Josias John Halleman, Executor. Sons: John, Robbert, Matthew. Legatee: Josias John Halleman. Witnesses: Absalom Atkinson and William Pittman.

Page 636: CUTHBERT WILLIAMSON. Inventory. Date ordered: 16 Jun. 1736. Rec.: Oct. 20, 1736. Hollum Sturdivant, Elizabeth Sturdivant, Administrators and John Rottenbury and Susanna Rottenbury, Administrators. John Threeweet, Sloman Wynne and William Parham, Appraisers.

Page 637: BENJAMIN ANDREWS of Surry. Will. Date: 14 Sept. 1736. Rec.: 20 Oct. 1736. Edward Bayley, Jr. and John Simmons,Jr. Executors. Son: William. Daughter: Ann Andrews. Witnesses: John Simmons, Jr., Robert Snipes and Edward Bayley,Jr.

Page 648: MARY CHAPMAN of Surry. Will. Date: 29 Aug. 1736. Rec.: 15 Dec. 1736. John Chapman, Executor. Daughters: Mary Pierce and Sarah Barrow of North Carolina; Mary Donaldson and child; and Ann Foster. Grandchildren: Hannah and Mary Bamer (not 21). Sons: John Chapman, and William Taylor of Ireland. Witnesses: Sarah Fort and Deborah King.

Page 648: EDWARD BA(Y)LEY of Surry. Will. Date: 7 Sept. 1735. Rec.: 15 Dec. 1736. Thomas and Edward Bayley, Executors. Sons: Thomas and edward. Daughters: Elizabeth, Hanah, Jane Bayley; Mary, wife of Samuel Briggs; Faith, widow of Joseph Blackburn, dec'd.; Sarah, wife of Benjamin Andrews. Friends: Nicholas Maget, Robert Watkins and John Chapman. Witnesses: Nicholas Magett, William Newsum and John Chapman.

Page 653: RICHARD ROSE of Surry. Will. Date: 20 Oct. 1736. Rec.: 15 Dec. 1736. Jane Rose, Executrix. Sons: Thomas and Richard. Daughter: Jane Rose and heir, grand-daughter: Hannah (not of age). Wife: Elizabeth. Witnesses: John Nicolson and John Ogburn.

Page 653: WILLIAM RAY. Inventory. Date: ----. Rec.: 15 Dec. 1736. Martha Ray, Executrix.

Page 654: JOHN HOLLOWMAN. Inventory. Date ordered: 20 Oct. 1736. Rec.: 16 Feb. 1736. Josiah John Holliman, Administrator. James Washington, Richard Blow and Sammuel Lancester, Appraisers.

Page 655: MARY HOLLOWMAN. Inventory. Date: ----. Rec.: 16 Feb. 1736. Josiah John Holliman, Executor. James Washington, Richard Blow and Sammuel Lancester, Appraisers.

Page 656: JOHN BAGLEY of Southwark Parish, Surry. Will. Date: 11 Dec.

(Page 656 - BAGLEY cont'd.): 1736. Rec.: 16 Feb. 1736. Elizabeth Bagley, Executrix. Sons: Thomas and Peter. Wife: Elesabeth. Witnesses: Richard Bullock, John Jones and Judah Jones.

Page 657: BENJAMIN ANDREWS. Inventory. Date: ----. Rec.: 16 Feb. 1736. John Simmons, Jr. and Edward Bailey, Executors. John Moring, John Griffith and Christopher Moring, Appraisers.

Page 658: RICHARD ROSE. Inventory. Date: ----. Rec.: 16 Feb. 1736. Jane Rose, Executrix.

Page 665: JOHN BAGLY. Inventory. Date: 12 Mar. 1736/37. Rec.: 16 Mar. 1736. Elizabeth Bagley, Executrix.

Page 666: EDWARD BAYLEY. Inventory. Date: ----. Rec.: 16 Mar. 1736. Thomas and Edward Bayley, Executors.

Page 669: WILLIAM BLUNT. Inventory. Date ordered: 16 Mar. 1736. Rec.: 20 Apr. 1737. Elizabeth Blunt, Administratrix. John Andrews, Samuel Magget and William Briggs, Appraisers.

Page 670: HINCHA GILLIAM of Southwark Parish, Surry. Will. Date: 3 Jan. 1736/37. Rec.: 20 Apr. 1737. Faith Gilliam, Executrix. Daughters: Elizabeth and Ann Gilliam. Sons: Hincha, John and Samuel. Legatee: Ose Taply. Brother: John. Mentions: Child not of age. Witnesses: Richard Blunt, John Gilliam and William Briggs.

Page 675: CHRISTOPHER CLINCH of Southwark Parish, Surry. Will. Date: 13 Dec. 1736. Rec.: 20 Apr. 1737. William Clinch, Executor. Wife: Hanah. Sons: William, James, Joseph John. Daughters: Elizabeth Holt; Mary, and Margaret Clinch. Witnesses: Robert Warren and Richard Rowell.

Page 680: DANIEL TURNER. Inventory. Date: 17 May 1736. Rec.: 20 Apr. 1737. Sarah Turner, Executrix. James Chappell, Robert Jones and James Jones, Appraisers.

Page 686: JOHN ATKINSON of Surry. Will. Date: 17 Apr. 1736. Rec.:18 May 1737. Elizabeth Atkinson, Executrix. Sons: Absalom, John, Aaron, Reubin, Amos, Daniel and Jacob. Wife: Elizabeth. Mentions: land in Isle of Wight County adjoining Christopher Atkinson. Witnesses: William Little, John Waller and Thomas Atkinson.

Page 693: WILLIAM PHILLEPS. Inventory. Date: 2 Apr. 1737. Rec.: 18 May 1737. Nathaniel Harrison, Administrator. Joshua Nicholson, Charles Lucas and Mickell Casely, Appraisers.

Page 695: WILLIAM MARTIN. Inventory. Date ordered: 15 Dec. 1736. Rec.: 18 May 1737. Sarah Martin, Administratrix. Sloman Wynne, John Wynne and Hollum Studvant, Appraisers.

Page 696: HINCHA GILLIAM. Inventory. Date ordered: 20 Apr. 1737. Rec.: 18 May 1737. Faith Gilliam, Executrix. (Includes property in Brunswick County). Richard Blunt, David Jones and William Cook, Appraisers.

Page 697: Capt. THOMAS EDMUNDS. Inventory. Date: ----. Rec.: 18 May 1737. Anne Edmunds, Administratrix. Howell Briggs, Richard Blunt and Samuel Maget, Appraisers.

Page 700: JOHN DOBY of Southwark Parish, Surry. Will. Date: 3 July 1735. Rec.: 15 June 1737. Anne Doby, Executrix. Wife: Anne. Sons: Peter and Robert. Mentions: land in Prince George County. Witnesses: Thomas Eldridge and Thomas Eldridge, Jr.

Page 701: THOMAS BROWN of Surry. Planter. Will. Date: 4 Sept. 1735.

(Page 701 - BROWN cont'd.): Rec.: 15 June 1737. John Cargill, Executor. Wife: Mary. Grandson: William Butterell. Daughter: Ann Mexodum. Friend: Nathaniel Harrison. Witnesses: Thomas Hamlin and Barnaby Tate.

Page 702: Mrs. MARY CHAPMAN. Inventory. Date: 17 May 1737. Rec.: 15 June 1737. John Chapman, Executor. Mentions: legacies to Mary Donaldson, John Chapman, Mary Pierce and Sarah Barrow-property in North Carolina.

Page 703: Capt. THOMAS HILL. Inventory. Date: 15 Jan. 1736/37. Rec: 15 June 1737. Priscilla Hill, Executrix. William Seward, Samson Willson and John Holt, Appraisers.

Page 707: JOHN DOBY. Inventory. Date: 18 July 1737. Rec.: 20 July 1737. Anne Doby, Executrix.

Page 711: THOMAS COGGIN. Inventory. Date: ----. Rec.: 20 July 1737. Elizabeth Coggin, Administratrix. Roger Delk, Newitt Edwards and John Glover, Appraisers.

Page 713: ARTHUR ALLEN. Account Current. Date: 1728. Rec.: 20 July 1737. Arthur Smith, Jr., wife: Elizabeth Smith and James Bray, Administrators.

Page 714: Mr. CHRISTOPHER CLINCH. Inventory. Date: ----. Rec.: 20 July 1737. William Clinch, Ex. Henry Watkins, Robert Warren and Richard Rowell, Appraisers. (Note: Henry Watkins, Executor.)

Page 725: MARY DAVIDSON of Surry. Will. Date: 2 May 1737. Rec.: 21 Sept. 1737. William Clemmons, Executrix. Sons: John and William Clemmons. Grandson: William Clements (not of age) Grand-daughter: Elizabeth Boykin (not of age). Friends: Mr. Nicholas Maget, Mr. George Cryer and Mr. Samuel Thompson. Witnesses: Edward Wesson and Joseph Clarke.

Page 729: ELIZABETH HOLT of Lawnes Creek Parish, Surry. Will. Date: 13 June 1737. Rec.: 21 Sept. 1737. Charles Holt, Executor. Daughters: Tapphenas Newsom; Anne Holt and Mary Holt. Son: Charles. Witnesses: William Edwards and Mary Piland.

Page 730: SAMUEL BRIGGS of Surry. Will. Date: 26 Mar. 1736. Rec.: 21 Sept. 1737. Mary Briggs, Executrix. Sons: William, Henry, Thomas; Robert, Nathaniel (not 21); Benjamin (not 18). Daughters: Faith Gilliam; Sarah Collier; Mary Edmunds; Anne, Lucy and Hannah Briggs (not of age). Friend: Thomas Edmunds. Wife: Mary. Witnesses: Thomas Edmunds, Richard Blunt and James Anderson.

Page 732: JOHN MOSS. Account Current. Date: ----. Rec.: 21 Sept. 1737. Martha Moss, Executrix. Nicholas Magett and William Edwards, Auditors.

Page 733: THOMAS BROWNE. Inventory. Date: 20 July 1737. Rec.: 21 Sept. 1737. John Cargill, Executor. Robert Grimmer, John Griffith and Jon Mooring, Appraisers.

Page 734: MARY BROWN of Southwark Parish, Surry. Will. Date: 22 Sept. 1736. Rec.: 20 July 1737. Thomas Hamlin, Executor. Sister-in-law: Faith Blackbun. Legatees: Anne Macshoden; Elizabeth Cooper; Sarah Dugar; Faith, Mary, and William Blackbun, children of sister-in-law. Friend: Thomas Hamlin. Dec'd husband. Witnesses: Robert Grimer and Elizabeth Cooper.

Page 735: JOHN COLLIER. Account Current. Date: ----. Rec.: 19 Oct. 1737. Mo. Johnson and Thomas Collier, Executors. Will Ray and Will Edwards, Auditors.

Page 747:   WILLIAM GRAY. Inventory. Date: 5 Oct. 1737. Rec.: 19 Oct. 1737. William, Robert, Joseph and Thomas Gray, Executors.

Page 747:   SAMUEL BRIGGS. Inventory. Date ordered: 21 Sept. 1737. Rec: 19 Oct. 1737. Mary Briggs, Executrix. Mentions: legacies to William, Henry, Robart, Nathaniel, Benjamin, Ann, Lawse, Hanah Briggs. Richard Blunt, James Anderson and Andrew Lester, Appraisers.

Page 749:   ELIZABETH HOLT. Inventory. Date: 17 Oct. 1737. Rec.: 19 Oct. 1737. Charles Holt, Executor.

Page 750:   MARY DAVIDSON. Inventory. Date: 17 Oct. 1737. Rec.: 19 Oct. 1737. William Clemmons (Clements), Executor. George Piland, Samuel Judkins and John Davis, Appraisers.

Page 759:   SAMUEL SANDS. Account Current. Date: ---. Rec: 16 Nov. 1737. Lenard Oney, Administrator. William Edwards, Nicholas Edmunds, Auditors.

Page 761:   JOHN KING. Inventory. Date: 12 Nov. 1737. Rec.: 16 Nov. 1737. Faitha King, Administratrix. Joseph John Clinch, Blanks Moody and Zacharias Madderna, Appraisers.

Page 762:   JOHN ATKINSON. Inventory. Date: 15 Aug. 1737. Rec: 17 Nov. 1737. Elizabeth Atkinson, Executrix.

Page 763:   THOMAS LANE. Inventory. Date: ----. Rec: 17 Nov. 1737. Mary Hart, Executrix.

Page 766:   ROBERT FLAKE. Account Current. Date: 1724. Rec.: 21 Dec. 1737. William Braddy, Administrator.

Page 766:   CUTHBERT WILLIAMSON. Account Current. Date: ----. Rec.: 21 Dec. 1737. Hollum and Elizabeth Sturdivant, Administrators; John Rottenbury and Susannah Rottenbury, Administrators.

Page 769:   WILLIAM MARTIN. Account Current. Date: ----. Rec.: 21 Dec. 1737. Sarah Martin, Administratrix.

Page 770:   BRAY HARGRAVE. Account Current. Date: 1727. Rec.: 21 Dec. 1737. Mary Hargrave, Administratrix.

Page 777:   WILLIAM TAYLOR. Account Current. Date: ----. Rec.: 18 Jan. 1737. Etheldred Taylor, Executor. Mentions: legacy to Capt. Ruffin; parts of estate to Samuel, Henry and Etheldred Taylor. William Gray and William Skipwith, Auditors.

Page 778:   DANIEL EPPES, JR. Account Current. Date: ----. Rec.: 18 Jan. 1737. Francis and Mary Mabry, Administrators. William Gray and William Skipwith, Auditors.

Page 790:   MARY BROWN. Inventory. Date: ----. Rec.: 18 Jan. 1737. Thomas Hamlin, Executor.

Page 796:   JOHN CARR of Southwark Parish, Surry. Carpenter. Will. Date: 9 Jan. 1737. Rec.: 15 Feb. 1737. Richard Ransom, Executor. Legatees: Friend: Matthew Current of Prince George County; Richard Ransom of Brunswick County. Witnesses: Ellin Rookings, Stephen Mercer, Richard Steward and James Watts.

Page 797:   AUGUSTIN BERRIMAN. Account Current. Date: 1736. Rec.: 15 Feb. 1737. Ann Berriman, Executrix.

Page 806:   JOSEPH SEAT of Southwark Parish, Surry. Will. Date: 27 Nov. 1737. Rec.: 15 Mar. 1737. Edward Bayley, and Joseph Seat, Executors. Sons: Joseph; Marchell (unmarried); Thomas;

(Page 806 - SEAT cont'd.): Bilusson; and James. Daughter: Mary Rose. Wife: Mable. Witnesses: Christopher Moring, Jr., William Partin and Elesbath Hux.

Page 807: THOMAS ANDRUS of Surry. Will. Date: 21 Jan. 1736. Rec.: 15 Mar. 1737. John Andrus, Executor. Sons: John and Thomas. Daughters: Ollef, Martha; Jean Andrus; Lucy Snipes; Mary Thornton. Wife: (not named). Witnesses: John Simmons, Thomas Bayley and Edward Bayley.

Page 812: WILLIAM PULLY of Southwark Parish, Surry. Will. Date: 29 Mar. 1738. Rec.: 19 Apr. 1738. Mary Pully, Executrix. Son: William. Daughters: Marther Moss and Hanah Clark. Grandson: William Pully. Wife: Mary. Witnesses: William Rookings, William Speed and Mathew Huberd.

Page 812: PETER LEATH of Southwark Parish, Surry. Will. Nunc. Will. Date: 13 Feb. 1737. Rec.: 19 Apr. 1738. Sarah Leath, Executrix. Son: John. Daughter: Elizabeth. Wife: Sarah. Witnesses: John Jackson, John Parham and Anthony Rackly.

Page 826: JOHN SIMMONS of Surry. Will. Date: 18 Oct. 1737. Rec.: 19 Apr. 1738. Rebeckah and William Simmons, Executors. Wife: Rebeckah. Sons: William and John. Daughter: Mary Simmons. Friend: Mr. Robert Gray. Mentions: land in Brunswick and Isle of Wight Counties. Witnesses: Benjamin Simmons, John Davis and Joseph Andrus.

Page 828: JOHN HOLLIMAN. Account Current. Date: -----. Rec.: 19 Apr. 1738. Josiah John Holliman, Administrator. James Washington and William Rookings, Auditors.

Page 829: MARY HOLLIMAN. Account Current. Date: -----. Rec.: 19 Apr. 1738. Josiah John Holliman, Executor. James Washington & William Rookings, Auditors.

Page 847: JEREMYAH ELLESS (JEREMIAH ELLIS). Inventory. Date: ---- Rec.: 17 May 1738. Elizabeth Ellis, Administratrix. Holon Studyvant, William Jones and William Pettway, Appraisers.

Page 848: PETER LEATH. Inventory. Date: 29 Apr. 1738. Rec.: 17 May 1738. Sarah Leath, Executor. Will Parham, Matthew Parham and John Parham, Appraisers.

Page 849: WILLIAM PULLY, SR. Inventory. Date: 15 May 1738. Rec.: 17 May 1738. Mary Pully, Executrix.

Page 862: WILLIAM PARR. Inventory. Date: 18 Mar. 1737. Rec.: 21 Jun. 1738. William Eppes, Administrator. Henry Mitchell, Nathaniel Howell and Matthew Gibbes, Appraisers.

Page 870: JOHN CARR. Inventory. Date: 16 Feb. 1737. Rec.: 21 June 1738. Richard Ransom, Executor. L. Delony, Thomas Allstin and Thomas Clarke, Appraisers.

Page 878: WILLIAM BLUNT. Account Current. Date: -----. Rec.: 19 Jul. 1738. James and Elizabeth Rookings, Administrators. Thomas Gray and James Washington, Auditors.

Page 881: THOMAS ANDREWS. Inventory. Date: -----. Rec.: 16 Aug. 1738. John Andrews, Administrator.

Page 881: JOHN BARLOW. Account Current. Date: 1729. Rec.: 16 Aug. 1738. Thomas Avent, Administrator. William Browne, Jr. & Henry Taylor, Auditors.

Page 887: WILLIAM RAWLINGS. Account Current/Sale: Date 1 Mar. 1737. Rec.: 16 Aug. 1738. William Simmons, Sheriff.

Page 901:   JOSEPH SEAT. Inventory. Date: ----. Rec.: 20 Sept. 1738.
             Edward Bayley and Joseph Seat, Executors.

Page 902:   JOHN GILLUM of Surry. Will. Date: 9 Aug. 1738. Rec.:20
             Sept. 1738. Sarah and John Gillum, Executors. Sons: John,
             Hinche, Burrell, Levi, Isom and Hansill. Wife: Sarah.
             Daughters: Sarah, Amy, Mary, Milley, Tabith, and Leada.
             Witnesses: John Dunn, Thomas Dunn and Mo. Johnson.

Page 903:   HENRY BRIGGS. Inventory. Date: ----. Rec.: 17 Jan. 1738.
             William Briggs, Administrator. Andrew Lester, James Ander-
             son and Rubin Cook, Appraisers.

Page 919:   JAMES COOPER. Account Current. Date: -----. Rec.: 17 Jan.
             1738. Elizabeth Cooper, Executrix. Robert Gray. and Will-
             iam Skipwith, Auditors.

Page 6:   EDWARD THROWER. Will. Date: 13 Nov. 1738. Rec.: 21 Feb.
           1738. William Gilliam, Executor. Wife: Tabitha. Sons:
           William, John, and Edward (not of age). Mentions: children
           and brother's estate. Witnesses: Francis Waker and David
           Sinckler.

Page 12:   JOHN GILLUM. Inventory. Date: 2 Nov. 1738. Rec.:   21
           Feb. 1738. Sary (Sarah) and John Gillum, Executors. Moses
           Johnson, Robert Webb, Jr. and Walles Jones, Appraisers.

Page 15:   NATHANEIL PHILLIPS of Surry. Will. Date: 22 Feb. 1729/30.
           Rec.: 21 Feb. 1738. Nathaniel Clanton, Executor. Legatee:
           Nathanell Clanton. Witnesses: Edward Clanton, Thomas Don
           and Sarey Clanton.

Page 16:   MARY TYUSS. Account Current. Date: 1735. Rec.: 21 Feb'y
           1738. John Tyus, Administrator. William Skipwith and Wil-
           liam Short, Jr., Auditors.

Page 18:   MARIOTT CRIPPS. Inventory. Date ordered: 16 Aug. 1738.
           Rec.: 21 Feb. 1738. William Cripps, Administrator. James
           Washington, Samuel Magett and Bartholomew Figuers, Apprais-
           ers.

Page 19:   MARIOTT CRIPPS. Account Current. Date: ----. Rec.: 21
           Feb. 1738. William Cripps, Administrator.

Page 35:   WALTER COCKE of Southwark Parish, Surry. Will. Date: Aug.
           1, 1735. Rec.: 21 Mar. 1738. Thomas Cocke, Executor. Sons:
           Thomas and John. Daughter: Anne Hamlin. Witnesses: Henry
           Berry, John Ware and Francis Hagood.

Page 36:   ALCE SHOCKEY of Southwark Parish, Surry. Will. Date: 17
           Feb. 1736/5. Rec.: 21 Mar. 1738. Daughters: Meley Ellis,
           Elizabeth Bullock, Agnes Barker, and Mary Shockey. Grand-
           son: Richard Ellis. Grand-daughters: Mary Ellis, Marry
           Barker, Agness Barker, Alce Bullock and Mary Bullock. Wit-
           nesses: Benjamin Reekes, Elizabeth Saffold. Mary Shockey,
           Executrix.

Page 47:   ALLEN WARRIN. Account Current. Date: ----. Rec.: 21 Mar.
           1738. John and Anne (alias Warrin) Little, Executors.
           Mentions: son Allen. William Rookings and Robert Gray,
           Auditors.

Page 48:   ELIZABETH CHAMPION. Account Current. Date: ----. Rec.:
           21 Mar. 1738. Charles Champion, Administrator. William
           Rookings and Robert Gray, Auditors.

Page 51:   JOHN PERSON. Will. Date: 8 Aug. 1721. Rec.: 21 March
           1738. Thomas Person, Executor. Sons: John, Thomas, Fran-
           cis, Joseph, Benjamin, Samuel, William and Jacob. Grand-
           children: Joseph and Avarelah Tuke. Daughters: Mary and
           Elizabeth Person. Wife: Sarah. Mentions: some children
           are minors,; land in Isle of Wight County. Witnesses:
           William Crips (age 62), Sampson Laneer (age 56), John Glover
           (age 50), and Robert Jordan (age 32) swear to handwriting.

Page 53:   ROBERT LAN(D)CASTOR of Lawnes Creek Parish, Surry. Will.
           Date: 12 Nov. 1738. Rec.: 18 Apr. 1739. Samuel Lancas-
           tor, Executor. Sons: Samuel, William; and Joseph (not 21).
           Daughters: Elizabeth, Mary and Anne. Friend: William An-
           drews. Witnesses: John Little (Littell) and William Hart.

Page 54:   NATHANIELL PHILIPS. Inventory. Date: 14 Apr. 1739. Rec.:
           18 Apr. 1739. Nathaniel Clanton, Executor.

Page 56:   EDWARD THROWER. Inventory. Date: ----. Rec.: 16 May
              1739. William Gilliam, Executor. George Booth, Thomas
              Wynne and William Winfield, Appraisers.

Page 57:   WILLIAM BREWTON of Lawnes Creek Parish, Surry. Will. Date:
              18 July 1737. Rec.: 16 May 1739. Sarah Brewton and Charles
              Binns, Executors. Sisters: Mary and Anne. Daughters:
              Martha, Sarah and Elizabeth. Wife: Sarah. Friend: Char-
              les Binns. Witnesses: Thomas Binns, Joseph Bridges and
              George Brewton.

Page 61:   EDWARD TATUM of Surry. Will. Date: 3 Sept. 1736. Rec.:
              16 May 1739. Peter Tatum, Executor. Sons: Nathanell and
              Peter. Daughters: Ruth and Elizabeth Tatum. Wife: Re-
              beckah. Witnesses: Christopher Tatum and Peter Tatum.

Page 61:   ROBERT LANCASTER. Inventory. Date: ----. Rec.: 16 May
              1739. Samuel Lancaster, Executor.

Page 62:   Mr. WALTER COCKE. Inventory. Date: 14 May 1739. Rec.: 16
              May 1739. Thomas Cocke, Executor.

Page 62:   RICHARD ROSE. Account Current. Date: ----. Rec.: 16 May
              1739. Returned by John Nicolson and Thomas Bayley. Men-
              tions: legacy paid to granddaughter: Hannah Rose. William
              Brown, Jr. and Jones Stokes, Auditors.

Page 64:   ELCE (ALICE) SHOCKY. Inventory. Date: ----. Rec.: 16 May
              1739. Mary Shockey, Executrix.

Page 67:   SOLOMON HARRISON of Surry. Will. Date: 11 Mar. 1736/37.
              Rec.: 18 July 1739. Mary Harrison, Executrix. Sons: John;
              William, Benjamin and Henry (not 20). Wife: Mary. Daugh-
              ter: Martha (not 18). Witnesses: William Rookings and
              William Dewell.

Page 68:   JOHN PERSON. Inventory. Date ordered: 21 Mar. 1738. Rec.:
              18 July 1739. Thomas Person, Executor. Joseph John Clinch,
              Joseph Witherington and John Moring, Appraisers.

Page 71:   THOMAS COGGING. List of Bills due. Date:----. Rec.: July
              18, 1739. Bills are in the hands of John Ruffin by Court
              order.

Page 74:   WILLIAM BRUTON. Inventory. Date:----. Rec.: 18 Jul. 1739.
              Sarah Bruton, and Charles Binns, Executors.

Page 75:   EDWARD TATUM. Inventory. Date: ----. Rec.: 18 Jul. 1739.
              Peter Tatum, Executor.

Page 87:   SOLOMON HARRISON. Inventory. Date: 18 Sept. 1739. Rec.:
              17 Oct. 1739. Mary Harrison, Executrix. Thomas Allstin,
              William Rookings and James Rookings, Appraisers.

Page 89:   MARY DAVIDSON. Account Current. Date:----. Rec.: 17 Oct.
              1739. William Clemons, Executor. Mentions: legacies to
              grandchildren: William Clemons and Elizabeth Boykin. Sons:
              John and William Clemons. Robert Jones, Jr. and Joseph Ma-
              son, Auditors.

Page 90:   THOMAS DREW. Inventory. Date: 3 Apr. 1739. Rec.: 17 Oct.
              1739. Judith Drew, Administratrix, of William Drew, Execu-
              tor of Thomas Drew. John Thompson, John Crafford and John
              Beryman, Appraisers.

Page 92:   HENRY HART of Lawnes Creek Parish, Surry. Will. Date: 8
              Nov. 1734. Rec.: 21 Nov. 1739. Thomas, Henry, John and
              Joseph Hart, Executors. Sons: Thomas, John (in North Car-
              olina); Joseph and Henry. Daughters: Lucy and Lidya.

(Page 92 - HART cont'd.): Wife: (not named). Mentions: 6 eldest daughters. Witnesses: Charles Binns, Henry Hart and William
Jordan.

Page 93:   HENRY BRIGGS of Surry. Will. Date: 22 Jan. 1738. Rec.:
21 Nov. 1739. James Chappell, Executors. Grandsons: Henry
Bedingfeld, James Chappell and Thomas Chappell. Daughters:
Mary Bedingfeld, Ann Barten, Jane Day, Hannah Hill, Priselah Barker and Elizabeth Chappell. Son-in-law: James Chappell. Grandaughter: Reabaco Chappell. Witnesses: John
Rossor, John Jarrad and James Chappell, Jr.

Page 98:   JOHN PERSON. Account Current. Date: ----. Rec.: 21 Nov.
1739. Thomas Person, Executor. Mentions: Sarah Person's
dower. Charles Binns and Kennith McKenzie, Auditors.

Page 100:   JOHN FLOOD of Southwark Parish, Surry. Will. Date: 4 Oct.
1739. Rec.: 21 Nov. 1739. Nicholas Edmunds granted Administration. Sister: Fortune Flood. Friend: Nicholas Edmunds. Witnesses: William Simmons (age 34), Richard Davis, Charles Simmons (age 17), John Davis and Anne Hamlin.

Page 100:   MICKELL CASELY of Southwark Parish, Surry. Will. Date: 23
July 1739. Rec.: 21 Nov. 1739. Elizabeth Casely, Execu-
trix. Son: Mickel (Michael) - (not of age). Daughters:
Mary, Sarah and Martha. Father-in-law: William Moss.
Wife: Elizabeth. Friends: Charles Lucas and Joshua Nicol-
son. Witnesses: Joshua Nicolson and William Moore.

Page 102:   HANNAH CLINCH of Southwark Parish, Surry. Will. Date: 10
Apr. 1739. Rec.: 16 Jan. 1739. Joseph John Clinch, Executor. Daughters: Mary, and Mary Clinch. Sons: James, Joseph John. Witnesses: Richard Cock, John Holt and Thomas
Holt.

Page 107:   THOMAS CARTER. Inventory. Date ordered: 16 Jan. 1739.
Rec.: 25 Feb. 1739. Bartholomu Figuars, Administrator.
John Andrews, Samuel Magett and Robert Junkins, Appraisers.

Page 111:   FRANCIS SHARP of Lawnes Creek Parish, Surry. Will. Date:
14 Aug. 1739. Rec.: 20 Feb. 1739. Jacob Sharp, Executor.
Sons: Francis, Jacob. John and William. Daughters: Sarah
Sharp, Mary; Elizabeth Garris; and Comfort King. Friend:
Mr. Charles Binns. Witnesses: Thomas Bell, William Evans
and Mary Bell. Mentions: lots in Williamsburg, and land
in Isle of Wight County.

Page 113:   JOHN ELLIS of Albemarle Parish, Surry. Will. Date: 10 Jan.
1739. Rec.: 20 Feb. 1739. Mary Ellis, Executrix. Wife:
Mary. Daughter: Mildred Ellis (not 18). Child in esse.
Witnesses: Andrew Lester, Morris Pritchett and Richard
Blunt.

Page 116:   WILLIAM SHARINTON of Albemarle Parish, Surry. Will. Date:
-----. Rec.: 19 Mar. 1740. Richard Rives, Executor. Leg-
atee: Richard Rives. Witnesses: Christopher Golightly,
William Pettway and William More.

Page 127:   JOHN GRANTHAM of Southwark Parish, Surry. Will. Date: 16
Jan. 1737/38. Rec.: 19 Mar. 1739. Sarah and Thomas Grantham, Executors. Sons: Thomas and Steven. Wife: Sarah.
Daughter: Sarah Grantham. Witnesses: Robert Snipes, Han-
er Fichet and Christopher Moring, Jr.

Page 133:   JOHN GILLIAM. Account Current. Date: ----. Rec.: 19 Mar.
1739. Sary and John Gilliam, Executors. R. Hamlin and
Robert Gray, Auditors.

Page 133:   ELIAS FORT of Southwark Parish, Surry. Will. Date: 20 Sept.

24

(Page 133 - FORT cont'd): 1732. Rec.: 19 Mar. 1739. Holiday Fort, Executor. Sons: John and Holiday. Grandson: John Fort. Daughters: Phillis Pennington, Mary Foster, Alice Foster, and Faith King. Wife: Sarah. Witnesses: John Chapman, John Bynum and Joseph Andrews.

Page 137: JOHN ELLIS. Inventory. Date: 28 Feb. 1739. Rec.: 19 Mar. 1739. Mary Ellis, Executrix. Richard Blunt, Edmund Ruffin and Andrew Lester, Appraisers.

Page 142: HENRY BRIGGS. Inventory. Date: 18 Mar. 1739/40. Rec.:19 Mar. 1739. James Chappell.

Page 142: FRANCIS RAY of Southwark Parish, Surry. Will. Date: 29 Apr. 1738. Rec.: 19 Mar. 1739. William Rawlings, next of kin, granted administration; the widow refused. Son: William (not 18). Wife: Affiah. Child in esse. Witnesses: William Cooper, Francis Ray and Benjamin Reeks.

Page 149: HINCHA GILLAM. Account Current. Date: ----. Rec.: 16 Apr. 1740. Willut and Faith Roberts, Executors. John Mason,Jr. and Bartholomew Figures, Auditors.

Page 151: ELIAS FORT. Inventory. Date: ----. Rec.: 16 Apr. 1740. Hollyday Fort, Executor. Mentions: Widow; legacies to John Fort, Phillis Pennington, Mary Foster, Faith King and Holiday Fort. Edward Bayley, Joseph Andrews and James Davis, Appraisers.

Page 152: WILLIAM SERGENTON. Inventory. Date: 6 Apr. 1740. Rec.: 16 Apr. 1740. Richard Rives, Executor.

Page 153: JOHN GRANTHAM. Inventory. Date: ----. Rec.: 16 Apr.1740. Sarah and Thomas Grantham, Executors. Edward Bayley, Christopher Moring, Jr. and Joseph Andrews, Appraisers.

Page 153: JOHN CARR. Account Current. Date: 1738. Rec.: 16 April 1740. Richard Ransom, Executor.

Page 172: TABITHA THROWER. Inventory. Date: ----. Rec.: 21 May 1740. William Gilliam, Administrator. George Booth, Peter Green and William Winfeild, Appraisers.

Page 175: HANNAH CLINCH. Inventory. Date: 22 Jan. 1739. Rec.: May 21, 1740. Joseph John Clinch, Executor. Gilbert Gray, Richard Andrews and Robert Gray, Appraisers.

Page 179: JOHN GRAVES, JR. Inventory. Date ordered: 16 April 1740. Rec.: 16 July 1740. John Groves, Administrator. Samuel Maget, Bartholomew Figures and Robert Judkins, Appraisers.

Page 199: WILLIAM EDMUNDS of Surry. Will. Date: 19 Feb. 1730. Rec.: 16 July 1740. Mary Edmunds, Executrix. Sons: William,David, John Edmongray (not 18). Daughters: Mary, Sarah, Susannah, Elizabeth, Faith, Fillis and Christian; Wife: Mary. Witnesses: Richard Parker and Nathaniel Moss.

Page 202: THOMAS BAGE. Inventory. Date: 14 July 1740. Rec.: 16 Jul. 1740. Elizabeth Bage, Administratrix. Richard Andrews, Henry Watkins and Robert Warren, Appraisers.

Page 205: HENRY HART. Inventory. Date: ----. Rec.: 16 July 1740. Thomas, Henry, John and Joseph Hart, Executors.

Page 208: FRANCIS RAY. Inventory. Date: 26 Mar. 1740. Rec.: 16 Jul. 1740. William Rawlings, Administrator. Benjamin Reeks, John Justise and Thomas Bedingfeld, Appraisers.

Page 210: THOMAS HUSKEY. Inventory. Date: 7 Aug. 1740. Rec.: Sept.

(Page 210 - HUSKEY cont'd.): 17, 1740. Thomas (John) Threewitt, Administrator - (each name mentioned once.) Thomas Wynne, Stephen Housman and Edward Ackles.

Page 210:   MICHAEL CASELY. Inventory. Date: 17 Sept. 1740. Rec.: 17
Sept. 1740. Elizabeth Casely, Executrix.

Page 215:   JOHN BARKER of Southword (Southwark) Parish, Surry. Will.
Date: 11 Apr. 1736. Rec.: 17 Sept. 1740. Mary Bishop, Executrix. Sister: Mary Brker (Ex.). Brother: Josuway
Brker. Mentions: 3 brothers. Witnesses: Josiah Barker
and Faith Barker.

Page 219:   JOHN OWIN. Inventory and Sale. Date: 6 Aug. 1740. Rec.:
15 Oct. 1740. Roger Delk, Administrator. Joseph Hancock,
Thomas Davidson and Newitt Edwards, Appraisers.

Page 222:   WILLIAM EDMUNDS. Inventory. Date: 15 Oct. 1740. Rec.:
15 Oct. 1740. Mary Edmunds, Executrix. Thomas Peters,John
Hunt and George Wych, Appraisers.

Page 223:   SAMUEL JUDKIN of Southwark Parish, Surry. Will. Date: 13
April 1740. Rec.: 15 Oct. 1740. Ann and Samuel Judkin,
Executors. Son: Samuel. Wife: Anne. Daughters: Anne
Champian; and Sarah Holt. Granddaughters: Lucy Champian
(not 18) and Lucy Holt. Witnesses: William Edwards, Char-
les Holt and Nicholas Judkin.

Page 224:   JOHN FLOOD. Inventory. Date: 12 Dec. 1739. Rec.: 15 Oct.
1740. Nicholas Edmunds, Administrator. William Rookings,
John Griffith and Thomas Allstin, Appraisers.

Page 229:   JOHN BARKER. Inventory. Date: 15 Oct. 1740. Rec.: 15 Oct.
1740. James Bishop, Executor. Thomas Bedingfild, Richard
Blunt and Edmund Ruffin, Appraisers.

Page 230:   JAMES RANSOM of Surry. Will. Date: 19 May 1740. Rec.: 15
Oct. 1740. Grissell Ransom, Charles Binns and John Ruffin,
Executors. Daughters: Mary, Catherine and Elizabeth.
Father and Mother: (not named). Wife: Grissell. Sons:
James and Gwathmy. Legatee: Elizabeth Smith (not of age).
Friends: James Baker, Charles Binns and John Ruffin. Wit-
nesses: Arthur Smith and James Carrell.

Page 231:   HARRY FLOYD of Surry. Will. Date: 18 Dec. 1739. Rec.: 15
Oct. 1740. Robert Nicholson, Executor. Daughters: Anne
Floyd (in England) and Elizabeth Nicholson. Grandchildren:
Henry, Robert, Mary, George, James and Anne Nicholson. Son-
in-law: Robert Nicholson. Friend: Col. John Allen. Wit-
nesses: Thomas Hamlin, L. Delony and Elizabeth Rookings.

Page 242:   WILLIAM FITCHIT. Inventory. Date: 11 Oct. 1740. Rec.: 19
Nov. 1740. Mary Fitchett, Administratrix. John Tyus, John
Moring and Joseph Witherington, Appraisers.

Page 250:   WILLIAM COOK of Surry. Will. Date: 1 May 1740. Rec.: 19
Nov. 1740. James Cook, Executor. Sons: William, Rubin,
and James. Daughters: Elizabeth, wife of Thomas Tomlinson;
Rebeccah, wife of James Anderson; Sarah, wife of Henry Mitch-
ell; Mary, wife of William Briggs; Susana, wife of Miell
Hill; Hannah, wife of Richard Gary; Amy, wife of John Mac-
lin. Witnesses: John Barker, William Brewer and Thomas
Lanier.

Page 254:   EDWARD STEPHENS. Inventory. Date: 2 May 1740. Rec.: 19
Nov. 1740. Rebecah Stephens, Administratrix. Christopher
Tatum, William Shands and Robert Doby, Appraisers.

Page 254:   SAMUEL JUDKIN. Inventory. Date: 18 Nov. 1740. Rec.: 9

(Page 254 - JUDKIN cont'd.): Nov. 1740. Samuel and Anne Judkin, Executors.

Page 257: WILLIAM LITTLE of Lawnes Creek Parish, Surry. Will. Date: 29 Sept. 1740. Rec.: 19 Nov. 1740. William and Benjamin Little, Executors. Sons: 1st, William; 2nd, John; 3rd, Benjamin. Daughters: Latherine (Catherine?) and Patience Little. Wife: (not named). Mentions: mullatto boy, James Bruce, to be free at age of 21. Witnesses: Thomas Pretlow, Jr., John Atkeison and Martha Price.

Page 259: WILLIAM GILBERT of Albemarle Parish, Surry. Will. Date: 3 Feb. 1739. Rec.: 19 Nov. 1740. Joannah Gilbert, Executrix. Wife: Joanah. Sons: John, James and William. Daughters: Mary, Elizabeth, Martha, Hanah and Ann Gilbert. Witnesses: Thomas Culum, John Cooper and Thomas Cooper. Mentions: land in Brunswick County.

Page 265: JOHN ROBARDS of Albemarle Parish, Surry. Will. Date: 11 Sept. 1740. Rec: 21 Jan. 1740. William Shands and William Pettway, Executors. Grandson: John Shans. Granddaughter: Mary Shands and Elizabeth Pettway. Daughters: Nazereth Shands and Elizabeth Pettway. Sons-in-law: William Shands and William Pettway. Legatees: Susanno Epps, Mary Pettway, Elizabeth Pettway, cousin of daughter Elizabeth. Witnesses: Robert Wynne, Peter and John Hawthorn.

Page 267: WILLIAM LANCASTER. Inventory. Date: 11 Oct. 1740. Rec: 21 Jan. 1740. Mary Lancaster, Administratrix. William Rose, Bartholomew Figures and Samuel Maget, Appraisers.

Page 275: WILLIAM LITEL (LITTLE). Inventory. Date: ----. Rec.: 18 Mar. 1740. William and Benjamin Littel, Executors.

Page 277: WILLIAM COOK. Inventory. Date: ----. Rec.: 18 Mar. 1740. James Cook, Executor.

Page 289: WILLIAM GILBART. Inventory. Date: ----. Rec.: 18 Mar.1740. Hannah Gilbert, Executrix.

Page 297: WILLIAM WILLIAMS of Southwark Parish, Surry. Will. Date: 17 Nov. 1740. Rec.: 15 Apr. 1741. Lewis Williams, Executor. Sons: Lewis, William and John. Daughters: Hester (not of age); Ledia, Anne, Katheron, Mary, Hanah, Unity and Faith. Friends: William Edwards and Mr. William Newsum. Witnesses: William Edwards and John Johnson.

Page 304: EDWARD STEPHENS. Account Current. Date: ----. Rec.: April 15, 1741. Benjamin and Rebeka Moss, Administrators. Samuel Weldon, and James Washington, Auditors.

Page 305: FRANCIS SHARP. Inventory. Date ordered: 20 Feb. 1739. Rec.: 15 Apr. 1741. Jacob Sharp, Executor. Samuel Maget, Thomas Bell and Joseph Witherington, Appraisers.

Page 307: JOSEPH SEAT. Inventory. Date: 10 Apr. 1741. Rec.: 15 Apr. 1741. Marshall Seat, Administrator. Edward Bayley, Henry Watkins and Christopher Moring, Jr., Appraisers.

Page 319: THOMAS ELDRIDGE of Albemarle Parish, Surry, Attorney at Law. Will. Date: 17 Aug. 1739. Rec.: 20 May 1741. Judith Eldridge, Executrix. Wife: Judith. Sons: William (not 21); Richard and Thomas. Daughters: Judith, Elizabeth, Mary, Ann and Martha. Grandchildren: Thomas and Jane Eldridge (not 21). Mentions: land in Prince George, Brunswick and Henrico Counties. Codicil. Witnesses: (none).

Page 327: WILLIAM CLEMENTS of Southwark Parish, Surry. Will. Date: 26 Apr. 1741. Rec.: 20 May 1741. Alice Clements, Execu-

(Page 327 - CLEMENTS cont'd.): trix. Wife: Ales (Alce). Daughters: Lucy and Elizabeth. Sons: Samuel, William and Henry. Legatee: Samuel Thompson. Mentions: none of children are of age. Witnesses: Mary Davis and Samuel Thompson.

Page 332: JANE LATHER of Surry. Will. Date: 28 Jan. 1740/41. Rec: 20 May 1741. Thomas Collier, Executor. Granddaughters: Rebecah and Priscilla Andrews. Daughter: Martha Andrews. Sons: Thomas and John Collier. Witnesses: Nicholas Maget, Peter Warren and Benjamin King.

Page 335: WILLIAM HOWELL. Account Current. Date: ----. Rec.: 21 May 1741. Joseph John Snipes and wife Mary, who was an Howell, return. Mentions: legacy to wife; daughter Joanna; Elizabeth; children. William Rookings and Moses Johnson, Auditors.

Page 338: CHRISTIAN KNOTT. Inventory. Date: 1 July 1741. Rec.: 15 July 1741. Gregory Rawlings, Administrator. William Rookings, Thomas Allstin and James Rookings, Appraisers.

Page 345: WILLIAM WILLIAMS. Inventory. Date: ----. Rec.: 15 July 1741. Lewis Williams, Executor. William Batts, Nicholas Thompson and Joseph Hart, Appraisers.

Page 350: JANE LATHER. Inventory. Date ordered: 20 May 1741. Rec: 15 July 1741. Thomas Collier, Executor. Robert Watkins, Edward Bayley and Henry Watkins, Appraisers.

Page 355: HENRY SAVAGE. Account Current and Sale. Date: 8 May 1741. Rec.: 15 July 1741. Robert Wynne, Sub-Sheriff. Purchasers include: Mary and Lovelace Savage. Amount due from Henry Savage's estate mentioned.

Page 355: JOHN SIMMONS, JR. Inventory. Date; ----. Rec.: 16 Sept. 1741. Rebecca and William Simmons, Executors. Includes property in Brunswick County. Edward Bayley, Robert Watkins and Henry Watkins, Appraisers.

Page 359: JOHN OWIN. Account Current. Date: 1740. Rec: 16 Sept.1741. Roger Delk, Administrator. Mentions: widow and two children. Robert Gray and Thomas Eldridge, Auditors.

Page 362: Capt. HENRY BROWNE. Account Current. Date: 1734. Rec: 16 Sept. 1741. William Browne, Jr., Executor. Mentions: the widow; legacies to - William Rogers and Edward Harris. Charles Binns and James Gee, Auditors.

Page 364: WILLIAM SHORT of Southwark Parish, Surry. Will. Date: 10 April 1736. Rec: 16 Sept. 1741. William Short, Executor. Sons: William and Thomas. Daughter: Mary Harris. Granddaughters: Susanna Short, daughter of Thomas Short; Sarah, Mary and Martha Short, daughters of William Short. Grandsons - William Harris, son of William (Harris?) (not 18); Thomas Harris (not 18), and William Short, son of William Short. Wife: Susana. Kinsman: Benjamin Heath. Witnesses: William Heeth, Richard Jones and Richard Bullock. Mentions land in Prince George County.

Page 382: PETER RANDOL (RANDALL). Inventory. Date: 1741. Rec: 21 Oct. 1741. Mary Randol, Administratrix. Thomas Vines, Thomas Mathis and Thomas Jones, Appraisers.

Page 384: JOHN CANNON of Southwark Parish, Surry. Will. Date: July 11, 1741. Rec: 21 Oct. 1741. John Justice, Executor. Wife: Joanna. Friend: John Justice. Daughter: Joanna Justice. Granddaughters: Joanna Scarbrough, Jaen Justice, Mary Justice (not of age); Elizabeth, Lydia and Sarah Justice. Great-granddaughter: Joannah Scarbrough. Grandson: John

(Page 384 - CANNON cont'd.): Justice, Jr. Cousin: Cannan, son of Benjamin Cooper. Legatee: William Scarbrough. Witnesses: Joshua Nicolson and John Collier.

Page 388: ELIZABETH ANDRUS of Surry. Will. Date: 29 Nov. 1735. Rec: 18 Nov. 1741. Bartholomew Andrus, Executor. Cousin: Bartholomew Andrus, son of Robert (Andrus). Former Husband: Nathaniel Roberts (will dated, 19 April 1693). Legatees: Marget Tuther, daughter of George; and Mary Long, widow of George. Witnesses: Henry Sowerby and Robert Jordan.

Page 389: JOHN COLLIER. Account Current. Date: ----. Rec.: 18 Nov. 1741. Moses Johnson and Thomas Collier, Executors. Mentions: legacy to Moses Johnson. James Chappell and Robert Jones, Jr., Auditors.

Page 397: WILLIAM SHORT. Inventory. Date: ----. Rec.: 20 Jan. 1741. William Short, Executor.

Page 397: JOHN CANNON. Inventory. Date: ----. Rec.: 17 Feb. 1741. John Justice, Executor.

Page 398: ELEANOR MABURY. Account Current. Date: ----. Rec: 17 Feb. 1741. Francis Mabury presents. Thomas Gray and Lemuel Cocke, Auditors.

Page 399: WILLIAM WRAY. Account Current. Date: ----. Rec: 21 April 1742. Martha Ray, Executrix. John Mason, Jr. and Robert Jones, Jr., Auditors.

Page 399: HENRY BROWN. Division. Date: 21 Nov. 1741. Rec: 21 Apr. 1742. Lemuel Cocke and wife, Jane, Henry, Ann, and Rebeccah Brown: 1/4 each.

Page 400: JOHN ALLEN of Surry, Gent. Will. Date: 5 Mar. 1741. Rec: 21 Apr. 1742. James Baker, Gent., Executor. Nephews: James Bridger (not 25); William Allen, son of Joseph Allen, dec'd. (not 21). Neice: Catherine Cocke. Nephew: James Allen. Housekeeper: Mrs. Mourning Thomas. Friends: Mr. James Baker and Capt. John Ruffin. Mentions: wife and child are dead; wife's sisters, Mrs. Rascow and Mrs. Daingerfield; Miss Mary Rascow, daughter of Col. William Rascow; James Harrison (not 22). Brother: Joseph, dec'd. Witnesses: Thomas Wharton, Patrick Adams, Augustine Claiborne, James Harrison, James Boyd and Charles Henry Jones.

Page 402: JOHN BARKER. Will. Date: 21 May 1725. Rec: 21 Apr. 1742. Mary Morris, Executrix (late Barker). Sons: John and Christopher. Daughter: Mary Barker. Wife: (unnamed). Mentions: 5 children. Witnesses: John Collier, Nicholas Cocke and Joshua Nicolson.

Page 403: THOMAS HUSKEY. Account Current. Date: ----. Rec.: 16 Jun. 1742. John Threewett, Administrator. William Mearns and Thomas Mitchell, Auditors.

Page 403: THOMAS DREW of Lawnes Creek Parish, Surry. Will. Date: 13 Feb. 1737/38. Rec: 21 Apr. 1742. David Drew, Executor. Sons: David, Thomas and John. Daughters: Mary, and Faith (not 18). Friends: Charles Binns and Benjamin Bell. Witnesses: Charles Binns, William Hart, Benjamin Bell and Thomas Binns.

Page 404: NATHANIEL HOWELL of Surry. Will. Date: 1 Apr. 1741. Rec: 16 June 1742. Susanna Howell granted Administration. Sons: John, William, Thomas and Nathaniel. Daughters: Mary Chambers; Ann Howell. Wife: Susannah. Witnesses: Christopher Tatum and Henry Mitchell.

29

Page 405:   Mrs. MARY KNOTT. Inventory. Date: 12 Feb. 1740/41. Rec: 16 June 1742. Alexander Finnie, Administrator. William Rookings, Thomas Allstin and Robert Grimer, Appraisers.

Page 406:   JOHN BARKER. Inventory. Date: 4 May 1742. Rec: 16 June 1742. Caleb Ellis, Thomas Bedingfield and Josiah Barker.

Page 406:   ELIAS FORT. Account Current. Date: ----. Rec: 21 July 1742. Holiday Fort, Executor. William Cocke and Moses Johnson, Auditors.

Page 407:   WILLIAM WILLIAMS. Account Current and Sale. Date: ----. Rec: 21 July 1742. Lewis Williams, Executor. Mentions legacies to: John Bennet, Thomas Waller, Ann Williams and Mary Savidge; maintenance of Hester, John and Faith Williams. William Clinch and William Edwards, Auditors.

Page 408:   SAMUEL DEAN. Inventory. Date: 28 Jan. 1741/42. Rec: July 21, 1742. William Eppes, Administrator. William Cook, William Shands and David Jones, Appraisers.

Page 409:   MARMADUKE GRESWITT. Will. Date: 31 Jan. 1741/42. Rec.: 18 Aug. 1742. Wife: Mary Greswitt, Executrix. Sons: George, and Thomas Gruswitt. Wife: Ann. Legatees: Walter Gruswitt and Daniel Guttre. Mentions: 3 sons. Witnesses: Nathaniel Briggs, Stephen Hamlin and James Jones.

Page 410:   LEMUEL HARGRAVE of Surry. Will. Date: 2 May 1740. Rec: 15 Sept. 1742. Samuel Hargrave, Executor. Sons: Samuel, Benjamin (dec'd). and Joseph. Grandsons: Jesse Hargrave and Samuel Hargrave. Son-in-law: Anselm Bailey. Mentions: land south of Roanoak River in North Carolina. Witnesses: Arthur Pollard, Joseph Hancock and Sarah Berriman.

Page 411:   JOSEPH PRETLOW. Inventory. Date: 18 Dec. 1740. Rec: 15 Sept. 1742. William Drew, Newitt Edwards and John Glover, Appraisers.

Page 412:   JOSEPH PRETLOW. Account Current. Date: ----. Rec: Sept. 15, 1742. Samuel and Sarah Hargrave, Administrators. Lemuel Cocke and William Short, Auditors.

Page 412:   THOMAS BAGE. Account Current. Date: 1740. Rec: 17 Nov.1742. Elizabeth Bage presents.

Page 413:   AMEY WORDEN of Southwark Parish, Surry. Will. Date: 26 Oct. 1741. Rec: 17 Nov. 1742. William Seward, Executor. Son: James. Daughters: Heluneh and Mary Bittle. Grandson: John Worden, son of James (Worden). Granddaughter: Mourning Minitry Newsom. Witness: John Avery.

Page 414:   DAVID SEBRELL of Southwark Parish, Surry. Will. Date: 7 Nov. 1742. Rec: 17 Nov. 1742. Joseph Hancock, Executor. Nephew: Nathaniel Sebrell (not 21). Sister: Susannah Hancock and Sarah Wilson. Brother-in-law: Joseph Hancock. Witnesses: William Seward and William Drew.

Page 415:   WILLIAM BATTS of Southwark Parish, Surry. Will. Date: 31 Dec. 1741. Rec: 17 Nov. 1742. William Batts and Mrs. Batts (widow, not named), Executors. Wife: (unnamed). Sons: John and William. Daughters: Martha, Mary and Elizabeth. Grandson: William Lain. Witnesses: Charles Binns, Henry Holt and David Drew.

Page 416:   MARMADUKE GRESSWITT. Inventory. Date: ----. Rec: 15 Dec. 1742. Ann Grisswitt, presents. George Briggs, Simon Murfee and Henry Sawrey, Appraisers.

Page 416:   DANIEL TURNER. Account Current. Date: 1738. Rec: 15

(Page 416 - TURNER cont'd.): Dec. 1742. Thomas and Sarah Wallace, Executors. Robert Jones, Jr. and John Newsom, Auditors.

Page 417:   GEORGE RANDALL. Inventory. Date: ----. Rec.: 17 January
1742. Mary Randall presents. William Raney, Robert Farrington and Edward Farrington, Appraisers.

Page 418:   Mr. JAMES RANSOM. Inventory. Date: ----. Rec.: 19 Jan.
1742. Grisell Ransom, Executor. John Ruffin, Charles
Binns and James Baker, Appraisers.

Page 419:   Mrs. AMY WORDEN. Inventory. Date: 20 Nov. 1742. Rec.: 16
Feb. 1742. William Seward, Executor. William Drew, Joseph
Hancock and Thomas Davidson, Appraisers.

Page 420:   AMY WORDEN. Account Current. Date: ----. Rec.: 16 Feb'y.
1742. William Seward, Executor. Legatees: James Worden;
John Worden, son of James; Mourning Menitree Newsom. Lemuel
Cocke and William Skipwith, Auditors.

Page 421:   DAVID SEBRELL. Inventory. Date: 2 Nov. 1742. Rec.: 16 Feb.
1742. Joseph Hancock, Executor. William Drew, Thomas Davidson and Francis Price, Appraisers.

Page 422:   TRISTRAM MOOR, late of Isle of Wight County. Account Current. Date: 1739. Rec.: 16 Feb. 1742. Booz Little for
Ann Little, Administrator.

Page 422:   WILLIAM SHARP. Inventory. Date: ----. Rec.: 16 Mar. 1742.
Charles Binns, Administrator. Samuel Maget, Thomas Bell &
William Evans, Appraisers.

Page 423:   JAMES JONES of Albemarle Parish, Surry. Will. Date: 22
Aug. 1742. Rec.: 16 Feb. 1742. James, Howell Jones (both
underage), Sarah Jones, Executors. Richard Blunt granted
Administration. Sons: James, Howell, John and Thomas(none
20). Daughter: Elizabeth. Child in esse. Brother: Robert.
Cousin: Robert Jones. Wife: Sarah. Mentions: land in
Prince George, Isle of Wight and Brunswick Counties. Wit-
nesses: Robert Jones, Robert Jones, Jr. and Richard Jones.

Page 426:   JAMES JONES. Inventory. Date: ----. Rec.: 16 Mar. 1743.
Richard Blunt, Executor.

Page 427:   JOHN JOHNSON of Brunswick. Will. Date: 11 June 1742. Rec:
20 Apr. 1743. John Scott, Gent., granted Administration.
Sons: John, Peter, Richard; and Levetor (not of age).
Daughters: Hannah Woodward, Rosemond Underwood, and Betty
Sollowman. Grandson: John Johnson, son of Thomas, dec'd.
Mentions: land in Surry County. Witnesses: William Renn,
William Minton and Sarah Renn.

Page 428:   BURWELL GREEN. Account Current. Date: 1738. Rec: 26 Apr.
1743. Ann Green, Administratrix. Thomas Gray and John
Mason, Jr., Auditors.

Page 429:   JOANNAH JOICE FLOYD. Will. Date: 21 Oct. 1720. Rec: 18
May 1743. Robert Nicholson granted Administration, Capt.
Thomas Cocke refused. Son: Robert Nicholson. Daughters:
Joice Nicholson, Ann Nicholson and Elizabeth --. Mentions:
children not of age; John Nicholson. Friends: Capt. Henry
Harrison; Capt. Thomas Cocke, son of Mr. Walter (Cocke?).
Witnesses: Nicholas Cocke, Mary Dawson and Mary Allstin.

Page 430:   SAMUEL SOWERSBY. Inventory. Date: 16 May 1743. Rec.: 18
May 1743. Jean Sowersby, Administratrix. William Simmons,
Joshua Nicolson and Charles Lucas, Appraisers.

Page 433:   NATHANIEL HOWELL. Inventory. Date: ----. Rec.: 15 June

(Page 433 - HOWELL cont'd.): 1743. Susanna Howell, Executrix. James Mason, Timothy Ezell, Peter Hawthorn and John Mason, Appraisers.

Page 433: RICHARD JOHNSON. Inventory. Date: ----. Rec.: 15 June 1743. Lemuel Cocke, William Short and Richard Bullock, Appraisers.

Page 434: Col. JOHN ALLEN, Gent. Inventory. Date: 1742. Rec: 20 Jul. 1743. James Baker, Executor.

Page 442: WILLIAM BATTS. Inventory. Date: ----. Rec.: 20 Jul. 1743. Mary Batts, Executrix. Joseph Hart, Thomas Lane and Nicholas Thompson, Appraisers.

Page 443: JOHN HAWTHORNE. Inventory. Date: ---- Rec.: 20 July 1743. Francis Mabry, Henry Mitchell and James Mason, Appraisers.

Page 444: LEWIS SOLOMON of Surry. Will. Date: 11 Dec. 1742. Rec: 20 July 1743. Martha Solomon, Executrix. Sons: William, and Lewis. Daughters: Mary Hill and Martha Solomon. Wife: Martha. Witnesses: Thomas Avent, John Owens and William Barlow.

Page 445: JOHN JONES of Southwark Parish, Surry. Will. Date: 9 Mar. 1742/43. Rec.: 17 Aug. 1743. Sarah Jones, Executrix. Daughters: Mary, Betty, and Rebecca Jones. Wife: Sarah. Brother: Richard. Wife's Father: William Batts. Friend: Holms Boyseau. Mentions: land in Isle of Wight County. Witnesses: David and Richard Jones and John Goodwyn.

Page 446: JOHN COCK. Sale. Date: 8 Aug. 1741. Rec.: 17 Aug. 1743. Robert Wynne, Sheriff. Mentions: paid Lemmon Cock her part in full.

Page 447: DANIEL VASSER. Sale. Date ordered: 19 Oct. 1741. Rec.:17 Aug. 1743. Robert Wynne, Sheriff. Mentions: paid John Coker and wife their part of estate.

Page 448: EDWARD SCARBROUGH. Inventory & Account Current. Date:1742. Rec.: 17 Aug. 1743. Robert Wynne, Sheriff.

Page 448: JAMES JONES. Additional Inventory. Date: ----. Rec.: 21 Sept. 1743. Richard Blunt and James Jones, Executors.

Page 449: AUGUSTINE HUNNICUT of Southwark Parish, Surry. Will. Date: 14 July 1743. Rec.: 19 Oct. 1743. John and Robert Hunnicutt, Executors. Wife: (not named). Sons: Robert (not 21), Augustine and John. Daughters: Martha and Mary. Witnesse : William Seward.

Page 450: RICHARD LEWIS. Inventory. Date: ----. Rec.: 19 October 1743. William Simmons, Executor.

Page 451: THOMAS EDMONDS, Gent. Account Current. Date: 1737. Rec.: 19 Oct. 1743. Edmund and Ann Ruffin, Administrators. John Mason, John Cargill and James Chappell, Auditors.

Page 452: FRANCIS SHARP. Account Current and Sale. Date: ----. Rec: 21 Dec. 1743. Jacob Sharp, Executor. Mentions: legacies to sons: Francis, John, William and Jacob; daughters: Comfort, Elizabeth, Sarah and Mary. Charles Binns, William Hart and Joseph Hart, Auditors.

Page 453: WILLIAM BATTS. Account Current and Sale. Date: 1742. Rec: 21 Dec. 1743. Mary Batts, Executrix. Mentions: legacies to Executor, William Batts, Mary Batts, Jr., Elizabeth Batts, John Batts and Martha Lane. Charles Binns, Auditor.

Page 454:   JOHN JONES. Inventory. Date ordered: 17 Aug. 1743. Rec: 21 Dec. 1743. Sarah Bard and Benjamin Baird, return. James Gee, John Goodwyn and William Cook, Appraisers.

Page 456:   LEWIS SOLOMAN. Inventory. Date: ----. Rec.: 21 December 1743. Mar'a Soloman returns.

Page 456:   JOHN JONES. Inventory. (Isle of Wight County). Date: 16 Dec. 1743. Rec.: 21 Dec. 1743. Sarah Bard returns. John Tharp, Owin Myrick and John Myrick, Appraisers.

Page 456:   TRUSTRAM MOORE. Account Current. Date: ----. Rec.: 21 Dec. 1743. Booz Little for Ann Little, Administrator.

Page 457:   CARTER CRAFFORD of Southwark Parish, Surry. Will. Date: 5 Aug. 1743. Rec.: 16 Feb. 1743. John and Carter Crafford, Executors. Sons: John and Carter. Daughters: Faith Hart; and Constant. Wife: (not named). Witnesses: John Ruffin and Daniel Hudson.

Page 458:   HANNAH OWIN. Inventory. Date: ----. Rec.: 15 Feb. 1743. Bartholomew Figures, Administrator. John Andrews, Benjamin Ellis and John Groves, Appraisers.

Page 459:   THOMAS PEEBLES. Inventory. Date: ----. Rec.: 15 February 1743. Sarah Peebles, Administratrix. Nicholas Partridge, John Tomlinson and Edward Weaver, Appraisers.

Page 460:   WILLIAM FITCHET. Account Current. Date: 1743. Rec.: 15 Feb. 1743. Richard Cocke, returns. Mentions: widow and children. John Nicholson and John Newsom, Auditors.

Page 460:   MICHAEL HARRIS of Southwark Parish, Surry,- Weaver. Will. Date: 7 Jan. 1739/40. Rec.: 21 Mar. 1743. John Harris, Executor. Son: John. Daughter: Mary. Wife: (not named). Witnesses: Samuel Thompson, John Davis and William Merriott.

Page 461:   SUSANNA SHORT of Southwark Parish, Surry. Will. Date: 3 Dec. 1743. Rec.: 21 Mar. 1743. Thomas Short, William Harris, Executors. Daughter: Mary Harris. Grandsons: William Harris (not 21); and Thomas Harris. Son: Thomas. Granddaughter: Susanna Short. Witnesses: William Short, John Woobank and Richard Bullock.

Page 463:   Capt. WILLIAM BROWNE, JR. Nunc. Will. Date: ----. Rec.: 18 Apr. 1744. Mary Browne, widow, Executrix. Wife: Mary. Daughter: mary. Mentions: children; Henry Browne, orphan (no accn't. by gdn.) Friends: Mr. William Eaton, Capt. Richard Cocke and James Balflour. Forgives debts of: Elizabeth Cobbs, Elizabeth Bage and Lewis Parham. Witnesses: James Balflour and Elizabeth Tute, widow.

Page 464:   HENRY WATKINS. Inventory. Date: 21 Feb. 1743. Rec.: 18 Apr. 1744. Robert Gray, John Nicholson and Gilbert Gray, Appraisers.

Page 465:   Mr. CARTER CRAFFORD. Inventory. Date: 6 Apr. 1744. Rec: 18 Apr. 1744. John and Carter Crafford, Executors. Thomas Binns, William Drew and John Newsum, Appraisers.

Page 466:   JOHN CARGILL, Gent. Inventory. Date: 12 Apr. 1744. Rec.: 18 Apr. 1744. Elizabeth Cargill, Administratrix. Robert Gray, Joseph John Clinch and John Nicholson, Appraisers.

Page 468:   ELIAS FORT. Additional Account Current. Date: 1743. Rec: 18 Apr. 1744. Holyday Fort, Executor. Mentions: expenses for burying the widow; division into 6 parts.

Page 468:   SUSANNA SHORT. Inventory. Date: 17 Apr. 1744. Rec: 18 Apr. 1744. Joshua Nicolson, Robert Lanier and Richard Bullock, Appraisers.

Page 469:   BENJAMIN CLARK. Inventory. Date: 13 Apr. 1744. Rec.: 16 May 1744. Elizabeth Clark, Administratrix. Thomas Binns, Nicholas Faulcon and Benjamin Holt, Appraisers.

Page 470:   GEORGE BARKER. Inventory. Date: ----. Rec.: 16 May 1744. Agnes Barker returns. James Anderson, John Averis and Thomas Bedingfield, Appraisers.

Page 470:   AUGUSTINE HUNNICUTT. Inventory. Date: 31 Mar. 1743/44. Rec.: 16 May 1744. John and Robert Hunnicutt, Executors.

Page 471:   MICHAEL HARRIS. Inventory. Date: 30 Apr. 1744. Rec.: 16 May 1744. J. H.,(?), Executor. Robert Gray, Joseph John Clinch and Thomas Warren, Appraisers.

Page 472:   ROBERT PARTIN. Inventory. Date: 7 Apr. 1744. Rec.: 16 May 1744. William Rookings, Thomas Clark and James Rookings, Appraisers.

Page 473:   WILLIAM HART of Surry. Will. Date: 27 Apr. 1744. Rec.: 18 July 1744. Robert Hart, Executor and Mrs. William Hart (not named), Executrix. Sons: Robert, William, John, Moses and Thomas. Wife: (not named). Daughters: Lucy, Mary, and Sarah. Mentions: some of the children not of age; Lucy, Mary, Sarah, Thomas - the youngest children. Witnesses: Charles Binns, John Evans and Thomas Hart.

Page 474:   WILLIAM MOORE of Surry. Will. Date: 4 Apr. 1744. Rec.: 18 July 1744. Elizabeth and William Moor, Executors. Sons: William and Eppes. Grandsons: William, Francis, Daniel, and Richard Eppes. Granddaughter: Sarah Eppes. Grandchildren: Robert, Ann, Selah, William, John and Phebe Pettaway. Daughters: Mary Pettaway, Susanna Eppes and Elizabeth Pettaway. Wife: Elizabeth. Mentions: wife's seven children. Witnesses: Christopher Tatum, George Rives and Richard Rives.

Page 475:   GEORGE RANDALL. Account Current. Date: 1743. Rec.: 18 July 1744. Mary Randall, Administratrix. Thomas Eldridge and James Balfour, Auditors.

Page 476:   ELIZABETH EDWARDS of Surry. Will. Date: 13 July 1744. Jane Edwards, Executrix. Father: (not named). Brother: Thomas Edwards. Sister: Jane Edwards. Witnesses: Charles Binns, Allen Warren, Jr. and Bruten Kae.

Page 476:   WILLIAM MOORE. Inventory. Date: 10 Aug. 1744. Rec.: Sept. 19, 1744. Elizabeth and William Moore, Executors.

Page 477:   JOHN COATES of Albemarle Parish, Surry. Will. Date: Apr. --, 1744. Rec.: 18 July 1744. Mary Coates, Executrix. Wife: Mary. Sons: Joseph (not 21); and John. Witnesses: William Willie, Henry Mitchell and Henry Mitchell, Jr. Further proven: 19 Sept. 1744.

Page 478:   THOMAS PEEBLES. Account Current. Date: ----. Rec.: Sept. 19, 1744. Richard Hamlin and W. Edwards, Auditors.

Page 479:   THOMAS WEATHERS of Albemarle Parish, Surry. Will. Date: 26 Apr. 1744. Rec.: 17 Oct. 1744. Lidia and William Weathers, Executors. Sons: William, Benjamin, Thomas, Michael, John, Isaac and Reubin. Daughter: Susanna. Wife: Lidia. Witnesses: Edward Pettway, William Pettway and Richard Rives.

Page 480: WILLIAM GRAY. Account Current. Date: 1736. Rec.: 17 Oct. 1744. William, Robert, Joseph and Thomas Gray, Executors. Mentions: legacies to William, Robert, Joseph, and Thomas Gray; Lucy Briggs; Edmund and James Gray. Benjamin Edwards and Richard Hamlin, Auditors.

Page 481: JOHN BAMER. Account Current. Date: 7140. Rec.: 21 Nov. 1744. Henry and Anne Foster return. B. Edwards and John Ruffin, Auditors.

Page 482: THOMAS CARTER. Account Current. Date: ----. Rec.: 19 Dec. 1744. Bartholomew Figures, Administrator. Thomas Gray and John Newsum, Auditors.

Page 483: BENJAMIN CLARK. Account Current. Date: ----. Rec.: 19 Dec. 1744. Elizabeth Clark, Administratrix. John Newsum and Thomas Gray, Auditors.

Page 483: JOHN MANGUM. Inventory. Date ordered: _ Aug. 1744. Rec.: 20 Dec. 1744. Olive Mangum, Administratrix. Samuel Maget, Robert Jurkins and Bartholomew Figures, Appraisers.

Page 484: JOSHUA PROCTOR. Inventory. Date ordered: 16 May 1744.Rec: 20 Dec. 1744. Mary Proctor, returns. James Nicholson, Benjamin Jordon and Robert Judkins, Appraisers.

Page 485: THOMAS TAYLOR of Surry. Will. Date: 4 Feb. 1743. Rec.: 16 Jan. 1744. Thomas and John Taylor, Executors. Sons: John and Thomas. Daughters: Elizabeth Chamless and Katherine Hobbs. Legatee: Mary Tomlinson, wife of John Tomlinson. Witnesses: James Gee, Wyke Hunnicutt and Charles Gee.

Page 486: ALLEN WARRIN (WARREN) of Southwark Parish, Surry. Will. Date: 15 Mar. 1737/38. Rec.: 16 Jan. 1744. Wife: (not named). Son: Benjamin. Witnesses: Thomas Warren, John Warren and Thomas Barham.

Page 486: BENJAMIN ROGERS. Inventory. Date: 8 Nov. 1744. Rec.: 16 Jan. 1744. Benjamin Ellis, Administrator. Robert Judkins, Samuel Maget and James Nicholson, Appraisers.

Page 487: THOMAS TAYLOR. Inventory. Date: 18 Feb. 1744/45. Rec.: 20 Feb. 1744. Thomas and John Taylor, Executors.

Page 488: JOANNAH JOYCE FLOYD. Inventory. Date: 20 Feb. 1744/45. Rec.: 20 Feb. 1744. Robert Nicolson, Executor.

Page 488: THOMAS REEKS of Surry. Will. Date: 15 Feb. 1744. Rec.: 20 Feb. 1744. John Phillips, Executor. Sisters: Elizabeth Collier, Mary Dawson, Sarah Howse and Faith Dudley. Brother: John Phillips. Nephew: William Collier, son of Elizabeth. Witnesses: John Jarret, Anne Jarret and George Barrick.

Page 489: SAMUEL LANCASTER. Inventory. Date: 11 Feb. 1744. Rec.: 20 Feb. 1744. Robert Hart, Charles Holt and Thomas Bell, Appraisers.

Page 490: ALLEN WARREN. Inventory. Date: 19 Feb. 1744/45. Rec: 20 Feb. 1744. Benjamin Warren, Executor.

Page 492: JAMES ALLEN of Southwark Parish, Surry. Will. Date: 16 Aug. 1744. Rec.: 20 Mar. 1744. Benjamin Cocke, Executor. Sister: Catherine Cocke. Brother-in-law: Benjamin Cocke. Legatees: Thomas and James Bray; William Allen; Arthur Smith; Frances and Elizabeth Bray; James and Joseph Bridger; John Cornwall (not 21), son of Jacob; and sisters.: Mary, Mourning. Witnesses: William Shelley and Richard Smith.

Page 493: THOMAS WEATHERS. Inventory. Date ordered: 21 Mar. 1744.

35

(Page 493 - WEATHERS cont'd.): .Rec. 20 Mar. 1744. William Pettway, Edward Pettway and Richard Rives, Appraisers.

Page 493:   WILLIAM EDWARDS of Southwark Parish, Surry. Will. Date: 10
Feb. 1744/45. Rec.: 20 Mar. 1744. Sarah Edwards, Executrix.
Wife: Sarah. Daughters: Mary, Elizabeth, Hannah, Sarah &
Rebecca (youngest). Mentions: none of children are of age.
Witnesses: William Holt, Thomas Warren and Samuel Thompson.

Page 495:   ROGER WILLIAMS of Southwark Parish, Surry. Will. Date: 7
Aug. 1744. Rec.: 20 Mar. 1744. Catharine Williams Execu-
trix. Wife: Catharine. Son: Thomas. Daughters: Elizabeth
Bage; Mary Lancaster, wife of Lawrence Lancaster; and Jane
Williams. Granddaughter: Elizabeth Lucy Bage. Witnesses:
William Jordan, John Sharpe and Robert Gray.

Page 496:   THOMAS REEX. Inventory. Date: ---. Rec.: 20 Mar. 1744. John
Phillips, Executor.

Page 496:   JOHN HEWETT. Inventory. Date ordered: 20 Feb. 1744. Rec:
20 Mar. 1744. William Shandes, John Goodwyn and Christopher
Tatum, Appraisers.

Page 497:   ROGER WILLIAMS. Inventory. Date: 10 Apr. 1745. Rec.: 17
Apr. 1745. Catharine Williams, Executrix.

Page 498:   SARAH BRUTON of Southwark Parish, Surry. Will. Date: 10
Mar. 1744. Rec.: 17 Apr. 1745. James Dering, Sarah and
Elizabeth Bruton, Executors. Daughters: Mary, Martha, Sa-
rah and Elizabeth (in descending order of age). Friend:
James Dering. Witnesses: Charles Binns and John Seward.

Page 498:   CARTER CRAFFORD. Inventory. Date: ----. Rec.: 17 April
1745. John and Carter Crafford, Executors.

Page 499:   WILLIAM HART. Inventory. Date: ----. Rec.: 17 Apr. 1745.
Mary and Robert Hart, Executors.

Page 500:   Capt. WILLIAM EDWARDS. Inventory. Date: 10 May 1745. Rec:
15 May 1745. Sarah Edwards, Executrix. Thomas Binns, Nicholas Faulcon and Samuel Judkins, Appraisers.

Page 501:   NICHOLAS MAGET of Southwark Parish, Surry. Will. Date: 18
Nov. 1743. Rec.: 15 May 1745. Samuel Maget, Executor.
Wife: Ann. Sons: Nicholas (not 21), Samuel. Sons-in-law:
Robert Judkins, Blanks Moody. Daughters: Fortune Watkins,
and Jane Sowerby. Legatees: --- Wager, son of Robert;
Nicholas Maget, son of Samuel; Charity Pernilum Moody, dau.
of Blanks Moody; John Spratley (not of age), son of John,
dec'd. of James City County; and Benjamin King. Witnesses:
Deborah King, William Browne, Jr. and Benjamin King.

Page 502:   JOHN HAWTHORN. Account Current. Date: 1744. Rec.: 15 May
1745. Rebecca Hawthorn presents. Thomas Gray and W. Edwards, Auditors.

Page 503:   GEORGE PILAND of Southwark Parish, Surry. Will. Date: 3 Dec.
1743. Rec.: 17 Jul. 1745. Mary and Richard Piland, Executors.
Wife: Mary. Daughters: Mary, Martha and Prissillah.   Son:
Richard. Witnesses: William Edwards and Samuel Judkins.

Page 504:   NICHOLAS MAGET. Inventory. Date: 17 May 1745. Rec.: 17 Jul.
1745. Samuel Magett, Executor. Joseph John Clinch, William
Clinch and John Nicholson, Appraisers.

Page 506:   DAVID DUNCAN of Albemarle Parish, Surry. Will. Date: --1744.
Rec.: 17 Jul. 1745. Nathaniel Duncan, Executor. Sons: Nath-
aniel, David, John, Peter and Daniel. Wife: Elizabeth. Dau.
Jennet. Mentions: children (except Nathaniel) not 21. Wit-

(Page 506 - DUNCAN cont'd.): nesses: Hugh Ivey and John Hays.

Page 507:   SARAH BRUTON. Inventory. Date: 15 Aug. 1745. Rec.: 21 Aug.
              1745. Elizabeth, and Sarah Bruton, and James Dering, Execu-
              tors.

Page 508:   WALTER WHITE of Southwark Parish, Surry. Will. Date: 23
              Sept. 1743. Rec.: 18 Sept. 1745. Hannah White, Executrix.
              Wife: Hannah. Children: Benjamin, Henry, Lucy, Joe and Nan-
              ny. Witnesses: Richard Cocke, James Maddra and James Clinch.

Page 509:   Mr. GEORGE PILAND. Inventory. Date: 12 Oct. 1745. Rec.: 16
              Oct. 1745. Mary and Richard Piland, Executors. William Holt,
              Nicholas Faulcon and Samuel Judkins, Appraisers.

Page 510:   WILLIAM MALONE of Southwark Parish, Surry. Will. Date: May
              3, 1736. Rec.: 16 Oct. 1745. Anne Malone, Executrix. Sons:
              William, and John. Wife: Anne. Daughters: Elizabeth, Sarah,
              Anne, Amey, Hannah, Agnes and Milley. Witnesses: Robert and
              Thomas Wynne.

Page 512:   WILLIAM MALONE. Inventory. Date: 12 Oct. 1745. Rec.: Oct.
              16, 1745. Anne Malone, Executrix.

Page 513:   Capt. WILLIAM BROWNE. Inventory. Date: ----. Rec.: 20 Nov.
              1745. Mary Browne returns. Mentions: property in Brunswick
              County.

Page 515:   ROGER WILLIAMS of Southwark Parish, Surry. Will. (See Page
              495 - identical Will.)

Page 518:   WALTER WHITE. Inventory. Date: ----. Rec.: 19 Mar. 1745.
              Joseph John Clinch and Richard Andrews, Appraisers.

Page 519:   JOHN JOHNSON. Inventory. Date: 12 Mar. 1745. Rec.: 19 Mar.
              1745. Mary Johnson, Administratrix. William Marriott, Ben-
              jamin Warren and Henry Davis, Appraisers.

Page 521:   PETER GREEN of Albemarle Parish, Surry. Will. Date: 17 Dec.
              1745. Rec.: 19 Mar. 1745. Mary Green, Executrix. Sons: Na-
              thaniel, Frederick, Peter and Mildend. Daughters: Olive,
              Elizabeth and Jane Green. Wife: Mary. Witnesses: Robert Far-
              rington, Nathaniel Green and Rebecca Epps.

Page 522:   JOSEPH PETTWAY. Will. Date: 1745. Rec.: 19 Mar. 1745. Will-
              iam and Joseph Pettway, Executors. Daughter: Jane Pettway.
              Sons: William, Joseph and Micajah. Mentions: land in Bruns-
              wick County. Witnesses: Thomas Wrenn and John Hancock.

Page 523:   JOHN JEFFRES, JR. of Surry. Will. Date: 24 Dec. 1745. Rec:
              19 Mar. 1745. Joseph Jeffres, Executor. Sons: Joseph, John;
              Richard (not 21). Daughters: Lucy, and Rebecca Jeffres.
              Father: (not named). Witnesses: Samuel Maget, Arthur Rich-
              ardson and William Owen.

Page 525:   THOMAS DREW. Inventory. Date: ----. Rec.: 17 March 1745.
              David and John Drew, Executors.

Page 526:   WILLIAM HEATH of Surry. Will. Date: 8 Nov. 1745. Rec.: 16
              Apr. 1746. Elizabeth Heath, Executrix. Sons: John, Thomas
              and William. Daughters: Mary and Rebecca Heath; Sarah, wife
              of Peter Tatum; Elizabeth, wife of Roger Taylor. Wife: Eli-
              zabeth. Grandson: John Heath, son of Abraham, dec'd. Grand-
              daughter: Sarah, daughter of Adam Heath. Witnesses: James
              Gee, Henry Gee and James Gee, Jr.

Page 528:   Capt. THOMAS GOODMAN. Inventory. Date: 11 Apr. 1746. Rec.:
              16 Apr. 1746. Mrs. Elizabeth Goodman, widow, Administratrix.
              Thomas Allstin, Peter Warren and John Allstin, Appraisers.

Page 529:   STEPHEN PEPPER of Albemarle Parish, Surry. Will. Date: Mar.
             1, 1739/40. Rec.: Apr. 16, 1746. Jane Petter, Executrix.
             Son: Stephen (not 18). Wife: Jane. Mentions: all of my child-
             ren. Witnesses: Bartholomew Figures and John Figures. Cod-
             dicil: Daughters - Elizabeth, Sarah, Rebecca and Jucoy Pep-
             per. Witnesses: William Rose and Arthur Richardson.

Page 530:   ROBERT GOOD. Inventory. Date ordered: 14 Dec. 1745. Rec.:
             16 Apr. 1746. John Yuille, Administrator. Joseph Mason,
             Thomas Atkins and John Hay, Appraisers.

Page 531:   RICHARD ROWELL of Southwark Parish, Surry. Will. Date: 18
             Oct. 1743. Rec.: 16 Apr. 1746. Mary Rowell, Executrix. Wife:
             Mary. Sons: Robert, and Richard (not of age). Mentions:
             land in Brunswick County. Witnesses: Joseph John and Will-
             iam Clinch.

Page 533:   JOSEPH PETTWAY. Inventory. Date: 21 May 1746. Rec.: 21 May
             1746. Augustine Hargrave, William Evans and John Hancock,
             Appraisers.

Page 535:   JOHN BELL of Albemarle Parish, Surry. Will. Date: 19 April
             1746. Rec.: 18 June 1746. Hannah Bell, Executrix. Sons:
             John, Burrell, Benjamin, Balaam, and James. Daughters: Ann
             Parham, Hannah Thompson; Mary Bell (not 21). Wife: Hannah.
             Witnesses: Silvanus Stokes, Jr., Edward Shalton and Charles
             Judkins.

Page 536:   JOHN JEFFERSS. Inventory. Date: 12 June 1746. Rec.: 18 Jun.
             1746. Bartholomew Figures, Benjamin Ellis and Samuel Maget,
             Appraisers.

Page 538:   WILLIAM HEETH. Inventory. Date: 1 June 1746. Rec.: 18 Jun.
             1746. Elizabeth Heeth, Executrix.

Page 539:   GEORGE RIVES of Albemarle Parish, Surry. Will. Date: 14 May
             1746. Rec.: 20 Aug. 1746. John Rives, refuses, Frances Rives
             is granted Administration. Wife: Frances. Sons: George,
             John, Christopher and Timothy. Daughters: Judith and Fran-
             ces Rives. Brothers: Timothy and William. Mentions: land in
             Prince George and Brunswick Counties; George, Christopher
             and Timothy - sons of wife Frances not 18. Witnesses:
             Thomas Davis, Peter Hawthorn and Christopher Tatum.

Page 541:   Mr. JOHN BELL. Inventory. Date ordered: 18 June 1746. Rec:
             20 Aug. 1746. John Stevens, William Ezell and Ephraim Par-
             ham, Appraisers.

Page 543:   ARTHUR TAYLOR. Receipt. Date: 8 Nov. 1740. Rec. 17 Sept.
             1746. His share of John Taylor's estate. Nicholas and Ann
             Maget, Administrators. Witnesses: Peter Warren and Benja-
             min Clark.

Page 543:   STEPHEN PEPPER. Inventory. Date: ---. Rec.: 20 Aug. 1746.

Page 544:   RICHARD ROWELL. Inventory. (Surry and Brunswick Counties).
             Date: ---. Rec.: 20 Aug. 1746. Joseph John Clinch, John
             Watkins and Gilbert Gray, Appraisers (Surry County). Rich-
             ard Ledbetter, John Wallton and Richard Ledbetter, Jr. Ap-
             praisers (Brunswick County.)

Page 545:   Mr. JAMES ALLEN. Inventory. Date: - May 1745. Rec.: 17 Sep.
             1745. Benjamin Cocke, Executor.

Page 547:   Mr. HENRY WATKINS. Additional Inventory. Date ordered: 17
             Sept. 1746. Rec.: 15 Oct. 1746. Joseph John Clinch, Gilbert
             Gray and Charles Holsworth, Appraisers.

Page 547:   JOHN WOMBWELL of Isle of Wight Co. Will. Date: - Dec.1741.

(Page 547 -WOMBWELL cont'd.): Rec.: 21 Jan. 1746. Mary Wombell, widow, Executrix. Sons: Benjamin (eldest, Joseph (second), Joshua and John. Daughters: Martha and Mary Wombell (not of age). Wife: Mary. Witnesses: William Brady, Edward Pittman, William Flake, John Giles and Matthew Jordan.

Page 549: Mr. GEORGE RIVES. Inventory. Date ordered: 20 Aug. 1746. Rec.: 21 Jan. 1746. Frances Rives, Administratrix. Henry Mitchel, Hartwell Marrable and Edward Pettway, Appraisers.

Page 550: JAMES DAVIS, SR. of Southwark Parish, Surry, Planter. Will. Date: 4 Sept. 1746. Rec.: 21 Jan. 1746. Henry and Robert Davis, Executors. Sons: Henry, Robert, James, Thomas,John and Nathaniel. Daughters: Ann Nicholson and Jane Warren. Wife: Elizabeth. Mentions: land in Isle of Wight County. Witnesses: Thomas Warren, John Warren and John Slate.

Page 552: PETER GREEN, Gent. Inventory. Date ordered: 19 May 1745. Rec.: 18 Feb. 1746. Henry Freeman, William Winfield and George Robertson, Appraisers.

Page 553: WILLIAM RICHARDSON of Surry. Will. Date: 4 Feb. 1742. Rec: 18 Feb. 1746. William Richardson, Executor. Sons: William, and Joseph. Wife: Martha. Daughters: Mary Wynne; Susanna, Betty, and Patty Richardson. Witnesses: Robert Farrington, Joshua Ellis and Mary Green.

Page 554: WILLIAM MOSS. Inventory. Date: 17 Mar. 1746/47. Rec.: 18 Mar. 1746. John Mason, Jr., Robert Jones and Thomas Adkins, Appraisers.

Page 554: GEORGE WILLS. Inventory. Date: 28 Jan. 1746. Rec: 18 Mar. 1746. Joshua Nicolson, Administrator. John Collier, Henry Collier and Thomas Sowerby, Appraisers.

Page 555: JAMES BRUCE, Gardner. Inventory. Date: 23 Feb. 1746/47. Rec.: 18 Mar. 1746. Patrick Adams, Administrator. John Avery, Edward Bayley and John Jarret, Appraisers.

Page 555: HUGH HUNNIFORD of Lawnes Creek Parish, Surry. Will. Date: 12 Nov. 1735. Rec.: 18 Mar. 1746. Jane Hunniford, Executrix. Wife: Jane. Witnesses: Charles Binns and Thomas Binns.

Page 556: CHARLES WHITE of Southwark Parish, Surry. Will. Date: 28 Mar. 1747. Rec.: 15 Apr. 1747. James Clinch and Robert White the Executors. Grandchildren: Charles, Mary Holsworth (not 18), children of Charles; and William Clinch. Son: Robert. Daughter: Jane Clinch. Son-in-law: James Clinch. Witnesses: Richard Cocke, Hartwell Cocke and Katherine Piland.

Page 557: WILLIAM RICHARDSON. Inventory. Date: ----. Rec.: 15 April 1747. William Green, Henry Freeman and William Green, Jr., Appraisers.

Page 558: HUGH HUNNIFORD. Inventory. Date: ----. Rec.: 19 May 1747. Jane Hunniford, Executrix.

Page 559: MARY JONES. Inventory. Date: 13 May 1747. Rec.: 19 May 1747. James Anderson, Thomas Bedingfield and Josias Barker, Appraisers.

Page 559: RICHARD BLUNT of Surry. Will. Date: 12 Apr. 1747. Rec: 16 June 1747. Ann Blunt, Executrix. Sons: Richard, John and Benjamin (not of age). Wife: Ann. Daughters: Mary Irby, Elizabeth and Lucy Blunt. Cousin: William Blunt. Legatees: Mr. Nicholas Edmunds and John Irby. Witnesses: Robert Nicolson, William Brown and Benjamin Ellis. Mentions: land in Isle of Wight and Brunswick Counties.

Page 561: CHARLES WHITE. Inventory. Date: 13 May 1747. Rec: 16 June 1747. James Clinch and Robert White present. John Nicolson, John Watkins and Gilbert Gray, Appraisers.

Page 562: JOHN WOMBWELL. Inventory. Date ordered: 21 Jan. 1746. Rec: 16 June 1746. Mary Wombwell, Executrix. Benjamin Bell, William Little and John Gwaltney, Appraisers.

Page 563: ARTHUR SHERROD. Inventory. Date: ordered: 16 June 1747. Rec: 21 July 1747. Charles Mabry, Administrator. Charles Holt, Augustine Hargrove and William Mangum, Appraisers.

Page 563: ELIZABETH HURDLE of Lawnes Creek Parish, Surry. Will. Date: 6 May 1747. Rec.: 15 Sept. 1747. John Madra, Executor. Daughters: Joanna Madra; and Christian Hurdle. Grandson: John Madra. Legatee: William Madra. Witnesses: James Bridger and Thomas Davidson.

Page 564: HENRY BEDINGFIELD of Albemarle Parish, Surry. Will. Date: 30 Apr. 1747. Rec.: 15 Sept. 1747. Nathaniel Bedingfield, Executor. Wife: Isabel. Sons: Thomas and Nathaniel. Witnesses: William Willie and Peter Hawthorn.

Page 565: JOHN RICHARDSON of Albemarle Parish, Surry. Will. Date: 11 Aug. 1747. Rec.: 20 Oct. 1747. Elizabeth Richardson, Executrix. Sons: Hopkin, Hardy and John. Wife: Elizabeth. Witnesses: Olive Mangum and Samuel Maget.

Page 566: ELIZABETH HURDLE. Inventory. Date: 1 Oct. 1747. Rec.: 20 Oct. 1747. John Maddarra, Executor. Joseph Hancock, Roger Delk and Francis Price, Appraisers.

Page 567: EDMOND HOWELL. Inventory. Date: 14 Aug. 1747. Rec.: 20 Oct. 1747. Olive Howell, Administratrix. John Newsum, John Crafford and Carter Crafford, Appraisers.

Page 568: WILLIAM BROWNE of Southwark Parish, Surry. Will. Date: 3 July 1746. Rec.: 19 Jan. 1747. Henry Browne, Gen., Executor. Grandsons: Henry, and William Browne (the latter not 18); Philip, William and John Edloe; Henry Edloe, dec'd. Granddaughters: Jane, Rebecca and Mary Edloe; Ann Browne, daughter of Henry; Ann Browne, daughter of William; Rebecca, Elizabeth and Martha Browne; Lucy Gray, daughter of William; Mary Eaton. Daughter-in-law: Mary Browne. Great-grandson: Henry Cocke, son of Lemuel. Mentions: land where his grandson, Henry Browne's father lived, land in Isle of Wight and Brunswick Counties. Witnesses: Patrick Adams, Richard Cocke and Peter Warren.

Page 571: JOHN RICHARDSON. Inventory. Date ordered: 20 Oct. 1747. Rec.: 19 Jan. 1747. Elizabeth Richardson, Executrix. Benjamin Ellis, Thomas Alsobrook and James Nicholson, Appraisers.

Page 571: JAMES CLINCH. Inventory. Date: 4 Feb. 1747/48. Rec.: 15 Mar. 1747. Jane Clinch presents. Zacha's Madderra, William Smith and James Davis, Appraisers.

Page 573: JETHRO BARKER of Albemarle Parish, Surry. Will. Date: 25 Jan. 1744. Rec.: 15 Mar. 1747. Jehu Barker, Executor. Sons: John, Jethro, Henry and Jehu. Daughters: Jane Field and Mary Andross. Granddaughters: Agnes, Mary and Elizabeth, daughters of George; Sarah, daughter of Jehu. Witnesses: Nicholas Partridge, Hugh Ivie and Nicholas Partridge, Jr.

Page 574: WILLIAM BRIGGS of Albemarle Parish, Surry. Will. Date: 8 Feb. 1747/48. Rec.: 19 Apr. 1748. Mary Briggs, Executrix. Brother: Thomas. Wife: Mary. Cousin: Hinchia Gilliam. Sons: John, William and Henry (not 21). Daughters: Eliza-

(Page 574 - BRIGGS cont'd:): beth, Mary Chappell; Amey, Rebecca, Lucy
Briggs (not 21). Mentions: land in Brunswick County. Wit-
nesses: John Hay, Edmond Ruffin, Willott Roberts and John
Irby.

Page 576: JAMES DAVIS. Inventory. Date: 18 Apr. 1748. Rec.: 19 Apr.
1748. Henry and Robert Davis, Executors. William Marriott,
John Harris and William Marriott, Jr., Appraisers.

Page 577: JETHRO BARKER. Inventory. Date: 14 Apr. 1748. Rec.: 19
Apr. 1748. Jehur Barker, presents.

Page 577: NICHOLAS COCKE of Surry. Will. Date: 4 Apr. 1748. Rec.: 19
Apr. 1748. William Cocke, Executor. Sons: William and John.
Daughters: Frances Simmons, Ann Woddrop; Elizabeth, Martha
and Catherine Cocke. Granddaughters: Lucy, Sarah Simmons;
Susanna Cocke; Elizabeth Woddrop. Friend: Col. Thomas
Cocke. Witnesses: James Rae, Howell Briggs, Joseph Munford
and Robert S. Woobank.

Page 579: RICHARD BLUNT, Gent. Inventory. Date ordered: 16 Jun.1747.
Rec.: 19 Apr. 1748. Ann Blunt, Executrix. Benjamin Ellis,
Willott Roberts and Edmund Ruffin, Appraisers, (Surry Co.);
- Clement Read, James Parish, and John Ingram, Appraisers.
(Brunswick Co.);- Howell Edmunds, James Ridley and Newitt
Drew, Appraisers (Isle of Wight Co.).

Page 582: DAVID FLOWERS. Inventory. Date ordered: 15 Mar. 1747. Rec:
19 Apr. 1748. John Mooring, Richard Proctor and Joshua
Proctor, Appraisers.

Page 582: FREDERICK BRYAN of Southwark Parish, Surry. Will. Date:
23 Feb. 1747. Rec.: 17 May 1748. Martha Bryan, Executrix.
Wife: Martha. Brother-in-law: John Ruffin. Mentions:
Children. Witnesses: James Baker and John Ruffin.

Page 583: GEORGE TALLETT. Inventory. Date: 21 Mar. 1747. Rec.: 17
May 1748. William Cornwell, Administrator. John Drew,
Abraham Mitchell and John Berryman, Appraisers.

Page 584: THOMAS JONES. Inventory. Date ordered: 17 May 1748. Rec:
21 June 1748. Sarah Jones, Administratrix. James Chappell,
James Chappell, Jr. and Robert Jones, Appraisers.

Page 584: JOHN PRICE of Surry. Will. Date: 10 June 1747. Rec.: 21
June 1748. Stephen Simmons, Executor. Wife: (not named).
Son-in-law: Stephen Simmons. Witnesses: Nicholas Thompson,
John Drew and Daniel Sebrell.

Page 585: WILLIAM BRIGGS. Inventory. Date ordered: 19 Apr. 1748.
Rec.: 21 June 1748. Mary Briggs, Executrix. David Jones,
John Goodwyn and John Irby, Appraisers.

Page 588: Mr. FREDERICK BRYAN. Inventory. Date: 16 July 1748. Rec:
19 July 1748. John Crafford, William Drew and John Newsum,
Appraisers.

Page 589: Capt. WILLIAM BROWNE, Gent. Inventory. Date: 22 Feb. 1747/
48. Rec.: 16 Aug. 1748. Henry Browne, Executor. Joseph
John Clinch, William Clinch and Peter Warren, Appraisers
(Surry Co.); Micajah Edwards, Henry Blunt and John Thomas,
Appraisers (Isle of Wight Co.); James Parish, Walter Camp-
bell and Drury Stith, Appraisers (Brunswick Co.).

Page 594: WILLIAM BRIGGS. Inventory. (Brunswick Co.). Date ordered:
17 May 1748. Rec.: 16 Aug. 1748. Mary Briggs, Executrix.
Nicholas Edmunds, James Parish and John Ogborn, Appraisers.

Page 595: THOMAS DAVIS of Albemarle Parish, Surry. Will. Date: 25 Aug.

41

(Page 595 - DAVIS cont'd.): 1748. Rec.: 18 Oct. 1748. Rebecca Davis, Executrix. Son: Thomas. Son-in-law: William Bird. Dau.: Elizabeth Ellis. Wife: Rebecca. Witnesses: John Bennett and Peter Hawthorn.

Page 596:   ANN BERRYMAN of Surry. Will. Date: 11 Aug. 1748. Rec.: 15 Nov. 1748. John Berryman, Executor. Sons: John, Joseph and William. Daughters: Lucy, Ann and Margaret Berryman. Witnesses: Joseph Edwards and John Edwards.

Page 597:   SAMUEL SEBRELL of Southwark Parish, Surry. Will. Date: 19 Aug. 1746. Rec.: 20 Dec. 1748. Moses Sebrell, Executor. Wife: Mary. Sons: Benjamin, Daniel, Moses, Joseph and Samuel. Daughters: Lidia Wigs; Naomi, and Elizabeth Sebrell. Grandson: Benjamin Wigs (not 20). Friends: Jacob Cornwel, Thomas Pritlow, Jr., and Anselm Baley, Jr. Witnesses: William Cornwell, John Champion and Jesse Hargrave.

Page 599:   MORRIS PRITCHARD, Overseer, of Surry. Will. Date: 9 Nov. 1748. Rec.: 20 Dec. 1748. Elizabeth Pritchard, Executrix. Wife: Elizabeth. Sons: John, Richard and Casey. Friends: John Watts and John Gillam. Mentions: children (or child) not of age; land on the Roanoke River. Witnesses: Ann Prescott, Rachell Prescott and Samuel Peete.

Page 601:   ANN BERRYMAN. Inventory. Date: 2 Dec. 1748. Rec.: 20 Dec. 1748. John Berryman, Executor. William Drew, John Thompson and Carter Crafford, Appraisers.

Page 601:   THOMAS GOODMAN and wife, ELIZABETH. Inventory. Date: 11 Oct. 1748. Rec.: 20 Dec. 1748. Administrator not named. Peter Warren, John Watkins and Thomas Collier, Appraisers.

Page 603:   JOHN GWALTNEY, JR. Inventory. Date: ----. Rec.: 20 Dec. 1748. Mary Gwaltney, Administratrix. William Little,John Little, and James Sampson Clark, Appraisers.

Page 604:   RICHARD DAVIS. Inventory. Date: 30 Dec. 1748. Rec.: 17 Jan. 1748. John Thompson, John Moring and James Davis, Appraisers.

Page 605:   SAMUEL SEBRELL. Inventory. Date: 12 and 13 Jan. 1748/49. Rec.: 17 Jan. 1748. Moses Sebrell, Executor. Legacies: to Mary (widow), Daniel, Samuel, Moses, Naomi, Joseph, Benjamin, Elizabeth Sebrell; Benjamin Wiggs. Mentions: silver spoons marked: $_S{}_M$ and $_C{}_M{}_T$. William Seward, Benjamin Cocke and William Drew, Appraisers.

Page 607:   MARY SEBRELL. Will. Date: (none). Rec.: 17 Jan. 1748. Jesse Hargrave granted Administration. Samuel Sebrell, heir at law refusing. Sons: Joseph, Benjamin (not 21), Samuel and Moses. Daughter. Naomi Sebrell. Witnesses: (none).

Page 608:   THOMAS DAVIS. Inventory. Date: ----. Rec.: 21 Mar. 1748. Rebecca Hawthorn, Administratrix.

Page 609:   SILVANUS STOKES of Surry. Will. Date: 18 May 1742. Rec: 21 Mar. 1748. Jones and Silvanus Stokes, Executors. Sons: Jones (eldest), Silvanus (second). Daughter: Martha Ezell. Grandchildren: Jones, Silvanus, Hamlin and Jones Stokes, sons of Jones; Marcus, Silvanus, sons of Silvanus; Agnes Freeman, daughter of son, Hamlin Stokes; Agnes Ezell. Witnesses: Samuel, John and David Stokes.

Page 611:   Capt. NICHOLAS COCKE. Inventory. Date: 5 May 1748. Rec: 18 Apr. 1749. William Cocke, Executor. William Rookings, James Rookings and Thomas Allstin, Appraisers.

Page 614: SAMUEL BROWNE. Inventory. Date: 11 Apr. 1749. Rec.: 16 May 1749. William Browne, Administrator. William Little, John Little and Robert Hart, Appraisers.

Page 615: EDWARD TAYLOR. Inventory. Date: 28 Apr. 1749. Rec.: 20 June 1749. John Whitaker, Administrator. William Drew, Dolphin Drew and Thomas Brantley, Appraisers.

Page 616: THOMAS WASHINGTON. Inventory. (Brunswick Co.). Date: 2 June 1749. Rec.: 20 June 1749. Agnes Washington, Administratrix. William Mosely, Benjamin Mosely and Thomas Clanton, Appraisers.

Page 617: SILVANUS STOKES. Inventory. Date ordered: 21 March 1748. Rec.: 20 June 1749. Jones and Silvanus Stokes, Executors. Gregory Rawlings, Robert Webb and Thomas Moore, Appraisers.

Page 619: JAMES WYCHE of Albemarle Parish, Surry. Will. Date: 24 Feb. 1748. Rec.: 20 June 1749. James Wyche, Executor. Daughters: Amey Jackson, wife of Ambrose Jackson; Tabitha Lucas; Martha Bridges; Elizabeth Johnson; Sarah, Ann, Frances and Rebecca Wyche. Sons: James (eldest), and Nathaniel. Wife: Elizabeth. Witnesses: James Ferrell and William Pettway.

Page 621: THOMAS WASHINGTON. Inventory. Date: 27 Jan. 1748. Rec: 15 Aug. 1749. Christopher Moring, Jr., Edward Bailey and Benjamin Reeks, Appraisers.

Page 622: MORRIS PRITCHARD. Inventory. Date: 26 June 1749. Rec: 15 Aug. 1749. Elizabeth Pritchard, Executrix. Moses Johnson, Richard Avery and Thomas Gilliam, Appraisers.

Page 623: CHARLES MAYBRY. Will. Date: 16 Mar. 1749. Rec.: 15 Aug. 1749. Charles and Elizabeth Mabry, Executors. Sons: Charles (Executor), Francis, William, Ebill and Cornelieus. Daughters: Elizabeth, Rebeccah, Emidie, (illegible); and Mary Battle. Wife: Rebeccah (Executrix). Witnesses: John Hargrove and Nathaniel Clanton.

Page 624: EDWARD LONG. Will. Date: 12 May 1749. Rec.: 15 Aug. 1749. Edward Long, Executor. Sons: William, George, Thomas, Lewis, and Edward. Daughters: Mary Long; Mary Ann Long; Frances Moore, daughter of Edward Long. (First two daughters not 21). Witnesses: Henry Savidge and Mercy Long.

Page 625: CHARLES MABRY. Inventory. Date: 16 Sept. 1749. Rec: Sept. 19, 1749. Charles and Rebeccah Mabry return. Moses Johnson, Charls Gillum, and Charls Battell, Appraisers.

Page 626: JOHN DEWELL. Inventory. Date: 3 Sept. 1749. Rec.: 19 Sep. 1749. Benjamin Cocke, Administrator. William Cocke, William Rookings and James Rookings, Appraisers.

Page 627: THOMAS BEARD (BAIRD) of Surry. Will. Date: 20 Sept. 1741. Rec.: 17 Oct. 1749. William Rookings granted Administration. Legatee: William Rookings of Surry. Witnesses: John Harper, Anne Williams and Elizabeth Dugall.

Page 628: JOHN WATKINS of Southwark Parish, Surry. Will. Date: 18 Jun. 1749. Rec.: 16 Jan. 1749. Mary Watkins, Executrix. Son: John. Mother-in-law: (not named). Wife: Mary. Child in esse. Witnesses: Robert Wager, Thomas Bage and Benjamin Nicholson.

Page 629: SAMUEL CHAPPELL, Planter, of Surry. Will. Date: 1748. Rec: 21 Nov. 1749. Elizabeth Chappell, Executrix. Sons: Samuel, Thomas, James, John, Robert, Benjamin and Drury. Daughters: Elizabeth, Sarah, Bethiah, Mary, Emelia and Nancy. Wife:

43

(Page 629 - CHAPPELL cont'd:) Elizabeth. Mentions: land in Occhineachy Neck, North Carolina. Witnesses: Samuel Peete, Robert Jones and James Chappell.

Page 630: EDWARD LONG. Inventory. Date: ----. Rec.: 21 Nov. 1749. Zecha. Madray, William Crews and John Madray, Appraisers.

Page 631: THOMAS WALLIS, SR. of Albemarle Parish, Surry. Will. Date: 6 Aug. 1745. Rec.: 16 Jan. 1749. Ann Wallis, Executrix. Sons: James, John, Thomas and William. Daughter: Martha. Wife: Ann. Grandson: Frederick Roberts. Witnesses: Stephen Hamlin and James Marsengill.

Page 632: JOHN THREEWETS of Surry. Will. Date: 14 Nov. 1749. Rec.: 20 Mar. 1749. John Threewets, Executor. Sons: Peter, Joel, Edward and John. Son-in-law: Robert Newman. Daughter: Lucy Threewets. Wife: Ann. Witnesses: Robert Newman, John Threewett, Jr., and Thomas Oliver. (Mentions land in Brunswick County).

Page 634: BENJAMIN CARRELL of Southwark Parish, Surry. Will. Date: 20 Nov. 1745. Rec.: 20 Mar. 1749. Joice Carrell, Executrix. Wife: Joice. Sons: Joseph and Benjamin (not 21). Daughters: Mary and Katherine. Witnesses: William Seward and Jordan Thomas.

Page 635: CHARLES BINNS of Surry. Will. Date: 16 Oct. 1749. Rec.: 20 Mar. 1749. Judith Binns, Executrix. Son: Charles (not 21). Daughters: Elizabeth, Martha and Lucy Binns (not 18). Child in esse. Nephew: Thomas Binns. Brother: Thomas Eldridge. Wife: Judith. Legatees: Sally Binns, Sarah Lands, Jean Gwaltney and John Champion. Witnesses: William Batts, John Newsum, John Harris, and Joseph Newsum. Mentions: land in Nansemond County.

Page 638: WILLIAM CRIPS of Albemarle Parish, Surry. Will. Date: 8 Aug. 1749. Rec.: 20 Mar. 1749. Anselm Bailey, Jr. (Quaker), Thomas Bell, Executors. Legatees: Richard Fealds; William Ward, son of Benjamin; Green Fields, son of Richard; Elizabeth, widow of brother, John Crips. Grandson: Thomas Myas (not 21). Nephews: Mary Crips and Ann Fealds. Witnesses: Samuel Thompson, Benjamin Clark and Benjamin Bailey, Jr.

Page 640: ROBERT ATKINSON of Albemarle Parish, Surry. Will. Date: 28 Aug. 1749. Rec.: 20 Mar. 1749. William and Benjamin Atkinson, Executors. Sons: William, Benjamin, Robert, John, and James. Wife: (not named). Mentions: land in Southampton County. Witnesses: Benjamin Bailey and Benjamin Gray.

Page 641: JOHN GROVES. Inventory. Date: 16 Jan. 1749. Rec: 20 Mar. 1749. Benjamin Ellis, Samuel Magget and John Andrews, Appraisers.

Page 643: JOHN PHILLIPS. Inventory. Date: ----. Rec.: 20 Mar. 1749. George Cryer and Robert Wager, Appraisers.

Page 643: SAMUEL CHAPPEL. Inventory. Date ordered: 21 Nov. 1749. Rec.: 20 Mar. 1749. Elizabeth Chappel returns. Howell Jones, Nicholas Partridge and John Barker, Appraisers.

Page 644: JOHN SEWARD. Inventory. Date: ----. Rec.: 20 Mar. 1749. John Holt, Christopher Tharpe and Thomas Davidson, Appraisers.

Page 644: JOHN PRICE. Inventory. Date: ----. Rec.: 20 March 1749. Stephen Simmons, Executor.

Page 645: JOHN DAVIS. Inventory. Date: 1 Sept. 1749. Rec.: 20 Mar. 1749. Dolphin Drew, Carter Crafford and Newet Edwards, Appraisers.

Page 646:   WILLIAM GREEN, SR. of Surry. Will. Date: 28 Nov. 1749.
              Rec.: 15 May 1750. Mary Randall, Executrix. Sons: Burrell,
              Benjamin and William. Daughters: Mary Randall, widow; and
              Elizabeth Hunt. Witnesses: Robert Farrington, Daniel Knight
              and William Wynne.

Page 647:   JOSEPH WREN, SR., Planter, of Surry. Will. Date: 23 Dec.
              1749. Rec.: 15 May 1750. James Wren, Executor. Sons:
              Thomas, Joseph, William, George, John and Francis. Daugh-
              ters: Susanna Heath and Elizabeth Rawser. Granddaughter:
              Susanna Rawser, daughter of Elizabeth Rawser. Daughter:
              Mary Daniel. Son: James. Witnesses: Samuel Peete, Laza-
              rus Drake and John Hinds.

Page 648:   WILLIAM MABRY of Albemarle Parish, Surry. Will. Date: 13
              Jan. 1749. Rec.: 15 May 1750. Robert Eeckle (not 21), Ex-
              ecutor. Administration granted to Edward Eckles. Legatee:
              Robert Eacolls (Eckles). Witnesses: Thomas Wynne, William
              Tucker, John Jackson and Robert Jackson.

Page 649:   GRACE BARKER of Southwark Parish, Surry. Will. Date: 19
              Feb. 1741. Rec.: 15 May 1750. Richard Barker, Executor.
              Brother: Josiah Barker. Cousins: Richard, John and Josiah
              Barker; Mary Bishop; William, Joshua and Joel Barker. Leg-
              atees: Elizabeth Barker, daughter of Josiah; James Bishop,
              son of May; Faith and Elizabeth Barker. Witnesses: Robert
              Lanier, Josiah Barker and Josiah Barker.

Page 650:   JOHN THREEWITT. Inventory. Date: ----. Rec.: 15 May 1750.
              Henry Sturdivant, John Rottenbury and Slomon Wynne, Apprais-
              ers. John Threewitt, Executor.

Page 651:   JAMES WYCH. Inventory. Date: ----. Rec.: 15 May 1750.
              Joseph Thorp, Major Tillar and Samuel Alsobroo, Appraisers.

Page 652:   JOSEPH MASON. Inventory. Date ordered: 20 Mar. 1749. Rec:
              15 May 1750. Phebe Mason, Executrix. Robert Jones, Howell
              Jones and Nicholas Partridge, Appraisers.

Page 653:   SARAH WEST of Southwark Parish, Surry. Will. Date: 20 Aug.
              1744. Rec.: 19 June 1750. Thomas Hudgens and wife, Sarah,
              Executors. Son: Nicholas Lanier. Daughters: Mary Hill;
              and Sarah West (Executrix). Witnesses: Thomas Allstin and
              William Rookings.

Page 654:   Mr. JOHN RIVES. Inventory. Date ordered: 15 May 1750.
              Rec.: 19 June 1750. Sarah Rives, Administratrix. Edward
              Pettway, Peter Poythress and Henry Mitchell, Appraisers.

Page 655:   DANIEL VASSER. Account Current and Sale. Date: 19 Oct.
              1741. Rec.: 19 June 1750. Robert Wynne, Sub-Sheriff.
              (Records says Thomas Vasser Estate).

Page 655:   JOHN COCKE. Account Current and Sale. Date: 8 Aug. 1741.
              Rec.: 19 June 1750. Mentions: paid Lemuel Cocke his part.
              Robert Wynne, Sub-Sheriff.

Page 656:   JOHN JOHNSON. Account Current. Date: 1747. Rec.: 19 June
              1750. Mary Johnson, Administratrix. Mentions: widow and
              children. William Clinch and John Harris, Auditors.

Page 656:   WILLIAM MABRY. Inventory. Date: 4 June 1750. Rec.: 19 Jun.
              1750. Edward Eckles returns. Thomas Wynne, William Par-
              ham and John Freeman, Appraisers.

Page 657:   Mr. WILLIAM ROOKINGS. Inventory. Date: 4 June 1750. Rec:
              19 June 1750. Charles Lucas, Thomas Shrewsbery and John
              Collier, Appraisers.

Page 658:   ROBERT ATKINSON. Inventory. Date: 15 June 1750. Rec.: 19
              June 1750. Mary Atkinson, Executrix. Thomas Wren, John
              Hancock and Richard Blow, Appraisers.

Page 659:   JOHN BELL. Inventory. Date: ----. Rec.: 19 June 1750.
              Ephraim Parham, Thomas Moore and Robert Webb, Appraisers.

Page 660:   BENJAMIN EDWARDS, Gent. Inventory. Date ordered: 20 Mar.
              1749. Rec.: 17 July 1750. Henry Browne, Administrator.
              William Seward, William Seward, Jr. and William Drew, Ap-
              praisers.

Page 663:   BENJAMIN CARRELL. Inventory. Date: 23 Mar. 1749. Rec.: 17
              July 1750. Joice Carrell, Executrix. Mentions: estate at
              Hog Island, estate at John Carrell's in Isle of Wight Co.,
              and goods at Mr. Jordan Thomas's in Isle of Wight County.
              Benjamin Cocke, William Drew and Dolphin Drew, Appraisers.

Page 672:   ROBERT SMITH WOOBANK. Inventory. Date: 16 June 1750. Rec:
              17 July 1750. John Woobank, Administrator. Charles Lucas,
              Thomas Sowerby and Joshua Nicholson, Appraisers.

Page 673:   ROBERT GREEN of Albemarle Parish, Surry. Will. Date: 9 Aug.
              1750. Rec.: 18 Sept. 1750. John Mercy, and Thomas Bobbitt,
              Executors. Cousins: Thomas Bobbitt, Mary Sturdivant, Anne
              Threewitts, and John Mercy. Witnesses: Edward Pettway,
              William Green and Ann Threewitts.

Page 674:   SAMPSON WILSON. Inventory. Date: 17 Aug. 1749. Rec.: 18
              Sept. 1750. Sarah Wilson presents. William and Dolphin Drew
              and John Newsum, Appraisers.

Page 675:   JOSEPH HAN(D)COCK. Inventory. Date: 11 Aug. 1750. Rec.:
              18 Sept. 1750. William and Dolphin Drew and Thomas Davidson,
              Appraisers.

Page 676:   CHARLES PITT of Southwark Parish, Surry. Will. Date: 3 Jan.
              1748. Rec.: 16 Oct. 1750. Joseph Pitt, Executor. Wife:
              (not named). Daughters: Milia, Lucy (neither of age). Son:
              Joseph. Witnesses: William Edwards, Jr. and Joseph Clark.

Page 677:   RICHARD ANDREWS of Surry. Will. Date: 17 Sept. 1750. Rec:
              20 Nov. 1750. David and Richard Andrews, Executors. Sons:
              William, David and Richard. Daughters: Elizabeth Wren and
              Mary Murrell. Wife: Elizabeth. Witness: William Clinch.

Page 678:   SAUANNA HANCOCK of Southwark Parish, Surry. Will. Date: 5
              Nov. 1750. Rec.: 20 Nov. 1750. Nathaniel Sebrell, Executor.
              Sons: James, William and Henry Hancock (last two youngest);
              Nathaniel Sebrell. Daughter: Fanny Hancock. Granddaugh-
              er: Mary Sebrell. Witnesses: Jacob Bruce and Michael
              Smalley.

Page 679:   EDWARD SLATE of Lower Parish, Surry. (Old). Will. Date:
              9 July 1747. Rec.: 20 Nov. 1750. Mary and Edward Slate,
              Executors. Wife: Mary. Son: Edward. Grandsons: John
              George, Robert Slate and Robert Kee. Witnesses: Robert
              Little, Francis Little and James Griffin.

Page 680:   JAMES DEWELL of Southwark Parish, Surry. Will. Date: 27 Oct.
              1750. Rec.: 20 Nov. 1750. Ellen Rookings, Executrix.
              Brother: Thomas. Friend: Ellen Rookings. Witnesses:
              William Pully, Jr. and Richard Stewart.

Page 681:   JOSEPH GWALTNEY. Will. Date: 24 Oct. 1750. Rec.: 20 Nov.
              1750. Thomas Gwaltney, Executor. Aunt: Martha Gwaltney.
              Brothers: Thomas, William, Benjamin and James. Witnesses:
              Jacob Atkinson, Daniel Atkinson and Robert Hart.

Page 681:   NATHANIEL GREEN, SR. of Surry. Will. Date: 30 Nov. 1749.
             Rec.: 20 Nov. 1750. Benjamin Hunt, Executor. Legatees:
             Benjamin, William and John (Jr.) Hunt. Witnesses: Robert
             Farrington, Burrell Green and Daniel Knight.

Page 682:   FRANCIS LITTLE of Southwark Parish, Surry. Will. Date: 14
             Aug. 1745. Rec.: 20 Nov. 1750. Francis Little, Executor.
             Sons: Robert, Francis and Boaz. Wife: (not named). Daugh-
             ter: Sarah Fones, wife of Philip. Witnesses: John Ruffin,
             William Seward, Jr. and James Wilson, Jr.

Page 683:   ROBERT GREEN. Inventory. Date: ----. Rec.: 20 Nov. 1750.
             John Massey and Thomas Bobbitt, Appraisers.

Page 684:   RICHARD TOMLINSON, JR. Inventory. Date: 16 Oct. 1750. Rec:
             20 Nov. 1750. John Mason, Jr., Christopher Tatum and Ed-
             ward Lee, Appraisers.

Page 685:   THOMAS COCKE of Southwark Parish, Surry. Will. Date: June
             7, 1750. Rec.: Dec. 18, 1750. Lemuel and Thomas Cocke,
             Gent's., Executors. Daughter: Elizabeth Cocke. Sons: Lem-
             uel, Thomas and John (not 21). Wife: Hannah. Mentions:
             land in Brunswick County. Witnesses: William Short and
             Richard Jones.

Page 687:   JOHN SLEDGE of Albemarle Parish, Surry. Will. Date: 27
             Dec. 1749. Rec.: 18 Dec. 1750. Rebecca Sledge, Executrix.
             Sons: Charles (eldest), Daniel, Amos and John. Daughters:
             Ann Griffis and Sarah Sledge. Wife: Rebecca. Mentions:
             land in Brunswick County. Witnesses: Hugh Ivey and Thomas
             Ivey.

Page 688:   JAMES DEWELL. Inventory. Date: 1 Dec. 1750. Rec.: 18 Dec.
             1750. Robert Lanier, Charles Lucas and Thomas Sowersby,
             Appraisers.

Page 689:   JOHN COLLINS. Inventory. Date ordered: 20 Nov. 1750.
             Rec.: 18 Dec. 1750. James Rookings, Administrator. Robert
             Lanier, Charles Lucas and Thomas Sowersby.

Page 690:   JOHN THREEWETTS. Inventory. (Brunswick Co.). Date: ----.
             Rec.: 18 Dec. 1750. Thomas Jackson, Jr., James Parham and
             Abraham Peebles, Appraisers.

Page 690:   WILLIAM CRIPS. Inventory. Date ordered: 20 Mar. 1750.Rec:
             18 Dec. 1750. Robert Nicolson, Richard Blow and William Han-
             cock, Appraisers.

Page 691:   THOMAS WALLER. Inventory. Date: 29 Dec. 1750. Rec.: 19
             Feb. 1750. John Ruffin, Administrator. Thomas Holt, John
             Newsum and Thomas Binns, Appraisers.

Page 692:   WILLIAM PHILLIPS. Inventory. Date: 29 Dec. 1750. Rec: 19
             Feb. 1750. John Ruffin, Administrator. Thomas Holt, John
             Newsum and Thomas Binns, Appraisers.

Page 692:   JOSEPH REN. Inventory. Date: ----. Rec.: 19 Feb. 1750.
             Thomas Peters, Thomas Peters, Jr. present.

Page 693:   ANN PHILLIPS. Inventory. Date: 28 Sept. 1750 (ordered).
             Rec.: 19 Feb. 1750. Thomas Collier, John Collier and Rob-
             ert Wager, Appraisers.

Page 693:   RICHARD PARKER of Albemarle Parish, Surry. Will. Date: 3
             Apr. 1744. Rec.: 19 Feb. 1750. William Parker, Executor.
             Daughters: Ann Phillips, Faith Hunt, Judith Clements (wife
             of Benjamin), and Hannah Sisson. Sons: Richard and William.
             Grandson: Frederick Parker (not 21). Wife: Mary. Witnesses:
             Sarah Jones, Elizabeth Jones, Elizabeth Jones, Jr. Robert
             Jones, Jr.

47

Page 694:   THOMAS TOMLINSON of Surry. Will. Date: 31 January 1750.
            Rec.: 19 Mar. 1750. Benjamin Tomlinson, not 21; John Tom-
            linson to act while Executor is a minor. Sons: William,
            Thomas and Benjamin. Daughters: Sarah Carter, Elizabeth
            Moss and Amy Carter. Witnesses: Joseph Carter, Henry Gee
            and Joseph Carter, Jr.

Page 696:   CATHERINE DOLES of Isle of Wight County. Will. Date: 24
            Feb. 1749. Rec.: 19 Mar. 1750. John Alsobrook, who mar-
            ried Rachel Doles, Executor. Grandson: Peter Doles, son
            of daughter Rachel. Daughter: Rachel Doles. Codicil:
            Grandchildren: Martha and Benjamin Stephenson, children of
            daughter, Ann and her husband, Peter Stephenson. Witnesses:
            Laurence Lancaster and John Stephenson.

Page 696:   THOMAS HAMLIN. Inventory. Date: 19 Feb. 1750 (ordered).
            Rec.: 19 Mar. 1750. John Jarret, George Berrick and Thomas
            Collier, Appraisers.

Page 697:   JOSEPH GWALTNEY. Inventory. Date: 1 Mar. 1750/51. Rec.:
            19 Mar. 1750. James Sampson Clark, Michael Deloach and Wil-
            liam Little, Appraisers.

Page 698:   ROBERT WHITE. Inventory. Date: 13 Mar. 1750. Rec.: 19 Mar.
            1750. Gilbert Gray, Henry Browne and Peter Warren, Apprais-
            ers.

Page 699:   MARTHA GWALTNEY of Surry. Will. Date: 15 Nov. 1750. Rec:
            16 Apr. 1751. Thomas Gwaltney, Executor. Legatees: James
            and Thomas, sons of John Gwaltney. Witnesses: Benjamin and
            William Gwaltney.

Page 699:   PETER TATUM of Surry. Will. Date: 11 Mar. 1750. Rec.: 16
            Apr. 1751. Sarah Tatum, Executrix. Sons: Thomas and Edward.
            Wife: Sarah. Daughters: Sarah, Rebecca and Wenia Tatum.
            Witnesses: Thomas Young, Elizabeth Tatum and Mary Heeth.

Page 700:   ELIZABETH HEATH of Albemarle Parish, Surry. Will. Date: 19
            Mar. 1749. Rec.: 16 Apr. 1751. Thomas Heath, Executor.
            Sons: William, Adam, John and Thomas. Daughters: Eliza-
            beth Taylor; Mary Heath; Sarah Tatum; and Rebecca Tatum.
            Granddaughter: Winneford Heath, daughter of James. Witness-
            es: Abraham Heeth, Susanna Heath and James Gee.

Page 702:   RICHARD PARKER, JR. of Albemarle Parish, Surry. Will. Date:
            27 Jan. 1750/51. Rec.: 16 Apr. 1751. Sarah Parker, Execu-
            trix. Sons: Richard, Thomas, Peter, (William not 18);
            Drury and Frederick. Daughters: Sarah, Martha, Mary, Ann
            Parker (not of age). Wife: Sarah. Child in esse. Witness-
            es: George Hamilton, Samuel Peete and William Parker. Cod-
            icil: Witnesses: Samuel Peete, John Wyne and William Hunt.
            Mentions: land in Brunswick Co.; land in Northampton Co.,
            North Carolina.

Page 705:   THOMAS TOMLINSON. Inventory. Date: ----. Rec.: 16 April
            1751. John Tomlinson, Administrator.

Page 706:   PETER TATUM. Inventory. Date: 15 Apr. 1751. Rec.: 16 Apr.
            1751. Sarah Tatum, Administratrix.

Page 707:   Col. THOMAS COCKE. Inventory. Date: 2 Mar. 1750. Rec: 16
            Apr. 1751. William Clinch, How'l Briggs and Richard Jones,
            Appraisers.

Page 709:   Col. THOMAS COCKE. Inventory. (Black Water Qtr., Home
            House). Date: 2 Mar. 1750. Rec.: 16 Apr. 1751. Lemuel
            Cocke and Thomas Cocke, Executors.

Page 711:   MARY CLANTON of Albemarle Parish, Surry. Widow. Will. Date:

(Page 711 - CLANTON cont'd.): 16 Oct. 1750. Rec.: 21 May 1751. John Clanton, Executor. Sons: William, John and Nathaniel. Daughters: Wiggins, others unnamed. Mentions: Thomas Clanton, son of Edward Clanton of Brunswick, dec'd. Witnesses: Richard Avery and William Rogers.

Page 712: WALTER LASHLY of Surry. Will. Date: 8 Apr. 1748. Rec: 21 May 1751. Thomas Lashly, Executor. Sons: Walter, John, Thomas, Patrick, William and Joel. Wife: Hannah. Witnesses: John Barker and Drewry Parker.

Page 714: ALEXANDER DINKINS. Inventory. Date: 4 May 1751. Rec.: 21 May 1751. Lydia Dinkins, presents. Mo. Johnson, John Pennington, and John Pennington, Jr., Appraisers.

Page 715: CHRISTOPHER TATUM. Inventory. Date: 30 Apr. 1751. Rec.: 21 Aug. 1751. Joshua Tatum, Administrator. William Shands, Sr., William Doby and Thomas Young, Appraisers.

Page 717: ELIZABETH HEETH. Inventory. Date: 23 Apr. 1751. Rec: 21 May 1751. Thomas Heeth, Executor. Thomas Young, John and Christopher Tatum, Appraisers.

Page 719: THOMAS AVERIES. Inventory. Date: 18 May 1751. Rec.: 21 May 1751. Rebecca Averis, Administratrix. Thomas Bedingfield, Jethreu Barker and Robert Tucker, Appraisers.

Page 720: PETER GREEN. Account Current. Date: 1746. Rec.: 21 May 1751. Mary Farrington, Executrix. Thomas Gray and William Newsum, Auditors.

Page 722: BENJAMIN BROADRIBB of Surry. Will. Date: 3 May 1751. Rec: 21 May 1751. Benjamin Broadribb, Billison Snipes, Executors. Daughters: Priscilla, Mary and Susanna. Sons: John Fithugh, and Benjamin. Witnesses: Thomas Gray, John Powell and Samuel Snipes.

Page 723: THOMAS ADKINS of Albemarle Parish, Surry. Will. Date: 2 Apr. 1751. Rec.: 16 July 1751. John and Thomas Adkins, Executors. Sons: John and Thomas. Wife: Grace. Daughters: Elizabeth; and Mary Tomlinson. Grandchildren: Thomas and Richard Tomlinson, children of Mary (not 21). Mentions: land in Lunenburg County. Witnesses: Nathaniel Duncan, Richard Cotton and William Hunter.

Page 725: JOHN ROTTENBURY of Albermarle Parish, Surry. Will. Date: 24 Feb. 1750. Rec.: 16 July 1751. Susannah Rottenbury, Executrix. Daughters: Rachel, Elizabeth, Susanna, Lucy and Mary Rottenbury (not 21). Witnesses: John Edmunds, John Threewett and Matthew Sturdivant.

Page 727: SARAH JONES of Albemarle Parish, Surry. Will. Date: 4 Mar. 1750. Rec.: 16 July 1751. John Jones, Administrator; Howell Jones is dead, James Jones, heir at law, refuses. Sons: James, Howell, John; Edmunds (not 21). Daughter: Elizabeth Eldridge. Mentions: land in Brunswick County. Witnesses: Samuel Peete and Thomas Eldridge.

Page 729: HOWELL JONES of Albemarle Parish, Surry. Will. Date: 6 Apr. 1751. Rec.: 16 July 1751. John Jones, Executor. Brothers: James, John; and Edmunds (not 21). Sister: Elizabeth Eldridge. Brother-in-law: Thomas Eldridge. Mentions: Howell and Mary Jones, children of brother James; my part of mother's dower. Friend. William Willie. Witnesses: Thomas Eldridge, John Harris and Thomas Wynne.

Page 731: RICHARD PARKER. Inventory. Date: ----. Rec.: 16 Jul. 1751. Sarah Parker, Executrix. Mentions: corn in Brunswick Co. Mo. Johnson, James Runn and Benjamin Wyche, Appraisers.

Page 733:   WALTER LASHLY. Inventory. Date: 21 May 1751 (ordered).
              Rec.: 16 July 1751. Thomas Lashly, Executor. William Cook,
              John Barker and Henry Barker, Appraisers.

Page 733:   THOMAS WASHINGTON. Inventory. (Brunswick Co.) Date: 2 June
              1749. Rec. ----. Agnes Washington, Administratrix. Will-
              iam Mosely, Benjamin Mosely and Thomas Clanton, Appraisers.

Page 734:   MARTHA GWALTNEY. Inventory. Date: 18 May 1751. Rec.: 16
              July 1751. Thomas Gwaltney, Executor.

Page 735:   JOHN BENNET. Will. Date: 24 Jan. 1750/51. Rec.: 16 July
              1751. Edward Eppes, Executor. Friend and Brother: Edward
              Eppes, son of Mr. Daniel Eppes, Sr. Witnesses: (none).

Page 736:   CHARLES PITTS. Inventory. Date: 15 Nov. 1750. Rec: 16 Jul.
              1751. Joseph Pitts, Executor. John Newsum, John and Carter
              Crafford, Appraisers.

Page 737:   SUSANNAH HANCOCK. Inventory. Date: 20 Nov. 1750 (ordered).
              Rec.: 16 July 1751. William Seward, Jr., William and Dol-
              phin Drew, Appraisers.

Page 739:   JOHN BENNET. Inventory. Date: 3 Aug. 1751. Rec.: 20 August
              1751. Edward Eppes, Executor. James Mason, Peter Hawthorn
              and Harry Meachum, Appraisers.

Page 740:   THOMAS ADKINS. Inventory. Date: 13 Aug. 1751. Rec.: 20 Aug.
              1751. John Harrison, Edward Weaver and Francis Niblett,
              Appraisers.

Page 741:   MARY CLANTON. Inventory. Date: 25 July 1751. Rec.: 20 Aug.
              1751. Richard Avery, William Lofting and John Rachel, Ap-
              praisers.

Page 742:   THOMAS KING. Inventory. Date: 15 May 1750 (ordered). Rec:
              20 Aug. 1751. Thomas Eldridge, Executor. John Harrison,
              Nicholas Patridge and Thomas Adkins, Appraisers.

Page 743:   RICHARD CLANTON. Inventory. Date: 21 May 1751 (ordered).
              Rec.: 20 Aug. 1751. Howell Briggs, Administrator. Richard
              Avery, Thomas Briggs and Cornelius Lofting, Appraisers.

Page 744:   LAMBERT ZELLS, SR. Inventory. Date: 31 July 1751. Rec.:20
              Aug. 1751. Elizabeth Zells presents. John Pennington,
              Clement Hancock and John Pennington, Appraisers.

Page 745:   HENRY MITCHELL of Albemarle Parish, Surry. Will. Date: 16
              May 1750. Rec.: 15 Oct. 1751. Robert Mitchell, Executor.
              Wife: Sarah. Sons: Samuel (not 21); William, Daniel and
              Robert. Daughters: Mary Mitchell, Tabitha Mitchell, Eliza-
              beth Smith, Sarah Smith, Rebecca Mitchell and Amy Mitchell.
              Witnesses: Thomas Vaughan, Robert Berryman and Thomas Vines.

Page 747:   WILLIAM SMITH of Surry. Will. Date: 26 Jan. 1750. Rec: 15
              Oct. 1751. Isham and Josiah Smith, Executors. Sons: Cuth-
              bert, Isham, Josiah and William. Daughters: Sarah, Lucy
              and Susannah. Wife: Ann. Witnesses: Lawrence Gibbons,
              John Wilkerson and George Robertson.

Page 750:   BENJAMIN BELL of Surry. Will. Date: 16 May 1751. Rec.: 15
              Oct. 1751. Ann Bell, Executrix. Wife: Ann. Sons: John,
              Micajah and Benjamin (not of age). Daughters: Lucy, Martha
              and Ann. Witnesses: Robert Hart, Jane Little and Jacob
              Little.

Page 751:   EDWARD SLATE. Inventory. Date: 20 Nov. 1750 (ordered).Rec:
              15 Oct. 1751. Edward Slate, Executor. William Seward, Jr.,
              Dolphin Drew and William Drew, Appraisers.

Page 754:   ARTHUR JOHNSON. Inventory. Date: 30 Aug. 1751. Rec.: 19
             Nov. 1751. William Clinch, Administrator. James Davis,
             William Rose and Jonathan Ellis, Appraisers.

Page 755:   WILLIAM CREWS. Inventory. Date ordered: 16 July 1751. Rec:
             19 Nov. 1751. Margaret Crews, Administratrix. John Thomp-
             son, Zachariah Maddera and William Smith, Appraisers.

Page 756:   THOMAS BOOTH of Surry. Will. Date: 8 July 1751. Rec.: 19
             Nov. 1751. George Booth, Executor. Wife: Ann. Father:
             George. Witnesses: Henry Freeman, Robert Farrington and
             Joel Freeman.

Page 757:   WILLIAM NEWSUM of Southwark Parish, Surry. Will. Date: 23
             Oct. 1747. Rec.: 19 Nov. 1751. John and Joseph Newsum,
             Executors. Sons: John and Joseph. Daughters: Elizabeth,
             wife of Thomas Edwards; Mary, wife of William Holt. Grand-
             children: William and John Newsum. Witnesses: John Ruffin
             and Robert Ruffin.

Page 758:   RICHARD TOMLINSON of Albemarle Parish, Surry. Will. Date:
             17 Aug. 1751. Rec.: 19 Nov. 1751. Nathaniel and Alexander
             Tomlinson, Executors. Sons: William, Nathaniel, Richard
             (dec'd), Alexander, Thomas and Joseph. Daughters: Sarah
             Hobbs and Mary Mason. Witnesses: Thomas Young, William
             Young and James Glover.

Page 759:   GEORGE PASSMORE of Albemarle Parish, Surry. Will. Date:
             11 Aug. 1750. Rec.: 19 Nov. 1751. Matthew Gibbs, Executor.
             Son: John. Daughter: Parnel Gibbs. Son-in-law: Matthew
             Gibbs. Witnesses: Edward Pettway, John Coates and Joseph
             Coates.

Page 760:   RICHARD JORDAN. Will. Date: 27 Dec. 1749. Rec.: 19 Nov.
             1751. William Jordan, Executor. Sons: William, Benjamin
             and Joseph. Witnesses: William and John Cooper.

Page 762:   BENJAMIN BRIGGS (from index, will partially destroyed).
             Will. Date: 1750. Rec.: 19 Nov. 1751. James Jones, Exe-
             cutor. Nephews: Howell Jones, son of James and Hannah; el-
             dest son of Richard Lanier; Neice: Mary Jones, daughter of
             James and Hannah. Godson: John Blunt (not 18). Mother:
             (not named). Friends: Thomas Bedingfield, John Irby, Wil-
             liart Roberts, Jr. (not 18). Legatees: Edward Goodrick
             and wife, Ann; Richard Lanier and wife; James Jones and
             wife, Hannah. Witnesses: Leonard Claiborne, Jr., James
             Gray and Howell Briggs.

Page 763:   JOHN BELL. Account Current. Date: ----. Rec.: 19 Nov. 1751.
             Phebe Bell, Administratrix. Edmund Ruffin and William Har-
             ris, Auditors.

Page 764:   LAMBERT ZELLS. Account Current. Date: 1751. Rec.: 19 Nov.
             1751. Elizabeth Zells, Executrix. John Mason, Jr. Auditor.

Page 765:   LUCY BRIGGS. Inventory. Date ordered: 19 Nov. 1751. Rec:
             17 Dec. 1751. Mary Briggs, Administratrix. Edmund Ruffin,
             John Irby and Willat Roberts, Appraisers.

Page 766:   ELIZABETH ROBERTSON of Surry. Nunc. Will. Date: ----.
             Rec.: 17 Dec. 1751. Richard Hardy, Executor. Legatees:
             James Key (Kea)'s children: James, Dile, Ann; Catherine
             and Alexander Williams; Sally Hardy. Witnesses: Susanna
             Cheatham and James Kea present.

Page 766:   WILLIAM RICHARDSON. Account Current. Date: 1749. Rec: 20
             Aug. 1751. William Richardson, Executor. Mentions: child
             (or children) of testator. Peter Warren and William Drew,
             Auditors.

Page 767:   MARTHA MOSS. Account Current. Date: ----. Rec.: 20 Aug. 1751. John Peter, and N's. Massenburg, Auditors.

Page 768:   WILLIAM MABRY. Account Current. Date: 1751. Rec.: 21 Aug. 1751. Edward Echols, Administrator. John Edmunds and John Jones, Auditors.

Page 768:   RICHARD LEWIS. Account Current. Date: 1736. Rec.: 22 Aug. 1751. William Simmons, Executor.

Page 769:   GEORGE PASSMORE. Inventory. Date: 21 Dec. 1751. Rec.: 21 Jan. 1752. William Moore, Eppes Moore and Peter Hawthorne, Appraisers.

Page 769:   WILLIAM and ELIZABETH ROBERTSON. Inventory. Date: 20 Dec. 1751. Rec.: 21 Jan. 1752. Capt. Richard Hardy, Administrator. Joshua Nicolson, Charles Lucas and John Collier, Appraisers.

Page 770:   RICHARD JONES. Inventory. Date: 14 Jan. 1752. Rec.: 21 Jan. 1752. Thomas Jones presents. Charles Lucas, Robert Lanier and William Lanier, Appraisers.

Page 771:   MATTHEW WILKINSON of Surry. Will. Date: 28 Oct. 1750. Rec: 21 Jan. 1752. Joseph Ezell, Executor. Legatees: Elizabeth Phelce, daughter of Hannah; Thomas Phelce; George and William Ezell; Joseph Ezell, son of George. Brother: John. Witnesses: Nat'l. and Francis Felts, and William Ezell.

Page 772:   SAMUEL NORRIS. Will. Date: 1 Sept. 1751. Rec.: 21 Jan. 1752. John Mason, Jr., Executor. Sons: Thomas and John Norris. Witnesses: Edward Weaver, Richard Cotten and Giles Underhill.

Page 772:   JAMES ANDERSON of Southwark Parish, Surry. Will. Date: 9 Jan. 1750/51. Rec.: 21 Jan. 1752. Rebecca Anderson, Executrix. Sons: Thomas, James, Jordan and John. Wife: Rebecca. Daughters: Mary Eps; Lyddey Averiss; Faith and Priscilla. Son: William (not of age). Mentions: land in Amelia County. Witnesses: Lemuel Cocke, John Bishop and John Ray.

Page 774:   HENRY MITCHELL. Inventory. Date: 13 Dec. 1751. Rec.: 21 Jan. 1752. Richard Pepper, Thomas Butler and Thomas Vines, Appraisers.

Page 775:   HENRY LEE of Albemarle Parish, Surry. Will. Date: 16 Dec. 1751. Rec.: 18 Feb. 1752. Edward Lee, Executor. Sons: Edward and John. Wife: Ann. Grandson: Henry Meachum. Witnesses: John Adkins and Henry Porch.

Page 776:   ZACHARIAH (ZACHARIAS) MADDERA of Southwark Parish, Surry. Will. Date: 4 Mar. 1748/49. Rec.: 18 Feb. 1752. Johanna and John Maddera, Executors. Wife: Johanna. Sons: James, John, William and Joel. Daughters: Sarah, Elizabeth, Lucy, Priscilla, Martha and Ann. Grandsons: James Davis, Zachariah Maddera (not of age). Mentions: children by last wife (including John). Witnesses: Samuel Thompson, Jane Warren, Henry Savidge, Blanks Moody and Ann Thompson.

Page 777:   RICHARD TOMLINSON. Inventory. Date: 30 Dec. 1751. Rec.: 18 Feb. 1752. Nathaniel and Alexander Tomlinson, Executors.

Page 778:   THOMAS BOOTH. Inventory. Date: 30 Dec. 1751. Rec.: 18 Feb. 1752. George Booth, Executor. John Tyus, William Harper and Richard Hill, Appraisers.

Page 778:   SAMUEL NORRIS. Inventory. Date: 13 Feb. 1752. Rec.: 18 Feb. 1752. John Harrison, Edward Weaver and Nathaniel Norrington, Appraisers.

Page 779:   MATTHEW WILKINSON. Inventory. Date: ----. Rec.: 18 Feb.
1752. William Knight, Nathaniel Felts and Benjamin Adams,
Appraisers.

Page 779:   JAMES ANDERSON. Inventory. Date: 21 Jan. 1752. Rec.: 18
Feb. 1752. Rebecca Anderson, Executrix. Benjamin Baird,
Thomas Bedingfield and Richard Jones, Appraisers.

Page 781:   SAMUEL THOMPSON. Inventory. Date: 18 Aug. 1751 (ordered).
Rec.: 18 Feb. 1752. John Nicolson, Thomas Warren and Gilbert Gray, Appraisers.

Page 782:   CATHERINE DOLES. Inventory. Date: 19 Mar. 1750 (ordered).
Rec.: 18 Feb. 1752. John Andrews, William Waller and Arthur
Richardson, Appraisers.

Page 782:   HENRY BARKER. Account Current. Date: ----. Rec.: 18 Feb.
1752. John Peter, Executor. George Noble and Thomas Gray,
Auditors.

Page 783:   SAMUEL CHAPPELL. Account Current. Date: ----. Rec.: 18 Feb.
1752. Elizabeth Chappell, Executrix. Mentions: family.
John Peter and Thomas Gray, Auditors.

Page 783:   WILLIAM THOMPSON of Albemarle Parish, Surry. Planter. Will.
Date: 28 Dec. 1751. Rec.: 21 Apr. 1752. James Thompson,
Executor. Daughter: Sarah Killebrew. Wife: Mary. Son: James.
Witnesses: Thomas Pate, John Morgan and John Pate.

Page 783:   BENJAMIN BELL. Inventory. Date: 11 Dec. 1751. Rec.: 21 Apr.
1752. Ann Bell, Executrix.

Page 784:   HENRY LEE. Inventory. Date: 18 Feb. 1752 (ordered). Rec.:
21 Apr. 1752. Peter Hawthorne, William Moore and Edward
Eppes, Appraisers.

Page 784:   STEPHEN HALFORD. Inventory. Date: ----. Rec.: 21 April
1752. John Spratley, James Davis and Jonathan Ellis, Appraisers.

Page 785:   SARAH JONES. Inventory. Date: 18 July 1751. Rec.: 21 Apr.
1752. John Jones, Administrator. Nicholas Partridge, John
Jarrett and Jehu Barker, Appraisers.

Page 785:   SARAH JONES. Inventory (Brunswick Co.). Date: 19 December
1751. Rec.: 21 Apr. 1752. Mason Bishop, Nicholas Lanier and
John Mattris, Appraisers.

Page 786:   HOWELL JONES. Inventory. Date: 18 July 1751. Rec: 21 Apr.
1752. John Jones, Administrator. Nicholas Partridge, John
Jarrat and Jehu Barker, Appraisers.

Page 786:   BLANKS MOODY. Inventory. Date: 16 Mar. 1752. Rec: 21 Apr.
1752. Edward Bayley, William Rose and Henry Johnson, Appraisers.

Page 787:   BARTHOLOMEW ANDREWS. Inventory. Date: ----. Rec: 21 April
1752. Edward Bailey, William Rose and Christopher Mooring,
Jr., Appraisers.

Page 788:   THOMAS BOOTH. Inventory. Date: 1751. Rec.: 21 Apr. 1752.
George Booth, Executor. John Peter, Samuel Maget, Appraiser.

Page 788:   JOHN RIVES. Account Current. Date: 1750. Rec.: 21 Apr.1752.
Mentions: land in Prince George County; family; Timothy
Reives; Mrs. Francis Rives. Henry Browne and W. Edwards,
Auditors.

Page 789:   HOWELL JONES. Account Current. Date: 1750. Rec.: 16 June

(Page 789: - JONES cont'd.): 1752. John Jones, Executor. Mentions: legacies to Mary Jones, Howell Jones, Eliza Eldridge and John Jones.

Page 789: SARAH JONES. Account Current and Sale. Date: 1750. Rec: 16 June 1752. John Jones, Administrator. Robert Nicholson and Henry Blow, Auditors.

Page 793: JOHN SEWARD. Account Current. Date: 1749. Rec.: 16 June 1752. Thomas Cocke and William Seward, Auditors.

Page 795: SAMUEL SEBRELL. Account Current. Date: 1748. Rec.: 16 Jun. 1752. Sarah Sebrell, Administratrix of Moses Sebrell, the Executrix. Mentions: legacy to Lidia Wiggs; paid Samuel Sebrell his part of his father's estate; Daniel Sebrell; Jesse Hargrave for his wife; Jesse Hargrave for Benjamin Sebrell; Anselm Bailey for Joseph Sebrell; Moses Sebrell; Elizabeth Sebrell legacy in father's will. John Ruffin and Benjamin Cocke, Auditors.

Page 797: Rev. Mr. HENRY EELBECK. Inventory. Date: ----. Rec.: June 16, 1752. Edward Bailey, Robert Wager and James Davis, Appraisers.

Page 798: JOHN JEFFRYS, SR. of Albemarle Parish, Surry. Planter. Will. Date: 3 Nov. 1746. Rec.: 16 June 1752. Martha Jeffrys, Executrix. Daughters: Mary Powell and Martha Jeffrys. Grandsons: John Jeffrys and Benjamin Tan. Witnesses: Samuel Maget and William Owen.

Page 799: CATHERINE WILLIAMS of Surry. Will. Date: 7 Nov. 1749. Rec: 16 June 1752. Thomas Williams and Lawrence Lancaster, Executors. Son: Thomas. Daughters: Elizabeth Na(e)rns, and Mary Lancaster. Grandchildren: Burwell Sharpe (not 21) -Catherine Jane Bage; Mary Williams (not 15); Hartwell King Williams (not 15). Witnesses: Joshua Proctor, Robert Gray and Mary Fitchit.

Page 800: HANNAH COCKE, Widow of THOMAS COCKE, late of Surry, Gent., dec'd. Date: 20 Nov. 1751. Rec.: 16 June 1752. Thomas Cocke, Executor. Sons: Thomas and John. Witnesses (to will?) Benjamin Cocke and John Cocke, Sr.

Page 800: SAMPSON WILSON. Account Current. Date: 1752. Rec.: 16 Jun. 1752. Sarah Wilson, Administratrix. John Nicolson and Stephen Hamlin, Auditors.

Page 801: LUCY BRIGGS. Account Current. Date: 1752. Rec.: 16 June 1752. Mary Briggs, Administratrix. Richard Jones, and James Jones, Jr., Auditors.

Page 801: JOHN ROTTENBERRY. Inventory. Date: 8 Nov. 1751. Rec.: 21 July 1752. Thomas Olliver, Sloman Wynne, and Holin Sturdivant, Appraisers.

Page 802: JOSHUA ROWLAND of Surry. Will. Date: 15 June 1752. Rec.: 21 July 1752. Elizabeth Rowland, Executrix. Brother: John. Wife: Elizabeth. Son: William. Mentions: all my children. Witnesses: Sylvanus Stokes, William Rowland and Thomas Adkins.

Page 803: WILLIAM THOMPSON. Inventory. Date: 8 May 1752. Rec.: 21 July 1752. Henry Lee, Thomas Peete and Peter Avent, Appraisers.

Page 804: ANDREW BROWNE. Account Current. Date: 1752. Rec.: 21 Jul. 1752. Christopher Mooring, Jr. presents. Edward Bailey, John Collier and Joseph Jordan, Auditors.

Page 804:   ROBERT ROWELL. Inventory. Date: ----. Rec.: 21 Jul. 1752. Thomas Warren, William Marriott, Jr. and John Warren, Appraisers.

Page 804:   ROBERT WARREN of Southwark Parish, Surry. Will. Date: 9 Apr. 1751. Rec.: 21 July 1752. Mary Warren, Executrix. Son: Joseph. Wife: Mary. Daughters (in order of birth): Elizabeth, Mary, Martha and Sarah; infant lately born. Witnesses: Peter Warren and Thomas Warren.

Page 805:   JOHN ROTTENBERRY. Account Current. Date: 1751. Rec: 21 July 1752. Susanna Rottenberry, Executrix. Thomas Olliver and Sylvanus Stokes, Auditors.

Page 806:   RICHARD CLANTON. Account Current. Date: 1750. Rec: 21 Jul. 1752. Howell Briggs, Administrator. Mentions - family. Samuel Peete and Peter Warren, Auditors.

Page 807:   CATHERINE NUNN. Account Current. Date: --. Rec: 22 July 1752.

Page 808:   JOHN MYAS. Account Current. Date: --. Rec.: 22 July 1752.

Page 808:   JAMEA ANDERSON. Account Current. Date: 1751. Rec.: 22 Jul. 1752. Rebecca Anderson, Executrix. John Hay and John Nicolson, Auditors.

Page 809:   BENJAMIN BRIGGS. Inventory. Date: 20 July 1752. Rec.: 22 July 1752. Edmond Ruffin, John Irby and Thomas Beddingfield, Appraisers.

Page 810:   MARY WALLER. Inventory. Date: 15 June 1750. Rec.: 18 Aug. 1752. Edmund Waller, Administrator. John Newsum, Carter Crafford and Thomas Binns, Appraisers.

Page 811:   WILLIAM SMITH. Inventory. Date: ----. Rec.: 18 Aug. 1752. Thomas Vaughan, Thomas Butlar and Lawrence Gibbons, Appraisers.

Page 812:   ROBERT LONG. Inventory. Date: ---. Rec.: 18 Aug. 1752. Hannah Long, Administratrix. George Briggs, Joseph Ellis and Simon Murfee, Appraisers.

Page 813:   THOMAS EDWARDS. Inventory. Date: ---. Rec.: 18 Aug. 1752. Nicholas Thompson, Joseph Hart and Thomas Lane, Appraisers.

Page 814:   JOHN AVARY of Southwark Parish, Surry. Will. Date: 30 Jun. 1752. Rec.: 18 Aug. 1752. John Avary, Executor. Sons: Richard and John. Mentions: William Warren, son of Ann Matthews. David Minnitree, Witness.

Page 815:   Mrs. HANNAH COCKE. Inventory. Date: 13 Aug. 1752. Rec.: 18 Aug. 1752. William Short, Charles Lucas and John J'Anson, Appraisers.

Page 817:   MATTHEW HILL. Inventory. Date: ----. Rec.: 18 Aug. 1752. Bathiah Morris, Admin'r. Richard Pepper, Thomas Butler and Lawrence Gibbons, Appraisers.

Page 818:   DONALD MC INNISH. Inventory. Date: 21 Nov. 1751. Rec.: 18 Feb. 1752. William Willie, Administrator. John Hay, Robert Newsum and Benjamin Wyche, Appraisers.

Page 819:   ROBERT ATKINSON. Account Current. Date: ----. Rec.: 18 Feb. 1752. Mary Atkinson, Administratrix. William Seward, Jr. and Henry Browne, Auditors.

Page 819:   JOHN BRUCE of Surry. Will. Date: 16 Aug. 1752. Rec.: 26 Sept. 1752. Sarah Bruce and Jacob Bruce, Executors. Son:

(Page 819 - BRUCE cont'd.): James. Daughters: Elizabeth and her daughter, Elizabeth; Ann; Sarah and her son, Jacob Bruce. Thomas Taylor, David Brooke and Arthur Smith, Witnesses.

Page 820: JAMES MASON. Inventory. Date: ----. Rec.: 26 Sept. 1752. Mary Mason, Administratrix. Peter Hawthorne, William Petway and Robert Petway, Appraisers.

Page 821: HENRY MITCHELL. Account Current. Date: 1752. Rec.: 26 Sep. 1752. Robert Mitchell, Executor. James Chappell, Jr. and Thomas Oliver, Auditors.

Page 822: JOSEPH MASON. Account Current. Date: 1749. Rec.: 26 Sept. 1752. Phebe Ogburn, Administratrix. Mentions: widow and children. Thomas Cocke and Thomas Binns, Auditors.

Page 823: PARKS NICOLSON. Inventory. Date: ----. Rec.: 26 Sept. 1752. Ephraim Baird, Richard Bullock and Charles Lucas, Appraisers.

Page 824: RICHARD TOMLINSON. Account Current. Date: ----. Rec.: 21 Sept. 1752. Mary Tomlinson, Administratrix. Thomas Gray, Christopher Mooring, Jr. Auditors.

Page 824: WILLIAM EVANS of Surry. Will. Date: 14 Sept. 1752. Rec: 17 Oct. 1752. Priscilla Evans, Executrix. Son: William. Dau: Cilia Mabry. Wife: Priscilla. Witnesses: Charles Holt, Anthony Evans and Robert Gray.

Page 826: JOHN JEFFRES. Inventory. Date: ----. Rec.: 17 Oct. 1752. Martha Jeffres, Executrix. Samuel Maget, William Owen and Arthur Richardson, Appraisers.

Page 826: JOHN EDMONDS of Surry, Gardener. Will. Date: 22 Feb. 1752. Rec.: 17 Oct. 1752. John Ruffin, Gen., Executor. Legatee: William Ruffin, son of John (not 21). Friend: Robert Ruffin. Witnesses: Thomas Warren, John Little and James Newsum.

Page 827: JAMES BENNETT of Southwark Parish, Surry. Will. Date: 30 Dec. 1745. Rec.: 17 Oct. 1752. Samuel Bennett, Executor. Sons: William, James, John and Samuel. Daughters: Ann, Martha, Sarah and Bridget. Grandson: Thomas Bennett, son of William. Witnesses: Charles Binns; William Goodwynn, William Batts and William Clark.

Page 829: CATHERINE WILLIAMS. Inventory. Date: ----. Rec.: 17 Oct. 1752. Thomas Williams presents. James Jones, John Tyus and John Wilborn, Appraisers.

Page 830: WILLIAM CRIPPS. Account Current. Date: 1751. Rec: 17 Oct. 1752. Anselm Bailey, Executor. Mentions: funeral expenses of Elizabeth Cripps; legacies to - Mary Cripps and Thomas Myas. Thomas Gray and George Cryer, Auditors.

Page 832: JOHN GWALTNEY of Surry. Will. Date: 21 Oct. 1752. Rec: 21 Nov. 1752. Benjamin Gwaltney, Executor. Sons: Benjamin, Thomas and James. Daughters: Elizabeth Andrews, and Martha Braddy. Grandson: John Gwaltney. Witnesses: Michael Deloach, Sarah Deloach, John Womble, Mary Gwaltney and William Clark.

Page 834: WILLIAM GWALTNEY of Southwark Parish, Surry. Will. Date: 17 Oct. 1752. Rec.: 21 Nov. 1752. Thomas Gwaltney, Executor. Brothers: Benjamin, Thomas and James. Witnesses: Edward Brown and John Bamer.

Page 835: JACOB PATE of Surry. Will. Date: 15 June 1752. Rec: 21 Nov. 1752. Zillah Pate and William Clinch, Executors. Wife: Zillah. Children: (not named). Mentions: land in James City Co. Wit.: Robert Wager and Archibald Wager.

Page 836:   NICHOLAS MAGET, JR. Will. Date: 21 Aug. 1752. Rec.: 21
            Nov. 1752. Ann Maget, Executrix. Legatees: William Browne,
            son of Henry; Henry Browne, son of Henry. Mother: Ann.
            Witnesses: Robert Watkins and John Watkins.

Page 837:   ROBERT ROWELL. Account Current. Date: ----. Rec.: 21 Nov.
            1752. John Davis, Administrator. John J'Anson and Peter
            Warren, Auditors.

Page 838:   THOMAS ADKINS. Account Current. Date: ----. Rec.: 21 Nov.
            1752. John and Thomas Adkins, Executors. Robert Nicolson,
            and Richard Jones, Auditors.

Page 838:   WILLIAM JOHNSON. Will. Date: ----. Rec.: 19 Dec. 1752.
            Phebe Johnson, Executrix. Sons: William, Nathaniel; and
            Petway (not 21). Daughters: Elizabeth Cullum, Phebe Coop-
            er and Susanna Johnson. Wife: Phebe. Witnesses: John Tom-
            linson, Howell Briggs and Samuel Hays.

Page 840:   WILLIAM EVANS. Inventory. Date: 4 Dec. 1752. Rec.:19 Dec.
            1752. Robert Gray, Thomas Wilson and Samuel Maget, Apprais-
            ers.

Page 842:   THOMAS WASHINGTON. Account Current. Date: 1749. Rec: 19
            Dec. 1752. Mo. Johnson and Nicholas Massenburg, Auditors.

Page 844:   DANIEL EPPES of Albemarle Parish, Surry. Will. Date: 6
            Sept. 1749. Rec.: 16 Jan. 1753. William Willie and Edward
            Eppes, Executors. Wife: Mary. Son: Edward. Daughters:
            Elizabeth Knight and Mary Tatum. Grandson: Daniel Eppes
            (not 21). Witness: William Willie.

Page 845:   BENJAMIN ANDREWS. Account Current. Date: 1747. Rec.: 16
            Jan. 1753. Edward Bailey, Executor. James Claiborne and
            Gray Briggs, Auditors.

Page 846:   DANIEL EPPES. Inventory. Date: 17 Mar. 1753. Rec.: 20 Mar.
            1753. William Willie and Edward Eppes, Executors.

Page 847:   JOHN IVIE of Albemarle Parish, Surry. Will. Date: 5 Jan'y
            1750. Rec.: 20 Mar. 1753. Thomas Ivie, Executor. Sons:
            John (eldest), Thomas and William. Wife: Christian. Dau:
            Amy Ivie. Witnesses: John Paynter, Thomas Adkins, Jr. and
            William Wilkinson.

Page 849:   Col. THOMAS COCKE. Account Current. Date: 1750. Rec.: 20
            Mar. 1753. Lemuel Cocke and Thomas Cocke, Executors. Men-
            tions: division into equal parts to - Lemuel, Thomas and
            John Cocke. William Short and John Peter, Auditors.

Page 853:   WILLIAM JOHNSON. Inventory. Date ordered: 19 Dec. 1752.
            Rec.: 20 Mar. 1753. Phebe Johnson, Executrix. Nicholas
            Partridge, Reuben Baird and Nicholas Partridge, Jr. Apprai-
            sers.

Page 854:   JOYCE CARRELL. Inventory (at Hog Island). Date: 18 Feb.
            1752. Rec.: 20 Mar. 1753. William Seward, Jr. and Jordan
            Thomas, Administrators. William Drew, Thomas Davidson and
            Carter Crafford, Appraisers.

Page 857:   JOHN HARWOOD. Inventory. Date: 29 Apr. 1752. Rec.: 20
            Mar. 1753. Thomas Davidson, Administrator. William Seward,
            Jr., William Drew and Dolphin Drew, Appraisers.

Page 859:   WILLIAM GWALTNEY. Inventory. Date: 17 Mar. 1753. Rec.:20
            Mar. 1753. Thomas Gwaltney, Executor.

Page 859:   CHARLES MABRY. Account Current. Date: 1748. Rec.: 20 Mar.
            1753. Rebecca Mabry, and Charles Mabry, Executors. Mentions

                                    57

(Page 859 - MABRY cont'd.): legacies to: William Mabry, Rebecca Mabry, Elizabeth Mabry and David Turner. Moses Johnson and Thomas Gray, Auditors.

Page 860: JOHN WATKINS. Inventory. Date: 16 Jan. 1749 (ordered). Rec.: 20 Mar. 1753. Henry Browne, Charles Holdsworth and John Nicholson, Appraisers.

Page 861: JOHN AVARY. Inventory. Date: 5 Nov. 1753. Rec.: 20 Mar. 1753. John Avary presents. Charles Lucas, Thomas Sourby and William Moring, Appraisers.

Page 862: CHRISTOPHER MOORING, SR. of Southwark Parish, Surry. Will. Date: 27 Dec. 1751. Rec.: 20 Mar. 1753. Christopher Mooring, Executor. Sons: John, Christopher and William. Daughters: Mary Morris, Jane Collier and Lucy Collier. Son-in-law: Edward Bayley. Grandson: John Mooring, son of John. Mentions: lands in England; son Christopher to have his mother's Bible marked MS. Witnesses: John Avary, Sr., Stephen Lucas and John Simmons.

Page 864: JOHN BRUCE. Inventory. Date: 20 Dec. 1752. Rec.: 17 Apr. 1753. Thomas Holt, Thomas Edwards and Nicholas Faulcon, Appraisers.

Page 865: FORTUNE WATKINS of Southwark Parish, Surry. Will. Date: 4 Dec. 1752. Rec.: 17 Apr. 1753. Thomas Bage, Executor. Sons: Robert and William. Daughters: Rebecca Figgers, Charity Watkins and Elizabeth Bage. Witnesses: Nicholas Cryer and George Cryer.

Page 866: THOMAS EDWARDS. Account Current. Date: ----. Rec.: 17 Apr. 1753. Elizabeth Edwards, Administratrix. John Peter and Peter Warren, Auditors.

Page 866: JOHN IVIE. Inventory. Date: ----. Rec.: 15 May 1753. Thomas Ivy, presents.

Page 867: PHILLIP LIGHTFOOT, JR. Account Current. Date: 1747. Rec: 15 May 1753. William Lightfoot, Administrator. B. Harrison and John Peter, Auditors.

Page 868: WILLIAM ROOKINGS. Account Current. Date: 1750. Rec.: 15 May 1753. Ellin Rookings, Administratrix. Nicholas Massenburg and Moses Johnson, Auditors.

Page 870: SARAH JONES. Will Further Proven. Rec: 15 May 1753. Thomas Eldridge by oath. Mentions: legacy to Elizabeth, wife of Thomas Eldridge.

Page 870: WILLIAM CLEMENTS. Inventory. Date: 19 Dec. 1752 (ordered) Rec.: 16 May 1753. Peter Warren, Thomas Warren and Samuel Judkins, Appraisers.

Page 871: ELIZABETH CARGILL of Southwark Parish, Surry. Will. Date: 10 Jan. 1744. Rec.: 15 May 1753. Nicholas Massenburg who married Lucy Cargill, granted Administration. Daughters: Lucy and Elizabeth Cargill, (neither of age). Brothers: Nathaniel and Benjamin Harrison. Friends: Dr. Patrick Adams and Robert Jones, Jr. Witnesses: John Thompson, John Jarrat and Jean Crosle.

Page 872: FRANCIS FELTS. Inventory. Date: 16 June 1753. Rec.: 19 June 1753. Nathaniel Felts, Administrator. William Knight, Jeremiah Bullock and John Battle, Jr., Appraisers.

Page 873: HENRY HARRISON. Inventory. Date ordered: 21 Mar. 1748. Rec.: 19 June 1753. John Jarret, George Berwick and Thomas Collier, Appraisers.

Page 873:   HENRY HARRISON. Account Current. Date: ---. Rec.: 19 Jun.
1753.

Page 873:   MOSES SEBRELL. Account Current. Date: 1751. Rec.: 19 Jun.
1753. Sarah Murdaugh, Administratrix. Mentions equal por-
tions to: Samuel Sebrell, Daniel Sebrell, Joseph Sebrell;
Joseph Sebrell for Elizabeth Sebrell, Jesse Hargrave, Benjamin Sebrell, Jordan Thomas for Lydia Wiggs; portion for
the Administratrix. Mo. Johnson and David Hunter, Auditors.

Page 874:   RICHARD BARKER. Inventory. Date: 23 Dec. 1752. Rec.:   19
June 1753. John Peter, Administrator. Thomas Briggs, Caleb Ellis and James Bishop, Appraisers.

Page 875:   WILLIAM HOLT of Southwark Parish, Surry. Will. Date: 14
Mar. 1753. Rec.: 19 June 1753. Mary Holt and Francis Holt
are the Executors. Sons: Benjamin, William, Francis and
James. Daughters: Mary, Hannah and Martha. Wife: Mary.
Witness: William Edwards, Jr.

Page 876:   WILLIAM LONG. Will. Date: 3 Sept. 1753. Rec.: 18 Sept.
1753. Ann Long, Executrix. Wife: Ann. Witnesses: John
Thompson, John Philips and Mourning Moor.

Page 877:   JAMES CLINCH. Account Current. Date: 1747. Rec.: 18 Sept.
1753. John White and Jane White, Executors. David Hunter
and William Harris, Auditors.

Page 878:   MARY EDMUNDS of Albemarle Parish, Surry, widow. Will. Date:
30 July 1747. Rec.: 20 Nov. 1753. John Edmunds, Executor.
Daughters: Elizabeth Hines, Christian Hines, Phillis Norrington, and Faith Ballard. Son: John. Witnesses: Howell
Jones and Thomas Ren.

Page 879:   JAMES BOYD of Surry, Taylor (Tailor). Will. Date: 6 June
1753. Rec.: 20 Nov. 1753. Benjamin Ruffin, Executor. Wife:
Sarah. Friend: Col. James Baker. Witnesses: Thomas Clarke,
William Pulley, Jr. and Ann Leversedge.

Page 880:   WILLIAM PHILLIPS. Account Current. Date: 1750. Rec.: Dec.
18, 1753. John Ruffin, Administrator. Mentions: Benjamin
Phillips heir at law. Nicholas Massenburg and John Peter,
Auditors.

Page 880:   THOMAS WALLER. Sale and Account Current. Date: 1750. Rec:
18 Dec. 1753. John Ruffin, Administrator. Nicholas Massenburg and John Peter, Auditors.

Page 881:   RICHARD ANDREWS. Inventory. Date: ----. Rec.: 19 Nov. 1751.
Richard Andrews and David Andrews, Administrators. Hartwell
Cocke, Appraiser.

Page 884:   WILLIAM LONG. Inventory. Date: ----. Rec.: 15 Jan. 1754.
Henry Savage, John Moring and William Savage, Appraisers.

Page 885:   ANN CLACK. Inventory. Date: ----. Rec.: 15 Jan. 1754. David Jones, John Goodwyn and William Cook, Appraisers.

Page 885:   BENJAMIN RICKS. Nunc. Will. Date: 14 Nov. 1753. Rec.: 15
Jan. 1754. Elizabeth Ricks and Thomas Ricks, Executors.
Daughters: Sarah and Mary Ricks. Mentions: Charles and
Philemon Ricks (not 21); Thomas Ricks; wife; young sons.
Witnesses: William Safford and Amey Blanks.

Page 886:   SIMON MURFEY of Surry, Planter. Will. Date: 5 July 1753.
Rec.: 15 Jan. 1754. Simon Murfey and Elizabeth Murfey (now
Edwards), Executors. Wife: Elizabeth (Executrix). Sons:
Richard of Southampton Co., Arthur of Surry Co., and Simon.
Daughters: Catherine and Lucy Murfey; Elizabeth Hines and

(Page 886 - MURFEY cont'd.): Mary Magarrity. Grandchildren: Simon
Murfey; and James Murfey, son of Arthur. Witnesses: Samuel
Peete, Simon Murfey and Catherine Murfey.

Page 887:   RICHARD JONES. Account Current. Date: ----. Rec.: 15 Jan.
1754. Nicholas Massenburg and Benjamin Baird, Auditors.

Page 887:   THOMAS AVORIS. Account Current. Date: ----. Rec.: 15 Jan.
1754. Richard Harrison presents. Mentions: widow and 3
children. Nicholas Massenburg and Benjamin Baird, Auditors.

Page 888:   RICHARD BARKER. Account Current. Date: ----. Rec.: 15 Jan.
1754. John Peter presents. Nicholas Massenburg and Benjamin Baird, Auditors.

Page 889:   ROBERT LONG. Account Current. Date: 1753. Rec.: 15 Jan.
1754. Hannah Long presents. John Hay and James Jones, Auditors.

Page 890:   JAMES CLINCH. Additional -Account Current. Date: ----.
Rec.: 15 Jan. 1754. John White and Jane White, Administra-
tor/Administratrix.

Page 891:   EDWARD ELLIS of Southwark Parish, Surry. Will. Date: 15 Jan.
1742/43. Rec.: 20 Dec. 1748. (further proven on 19 Feb.
1754. Richard Puttney and Thomas Grantham, Executors.
Daughters: Elizabeth Ellis, Sarah Puttney and Mary Grantham.
Grandsons: James and Benjamin Puttney. Friend: Joshua Nicholson. Witnesses: John Avary, Jr., William Warren and
William Rawlings.

Page 893:   DAVID DREW of Surry. Will. Date: 14 Dec. 1753. Rec.: 19
Feb. 1754. Lucy Drew and Robert Hart, Executors. Wife:
Lucy. Son: David (not of age). Sister's son: John Watkins.
Witnesses: Samuel Bennett, Mary Williams and Mary Hart.

Page 894:   GEORGE CRYER, SR. of Surry. Will. Date: 20 Dec. 1753. Rec:
19 Feb. 1754. Ann Cryer and George Cryer, Executors. Wife:
Ann. Sons: Nicholas, George, William and Samuel. Friend:
William Clinch. Witnesses: Robert Wager, Mary Cryer and
William Clinch.

Page 895:   BENJAMIN HYDE. Inventory. Date: 19 Feb. 1754. Rec.: 19
Feb. 1754. David Hunter, Samuel Magget and Thomas Alsobrook, Appraisers.

Page 895:   CHRISTOPHER MORING. Inventory. Date: 13 Apr. 1753. Rec: 19
Feb. 1754. Christopher Moring, Executor. Mentions legatees
- Christopher, John and William Moring; Lucy and Jean Coll-
ier; Mary Morris. William Pulley, Jr., Henry Collier and
Thomas Sorsby, Appraisers.

Page 897:   BENJAMIN CARRELL. Account Current. Date: ----. Rec.: 16
Apr. 1754. Joice Carrell, Executrix, now deceased. William
Seward, Jr. and Jordan Thomas, Administrators. Thomas Holt,
Benjamin Cocke and William Drew, Auditors.

Page 898:   Mr. GEORGE CRYER. Inventory. Date: 15 Mar. 1754. Rec.: 16
Apr. 1754. Thomas Collier, Charles Holeworth and William
Marriott, Jr., Appraisers.

Page 900:   MOSES SEBRELL. Inventory. Date ordered: 15 Oct. 1751. Rec:
16 Apr. 1754. William Drew, Dolphin Drew and John Newsum,
Appraisers.

Page 1: BENJAMIN REECKS. Inventory. Date: ----. Rec.: 21 May 1754. Thomas Reeks, Executor.

Page 2: WILLIAM JOHNSON. Account Current. Date: ----. Rec.: 21 May 1754. Phebe Johnson, Executrix. Mentions: payments to Susanna Johnson, Thomas Cooper and William Johnson. Benjamin Ruffin and William Seward, Jr., Auditors.

Page 3: BENJAMIN BROADRIB. Account Current. Date: 1750. Rec. ____ Billison Snipes and Benjamin Broadrib, Executors.

Page 4: THOMAS PRETLOW. Will. Date: ----. Rec.----. Rebekah Pretlow, Executrix. Wife: Rebekah. Sons: Thomas, Joshua, John and Samuel. Sister: Ann Nail. Grandsons: William Pretlow and Thomas Newby. Mentions: Samuel Person as some relation. Witnesses: --- Cornwell and John Saunders.

Page 5: WILLIAM LONG. Inventory. Date: ----. Rec.: ----. Ann Long (presents inventory). Howell Briggs (Appraiser?)

Page 6: MATTHEW HILL. Account Current. Date: ----. Rec.: 18 Jun. 1754. Mentions: balance due Bethia Morris. John Hay and Nicholas Massenburg, Auditors.

Page 6: WILLIAM ROOKINGS. Additional Inventory. Date: ---. Rec.: ----. Ellen Rookings, Administratrix.

Page 7: JOHN DAVIS. Account Current. Date: ----. Rec.: 16 Jul. 1754. Ann Davis (presents AC).

Page 7: WALTER LASHLEY. Account Current. Date: 1752. Rec: 16 Jul. 1754. Thomas Lasley, Executor.

Page 8: BENJAMIN REEKS. Inventory. Date: 15 Jan. 1754. Rec.: 16 July 1754. Thomas Reeks, Executor. Mentions: property in Lunenburg County. William Safford, Philleman Russel and Henery Gill, Appraisers.

Page 8: ANN MAGIT (MAGGETT), widow of Surry County. Will. Date: 5 Sept. 1752. Rec.: 16 July 1754. Benjamin Taylor, Executor. Sons: Arthur Taylor, Benjamin Taylor; John Taylor and William Taylor (dec'd.). Daughter: Margret Gray, wife of Gilbert Gray. Grandchildren: Martha Taylor, William Wilson Taylor (son of William, dec'd.), Elizabeth Gray, John Taylor (son of John, dec'd.), Joseph Gray, Ann Taylor, Elizabeth Hancel and William Gray. Witnesses: George Cryer and Mary Cryer.

Page 10: ROBERT WARREN. Inventory. Date: 21 July 1752. Rec.: 16 July 1754. Samuel Thompson, John Harris and William Marriott, Jr., Appraisers.

Page 11: NICHOLAS MAGET. Inventory. Date: 21 Nov. ---. Rec.: 16 July 1754. William Clinch, Peter Warren and Charles Hodlsworth, Appraisers.

Page 11: DAVID LONG, Gent. of Surry. Will. Date: ----. Rec. ----. James Cocke and Henry Browne, Gent., Executors. Wife: Mary. Mentions: wife's father, Col. Benjamin Edwards. John Ruffin, --- Poythress, Hartwell Cocke and Thomas Cocke, Gent, swear to handwriting.

Page 12: JOHN SAMPSON CLARK. Will. Date: ---1752. Rec.: 20 Aug. 1754. Joice Clark and James Clark, Executors. Wife: Joice. Sons: Sampson, James and William. Daughters: Lucy, Anne, Patty, Mary, Elizabeth, Sarah and Amey Clark. Witnesses: --- Edwards, John Deloach and Jordan Thomas.

Page 14:   SIMON MURFEE. Inventory. Date: 15 Jan. 1754. Rec.: Sept. 17, 1754. James Jones of Sussex, presents. Joseph Ellis, Peter Hines and David Hines, Appraisers.

Page 14:   FORTUNE WATKINS. Inventory. Date: 30 Jan. 1754. Rec.: 17 Sept. 1754.

Page 15:   THOMAS WASHINGTON. Additional Account Current. Date: ---. Rec.: 17 Sept. 1754. William Short and John Peter, Auditors.

Page 16:   Col. THOMAS COCKE. Account Current. Date: 1753. Rec.: 17 Sept. 1754. Lemuel Cocke and Thomas Cocke, Executors. Mentions: Lemuel Cocke's share; Thomas Cocke's share; and John Cocke's share. William Short and John Peter, Auditors.

Page 17:   DAVID DREW. Inventory. Date: 10 Feb. 1754. Rec.: 19 Nov. 1754. Lucy Drew and Robert Hart, Executors.

Page 18:   JOHN COLLIER of Southwark Parish, Surry. Will. Date: Aug. 12, 1754. Rec.: Nov. 19, 1754. Samson Collier and Stephen Collier, Executors. Sons: Samson and Stephen. Daughters: Anne Morse and Elezabeth Collier. Witnesses: Henry Dugger, Christopher Moring and Benjamin Cheatham.

Page 19:   THOMAS PRETLOW. Inventory. Date: 10th mo., 29, 1754. Rec: 19 Nov. 1754. Thomas Pretlow and Rebekah Pretlow, Executors.

Page 21:   Grays Creek Tobacco Warehouse Inspection. (G.C.T.W.I.)

Page 21:   Cabbin Point Tobacco Warehouse Inspection. (C.P.T.W.I.)

Page 22:   JAMES MASON. Account Current. Date: 1752. Rec.: 19 Nov. 1754. John Jenkins and Mary Jenkins, Administrators. William Seward and Will Salter, Auditors.

Page 23:   JAMES BOYD. Inventory. Date: 1 Dec. 1753. Rec.: 19 Nov. 1754. --- Delony, Thomas Allstin and William Cocke, Appraisers.

Page 25:   JAMES BOYD. Account Current. Date: -----. Rec.: 19 Nov.1754. Benjamin Ruffin, Executor. Mentions: Anne Boyd. William Seward, Jr. and Will Salter, Auditors.

Page 26:   JETHRO BARKER of Surry. Will. Date: 3 Dec. 1754. Rec.: 17 Dec. 1754. John Barker, Executor. Sons: John and Jethro. Daughter: Elizabeth Sheffel. Granddaughter: Sarah Barker. Daughter-in-law: Alce Barker, widow. Witnesses: Lemuel Cocke and John Barker.

Page 27:   ROB. WHITE. Account Current. Date: -----. Rec.: 18 Dec.1754. Thomas Baley and wife, Mary, Administrators. Mentions: Payments from William White and Benjamin White. John Irby, Joseph Newsum and Mat. Marriott, Auditors.

Page 28:   JOHN GLOVER. Inventory. Date: 19 Feb. 1754. Rec.: 17 Dec. 1754. Mary Glover, Administratrix. Joseph Hart, Nicholas Thompson and Thomas Lane, Appraisers.

Page 29:   JAMES SAMPSON CLARK. Inventory. Date: 21 Nov. 1754. Rec: 18 Dec. 1754. Joice Clark and James Clark, Executors. Joseph Hart, Thomas Lane and Robert Hunnicutt, Appraisers.

Page 30:   JOHN THOMPSON of Southwark Parish, Surry. Will. Date: 27 Mar. 1754. Rec.: 21 Jan. 1755. Ann Thompson, Executrix. Sons: William, Robert, John and Samuel. Wife: Ann. Daughters: Elizabeth and Annor. Witnesses: Benjamin Cocke, Augustin Hunnicutt and John Hunnycutt.

Page 31:   ROBERT WAGER. Inventory. Date: 19 Nov. 1754. Rec.: 22 Jan.
1755. John Harris, Joseph Newsum and William Marriott, Jr.,
Appraisers.

Page 33:   JETHRO BARKER, SR. Inventory. Date: 17 Dec. 1754. Rec.:
15 Apr. 1755. Thomas Beddingfield, Benjamin Baird and Moses Hill, Appraisers.

Page 35:   JAMES MARLOW. Inventory. Date: -- Feb. 1752. Rec.: 20
May 1755. William Drew, William Seward, Jr. and Dolphin
Drew, Appraisers.

Page 36:   THOMAS PETTWAY of Cobham Town, Surry. Will. Date: 4 Apr.
1755. Rec.: 20 May 1755. Capt. Thomas Holt, Executor. Wife:
(unnamed). Sons: Edward and John (not 18). Father: Edward.
Brother-in-law: John Warren. Witnesses: Robert Narn, Samuel Judkins and James Edwards.

Page 37:   JOHN COLLIER. Inventory. Date: ---. Rec.: 20 May 1755.
Sampson Collier and Stephen Collier, Executors.

Page 38:   CHARLES CHAMPION. Inventory. Date: 15 Apr. 1755. Rec.: 17
June 1755. Thomas Wilson, John White and Arthur Holliman,
Appraisers.

Page 39:   THOMAS WASHINGTON. Account Current. Date: 1749. Rec: June
17, 1755. Mentions: Thomas Briggs and wife Agnis (her 3rd's)
and Thomas Washington, orphan. William Clinch and John Harris, Auditors.

Page 41:   JOHN THOMPSON. Inventory. Date: ----. Rec.: 15 July 1755.
Ann Thonpson, Executrix. Carter Crafford, John Crafford &
John Hunnicutt, Appraisers.

Page 42:   ALEXANDER MILLS (MILNE). Inventory. Date: ----. Rec: 16
July 1755. William Nicolson, Charles Lucas and Robert Lanier, Appraisers.

Page 43:   THOMAS PETTWAY. Inventory. Date: 12 June 1755. Rec.: 16
Sept. 1755. W. Edwards, Nicholas Faulcon and Samuel Judkins,
Appraisers.

Page 45:   CHARLES BINNS. Inventory. Date: Jan. 1750. Rec.: 16 Sept.
1755. Judith Binns, Executrix. John Hay and wife Judith,
Executors.

Page 48:   JOHN BRUCE. Account Current. Date: 1752. Rec.: 16 Sept.
1755. Sarah Bruce and Jacob Bruce, Executors. Mentions:
payments by will to Elizabeth Atkinson, Ann Allen and to
Sarah Bruce. William Seward, Jr. and Matt. Marriott, Auditors.

Page 49:   WILLIAM MARRIOTT, JR. of Southwark Parish, Surry. Will.
Date: 13 July 1755. Rec.: 16 Sept. 1755. Father: William,
Sr. Brothers: Matthias and Benjamin Marriott. Mentions:
land in Brunswick County. Witnesses: John Harris, William
Scarbrough and William Nicolson.

Page 49:   SAMUEL HARGRAVE of Surry. Will. Date: 14 June 1755. Rec: 16
Sept. 1755. Sarah Hargrave, Executrix. Wife: Sarah. Wife's
son: William Pritlow (not 21). Cousin: Samuel Hargrave.
Legatee: John Denson, son of James of Nansemond County.
Witnesses: John Ruffin and Benjamin Cocke.

Page 50:   GEORGE TALLET. Account Current. Date: 1747. Rec: 16 Sept.
1755. William Cornwell, Executor. William ----, and Matthias Marriott, Auditors.

Page 51:   Grays Creek Tobacco Warehouse Inspection.

Page 51:   Cabin Point Tobacco Warehouse Inspection.

Page 51:   ROBERT WAGER. Account Current. Date: ----. Rec.: 18 Nov.
             1755. Elizabeth Wager, Administratrix. Mentions: Eliza
             Dodd, heir of Rachel Wager, orphan of Nicholas and Mary.

Page 68:   BENJAMIN BRIGGS. Account Current. Date: ----. Rec.: 17 Aug.
             1756. James Jones, Executor. Joseph Newsum and Henry Coll-
             ier, Appraisers.

Page 72:   LEMUEL COCKE of Southwark Parish, Surry. Will. Date: 13
             Apr. 1756. Rec.: 17 Aug. 1756. Sons: Henry, Richard, Lem-
             uel and Thomas. Daughters: Betty, Anne and Sally Cocke.
             Wife: Jane. Brothers: John and Thomas. Mentions: land
             my father gave me; land in Brunswick County. Witnesses:
             Caleb Ellis, Jr., Richard Jones, Sr. and John Barker.

Page 75:   ANTHONY ATKINSON. Inventory. Date: ----. Rec.: 21 Sep. 1756.
             William Shell, William Scarbrough and Thomas Bedingfield,
             Appraisers.

Page 75:   MARY BRIGGS. Inventory. Date: ----. Rec.: 16 Nov. 1756.
             Thomas Bedingfield, Stephen Lucas and John Barker, Apprais-
             ers.

Page 76:   JOHN SIMMONS. Account Current. Date: ----. Rec.: 16 Nov.
             1756. Christopher and Rebeccah Moring present AC. Mentions:
             wife's legacy. John Peter and John Cocke, Auditors.

Page 78:   JOSEPH JOHN CLINCH. Account Current. Date: ----. Rec.: 17
             Nov. 1756. Elizabeth Rose, Administratrix.

Page 79:   JOSEPH JOHN CLINCH. Inventory. Date: 1750. Rec.: 17 Nov.
             1756. Henry Browne, John Harris and Peter Warren, Appraisers.

Page 83:   WILLIAM SMITH of Surry. Will. Date: 3 July 1755. Rec.: 18
             Jan. 1757. Elizabeth Smith, Executrix. Wife: Elizabeth.
             Sons: William, Henry and James. Daughters: Sarah Davis,
             Mary Davis and Judkins. Granddaughter: Elizabeth Smith.
             Witnesses: William Clinch and Thomas Warren.

Page 84:   JAMES CLARK of Surry. Will. Date: 9 Dec. 1756. Rec.: 15 Mar.
             1757. Wife deceased. Robert Hart granted Administration.
             Wife: (unnamed). Child in Esse. Witnesses: Bridget Bennet
             and Robert Hart.

Page 85:   WILLIAM SHORT of Southwark Parish, Surry. Will. Date: 24
             Dec. 1756. Rec.: 15 Mar. 1757. Daughters: Sarah Cocke, Mary
             Poythress and Martha Reade. Wife: Martha. Son: William.
             Nephew: William Harris. Grandchildren: William, Susannah,
             Sarah, Elizabeth Cocke (not of age); William, Eliza, Joshua
             Poythress (not of age). Legatees: Joshua Poythress; Rob-
             ert Reade's father, Given Reade. Mentions: land given to
             daughter Martha Reade by my father; land given to nephew
             William Harris by my father. Witnesses: John J'Anson,
             John Cocke and James Kee.

Page 87:   ANN JUDKINS of Southwark Parish, Surry. Will. Date: 12 Dec.
             1756. Rec.: 15 Mar. 1757. Samuel Judkins, Executor. Son:
             Samuel. Daughters: Ann Champion and Sarah Holt. Grand-
             children: Benjamin, Samuel, Charles, Lucy, Sarah and Mary
             Champion; Lucy, Henry, Ann, Charles, Samuel, Hannah, Sarah
             and William Holt; William and Mary Ann Judkins. Witnesses:
             Charles Thompson and Jane White.

Page 89:   ANN JUDKINS. Inventory. Date: 15 Mar. 1757. Rec.: 17 May
             1757. Charles Thompson, Thomas Wilson and John White, Ap-
             praisers.

Page 90: JAMES CLARK. Inventory. Date: 19 Mar. 1757. Rec.: 17 May 1757. Richard Rowell, Robert Hunnicutt and Thomas Lane, Appraisers.

Page 92: THOMAS SLADE. Inventory. Date: 18 Apr. 1757. Rec.: 18 May 1757. Matthias Marriott, John Warren and John Davis, Appraisers.

Page 93: THOMAS CLARK of Southwark Parish, Surry. Will. Date: 19 Apr. 1755. Rec.: 17 May 1757. James Clark, Executor. Sons: James and John (latter not of age). Daughters: Tabitha and Jane Clark (not of age). Witnesses: L. Deloney, Ellen Rooking and James Fawn.

Page 94: RICHARD PILAND of Southwark Parish, Surry. Will. Date: 12 Nov. 1756. Rec.: 17 May 1757. Mary Piland, Executrix. Wife: Mary. Sons: George, Robert, Nicholas and Benjamin. Daughters: Elizabeth Judkins, Mary and Martha Piland. Mother: (unnamed). Witnesses: Samuel Judkins and Benjamin Harrison.

Page 96: JANE HUNNIFORD of Surry. Will. Date: 23 Dec. 1754. Rec.:21 June 1757. William Davidson refuses Executorship. John Clark of Isle of Wight County, summoned for Administration. Cousin: William Davidson (in Carolina); Prudence Clark, daughter of John. Legatees: Bartlet Moreland Davidson and brother, Thomas Davidson; Thomas, William and John, sons of Thomas Davidson; and Allen Warren. Witnesses: William Hart, Thomas Hart, Robert Hart and Buford Pleasant.

Page 97: THOMAS CLARKE. Inventory. Date: 17 May 1757. Rec.: 21 Jun. 1757. William Cocke, William Pulley and Benjamin Bryan, Appraisers.

Page 98: RICHARD PILAND. Inventory. Date: 18 May 1757. Rec.: 21 Jun. 1757. Mary Piland, Executrix. Samuel Judkins, Thomas Lane and John Warren, Appraisers.

Page 100: WILLIAM CLARK of Surry, Planter. Will. Date: 14 Dec. 1756. Rec.: 19 July 1757. John Clark and Etheldred Clark, Executors. Wife: Mary. Sons: John, Etheldred and Jesse. Friend: Thomas Lane. Mentions: all my children. Witnesses: Thomas Lane, Thomas Presson and John Cocks.

Page 101: GEORGE WILLIAMS. Inventory. Date: 10 Dec. 1753. Rec.: 16 Aug. 1757. William Cocke, Thomas Sworsbery and Robert Lanier, Appraisers.

Page 102: GEORGE WILLIAMS. Account Current. Date: ---. Rec: 16 Aug. 1757. Benjamin Ruffin, Administrator. W. Edwards and John Watkins, Auditors.

Page 103: Grays Creek Tobacco Warehouse Inspection.

Page 104: JOHN CHAMPION of Surry. Will. Date: 25 Aug. 1755. Rec.: 20 Sept. 1757. Lucy Champion, Executrix. Sons: William (eldest), Hart, and John (none of age). Wife: Lucy. Child in esse. Mentions: land father left me. Witnesses: Richard Presson, Robert Hart and James Clark.

Page 105: SUS. HANCOCK. Account Current. Date: 1750. Rec.: 20 Sept. 1757. Mentions: payments to William Hancock; schooling for son Jimmy. John J'Anson, and John Watkins, Auditors.

Page 107: WILLIAM CLARK. Inventory. Date: 13 Oct. 1757. Rec.: 18 Oct. 1757. Nicholas Thompson, Robert Hunnicutt and Samuel Bennet, Appraisers.

Page 108: Grays Creek Tobacco Warehouse Inspection.

Page 109: Cabin Point Tobacco Warehouse Inspection.

Page 110:   JOHN CHAMPION. Inventory. Date: 20 Sept. 1757. Rec.: 15
             Nov. 1757. Richard Presson, Thomas Wilson and John White,
             Appraisers.

Page 112:   FORTUNE WATKINS. Account Current. Date: ----. Rec.: 15
             Nov. 1757. Thomas Bage, Executor. Mentions: part to Ex-
             ecutor; to Charity Watkins; to Robert Watkins; to William
             Watkins, being part of their father's estate. Richard
             Cocke and Henry Browne, Auditors.

Page 113:   MARY GRAY of Surry. Will. Date: 31 Mar. 1756.   Rec.: ---
             Daughter: Lucy Briggs, wife of Howell Briggs. Granddaugh-
             ter: Elizabeth Rose. Sons: William, Edmund, James; Will-
             iam Seward; Robert, Joseph, Thomas and James Gray. Wit-
             nesses: Gray Briggs, Susannah Gray and William Thorp.

Page 114:   JOHN EDWARDS of Surry. Will. Date: 25 Nov. 1757. Rec: 20
             Dec. 1757. Wife: Mary. Sons: William Phillip, John and
             Arthur. Daughter: Mourning. Sons-in-law: Augustine Hunn-
             icutt, David Elexander and John Berriman. Witnesses: Will
             Salter, Carter Crafford and Thomas Cogging.

Page 115:   NICHOLAS MANGUM. Inventory. Date: 17 May 1757. Rec.: 20
             Dec. 1757. Joseph Mangum presents. Robert Hart, William
             Cocke and John Little, Appraisers.

Page 116:   Capt. LEMUEL COCKE. Inventory. Date: 14 Feb. 1757. Rec:
             20 Dec. 1757. John Maclin, Thomas Briggs and Thomas Collyer,
             Appraisers.

Page 123:   THOMAS JOHNSON of Surry. Will. Date: 29 June 1756. Rec.: 17
             Jan. 1758. Henry Johnson, Executor. Sons: Henry and Thom-
             as Johnson. Daughter: Lucy. Wife: Elizabeth. Witnesses:
             Joseph Jordan and Samuel Clements.

Page 124:   JOHN EDWARDS. Inventory. Date: 30 Dec. 1757. Rec.: 21 Feb.
             1758. Edmund Waller, Nicholas Faulcon and John Newsum, Ap-
             praisers.

Page 125:   FRANCIS PERSON. Inventory. Date: 18 Feb. 1758. Rec: 21
             Feb. 1758. Richard Gray, Robert Hunnicutt and James Clark,
             Appraisers.

Page 128:   THOMAS JOHNSON. Inventory. Date: ----. Rec.: 21 Feb. 1757.
             Joseph Jordan, Jonathan Ellis and William Maget, Appraisers.

Page 129:   JOHN BARNES. Inventory. Date: ----. Rec.: 21 Feb. 1758.
             Jonathan Ellis, Joseph Jordan and Henry Johnson, Appraisers.

Page 130:   THOMAS TAYLOR of Surry, Planter. Will. Date: 21 Dec. 1755.
             Rec.: 21 Feb. 1758. William Taylor, Executor. Son: William.
             Wife: Elizabeth. Daughter: Lucy. Witnesses: Thomas Brantley
             and John Ingram.

Page 131:   THOMAS RESPESS of Southwark Parish, Surry. Will. Date: 26
             Nov. 1757. Rec.: 21 Feb. 1758. Ann Respess and Thomas Res-
             pess. Wife: Ann. Daughters:Mary and Ann. Sons: Richard,
             Thomas, Christopher and Robert. Witnesses: William Clinch,
             George Berrick and John Collier.

Page 132:   NATHANIEL GREEN. Inventory. Date: 20 Nov. 1750. Rec.:   21
             Mar. 1758. William Green, Administrator. Matthew Parham,
             Ephraim Parham and Robert Farrington, Appraisers.

Page 133:   SAMUEL THOMPSON. Account Current. Date: 1752. Rec.: 21 Mar.
             1758. Samuel Thompson, Administrator. Will Short and John
             Harris, Auditors.

Page 134:   JOHN CENNON. Inventory. Date: 20 Dec. 1757. Rec.: 21 Mar.

(Page 134 - CENNON cont'd.): 1758. Mentions: legacies to great-granddaughter, Joanna Scarbrow, granddaughter Joanna Scarbrow,
daughter, Joanna Jestis, John Justis, Jr. Christopher Moring, Henry Barns and Joseph Jordan, Appraisers.

Page 135:   JOANNA CANNON. Inventory. Date: 20 Dec. 1757. Rec.: 21
Mar. 1758. Christopher Moring, Henry Barns and Joseph Jordan, Appraisers.

Page 136:   JOHN BISHOP of Surry. Will. Date: 16 Jul. 1757. Rec.: 18 Apr
1758. Mary Bishop and Joseph Bishop, Executors. Sons: Joseph and David (youngest). Wife: Mary. Witnesses: Caleb
Ellis, Jr., James Bishop, Sr. and James Bishop, Jr.

Page 137:   THOMAS RESPESS. Inventory. Date: 21 Feb. 1758. Rec: 18 Apr
1758. John Collier, William Pully and John Jarrott, Appraisers.

Page 138:   GILBERT HAY of Surry. Will. Date: 14 Apr. 1758. Rec.: 18
Apr. 1758. Edward Weaver and James Holloway, Executors. Son-
in-law: John Griffis. Cousin: Gilbirt Hay, son of Charles.
Sister: Ruth Solowman, wife of William. Brother: Richard.
Legatees: Thomas, son of Edward Griffis and Edward Griffis;
Betty Prince, wife of Nicholas; Nathan, Henry and Nicholas
Prince; Jane Jarret, wife of Nicholas; Stephen Johnson;
Lucy Cotton, wife of John; James Holloway, son of John, Sr.;
Mary Weaver, wife of Edward; Edith Griffis, daughter of
Thomas; Betty Tatum. Godchildren: Gilbirt Hay, Lucy Cotton,
Richard Corlisly, Jane Jarret, Stephen Johnson, James Hol-
loway, Luccey Griffis and Betty Prince. Witnesses: William
Cooke, James Cook and John Johnson.

Page 140:   WILLIAM JORDAN. Will. Date: 18 Jan. 1758. Red.: 16 May
1758. Joseph Jordan, Executor. Cousins: Henry Jordan, son
of Joseph; Steven Jordan, son of Joseph; Jesse Jordan, son
of Joseph. Brother: Joseph Jordan. Witnesses: Richard
Wiggins and James Wiggins.

Page 142:   JOHN BARNES. Will. Date: 29 Oct. 1757. Rec.: 16 May 1758.
Thomas Sowersby and Henry Barnes, Executors. Sons: Samuel,
Benjamin (not of age); William and John. Wife: (unnamed).
Daughter: Lucy. Father: Henry. Witnesses: Joseph Jordan,
William Duell and Benjamin Barns.

Page 143:   MARY GRAY. Inventory. Date: June 1758. Rec.: 20 Jun. 1758.
Howell Briggs, Executor.

Page 144:   ANTHONY ATKINSON. Account Current. Date: Oct. 1757. Rec.:
July 19,1758. Michal Casely, Administrator. Mentions:
legacies to me (administrator), Martha Casely. John Cocke
and Benjamin Baird, Auditors.

Page 145:   JOHN BISHOP. Inventory. Date: ----. Rec.: 20 June 1758.
Joshua Barker, Thomas Bedingfield and Caleb Ellis, Appraisers.

Page 146:   BLANKS MOODY. Account Current. Date: ----. Rec.: 20 June
1758. Samuel Magott, Executor. Mr. William Edwards and
William Harris, Auditors.

Page 147:   BLANKS MOODY. Sale. Date: ----. Rec.: 20 June 1758. Samuel Magott, Executor. Purchaser: Mary Moody.

Page 148:   JOHN J'ANSON of Surry, Doctor. Will. Date: 9 May 1758.Rec:
20 June 1758. Lucy J'Anson,and James Belsches of Sussex,
Executors. Wife: Lucy. Son: Thomas (not 21). Daughter:
Mary J'Anson (not 21). Friend: Thomas Peter. Mentions:
land in Prince George County. Witnesses: Archibald Dunlop,
Henry Browne and Benjamin Cocke.

Page 150: WILLIAM JORDAN. Inventory. Date: 16 May 1758. Rec: June 20, 1758. Jonathan Ellis, Henry Barns and Stephen Collier, Appraisers.

Page 152: CHARLES LUCAS of Southwark Parish, Surry. Will. Date: 4 Aug. 1752. Rec.: 19 Jul. 1758. Stephen Lucas, Executor. Wife: Mary. Sons: John, Samuel, William and Stephen. Daughter: Mary Lucas. Grandchildren: Charles and Rebecca Lucas, children of William. Mentions: land in Brunswick County. Witnesses: Robert Jones, Jr. (of North Carolina), John Edmunds and John Simmons.

Page 155: JOHN SPRATLEY of Southwark Parish, Surry. Will. Date: 3 May 1758. Rec.: 19 July 1758. William Spratley, Executor. Sons: John, Walter; William, and Benjamin (not of age). Wife: (unnamed). Legatee: Duncan McGureman (my printice). Friends: William Spratley and Benjamin Bryan. Witnesses: Ken McKenzie, Thomas Harris and Thomas Warren.

Page 157: GILBIRT HAY. Inventory. Date: ----. Rec.: 15 Aug. 1758.

Page 158: WILLIAM SHORT. Inventory. Date: ----. Rec.: 15 Aug. 1758. Will Short, Executor.

Page 159: JOHN CRAFFORD of Surry. Will. Date: 31 July 1758. Rec.: 15 Aug. 1758. Carter Crafford and Mary Crafford, Executors. Wife: Mary. Children: Ann, Carter, and John (none 21). Brother: Carter Crafford. Mentions: land in Nansemond Co. Witnesses: Benjamin Newsum and William Newsum.

Page 160: WILLIAM SORSBY. Inventory. Date: 10 Aug. 1758. Rec.: 15 Aug. 1758. William Simmons, Jr., Sampson Collier and Richard Putney, Appraisers.

Page 161: JOHN CLARK. Inventory. Date: 27 July 1754. Rec.: 19 Sept. 1758. Benjamin Clark, Administrator. John Newsum, Nicholas Faulcon, Jr., and William Edwards, Jr., Appraisers.

Page 162: JOHN CRAFFORD. Inventory. Date: 21 Aug. 1758. Rec.: 19 Sept. 1758. Will Salter, John Drew, and Abr. Mitchell, Appraisers.

Page 165: Rev. PETER DAVIS. Inventory. Date: 18 July 1758. Rec.: 19 Sept. 1758. Edward Bailey, John Davis and Christopher Moring, Appraisers.

Page 166: JOHN CLARK. Account Current. Date: 1744. Rec.: 19 Sept. 1758. Benjamin Clark, Administrator. Capt. William Seward and Mr. John Watkins, Appraisers.

Page 167: Cabin Point Tobacco Warehouse Inspection.

Page 168: WILLIAM FAWN. Inventory. Date: 18 July 1758. Rec.: 21 Nov. 1758. William Nicholson, Henry Collier and Ephraim Baird, Appraisers.

Page 169: JOHN BARKER of Surry. Will. Date: 8 Aug. 1758. Rec.: 27 Nov. 1758. William Scarbrow, Executor. Legatees: Ann Thompson, daughter of Ann, formerly wife of John Thompson; Thomas Barker, son of Jethro and Elizabeth; child/children of Jethro Barker and of Elizabeth Sheffel. Witnesses: Drewry Barker and Robert Tucker.

Page 170: GILBIRT HAY. Account Current. Date: ----. Rec.: 21 Nov. 1758. William Edwards and Henry Collier, Auditors.

Page 171: DAVID MINENTREE of Southwark Parish, Surry. Will. Date: 30 Apr. 1758. Rec.: 21 Nov. 1758. Faith Minentree, Executrix. Wife: Faith. Daughters: Mary and Ann Minentree. Mentions:

(Page 171 - MINENTREE cont'd.): land given to wife by her brother. Witnesses: George Berrick, Henry Watkins and William Andrews.

Page 172:   Gray's Creek Tobacco Warehouse Inspection.

Page 173:   JOHN SPRATLEY, Gent. Inventory. Date: 25 Nov. 1758. Rec: 19 Dec. 1758. John Davis, Thomas Warren and John Warren, Appraisers.

Page 175:   SAMUEL BROWN. Inventory. Date: 18 Sept. 1758. Rec.: 19 Dec. 1758. Will Short, Administrator. John Cocke, William Harriss and James Kea, Appraisers.

Page 177:   JOHN BARKER. Inventory. Date: ----. Rec.: 19 Dec. 1758. Thomas Beddingfield, Moses Hill and Stephen Lucas, Appraisers.

Page 178:   JOHN PHILLIPS of Surry. Will. Date: 11 Aug. 1758. Rec.: 16 Jan. 1759. Carter Crafford, Executor. Sons: John, Hartwell, Arthur and Joseph. Daughters: Mary Warren; Elizabeth, Lucy, Sarah and Ann. Kinsman: Carter Crafford. Mentions: land in Southampton County. Witnesses: John Ruffin, John Regan and William Maget.

Page 180:   RICHARD PILAND. Account Current. Date: ---. Rec.: 16 Jan. 1759. Mary Piland, Executrix. William Harriss and Carter Crafford, Auditors.

Page 181:   CHARLES CHAMPION. Account Current. Date: 1756. Rec.: 16 Jan. 1759. Ann Champion, Administratrix. Thomas Harris and Joseph Newsum, Auditors.

Page 183:   JOHN PHILIPS. Inventory. Date: ----. Rec.: 20 Feb. 1759.

Page 184:   JOSEPH PETTWAY. Account Current. Date: 1746. Rec.: 20 Feb. 1759. Mentions: William and Joseph Pettway. W. Edwards and Robert Watkins, Auditors.

Page 185:   BENJAMIN HARRISON, Gent. of Surry. Will. Date: 14 Nov. 1758. Rec.: 20 Mar. 1759. Col. Nathaniel Harrison, Executor. Sons: Peter Cole Harrison and Nathaniel. Daughters: Susannah, Hannah and Ludwell Harrison. Wife: Susannah. Brother: Nathaniel. Friend: Nicholas Massenburg. Witnesses: Anne Bozman, Anne Rispis and William Moring.

Page 186:   JOSEPH SEBRELL of Surry. Will. Date: 21 Feb. 1759. Rec.: 20 Mar. 1759. Benjamin Sebrell, Executor. Brother-in-law: Jesse Hargrave. Brothers: Daniel, Samuel and Benjamin. Witnesses: William White, Exum Williamson and William Cocks.

Page 187:   WILLIAM CLARK. Account Current. Date: 1758. Rec.: 20 Mar. 1759. Daniel Driver, for wife Mary, Administratrix. W. Edwards and John Watkins, Auditors.

Page 189:   WILLIAM CORNWELL. Inventory. Date: 20 Mar. 1759. Rec.: 17 Apr. 1759. Mary Cornwell, Administratrix. William Drew, Abrm. Mitchell and Ctr. Crafford, Appraisers.

Page 191:   DAVID MINTREE. Inventory. Date: 31 Jan. 1759. Rec.: 15 May 1759. Henry Watkins, William Pully and John Jarret, Appraisers.

Page 193:   THOMAS TAYLOR. Inventory. Date: 21 Feb. 1758. Rec.: 15 May 1759. Mentions: legacy to William Taylor. William Drew, William Seward, Jr., and Wil Seward, Appraisers.

Page 195:   Capt. JOEL DUNN. Inventory. Date: 2 May 1759. Rec.: 15 May 1759. Will Cocke, Thomas Sowersby and William Simmons, Appraisers.

Page 196: THOMAS TAYLOR. Account Current. Date: ----. Rec.: 15 May 1759. William Taylor, Executor. Joseph Newsum and William Drew, Auditors.

Page 197: THOMAS WARREN of Surry. Will. Date: 25 Apr. 1759. Rec.: 19 June 1759. Lucy Warren, Executrix. Sons: John and Thomas. Daughters: Mary, Lucy and Rebecca Warren. Son-in-law: Richard Rowell. Mentions: land to poor of Southwark Parish; land given my mother by her father; land in North Carolina. Witnesses: John Warren, John Judkins, Jr. and John Harris.

Page 199: CHARLES LUCAS. Inventory. Date: 21 Dec. 1758. Rec.: 19 Jun. 1759. Stephen Lucas, Executor.

Page 200: BARTHOLOMEW ANDREWS. Account Current. Date: 1755. Rec.: 19 June 1759. Elizabeth Andrews, Executrix. Wil Short, and Walter Peter, Auditors.

Page 201: MARTHA BRYAN. Inventory. Date: 30 Apr. 1759. Rec.: 19 Jun. 1759. William Newsum, Carter Crafford and Benjamin Phillips, Appraisers.

Page 202: JAMES CLARK. Account Current. Date: ----. Rec.: 19 June 1759. Robert Hart presents. Mentions: John Clark, Jr. W. Edwards and Henry Collier, Auditors.

Page 204: RICHARD STEWART of Southwark Parish, Surry, Planter. Will. Date: 26 Apr. 1757. Rec.: 17 July 1759. Hannah Stewart, Executrix. Daughter: Hannah Stewart. Sons: Richard and James. Wife: Hannah. Friend: Thomas Sorsby. Witnesses: Stephen Mac'Thompson, John Matheson and Benjamin Stewart.

Page 205: JAMES KING. Inventory. Date: 1 Aug. 1759. Rec.: 18 Sept. 1759. Thomas Sowersby, Thomas Grantham and William Simmons, Appraisers.

Page 206: ROBERT LANIER. Account Current. Date: 1756. Rec.: 18 Sept. 1759. John Lanier presents. W. Cocke and Henry Collier, Auditors.

Page 207: JOHN SHARP of Surry. Will. Date: 21 Apr. 1759. Rec.: 18 Sep. 1759. Constant Sharp, Executrix. Son: Burrell (not of age). Daughters: Elizabeth, Mary and Cherry (none 21). Wife: Constant. Witnesses: Caleb Ellis, John Griffin and Elizabeth Griffin.

Page 208: ANSELM BAILEY, SR. of Surry. Will. Date: July 1754. Rec.: 16 Oct. 1759. Samuel Bailey and Elijah Bailey, Executors. Grandchildren: Hannah Hargrave, Elijah Bailey, Joseph Bailey and Samuel Bailey. Sons: Benjamin and Anselm. Daughter: Martha Hargrave. Mentions: Joseph Hargrave. Witnesses: Tryal Bailey, Benjamin Bailey, Jr., and Anselm Bailey, Jr.

Page 211: JOHN SHARP. Inventory. Date: 12 Oct. 1759. Rec.: 16 Oct. 1759. James Gray, Anthony Evans and Henry Davis, Appraisers.

Page 213: DONALD MC INNISH. Account Current. Date: 1750. Rec.: 16 Oct. 1759. William Willie, Administrator. Mentions: funeral charges of wife and two children. David Ralston and Henry Collier, Auditors.

Page 214: Gray's Creek Tobacco Warehouse Inspection.

Page 215: Cabin Point Tobacco Warehouse Inspection.

Page 215: WILLIAM COOPER of Surry. Will. Date: 4 Apr. 1756. Rec.: 20 Nov. 1759. William Cooper, Executor. Sons: John, William and George. Daughters: Elizabeth Barker; Mary, Hannah and Sarah. Grandchildren: Jesse Jurden, Jane Jurden and Howell

70

(Page 215 - COOPER cont'd.): Barker. Witnesses: John Justiss, Robert Rae and Joanna Justiss.

Page 217: ANSELM BAILEY. Inventory. Date: ----. Rec.: 18 Dec. 1759. Samuel Bailey and Elijah Bailey, Executors.

Page 217: JOSEPH SEBRELL. Inventory. Date: 20 Mar. 1759. Rec.: 19 Feb. 1760. William White, Samuel Bennet and Thomas Davis, Appraisers.

Page 219: MARY EDWARDS. Inventory. Date: 6 Dec. 1759. Rec.: 19 Feb. 1760. William Newsum, Ctr. Crafford and Edmund Waller, Appraisers.

Page 220: ANN JUDKINS. Account Current. Date: ----. Rec.: 15 April 1760. Mentions: legacies to Benjamin Champion, Lucy Champion, Lucy Holt, Charles Holt, Ann Champion and Samuel Judkins. David Raltston and John Austin Finne, Auditors.

Page 221: HENRY BARNES. Will. Date: 16 Apr. 1759. Rec.: 15 Apr. 1760. Naomy Barnes, Executrix. Sons: William, John, Benjamin and Henry. Daughter: Elizabeth. Wife: Naomy. Witnesses: Joseph Jordan, Stephen Grantham and John Davis.

Page 222: WILLIAM NICOLSON. Inventory. Date: ----. Rec.: 20 May 1760. William Harris, James Kee and Ephraim Baird, Appraisers.

Page 223: DANIEL SPENCE. Will. Date: 19 Apr. 1760. Rec.: 20 May 1760. John Peter of Surry, Merchant, Executor. Legatees: John Heath, son of Benjamin (dec'd.) of Prince George County; Alexander Belches, son of James; Thomas Peter, son of John. Mentions: land in Prince George County. Friend: James Belches. Witnesses: Abraham Bywater, John Hamlin and William Simmons.

Page 225: JOHN JUDKINS of Southwark Parish, Surry. Will. Date: 12 Dec. 1758. Rec.: 20 May 1760. Martha Judkins and William Judkins, Executors. Sons: Nicholas, William, Joseph, Samuel, Jesse and Charles (sons to be of age at 18). Daughters: Mary Barham, Ann Mourning and Sarah Barham. Grandchildren: Robert Barham; Philip, Frederick, Rebeccah and Patta Thomson. Wife: Martha. Mentions: Charles Barham and William Thomson. Witnesses: Joseph Newsum, James Davis, Samuel Judkins and John Warren.

Page 228: WILLIAM and ELIZABETH ROBINSON (ROBERTSON). Account Current. Date: ----. Rec.: 20 May 1760. Benjamin Baker, Administrator. Mentions: legacies paid to Katharine and Elia[r] Williams; James Kee's children. William Harrison and John Newsum, Auditors.

Page 229: WILLIAM FANN. Account Current. Date: ----. Rec.: 21 May 1760. John Austin Finne returns. Mentions: James Fann, son of William.

Page 229: JOHN JUDKINS. Inventory. Date: ----. Rec.: 17 June 1760. Martha and William Judkins, Executors.

Page 230: WILLIAM NICHOLSON. Additional Inventory. Date: 30 May 1760. Rec.: 17 June 1760. William Short, James Kee and Eaph'r. Baird, Appraisers.

Page 231: WILLIAM SORSBY. Account Current. Date: 1758. Rec.: 17 Jun. 1760. Ann Sorsby, Administratrix. Thomas Cocke, and Matt. Marriot, Auditors.

Page 232: LAMUEL COCKE. Account Current. Date: 1756. Rec.: 17 June 1760. Jane Cocke, Executrix. John Peter and John Austin Finne, Auditors.

Page 234:   WILLIAM EVENS. Account Current. Date: 1752. Rec.: 19 Aug. 1760. George Barrick and Priscilla Barrick, Executors. Mentions: legacy to son William. Thomas Wilson, John White and Joseph Holleman, Auditors.

Page 235:   Mrs. MARY MOODY. Inventory. Date: 20 July 1756. Rec.: 19 Aug. 1760. John Thompson, James Smith and William Maddera, Appraisers.

Page 236:   Mrs. MARY MOODY. Account Current. Date: ----. Rec.: 19 Aug. 1760. Henry Smith, Administrator. Etheldred Gray and Charles Thompson, Auditors.

Page 237:   HENRY BARNES. Inventory. Date: 17 May 1760. Rec.: 16 Dec. 1760. Christopher Moring, Stephen Collier and Thomas Grantham, Appraisers.

Page 238:   WILLIAM JUDKINS of Southwark Parish, Surry. Will. Date: 10 Dec. 1760. Joseph and Samuel Judkins, Executors. Sons: Joel, Thomas, Jordan, and Mark (not 19). Daughters: Hannah, Rebeccah and Sarah Judkins (not 19). Brothers: Joseph and Samuel Judkins. Mentions: land in Granville County, North Carolina. Witnesses: William Cocks, Charles Holt, Charles Thompson and William Evans.

Page 239:   MARY PILAND of Southwark Parish, Surry. Will. Date: 2 Dec. 1757. Rec.: 16 Dec. 1760. William Piland, Executor. Daughters: Mary Piland, Martha Johnson and Priscilla Clark. Grandchildren: Lucy Piland and George Piland. Son-in-law: William Piland.

Page 240:   Cabin Point Tobacco Warehouse Inspection.

Page 240:   Gray's Creek Tobacco Warehouse Inspection.

Page 241:   SAMUEL LANCASTER of Surry. Will. Date: 28 Dec. 1760. Rec.: 20 Jan. 1761. Joseph Holleman, Executor. Daughters: Silvia, and Elizabeth Lancaster. Wife: Elizabeth. Friend: Arthur Holleman. Witnesses: John White and Nathan Williford.

Page 242:   MARY PILAND. Inventory. Date: 16 Dec. 1760. Rec.: 20 Jan. 1761. John Davis, Samuel Judkins and Thomas Carrell, Appraisers.

Page 243:   WILLIAM JUDKINS. Inventory. Date: ----. Rec.: 20 Jan. 1761. Joseph Judkins and Samuek Judkins, Executors.

Page 244:   SAMUEL LANCASTER. Inventory. Date: 21 Jan. 1761. Rec.: 17 Feb. 1761. Charles Holt, Charles Thompson and Aaron Wall, Appraisers.

Page 245:   ELIZABETH ANDREWS. Inventory. Date: 17 Feb. 1761. Rec.: 17 Mar. 1761. Henry Johnson, James Davis, and Joseph Jordan, Appraisers.

Page 246:   WILLIAM SEWARD of Southwark Parish, Surry. Will. Date: 25 May 1759. Rec.: 17 Mar. 1761. Henry Seward, Executor. Sons: William and Henry. Daughter: Ann, wife of Jordan Thomas. Mentions: Elizabeth, now wife of Richard Hamlin; Henry Seward, a cripple; testator is aged. Witnesses: Thomas Taylor, William Taylor, Barnes Clary and Michael Smalley of North Carolina.

Page 249:   WILLIAM SEWARD. Inventory. Date: 23 Jan. 1761. Rec.: 17 March 1761.

Page 250:   JOSIAH BARKER of Southwark Parish, Surry. Will. Date: 23 Feb. 1760. Rec.: 17 Mar. 1761. John Barker, Executor. Sons: John, Arthur, Tiver and Lamuel. Daughter: Fathy Barker.

(Page 250 - BARKER cont'd.): Wife: Fathy. Grandchildren: William, son of Tiver Barker. Legatees: Sarah, Fathy and Mary Ellis: Grace Barker. Witnesses: Philip Reekes, Benjamin Emrey & Fathia Emrey.

Page 251:   JOHN GRIFFIN. Inventory. Date: 24 Feb. 1761. Rec.: 17 Mar. 1761. Caleb Ellis, Etheldred Gray and N. Maget, Appraisers.

Page 252:   WILLIAM BENNET. Inventory. Date: 17 Feb. 1761. Rec.: 21 Apr. 1761. Thomas Carrell, Nicholas Thompson and Richard Rowell, Appraisers.

Page 254:   JOHN BARKER. Account Current. Date: ----. Rec.: 19 May 1761. Etheldred Gray and George Cryer, Auditors.

Page 255:   JOSIAH BARKER. Inventory. Date: ---. Rec.: 16 June 1761.

Page 255:   DANIEL HUDSON of Surry. Will. Date: 25 July 1758. Rec.: 16 June 1761. John Ruffin, Executor. Nephew: John Crutchfield. Mentions: Martha, wife of John Ruffin. Witnesses: Augustin Hunnicutt, William Ruffin and Mary Haswell.

Page 256:   DANIEL HUDSON. Inventory. Date: ----. Rec.: 16 June 1761. John Ruffin, Executor.

Page 257:   JAMES KING. Account Current. Date: ----. Rec.: 16 Jun.1761. Elizabeth King, Administratrix. Mentions: Elizabeth King's thirds, child's part. George Kur and Robert Hunnicutt, Auditors.

Page 258:   JAMES BOARDMAN. Inventory. Date: 19 May 1761. Rec.: 21 Jul. 1761. Jonathan Ellis, Henry Johnson and William Magget, Appraisers.

Page 259:   HANNAH KERSEY. Inventory. Date: ----. Rec.: 21 Jul. 1761. William Short, William Harris and John Lanier, Appraisers.

Page 260:   WILLIAM MARRIOT. Inventory. Date: 6 Nov. 1755. Rec.: 21 July 1761. John Harris, John Davis and Joseph Newsum, Appraisers.

Page 261:   JOHN GRIFFIN. Account Current. Date: ----. Rec.: 18 Aug. 1761. Thomas Griffin, Administrator.

Page 261:   Gray's Creek Tobacco Warehouse Inspection.

Page 262:   Cabin Point Tobacco Warehouse Inspection.

Page 262:   JOHN SLATE. Inventory. Date: 20 Oct. 1761. Rec.: 17 Nov. 1761. William Maddera, William Smith and John Maddera, Appraisers.

Page 264:   MARTHA MANGUM of Southwark Parish, Surry. Will. Date: 6 Dec. 1761. Rec.: 15 Dec. 1761. John Brown and Aaron Wall, Executors. Daughter: Elizabeth Wall. Sons: John Brown; and Joseph Mangum. Mentions: Sarah Fitchit. Witnesses: William Cocks and John Little.

Page 265:   Cabin Point Tobacco Warehouse Inspection.

Page 265:   MARTHA MANGUM. Inventory. Date: ----. Rec.: 19 Jan. 1762. John Browne and Aaron Wall, Executors.

Page 266:   JOHN CRAFFORD. Account Current. Date: 1758. Rec.: 19 Jan. 1762. W. Edwards and Joseph Newsum, Auditors.

Page 267:   BENJAMIN MERRIOT. Inventory. Date: 28 Aug. 1761. Rec.: 19 Jan. 1762. John Harris, John Davis and John Warren, Appraisers.

Page 269:   JOHN PHILIPS. Account Current and Inventory. Date: -----.
            Rec.: 19 Jan. 1762. Carter Crafford presents. Mentions:
            payments to Arthur Philips, Joseph Philips, Joshua Wood,
            Moses Bennett, Micajah Exum, Hartwell Philips (orphan) and
            Allen Warren. David Ralston and John Harris. Auditors.

Page 271:   JOHN KEA. Inventory. Date: 16 Feb. 1762. Rec.: 16 March
            1762. Mary Savidge, Administratrix. Nicholas Thompson,
            Jesse Judkins and Charles Judkins, Appraisers.

Page 271:   DANIEL SPENCE. Inventory. Date: 8 and 9 Oct. 1760. Rec.:
            16 Mar. 1762.

Page 273:   JOHN CANNON. Account Current. Date: 1759. Rec.: 16 March
            1763. Mentions: legacies paid to Elizabeth Justice, Sarah
            Justice and Joannah Scarbrough. James Rod. Bradby and
            Christopher Moring, Auditors.

Page 274:   MARTHA BRYAN. Account Current. Date: 1762. Rec.: 16 March
            1762. Benjamin Ruffin, Administrator. Mentions: L. Bryan.
            W. Edwards, Benjamin Cocke, Jr., Auditors.

Page 275:   WILLIAM CREWS. Account Current. Date: ----. Rec.: 16 Mar.
            1762. William Maddera presents. Mentions: widow's third
            part. James Rod. Bradby and Christopher Moring, Auditors.

Page 276:   JOHN GLOVER. Account Current. Date: 1755. Rec.: 16 Mar.
            1762. Mary Glover, Administratrix. John Ruffin, Thomas
            Bailey, Jr., Auditors.

Page 277:   NEWITT EDWARDS of Southwark Parish, Surry. Will. Date: 5
            Nov. 1760. Rec.: 18 Mar. 1762. Etheldred Edwards, Executor.
            Sons: Thomas, William Newit, and Etheldred. Daughter:
            Elizabeth Edwards. Wife: Sarah. Granddaughter: Elizabeth
            Edwards. Son-in-law: William Thompson. Mentions: Benja-
            min and Faithy Hunnicutt. Witnesses: Thomas White, James
            Shelley and Skelton Delk.

Page 278:   THOMAS EDWARDS of Southwark Parish, Surry. Will. Date: 25
            Jan. 1761. Rec.: 18 May 1762. William Edwards, Executor.
            Daughters: Elizabeth Barham and Lucy Clark. Son: William.
            Grandson: Thomas Edwards. Witnesses: Thomas Binns, Thom-
            as Edwards and Nicholas Faulcon, Jr.

Page 279:   WILLIAM MACLIN of Surry. Will. Date: 16 Apr. 1762. Rec.:
            18 May 1762. William Maclin, Executor. Wife: Sary (Sarah).
            Daughter: Mary Breasie. Son: William. Brothers: James &
            John. Legatees: Nanny Breasie and Sackfield Macklin Brea-
            sie. Mentions: land in Lieunnenburg and Brunswick Co.'s.
            Witnesses: John Heath, Patrick Adams and Joseph Newsum.

Page 281:   CHARLES CLARY of Surry. Will. Date: 19 Jan. 1762. Rec.: 18
            May 1762. Son: Barnes. Daughter: Mourning Smith. Grandch:
            Jordan, Charles, William, Barnes, Silvia, Ann, Mary and Su-
            sannah Clary; Lucy and Mary Fiveash. Legatee: Martha Pitt-
            man. (Barnes Clary, Executor). Witnesses: James Taylor,
            Francis Little and William White.

Page 283:   CALEB ELLIS. Inventory. Date: 23 Mar. 1762. Rec.: 18 May
            1762. Stephen Lucas, James Adams and Joshua Barker, Ap-
            praisers.

Page 285:   CALEB ELLIS of Surry. Will. Date: 10 Aug. 1760. Rec.: 17
            May 1762. Caleb Ellis and Benjamin Ellis, Executors. Sons:
            Richard, Stephen, Caleb, Benjamin and Dann. Wife: Amelia.
            Daughters: Mary Cooper, and Amelia Shell. Witnesses: John
            Cooper and Richard Cooper.

Page 286:   WILLIAM KERSEY of Southwark Parish, Surry. Will. Date: 13

(Page 286 - KERSEY cont'd.): Nov. 1761. Rec.: 18 May 1762. Mary Kersey,
Executrix. Sister: Mary Kersey. Witnesses: William Short,
Charles Williamson and John Burges.

Page 287: ROBERT JORDAN. Inventory. Date: 17 Nov. 1761. Rec.: 18
May 1762. John Magget, James Davis and William Davis, Appraisers.

Page 288: JOHN AVORIES of Surry. Will. Date: 26 June 1761. Rec.: 15
June 1762. William Avories and William Pennington, Execu-
tors. Son: William. Daughters: Hannah Ezell, Sarah Jones,
An Jones (dec'd.), Amey Bishop. Sons-in-law: John Lashley,
William Pennington and wife, Mary, Sackey Pennington, John
Gibbs and wife, Elizabeth, Herman Bishop and wife, Amey, &
William Scarbro. Grandchildren: William Lashley; William
Ezell; Avories Bishop; James Jones; Frederick Scarbro (not
21); Lucy and John Avories, children of Thomas, dec'd.; Wil-
liam Scarbro; Ann Casely; Elizabeth Lesly; Mary Avories,
daughter of Thomas, dec'd.; ch. of An Jones, dec'd. Wit-
nesses: John Peter, Henry Cocke, William Lamb and James
Kee, Jr.

Page 290: EDWARD BAILEY of Surry. Will. Date: 26 Nov. 1758. Rec.: 15
June 1762. Thomas Bailey, Executor. Sons: Thomas (eldest),
Edward, William, John and Henry. Daughters: Mary, Sarah,
Ann and Lucy. Witnesses: George Berrick, Christopher Mor-
ing and Henry Duggin.

Page 292: WILLIAM HARGRAVE of Surry. Will. Date: 27 Apr. 1762. Rec.:
20 July 1762. Sons: Josiah and William. Wife: Sarah. Daughters: Silviah, Mary, Mourning and Sarah. Father: Augustine Hargrave. Friends: Edward Wotton and Hartwell Hargrave. Witnesses: Benjamin Bailey, Jr., Benjamin Hargrave
and Jesse Hargrave.

Page 293: THOMAS ALLSTIN of Southwark Parish, Surry. Will. Date: 18
Mar. 1759. Rec.: 20 July 1762. Mary Allstin, Executrix.
Wife: Mary. Goddaughter: Ann Barker. Friend: William Col-
lins. Witnesses: Stephen Thompson, Robert Watkins, Jr. &
William Pulley.

Page 294: RICHARD FUGLER. Inventory. Date: 23 Jan. 1762. Rec.: 20
July 1762. Benjamin Bryna, William Pulley and William Collins, Appraisers.

Page 295: JAMES BOARDMAN. Account Current. Date: ----. Rec.: 20 Jul.
1762. Elizabeth Boardman, Administratrix. John Day, William Ruffin, Auditors.

Page 296: Capt. JAMES SUMMERVILL. Inventory. Date: 26 July 1762. Rec:
17 Aug. 1762. James Belsches, Archibald Dunlop and John
Austin Finne, Appraisers.

Page 297: CHARLES CLARY. Inventory. Date: 18 May 1762. Rec.: 17 Aug.
1762. Wil Seward, Henry Seward and Francis Little, Appraisers.

Page 299: JOHN HUNNICUTT of Surry. Will. Date: 14 Mar. 1762. Rec.: 17
Aug. 1762. Robert Hunnicutt, Executor. Daughters: Martha,
Sarah and Mary (none 18). Godson: John Hunnicutt. Wife:
Faithy. Brother: Robert Hunnicutt. Witnesses: William
White, William Philips and Robert Hunnicutt.

Page 300: NEWIT EDWARDS. Inventory. Date: 18 May 1762. Rec.: 17 Aug.
1762. Robert Hunnicutt, Carter Crafford and James Taylor,
Appraisers.

Page 301: GEORGE CRYER of Surry. Will. Date: 26 Apr. 1762. Rec.: 17
Aug. 1762. Ann Cryer, Executrix. Daughter: Elizabeth.

(Page 301 - CRYER cont'd.): Wife: Ann. Friend: John Watkins. Witnesses: Patrick Adams, Robert Watkins and John Watkins.

Page 302:   WILLIAM THOMPSON. Will. Date: 14 Feb. 1762. Rec.: 17 Aug. 1762. Wife - Executrix. Children: Philip, Frederick, Patty and Becky Thompson. Son: Nathaniel. Wife: (unnamed). Brother: John Thompson. Witnesses: Thomas White, Etheldred Edwards and Thomas Edwards.

Page 302:   GEORGE CRYER. Inventory. Date: 17 Aug. 1762. Rec.: 19 Oct. 1762. John Collier, Thomas Collier and John Tarrett, Sr., Appraisers.

Page 304:   Gray's Creek Tobacco Warehouse Inspection.

Page 304:   Cabin Point Tobacco Warehouse Inspection.

Page 304:   THOMAS EDWARDS of Surry. Will. Date: 11 Apr. 1761. Rec.: 19 Oct. 1762. William Edwards and Benjamin Edwards, Executors. Sons: William, Benjamin and Etheldred (last not 21). Witnesses: Robert Hart, Thomas Hart and William D. Williams.

Page 306:   HANNAH KERSEY. Account Current. Date: 1762. Rec.: 19 Oct. 1762. William Kersey, Administrator. Wil Salter and Charles Binns, Auditors.

Page 306:   WILLIAM HARGRAVE. Inventory. Date: 20 July 1762. Rec.: 21 Dec. 1762. Edward Wootten, and Sarah Hargrave, Executors. Joseph Petway, David Andrews and Thomas Wrenn, Appraisers.

Page 307:   Gray's Creek Tobacco Warehouse Inspection.

Page 307:   HENRY BROWNE of Surry. Will. Date: 30 Oct. 1762. Rec.: 21 Dec. 1763. William Browne of Surry and John Edmunds of Sussex, Executors. Wife: Hannah. Sons: William, Henry, Benjamin Edwards Browne (first two not 21). Daughters: Mary and Elizabeth Browne. Friends: William Poythress of Prince George Co. and Hartwell Cocke of Surry Co. Mentions: land in Southampton and Brunswick Counties; lots in Cobham, Guilford and Petersburg. Witnesses: James Carter, John Hutchings, Jr. and John Collier.

Page 310:   JOHN AVORIES. Inventory. Date: ---. Rec.: -- 18, 1763. John Barker, James Adams and William Shell, Appraisers.

Page 312:   JOHN HUNNICUTT. Inventory. Date: 17 Aug. 1762. Rec.: Mar. 15, 1763. Nicholas Thompson, Thomas Lane and Richard Rowell, Appraisers.

Page 313:   HENRY SEWARD of Surry. Will. Date: 18 Mar. 1762. Rec.: 15 Mar. 1763. William Seward, Executor. Wife: (unnamed). Wife's brother: Joshua Nicholson. Brother: William Seward. All my children. Witnesses: Joseph Brookes, Richard Hamlin, Jr. and William Pretlow.

Page 314:   THOMAS EDWARDS. Inventory. Date: ----. Rec.: 15 Mar. 1763. William and Benjamin Edwards, Executors.

Page 314:   JOHN BARNES. Account Current. Date: ---. Rec.: 15 March 1763. Thomas Sorsby, and Sarah Barnes, Executors. John Ruffin, and Thomas Bailey, Jr., Auditors.

Page 316:   WILLIAM MACLIN. Inventory. Date: 25 Jan. 1763. Rec.: 19 Apr. 1763. William Maclin, Executor.

Page 317:   JOHN PETER of Surry. Will. Date: 14 Feb. 1763. Rec.: 19 Apr. 1763. Walter Peter, Mr. John Edmunds and Mr. William Short, Executors. Wife: Elizabeth. Sons: Thomas, John and Robert (none 21). Daughter: Jane Dunlop Peter. Child in esse.

(Page 317: - PETER cont'd.): Father: (unnamed). Brothers: Walter, Thomas, Alexander, Robert and David Peter. Mentions: partnership with brother Walter, in Brunswick County; sons to be educated in Glascow in North Britain under my father and brothers, Thomas and Alexander. Witnesses: Robert Dick, Daniel Fisher, David Scott and Katharine Cocke.

Page 323: BENJAMIN COCKE of Southwark Parish, Surry. Will. Date: 13 Mar. 1763. Rec.: 17 May 1763. Mr. Hartwell Cocke and Mr. William Acril, Executors. Daughter: Katharine Allen Bradby. Son: Allen. Daughter: Rebecca Cocke (not 21). Brother: Richard Cocke and his son, Hartwell. Mentions: Mr. William Salter, Mrs. Elizabeth Stith, Mr. Benjamin Cocke, Jr., Mrs. Elizabeth Thornton, Mrs. Rebecca Taliaferro, Mr. William Acril, Mr. William Edwards, Mr. William Nelson, Mr. Thomas Adams, and Benjamin Cocke, son of brother Richard. Mentions: land in Goochland, Albemarle and Buckinham Counties. Witnesses: Patrick Adams, William Nelson, Joseph Berriman and John Maddera. Codicil: mentions John Bradly, Joseph Berriman and Abraham Mitchell. Witnesses: Richard Cocke, John Bradly and Thomas Cogging.

Page 326: WILLIAM BENNET. Account Current. Date: 1761. Rec.: June 21, 1763. Mildred Bennet, Administratrix. Mentions: all my daughters.

Page 326: AUGUSTINE HARGRAVE of Surry. Will. Date: ---. Rec.: 21 June 1763. Hartwell and Augustine Hargrave, Executors. Sons: William, Hartwell, Augustine, Thomas and Hardy. Daughter: Katharine Hargrave. Wife: (unnamed). Mentions: Olive Hargrave. Witnesses: (none) ; Anselm and Benjamin Bailey swear to handwriting.

Page 328: JOHN THOMPSON of Southwark Parish, Surry. Will. Date: --- Rec.: 19 July 1763. Wife: Ann. Sons: John, Philip, Nathaniel and William Edloe Thompson. Daughters: Elizabeth, Rebeccah and Ann Cocke Thompson. Witnesses: (none); William Browne, Etheldred Gray swear to handwriting.

Page 329: Capt. WILLIAM PETRIE. Inventory. Date: 6 May 1763. Rec.: 19 July 1763. Thomas Holt, James Belches, and George Keer, Appraisers.

Page 330: HENRY BARNES. Account Current. Date: ---. Rec.: 19 July 1763. Neomy Barnes, Executrix. Mentions: legatees Henry Barnes and Thomas Dewell. Christopher Moring and William Ruffin, Auditors.

Page 331: WILLIAM THOMPSON. Inventory. Date: ----. Rec.: 16 Aug. 1763. Augustine Hunnicutt, Thomas Lane and William White, Appraisers.

Page 333: ELIZABETH ANDREWS. Account Current. Date: ----. Rec.: 16 Aug. 1763. William Warren, Administrator. Benjamin Cocke and William Harris, Auditors.

Page 334: Gray's Creek Tobacco Warehouse Inspection.

Page 334: Cabin Point Tobacco Warehouse Inspection.

Page 334: AUGUSTINE HARGRAVE. Inventory. Date: 21 June 1763. Rec.: 20 Sept. 1763. Hartwell Hargrave and Augustine Hargrave, Executors. George Berrick and Arthur Holleman, Appraisers.

Page 336: WILLIAM COCKE of Surry. Will. Date: 28 June 1763. Rec.: 20 Sept. 1763. James Belches and William Short, Executors. Wife: Sarah. Daughters: Susan, Sarah, Elizabeth and Martha Cocke (none 18). Son: William (not 21). Friends: James Belches and William Simmons. Witnesses: Robert Watkins,

(Page 336 - COCKE cont'd.): Francis Simmons, Peter DuBe and Lewis Pulley.

Page 339: JOHN WALL of Surry. Will. Date: 6 Aug. 1763. Rec.: 20 Sept. 1763. John Wall, Executor. Sons: John, Moses, William and Aaron. Daughters: Hannah Browne and Mary Cocks. Witnesses: Thomas Willson, George Berrick and Joseph Holleman.

Page 340: Gray's Creek Tobacco Warehouse Inspection.

Page 340: EDWARD BAILEY, SR. Inventory. Date: 15 June 1763. Rec.: 20 Dec. 1763. John Andrews, John Watkins and James Davis, Appraisers.

Page 342: EDWARD BAILEY, JR. Inventory. Date: 19 Mar. 1763. Rec.: 20 Dec. 1763. Thomas Bailey, Jr., Administrator. Christopher Moring, William Andrews and John Andrews, Appraisers.

Page 343: JOHN WALL. Inventory. Date: Dec. 1763. Rec.: 17 Jan. 1764. George Berrick, Charles Thompson and Arthur Holleman, Appraisers.

Page 345: HENRY SMITH of Surry. Will. Date: 20 Nov. 1763. Rec.: 17 Jan. 1764. James Smith and William Smith, Executors. Wife: Charity. Sons: John, Nicholas and Henry. Daughters: Sarah, Mary and Susanna. Brothers: James and William. Witnesses: William Clinch, William Lane and John Warren.

Page 346: SILVESTER AMISS of Surry. Will. Date: 4 Jan. 1763. Rec.: 17 Jan. 1764. Mary Amiss, Executrix. Wife: Mary. Daughters: Elizabeth Amiss, Mary Jordan and Sarah Amiss. Friend: Henry Watkins. Witnesses: Jonathan Ellis, Robert Andrews and Hannah Ellis.

Page 347: THOMAS GRIFFIS of Southwark Parish, Surry. Will. Date: 20 Oct. 1763. Rec.: 21 Feb. 1764. Sarah Griffis, Executrix. Wife: Sarah. Daughter: Sarah Haley. Grandchild: Cady Griffis Clark. Son: Thomas. Witnesses: Robert Watson, Richard Carter and James Cook. Codicil: Grandchild: James Haley.

Page 349: HENRY SMITH. Inventory. Date: 17 Jan. 1764. Rec.: 21 Feb. 1764. John Harris, Matthias Marriott and Joseph Warren, Appraisers.

Page 351: SILVESTER AMISS. Inventory. Date: 17 Jan. 1764. Rec.: 21 Feb. 1764. Jonathan Ellis, William Magget and William Davis, Appraisers.

Page 354: THOMAS GRIFFIS. Inventory. Date: ---. Rec.: 20 Mar. 1764.

Page 355: JOHN DREW of Surry. Will. Date: 14 Jan. 1764. Rec.: 20 Mar. 1764. Wife, Executrix. Wife: (unnamed). Grandch.: (unnamed) Daughters: Faithy, Betty and Martha. Witnesses: John Newsum, Edmund Waller and Wil Salter. Mentions: Children of Faithy and Betty.

Page 356: RICHARD PRESSON. Inventory. Date: 21 Feb. 1764. Rec.: 15 May 1764. Joseph Holleman, Arthur Holleman and David Holleway, Appraisers.

Page 358: CHARLES CLARY. Account Current. Date: ----. Rec.: 19 June 1764. Barnes Clary presents. Mentions: legacies to Mary Fiveash, Martha Pittman; Richard Smith his 1/4 interest of sales of personal estate; Silvah Clary, her 1/4 interest of same; Barnes Clary, my 1/2 interest of same. Walter Peter, and Joseph Holleman, Auditors.

Page 359: JOHN DREW. Inventory. Date: 20 Mar. 1764. Rec.: 21 Aug. 1764. Cloe Drew, Executrix. Carter Crafford, Robert Hunni-

(Page 359: - DREW cont'd.): cutt and William Newsum, Appraisers.

Page 361:   WILLIAM JORDAN. Will. Date: 16 Feb. 1764. Rec.: 21 August
            1764. Ann Jordan and James Jordan, Executors. Wife: Ann.
            Daughters: Mary Savidge and Jane Savidge. Son: James. Wit-
            nesses: W. Magget, Henry White and John Judkins, Jr.

Page 361:   JOHN THOMPSON. Account Current. Date: 1763. Rec.: 21 Aug.
            1764. Thomas Willson, Sheriff.

Page 363:   HENRY BROWNE, Gent. Inventory. Date: 21 Dec. 1762. Rec.: 21
            Aug. 1764. J. Edmunds and William Browne, Executors.(Surry
            County). John Collier, Charles Holdsworth and Thomas Bail-
            ey, Appraisers.

Page 370:   Mr. HENRY BROWNE. Inventory. Date: 16 Mar. 1763. Rec.: 21
            Aug. 1764. J. Edmunds and William Browne, Executors. (South-
            ampton County). J. Gray, Benjamin Ruffin and R. Kello, Ap-
            praisers.

Page 371:   HENRY BROWNE, Gent. Inventory. Date: 11 Feb. 1763. Rec.: 21
            Aug. 1764. J. Edmunds and William Browne, Executors.(Bruns-
            wick County). Nicholas Edmunds, Thomas Butler and Robert
            Briggs, Appraisers.

Page 372:   MARY LUCAS of Southwark Parish, Surry. Will. Date: 12 Jan.
            1760. Rec.: 21 Aug. 1764. John Lucas, Executor. Sons: David
            and Richard Hide; William, Stephen, John and Samuel Lucas.
            Daughters: Ann Yorborer and Mary Gillom. Granddaughter: Re-
            becca Hide, daughter of son, Benjamin Hide. Witnesses:
            Christopher Moring and John Marks.

Page 373:   Cabin Point Tobacco Warehouse Inspection.

Page 374:   Gray's Creek Tobacco Warehouse Inspection.

Page 374:   JOHN HOLT of Southwark Parish, Surry. Will. Date: 21 Sept.
            1759. Rec.: 16 Oct. 1764. Randolph Holt, Executor. Daugh-
            ters: Kezia, Elvira; Mary and Anna (not 20). Sons: John,
            Josiah (not 21); and Randolph. Grandson: John Randolph
            Wilkinson (not 12). Mentions: land in Sussex County and
            lot in Blanford. Witnesses: Patrick Adams, Elizabeth Tay-
            lor and Thomas Holt, Jr.

Page 376:   GILBERT GRAY of Surry. Will. Date: 8 Apr. 1758. Rec.: 18
            Dec. 1764. Margaret Gray, Executrix. Sons: Joseph, John and
            James. Daughters: Elizabeth Marriott, wife of Matthias;
            Sarah, Mary and Lucy Gray. Wife: Margaret. Witnesses: Rob-
            ert Gray, Hartwell Cocke, and George Dawson.

Page 378:   CHARLES HOLDSWORTH, SR. of Surry. Will. Date: 2 May 1764.
            Rec.: 18 Dec. 1764. Rebecca Holdsworth and Mr. John White,
            Executors. Sons: Charles, Thomas and William (the last two
            not of age). Daughters: Mary Banks; Eliz'a, Tabitha, Re-
            becca and Sarah (last four not of age). Grandchildren: Rob-
            ert White Holdsworth and Benjamin Banks. Child in esse.
            Wife: Rebecca. Mentions ch. by present wife. Friend: Col.
            Hartwell Cocke. Witnesses: William Underwood, John White,
            Philip West and Benjamin Clark.

Page 380:   CHARLES HOLDSWORTH. Inventory. Date: 2 Jan. 1765. Rec.:
            18 Jan. 1765. John Watkins, Robert Watkins and John Coll-
            ier, Appraisers.

Page 382:   JOHN MATTHEWSON. Inventory. Date: 1 Dec. 1764. Rec.: 15
            Jan. 1765. James Buchanan, John Heath and David Scott, Ap-
            praisers.

Page 383:   ROBERT PULLEY. Account Current. Date: -- Rec.: 19 Feb. 1765.
            Thomas Wilson, Sheriff.

Page 383:   GEORGE ANDERTON. Inventory. Date: 11 Aug. 1766. Rec.: 19
            Mar. 1765. Christopher Moring, John Lucas and William Bail-
            ey, Appraisers.

Page 384:   THOMAS BINNS. Will. Date: 2 Apr. 1765. Rec.: 18 June 1765.
            Elizabeth Binns, Executrix. Wife: Elizabeth. Witnesses:
            (none); John and Joseph Newsum and Martha Edwards swear to
            will.

Page 385:   NICHOLAS JUDKINS of Southwark Parish, Surry. Will. Date: 20
            May 1763. Rec.: 16 June 1765. John Judkins, Executor. Sons:
            John and Jacob. Wife: Elizabeth. Daughters: Mary, Eliza-
            beth, Martha and Ann Judkins. Mentions: portions of my
            father's estate. Witnesses: Henry Davis, Etheldred Gray
            and Anthony Evans, Jr.

Page 387:   JOSEPH PETTWAY. Inventory. Date: 18 June 1765. Rec.: July
            16, 1765. Joseph Holleman, David Andrews and Thomas Wrenn,
            Appraisers.

Page 388:   NICHOLAS JUDKINS. Inventory. Date: ---. Rec.: 16 Jul. 1765.
            John Judkins, Executor.

Page 389:   CALEB ELLIS. Account Current. Date: ---. Rec.: 16 Jul.1765.
            Thomas Bailey and Henry Howard, Auditors.

Page 390:   JOHN HOLT. Inventory. Date: ---. Rec.: 20 Aug. 1765. Ran-
            dolph Holt, Executor. Carter Crafford, Thomas Binns and
            Robert Hunnicutt, Appraisers.

Page 395:   THOMAS BINNS. Inventory. Date: 18 July 1765. Rec.: 18 Jul.
            1765. James Rod'l Bradby, John Newsum and Samuel Judkins,
            Appraisers.

Page 398:   EDWARD HARRISS of Surry. Will. Date: 17 Jan. 1760. Rec.:20
            Aug. 1765. Hopkin Harriss, Executor. Wife: Martha. Sons:
            Hopkin, John and William. Daughters: Martha Harriss and
            Hannah Pettway. Grandchildren: James Harriss; and Mary Hun-
            nicutt (not 21). Witnesses: Anselm Bailey, Jr., Thomas Wil-
            son and Charles Thompson.

Page 399:   BENJAMIN CLARK. Account Current. Date: ---. Rec.: 20 Aug.
            1765. Anselm Bailey, Administrator. Mentions: widow. Free-
            man Walker and Robert Hunnicutt, Auditors.

Page 400:   JOHN SPRATLEY. Account Current. Date: ---. Rec.: 20 Aug.
            1765. William Spratley, Executor. William Short, James Bel-
            sches, and Walter Peter, Appraiser.

Page 401:   JOHN LANIER of Southwark Parish, Surry. Will. Date: 14 Dec.
            1764. Rec.: 20 Aug. 1765. Wife: Priscilla. Sons: Robert and
            John. Daughter: Lucy Lanier. Brother: Robert Lanier. Men-
            tions: children to be educated. Witnesses: John Rivers,
            Hones Rivers and Jonn Rivers.

Page 403:   Cabin Point Tobacco Warehouse Inspection.

Page 403:   WILLIAM COCKE. Inventory. Date: 18 Nov. 1763. Rec.: 20 Aug.
            1765. James Belsches and William Short, Appraiser.

Page 404:   CHARLES BINNS. Sale. Date: --- Rec.: 15 Oct. 1765. Charles
            Binns, Executor.

Page 409:   CHARLES BINNS. Account Current. Date: ---. Rec.: 15 Oct.
            1765. Mentions: Mrs. Hay's death; Mr. John Jones' part in
            right of wife; Mr. John Jones as guardian of Lucy Binns,
            her part; Mr. John Jones as guardian of Martha Binns, her
            part; Charles Binns' part.

Page 409:   JOHN KEA. Account Current. Date: ----. Rec.: 15 Oct.1765. William Short and Thomas Bailey, Auditors.

Page 410:   HANNAH KERSEY. Account Current. Date: ----. Rec.: 15 Oct. 1765. James Belsches, Administrator. Thomas Bailey and David Scott, Auditors.

Page 411:   JOHN J'ANSON. Inventory. Date: 1759. Rec.: 15 Oct. 1765. James Belsches, Executor.

Page 412:   Gray's Creek Tobacco Warehouse Inspection.

Page 413:   JOHN HOLT. Inventory. (Sussex Co.). Date: 6 December 1764. Rec.: 20 May 1766. William Gilliam, Richard Hill and Josiah Freeman, Appraisers.

Page 414:   BENJAMIN CLARK of Surry. Will. Date: 16 Mar. 1766. Rec.: 17 June 1766. Lucy Clark and Matthias Marriott, Executors. Wife: Lucy. Son: James (not of age). Sisters: Ann Snips and Sarah Clark. Legatees: Benjamin Clark, son of Joseph; and Ann Snips' children: John, Lucy and Silvia. Witnesses: William Clinch and Matthias Marriott.

Page 415:   JANE COCKE of Surry. Will. Date: 13 Nov. 1765. Rec.: 17 June 1766. Henry Cocke, Executor. Sons: Richard (not of age), Lemuel, Thomas, and Henry. Daughter: Anne Cocke. Witnesses: John Edmunds, Stephen Lucas and Samuel Lucas.

Page 416:   MARMADUKE CHEATHAM. Will. Date: 30 Apr. 1762. Rec.: 17 Jun. 1766. John Cheatham and Joseph Cheatham, Executors. Wife: Susanna. Sons: John, James, Benjamin, and Joseph. Daughters: Sarah, Ann, and Elizabeth. Grandchildren: James Cheatham, son of John; Joseph Simmons, son of daughter, Ann. Legatee: John Dugger, son of Lydia Dugger, dec'd. Witnesses: Joseph Jordan, Henry Jordan and Mary Jordan.

Page 418:   BENJAMIN GRAY. Inventory. Date: 22 May 1766. Rec.: 15 July 1766. Christopher Clinch, Administrator. Henry Davis, Henry White and John Judkins, Jr., Appraisers.

Page 418:   ROBERT and MARY WARREN. Account Current. Date: 1754. Rec: 15 July 1766. Peter Warren presents. Mentions: legacies paid to Joseph Bishop in right of his wife; Joseph Warren; Patty, Sally and Lucy Warren. Executor's brother: Thomas Warren. James Belsches and William Simmons, Auditors.

Page 421:   WILLIAM HARGRAVE. Account Current. Date: ----. Rec.: 19 Aug. 1766. Sarah Hargrave and Edward Wooten, Executors. William Short and G. Kerr, Auditors.

Page 422:   JAMES CLEVELAND of Wouthwark Parish, Surry. Will. Date: 17 Dec. 1765. Rec.: 19 Aug. 1766. William Collins, Executor. Wife: Martha. Sons: William and John. Daughter: Peggy Cleveland. Child in esse. Witnesses: Mary Harrison, William Pulley, Sr., and William Simmons.

Page 423:   Gray's Creek Tobacco Warehouse Inspection.

Page 424:   Cabin Point Tobacco Warehouse Inspection.

Page 424:   WILLIAM ROSE. Will. Date: 19 Feb. 1760. Rec.: 21 Oct. 1766. Elizabeth Rose, Executrix. Wife: Elizabeth. Witnesses: Hannah Wilkinson, Elizabeth Johnson, Robert Gray, Philip Clinch and James Wilkinson.

Page 425:   JOHN LANIER. Inventory. Date: 15 Sept. 1766. Rec.: 21 Oct. 1766. James Belsches presents. William Harriss, William Short and John Burges, Appraisers.

Page 426: THOMAS DAVIS of Surry. Will. Date: 17 Mar. 1766. Rec.: 21
Oct. 1766. William and Thomas Davis, Executors. Wife: Mary.
Daughters: Mary and Sarah Davis. Sons: James, John, William,
Thomas; David and Joseph (in school). Friends: Robert Hart
and Thomas Wilson. Witnesses: Thomas Hart, Edward Brown
and Jesse Bennett.

Page 427: JAMES CLEVELAND. Inventory. Date: 27 Oct. 1766. Rec.: 21
Nov. 1766. Thomas Shrewsbury, William Pulley, Sr., and
Robert Watkins, Appraisers.

Page 429: EDWARD PETTWAY of Surry. Will. Date: 3 Oct. 1765. Rec.: 18
Nov. 1766. Sarah Pettway and Hartwell, Executors. Wife:
Sarah. Grandchildren: John and Edward Pettway; John Hart.
Daughters: Lucy Hart and Elizabeth Warren. Sons-in-law:
John Warren and Hartwell Hart. Witnesses: William Clinch,
and Nathaniel Sebrell.

Page 430: JOHN MEED of Surry. Will. Date: 22 Feb. 1765. Rec.: 18 Nov.
1766. Jane Meed, Executrix. Sons: Minor and John. Wife:
Jane. Daughters: Susanna and Sarah. Friends: Carter Craf-
ford, William Grimes and Page Blunt. Mentions: land in
Hanover County. Witnesses: Nathaniel Sebrell, Anselm Jones
and Wil Salter. Codicil. Date: 27 May 1766. Daughter:
Martha, born since making will. Witnesses: Wil Salter, Jr.,
Joseph Gray and Wil Salter.

Page 432: Gray's Creek Tobacco Warehouse Inspection.

Page 432: JOHN THOMPSON. Inventory. Date: 16 Dec. 1766. Rec.: 16 Dec.
1766. James Smith, John Lane and William Cane, Appraisers.

Page 433: GEORGE BERRICK of Surry. Will. Date: 17 Aug. 1765. Rec.:20
Jan. 1767. Wife: Priscilla (who is also Executrix). Witnesses: Thomas Bailey, John Jarratt, Jr. and John Bailey.

Page 433: WILLIAM ROSE. Inventory. Date: 1766. Rec.: 20 Jan. 1767.
Elizabeth Rose, Executrix.

Page 434: JOHN RIGGAN of Surry. Will. Date: 12 Dec. 1766. Rec.: 20
Jan. 1767. William and Benjamin Riggan, Executors. Sons:
William, Jesse and Benjamin. Daughter: Mary Riggan. Wit-
nesses: James Smith, John and William Lane.

Page 435: ROBERT WATKINS of Southwark Parish, Surry. Will. Date: 28
Nov. 1766. Rec.: 20 Jan. 1766. Philip Clinch, Executor.
Cousin: John Watkins, Jr. Mentions: Henry Watkins, Rebekah Bage, Ann Cryer, Thomas Bage, Jr., and John Watkins,
son of Jenkins Watkins. Witnesses: John Watkins, Ann Huse
and William Collins.

Page 436: WILLIAM MARRIOTT of Surry. Will. Date: 20 Sept. 1765. Rec:
20 Jan. 1767. Matthias Marriott, Executor. Sons: Thomas,
Matthias; and Benjamin (mentions land where he lived.).
Grandsons: William and John Marriott, sons of Benjamin -
(not 18); William Davis. Son-in-law: Henry Davis. Mentions: Stephenson Buxton and wife, Elizabeth, to enjoy the
house until grandson, William Marriott is 18; land in Brunswick County. Witnesses: John Harris, Margaret Gray and
Hannah Davis.

Page 437: BENJAMIN PHILIPS. Inventory. Date: 8 Dec. 1766. Rec.: 26
Jan. 1767. Wil Salter, Thomas Lane, and Joel Thompson, Appraisers.

Page 439: JOHN SLATE. Account Current. Date: 1765. Rec.: 20 Jan.
1767. Mentions: paid Priscilla Maddra her share of her
father's estate due by bond before her mother's marriage
with John Slate; John Slate's five (5) children. William
Harris, and John Jarratt, Jr., Auditors.

Page 440: WILLIAM ROYALL. Inventory. Date: 29 Jan. 1767. Rec.: Feb. 17, 1767. James Belsches, Administrator. Jonathan Ellis, Henry Watkins, and William Magot, Appraisers.

Page 440: JOHN WARREN of Surry. Will. Date: 16 Jan. 1767. Rec.: 17 Feb. 1767. Henry Davis, Jr., Executor. Brother: Frederick. Sister: Eadith Warren. Wife: Edith. Witnesses: John Wesson, Joseph Warren and Joseph Bishop.

Page 441: EDWARD PETTWAY. Inventory. Date: 18 Nov. 1766. Rec.: 17 Feb. 1767. James Price, Samuel Judkins and Nathaniel Sebrell, Appraisers.

Page 443: JAMES SAMPSON CLARK. Account Current. Date: ----. Rec.: 17 Feb. 1767. Joice and James Clark present. William Edwards and Joseph Newsum.

Page 444: MARY LUCAS. Inventory. Date: 21 Dec. 1764. Rec.: 17 Feb. 1767. John Lucas, Executor.

Page 445: RICHARD PRESSON. Account Current. Date: 1764. Rec.: 17 Feb. 1767. John Presson, Administrator. Wil Seward and Thomas Fenner, Auditors.

Page 446: BENJAMIN BRYAN. Inventory. Date: 21 Feb. 1767. Rec.: 17 Mar. 1767. Thomas Holt, Thomas Sorsby and Martin Baker, Appraisers.

Page 447: JOHN RIGGAN. Inventory. Date: ----. Rec.: 17 Mar. 1767. William and Benjamin Riggan, Executors.

Page 448: SARAH MADDERA of Surry. Will. Date: 23 Sept. 1766. Rec: 17 Mar. 1767. Daughter: Mary Warren. Mentions: John Davis the son of John. Son-in-law: Frederick Warren. Witnesses: John Wesson, Lucy Pyland and Martha Price.

Page 448: HENRY DAVIS of Surry. Will. Date: 18 Feb. 1767. Rec.: 17 Mar. 1767. Etheldred Gray, Executor. Sons: Benjamin, Isham, Randolph, Henry, William, Marriott and James. Daughters: Ann, Hannah, Betsey, Keziah and Sylvia. Brothers: John and James Davis. Witnesses: Thomas Marriott, John Judkins, Frederick Burdye and Etheldred Gray.

Page 450: JOHN WARREN. Inventory. Date: 16 Feb. 1767. Rec.: 17 Mar. 1767. Joseph Warren, John Warren and James Davis, Jr., Appraisers.

Page 452: JOHN CLARKE. Inventory. Date: 17 Mar. 1767. Rec.: 21 Apr. 1767. Nicholas Thompson, Richard Rowell and Henry Moring, Appraisers.

Page 453: HENRY DAVIS. Inventory. Date: 3 Apr. 1767. Rec.: 21 Apr. 1767. Etheldred Gray, Executor. William Maget, Henry White and John Judkins, Jr., Appraisers.

Page 456: FRANCIS HOLT. Inventory. Date: 29 Dec. 1766. Rec.: 22 Apr. 1767. William Nelson, William Berriman and James Taylor, Appraisers.

Page 458: BENJAMIN PHILIPS. Account Current. Date: 1766. Rec.: 19 May 1767. Thomas and Mary Shelly, Ex. of James Shelly, dec'd. Adm. of Benjamin Philips.

Page 459: GEORGE BERRICK. Inventory. Date: 18 May 1767. Rec.: 19 May 1767. Priscilla Berrick, Executrix.

Page 460: WILLIAM PRITLOW. Inventory. Date: 19 Aug. 1765. Rec.: 19 May 1767. Freeman Walker and Robert Hunnicutt, Appraisers.

Page 463:   THOMAS BARHAM. Inventory. Date: 6 Mar. 1765. Rec.: 19 May
             1767. Robert Hunnicutt, William Newsum and Edmond Walker,
             Appraisers.

Page 464:   Dr. KENNETH MC KENZIE. Inventory. Date: 27 Jun. 1766. Rec:
             19 May 1767. James Belsches and Thomas Sorsby, Appraisers.

Page 467:   JANE COCKE. Inventory. Date: 18 Aug. 1766. Rec.: 16 June
             1767. William Anderson, Stephen Lucas and Joshua Barker,
             Appraisers.

Page 471:   SAMUEL GILLUM of Brunswick County. Will. Date: 14 May 1767.
             Rec.: 16 June 1767. John Gillum, Executor. Brother: John.
             Mentions: land (willed) to me by my father. Witnesses:
             John Burgess, John Burrow and William Anthony.

Page 472:   JOHN DREW. Account Current. Date: 1764. Rec.: 16 Jun. 1767.
             Alice Drew, Executrix. Carter Crafford and William Ruffin,
             Auditors.

Page 474:   ROBERT WATKINS. Inventory. Date: 23 Feb. 1767. Rec.: June
             16, 1767. Thomas Bailey, Administrator. William Simmons,
             Thomas Sorsbury and William Collins, Appraisers.

Page 475:   BENJAMIN CARRELL. Inventory. Date: 11 Apr. 1767. Rec: 18
             Aug. 1767.

Page 476:   HENRY SEWARD. Inventory. Date: 15 Mar. 1763. Rec.: 18 Aug.
             1767. William Drew, James Holt and Francis Holt, Appraisers.

Page 480:   SAMUEL PRICE of Southwark Parish, Surry. Will. Date: 17
             Feb. 1767. Rec.: 18 Aug. 1767. Randolph Price, Executor.
             Brother: Randolph. Legatees: Silvere, Rebecah, Martha &
             Hannah Copland Price. Witnesses: Henry Moring, Nathan Da-
             vis and John Wesson.

Page 481:   WILLIAM MARRIOTT. Account Current. Date: 1765. Rec.: 18
             Aug. 1767. Matthias Marriott, Executor. Benjamin Cocke,
             Wil Seward and Nicholas Faulcon, Jr., Auditors.

Page 483:   Petition to lay of dower of MOURNING, relict of BENJAMIN
             MARRIOTT. Date: 18 Nov. 1766. Rec.: 18 Aug. 1767. Division
             by William Clinch, James Price and Joseph Newsum.

Page 484:   HENRY SEWARD. Account Current. Date: 1763. Rec.: 15 Sept.
             1767. William Seward, Executor. Includes: Account Current
             of William Seward; Account Current of Sarah Seward, widow
             of Henry. Benjamin Cocke and William Ruffin, Auditors.

Page 487:   JOHN THOMPSON of Southwark Parish, Surry. Will. Date: May
             8, 1767. Rec.: Sept. 15, 1767. William Clinch, Jr., Exe-
             cutor. Brothers: Nathan and William. Legatees: Rebecah,
             Ann Cocke, Nathan, William and Philip Thompson. Witnesses:
             Richard Rispus, Philip King and John Watkins, Jr.

Page 488:   Gray's Creek Tobacco Warehouse Inspection.

Page 488:   Cabin Point Tobacco Warehouse Inspection.

Page 489:   MARGARET GRAY of Southwark Parish, Surry. Will. Date: 27
             June 1767. Rec.: 17 Nov. 1767. John Gray, Executor. Sons:
             John, and James. Daughters: Lucy Gray and Mary Clinch.
             Friend: Matthias Marriott. Witnesses: (none); Hartwell
             Cocke, and Matthias Marriott swear to handwriting.

Page 490:   THOMAS JOHNSON of Surry. Will. Date: 18 Aug. 1766. Rec.:17
             Nov. 1767. Wife: (unnamed). Daughters: Elizabeth and Sar-
             ah Johnson. Friend: John Warren. Witnesses: Jesse Jud-
             kins, John Davis, Jr. and John Judkins, Jr.

Page 490:   JOHN COLLIER. Inventory. Date: 14 Dec. 1767. Rec.: 19
              Apr. 1768. John Collier, Administrator. John Watkins, Ben-
              jamin Moring and John Andrews, Appraisers.

Page 492:   BENJAMIN COLLIER. Inventory. Date: 17 Nov. 1767. Rec.:19
              Apr. 1768. John Watkins, Benjamin Moring and John Andrews,
              Appraisers.

Page 493:   THOMAS WILSON of Surry. Will. Date: 21 May 1761. Rec.: 19
              Apr. 1768. Thomas Wilson, Executor. Wife: Elizabeth. Sons:
              Thomas, John, William, James, Nicholas and Whitfield. Daus:
              Elizabeth Holleman; Ann Wilson and Mary Wilson. Friend:
              Joseph Holleman. Witnesses: William Maget, Etheldred Gray
              and Henry White.

Page 494:   SILVIAH LANCASTER. Nunc. Will. Date: 9 Nov. 1767. Rec.:
              19 Apr. 1768. Mother: Elizabeth Lancaster. Sister: Eliza-
              beth Lancaster. Witnesses: Thomas Betts and wife, Sarah,
              of Isle of Wight County (at whose house she died).

Page 495:   JOHN MEAD. Inventory. Date: 14 May 1767. Rec.: 19 April
              1768. Jane Mead, Executrix. John Clayton, John Laurence
              and John Day, Appraisers.

Page 497:   JOHN JARRETT, the Elder, of Southwark Parish, Surry County.
              Will. Date: 12 Feb. 1768. Rec.: 19 Apr. 1768. John and
              Nathaniel Jarrett, Executors. Wife: Ann. Sons: John and
              Nathaniel. Son-in-law: Nicholas Cryer. Grandchildren:
              Patty, William and Susanna Cryer (none 18). Witnesses:
              John Lucas and Benjamin Moring.

Page 499:   HANNAH SEWARD of Surry. Will. Date: 26 Nov. 1767. Rec: 19
              Apr. 1768. James Seward, Executor. Son: James. Witnesses:
              Robert Barradell, Philip Burt and William Collins.

Page 500:   PHILIP CLINCH. Inventory. Date: 27 Mar. 1767. Rec.: 19
              Apr. 1768. James Davis, Jonathan Ellis and William Maget,
              Appraisers.

Page 502:   SAMUEL PRICE. Inventory. Date: ----. Rec.: 19 Apr. 1768.
              Samuel Judkins, Thomas Adams and George Pyland, Appraisers.

Page 1:   BENJAMIN SAVIDGE of Surry. Will. Date: 8 Apr. 1768. Rec.:
             17 May 1768. Elizabeth Savidge, Executrix. Wife: Elizabeth.
             Sons: Joel, Benjamin, John and Andrew. Daughters: May
             Savidge, Sarah Smith and Hannah Citchen. Witnesses: Will-
             iam Riggan, Benjamin Riggan and James Smith.

Page 2:   MARGARET GRAY. Inventory. Date: 17 Dec. 1767. Rec.: 17
             May 1768. William Clinch, Samuel Judkins and Joseph Newsum,
             Appraisers.

Page 7:   PETER REDBURN of Surry. Will. Date: 3 Oct. 1761. Rec.:17
             May 1768. Henry Smith, Executor. Legatee: Henry Smith.
             Witnesses: Ann Moody and Benjamin Slade.

Page 8:   CHARLES KEA of Surry. Will. Date: 30 Aug. 1764. Rec.: 18
             May 1768. William Hart, Executor. Wife: (unnamed). Wit-
             nesses: Thomas and Robert Hart.

Page 9:   BENJAMIN SAVIDGE. Inventory. Date: 7 June 1768. Rec.: 21
             June 1768. Elizabeth Savidge, Executrix. John Batts, Will
             Madera and William Smith, Appraisers.

Page 10:   JOHN THOMPSON. Inventory. Date: 7 June 1768. Rec.: 19 Jul.
             1768. John Watkins,Jr., Executor. James Smith, John Batts
             and Will Madera, Appraisers.

Page 11:   GEORGE CRYER. Account Current. Date: 1753. Rec.: 16 Aug.
             1768. Anne and George Cryer, Executors. Thomas Bailey and
             John Watkins, Auditors.

Page 14:   ANNE THOMPSON. Inventory. Date: 2 Dec. 1767. Rec.: 16 Aug.
             1768. Robert Hunnicutt, Richard Gray and Willis Wilson, Ap-
             praisers.

Page 16:   Gray's Creek Tobacco Warehouse Inspection.

Page 17:   Cabin Point Tobacco Warehouse Inspection.

Page 18:   SAMUEL PRICE. Account Current. Date: ----. Rec.: 20 Sept.
             1768. Mentions: Payments to legatees - Silviah Price, Re-
             bekah Price, Martha Price and Hannah Copland Price. W. Ed-
             Wards and Thomas Fenner, Auditors.

Page 19:   WILLIAM BERRIMAN. Inventory. Date: 9 May 1768. Rec.: 20
             Sept. 1768. James Taylor, James Gray and William Taylor,
             Appraisers.

Page 22:   THOMAS SORSBY, the Elder, of Southwark Parish, Surry County.
             Will. Date: 14 Jan. 1765. Rec.: 18 Oct. 1768. Thomas Sors-
             by, Jr., Executor. Wife: Elizabeth. Daughters: Sarah
             Barns and Elizabeth White. Sons: Samuel, Thomas, Jr.;
             Stephen and Alexander (not 21). Friend: William Simmons.
             Mentions: land in Dinwiddie County. Witnesses: John An-
             drews, John Davis, Jr. and Duncan McGurriman.

Page 27:   THOMAS BINNS. Account Current. Date: ----. Rec.: 18 Oct.
             1768. Elizabeth Binns, Executrix. Carter Crafford, Wil
             Salter and James Baird, Auditors.

Page 30:   JOHN COOPER of Surry. Will. Date: 6 Nov. 1768. Rec.: 15 Nov.
             1768. John Cooper, Executor. Children: Richard, John, Alic
             and Mary Cooper. Witnesses: Richard Ellis, Benjamin Ellis
             and William Barker.

Page 32:   Gray's Creek Tobacco Warehouse Inspection.

Page 32:   PATRICK ADAMS of Surry. Will. Date: 18 Jul. 1768. Rec.:

(Page 32 - ADAMS cont'd.):   21 Feb. 1769. Col. Richard Baker, Executor.
Son: Alexander. Daughter: Mary Adams. Legatee: Mrs.
Elizabeth Boardman. Witnesses: John Andrews, Joseph Cary
and Lucy Andrews.

Page 35:   BENJAMIN SAVIDGE. Account Current. Date: ----. Rec.: Apr.
18, 1769. Elizabeth Savidge, Executrix. W. Edwards and
Dolphin Drew, Auditors.

Page 36:   ANTHONY EVANS. Inventory. Date: 21 Mar. 1769. Rec.: 16
May 1769. Etheldred Gray, Joseph Judkins and William Cocks,
Appraisers.

Page 40:   MARY HARRISON of Surry. (Ancient). Date: 8 Jan. 1768. Rec:
20 June 1769. Daughter: Martha Clevaland. Sons: William,
and Benjamin. Witnesses: Thomas Bailey, and William Collins.

Page 42:   JOHN CLARK. Account Current. Date: 1766. Rec.: 20 June
1769. Sarah Clark, Administratrix. Henry Cocke and James
Gilchrist, Auditors.

Page 43:   HENRY SMITH. Account Current. Date: ----. Rec.: 20 June
1769. James and William Smith, Executors. William Clinch,
Jr. and Joseph Holleman, Auditors.

Page 46:   FAITH MININGTREE. Account Current. Date: 1769. Rec.: 20
June 1769. William Andrews, Administrator. John Holt, and
Henry Moring, Auditors.

Page 48:   THOMAS DAVIS. Inventory. Date: 1766. Rec.: 18 July 1769.
William and Thomas Davis, Executors. Robert Hart, William
Hart and Edward Browne, Appraisers.

Page 51:   GEORGE CRYER. Account Current. Date: 1763. Rec.: 18 July
1769. Robert Watkins, dec'd. Estate. Mentions: Nicholas
Cryer, guardian to George and Elizabeth Cryer, orphans of
George Cryer, dec'd. William Simmons, John Heath and Thomas Fenner, Auditors.

Page 53:   EDWARD PETTWAY. Account Current. Date: ----. Rec.: 15 Aug.
1769. Sarah Pettway and Hartwell Hart, Executors.

Page 54:   THOMAS DAVIS. Account Current. Date: 1769. Rec.: 15 Aug.
1769. William and Thomas Davis, Executors. Mentions: legatees - Joseph and David Davis. James Kea, Jr. and Thomas
Fenner, Auditors.

Page 55:   Cabin Point Tobacco Warehouse Inspection.

Page 56:   Gray's Creek Tobacco Warehouse Inspection.

Page 56:   ROBERT LAYLAND of Southwark Parish, Surry. Will. Date: 6
Sept. 1769. Rec.: 19 Sept. 1769. Jeremiah Pierce, Executor. Legatee: Peggy Berriman (my wife's clothing). Witnesses: Samuel Webb and Nathaniel Berriman.

Page 57:   JOHN COOPER. Inventory. Date: ----. Rec.: 17 Oct. 1769.
John Cooper, Executor.

Page 58:   MARY HARGRAVE of Surry. Will. Date: 29 Aug. 1769. Rec.: 17
Oct. 1769. Augustine Hargrave, Executor. Sons: Thomas,
Augustine and Hardy. Daughter: Olive Hargrave. Witnesses:
Michael Blow and Aaron Wall.

Page 60:   JOHN WARREN. Account Current. Date: 1767. Rec.: 17 October
1769. Henry Davis, Executor. Mentions legacies paid to:
Frederick Warren and Edith Warren (sister), widow. Joseph
Holleman and John Watkins, Jr., Auditors.

87

Page 62: FRANCIS HOLT. Account Current. Date: ----. Rec.: 17 Oct. 1769. Barnes Clary, Administrator. Mentions: wife, dec'd.; son, James. Hamilton Usher St. George and Willis Wilson, Auditors.

Page 64: HENRY WATKINS of Surry. Will. Date: 18 Dec. 1769. Rec.: 17 Jan. 1770. Jonathan Ellis, Executor. Mentions: all my children when of age. Witnesses: William Clinch, James Gilchrist and Henry Duggar.

Page 66: Gray's Creek Tobacco Warehouse Inspection.

Page 66: ROBERT RAE of Surry. Will. Date: 10 Nov. 1768. Rec.: 16 Jan. 1770. James Rae and Francis Rae, Executors. Father: Francis. Mother: Elizabeth. Sisters: Mary and Lucy Rae. Brother: James. Witnesses: John Burgess, John Cooper and William Madera.

Page 68: WILLIAM TAYLOR of Southwark Parish, Surry. Will. Date: 8 Oct. 1769. Rec.: 20 Feb. 1770. James Taylor and Richard Scammell, Executors. Wife: Mary. Mentions: all of my children when of age. Witnesses: Samuel Webb, Barnes Clary and William Marlow.

Page 70: SAMUEL LUCAS of Southwark Parish, Surry. Will. Date: 18 Jan. 1770. Rec.: 17 Feb. 1770. Richard Cocke, Executor. Wife: Elizabeth. Sons: Thomas and Samuel (neither 21). Daughter: Sally Lucas (not 18). Child in esse. Nephews: Charles Lucas, son of Stephen; John Lucas, son of John. Neice: Mary Lucas, daughter of William. Brothers: Stephen, John and William. Friend: John Cocke. Witnesses: John Lucas, Richard Putney, William Simmons and William Hazelwood.

Page 74: WILLIAM JUDKINS. Account Current. Date: 1761. Rec.: 17 Feb. 1770. John and Samuel Judkins present. Mentions: board, etc. of Joel, Thomas, Jordan, Mark, Hannah, Rebecah, and Sarah Judkins. Thomas Cocke and Etheldred Gray, Auditors.

Page 77: REBECAH ANDERSON of Surry. Will. Date: 14 Oct. 1763. Rec: 20 Mar. 1770. William Anderson, Executor. Sisters: Sarah Rachel, Mary Bonner, Susanna Hill and Hannah Gary. Granddaughter: Charlotte Anderson. Son: William. Witnesses: John Edmunds, Moses Hill and John Johnson.

Page 78: ROBERT RAE. Inventory. Date: ----. Rec.: 21 March 1770. Thomas Jones, William Scarbrough and William Justiss, Appraisers.

Page 80: HENRY WATKINS. Inventory. Date: 16 Jan. 1770. Rec.: 20 Mar. 1770. Michael Nicholson, Nathaniel Sebrell and Robert Andrews, Appraisers.

Page 83: JOHN AVERISS. Account Current. Date: 1762. Rec.: 20 Mar. 1770. Mentions: deed of gift to John Averiss; legacies to William Averiss and John Justice. John Heath, and James Baird, Auditors.

Page 86: HENRY SEWARD. Add. Account Current. Date: ----. Rec.: 20 Mar. 1770. Will Seward, Executor. Allen Cocke and William Drew, Auditors.

Page 87: ROBERT WATKINS. Account Current. Date: ----. Rec.: 17 Apr. 1770. Thomas Bailey, Administrator. Mentions: Henry Howard, guardian of John Watkins; legacies to Anne Cryer, Rebecah Bage and Henry Watkins. John White, and Etheldred Gray, Auditors.

Page 91:	JOHN NEWSUM of Southwark Parish, Surry. Will. Date: 23 Dec. 1769. Rec.: 17 Apr. 1770. Robert Newsum, Executor. Sons: Francis and Robert. Wife: Martha. Daughter: Elizabeth Barrett. Grandson: John Newsum, son of Francis. Witnesses: Samuel Webb, Charles Reeks and Nicholas Faulcon, Jr.
Page 92:	ROBERT LAYLAND. Inventory. Date: Sept. 1769. Rec.: 15 May 1770. Josiah Wilson, Francis Moreland and Francis Little, Appraisers.
Page 94:	REBECAH ANDERSON. Inventory. Date: ----. Rec.: 19 June 1770. William Anderson, Executor.
Page 96:	JOHN GIBBONS, JR. Inventory. Date: 15 May 1770. Rec.: 17 July 1770. Richard Wrenn, William Evans and Lewis Pulley, Appraisers.
Page 97:	ANN COLLIER of Surry. Will. Date: 25 June 1770. Rec.: 17 July 1770. Samuel Moody, Executor. Son: Archibald Moody. Cousin: Mary Smith, daughter of Charity Collier. Sister: Charity Collier. Brother: Samuel Moody. Legatee: William Cryer, son of Nicholas. Friend: John Watkins. Witnesses: John and Mary Bartle and Tabitha Williams.
Page 98:	ROBERT BARHAM of Surry. Will. Date: 27 Mar. 1770. Rec.: 17 July 1770. William Barham, Executor. Son: William. Granddaughter: Elizabeth Barham (not of age). Witnesses: John Barham, Edmund Waller and William Ruffin.
Page 100:	JOHN NEWSUM. Inventory. Date: 19 Apr. 1770. Rec.: 17 Jul. 1770.
Page 101:	RANDOLPH HOLT of Surry. Will. Date: 4 Oct. 1765. Rec.--- Brother: Josiah. Sisters: Mary and Anna Holt. Friends: William Spratley and William Clayton. Witnesses: Patrick Adams, John Cocke and William Clayton.
Page 103:	WILLIAM TAYLOR. Inventory. Date: 23 Feb. 1770. Rec.: 18 Sept. 1770. Josiah Wilson, Jeremiah Pearce and Francis Little, Appraisers.
Page 106:	Gray's Creek Tobacco Warehouse Inspection.
Page 107:	Cabin Point Tobacco Warehouse Inspection.
Page 107:	WILLIAM MARRIOTT. Inventory. Date: 21 Jan. 1767. Rec.: 18 Sept. 1770. William Clinch, John Warren and Drury Warren, Appraisers.
Page 110:	PETER REDBURN. Inventory. Date: 17 May 1768. Rec.: 18 Sept. 1770. John Harris, Micajah Coggin and Drury Warren, Appraisers.
Page 111:	HARDAH (HARDY) HARGRAVE of Surry. Will. Date: 21 Sep. 1770. Rec.: 16 Oct. 1770. Michael Bailey, Executor. Brothers: Thomas and Augustine. Sister: Olive Hargrave. Witnesses: John Inman and Lucy Hargrave.
Page 112:	BENJAMIN HOLT. Will. Date: 14 Oct. 1770. Rec.: 20 Nov. 1770. Joseph Holt, Executor. Daughters: Lucy Barham and Ann Bell. Sons: Joseph, Michael and Philip. Witnesses: Charles Ricks and William Ward.
Page 114:	JOSEPH JORDAN of Surry. Will. Date: 11 Oct. 1770. Rec.: 20 Nov. 1770. Joseph Cheatham, Executor. Sons: Richard, William and Stephen. Wife: Hanah. Mentions: all of my children. Witnesses: John Presson, Jr., James Wiggans and Martha Casely.

Page 116: BENJAMIN HOLT. Inventory. Date: 8 Dec. 1770. Rec.: 18 Dec. 1770. George Pyland, Edmund Waller and Etheldred Lane, Appraisers.

Page 118: ALEXANDER SORSBY of Surry. Will. Date: 15 Oct. 1770. Rec: 15 Jan. 1771. Thomas Sorsby, Executor. Mother: Elizabeth Sorsby. Legatees: Elizabeth White, Samuel Sorsby; Stephen Sorsby; and Thomas Sorsby. Friend: William Collins. Witnesses: James Kee, Jr., David Putney and William Dawson.

Page 119: ARTHUR BARKER of Southwark Parish, Surry. Will. Date: ---. Rec.: 15 Jan. 1771. Daughters: Sarah and Maryanna Barker. Wife: Rebekah. Father-in-law: Thomas Jones. Mentions: children. Witnesses: Lemuel and Elizabeth Barker.

Page 120: JOSEPH JORDAN. Inventory. Date: ----. Rec.: 15 Jan. 1771. Jonathan Ellis, Stephen Collier and John Presson, Appraisers.

Page 123: Mrs. JANE COCKE. Account Current. Date: Nov. 1765. Rec.: 19 Feb. 1771. Henry Cocke presents. Mentions legatees: Richard Cocke; Lemuel Cocke estate due from Mrs. Jane Cocke as guardian; Ann Cocke; and Thomas Cocke.

Page 130: THOMAS ADAMS of Southwark Parish, Surry. Will. Date: 15 Dec. 1768. Rec.: 19 Feb. 1771, further proven. (18 Dec. 1770, recorded). Nicholas Faulcon, Jr., Executor. Sons: William, Nathaniel and James. Daughters: Martha, Rebecca and Ann Adams. Wife: Martha. Mentions: children not 19; land my grandmother lives on. Witnesses: Samuel Judkins, Sr., and George Gardner.

Page 132: JOHN HARRIS of Surry. Will. Date: 26 Dec. 1770. Rec.: 19 Mar. 1771. Rev. Mr. McRae and Michael Nicholson of Surry, Executors. Daughters: Pamelia MacRae; Mary Harris and Anne Kennon Harris (not of age). Sons: Kennon, Eldridge; and Richard (not of age). Legatee: Rev. Christopher MacRae of Southwark Parish, Surry County. Friend: William Eldridge of Sussex County. Witnesses: John Wesson, Micajah Madera and Richard Rispes.

Page 136: HARDY HARGRAVE. Inventory. Date: 18 Mar. 1771. Rec.: 19 Mar. 1771. Michael Bailey presents. Benjamin Hargrave, William Evans and Lewis Pulley, Appraisers.

Page 137: THOMAS ADAMS. Inventory. Date: 13 Mar. 1771. Rec.: 19 Mar. 1771. Samuel Judkins, Randolph Price and George Gardner, Appraisers.

Page 139: THOMAS LANE of Surry. Will. Date: 5 Mar. 1770. Rec.: 19 Mar. 1771. Mary Lane, Executrix. Wife: Mary. Daughter: Sally Lane. Sons: Thomas and Etheldred. Brother: John. Witnesses: Thomas, John and William Bailey.

Page 141: JOHN COLLIER. Account Current. Date: 1768. Rec.: 19 Mar. 1771. John Collier, Administrator. Mentions division: widow Lucy, 1/3 part; Lucy Collier, 1/4 of remainder; Robert Andrews, in right of his wife Mary, 1/4 of same; Benjamin Collier, dec'd, heirs 1/4 of same; my (administrator) share 1/4 of same. Thomas Cocke and William Clinch, Auditors.

Page 143: JOHN HARRIS. Inventory. Date: 20 Mar. 1771. Rec.: 21 May 1771. Christopher McRae and Michael Nicholson, present.

Page 144: JOHN KERR. Will. Date: 30 Dec. 1770. Rec.: 21 May 1771. Robert and Samuel Kerr, executors. Mother: (unnamed). Brother: Robert Kerr. Sister: Margaret Kerr. Mentions: partnership of Samuel and George Kerr. Friend: George Kerr.

(Page 144 - KERR cont'd.): Cousin: Mr. Samuel Kerr asked John Kerr if
he left anything to his half-brother, Hugh Kerr and he said
no. Witnesses: (none).

Page 145:   JOHN AVORIS. Account Current. Date: ----. Rec.: 21 May
1771. William Pennington, Executor. Mentions legacies to:
Frederick and William Scarbrough; payments to William Avoris, 1/6 part; John Ezell, 1/6 part; Sarah Jones, 1/6 part;
John Gibbs, 1/6 part; Herman Bishop, 1/6 part; my (executor)
1/6 part. John Hay and William Henderson, Auditors.

Page 146:   CHARLES LUCAS. Account Current. Date: ----. Rec.: 21 May
1771. Stephen Lucas, Executor. Mentions: legacy to Rebekah Lucas. William Simmons and Thomas Fenner, Auditors.

Page 149:   JOSEPH PETTWAY. Account Current. Date: ----. Rec.: 21 May
1771. Hannah Coaker, Administratrix. Joseph Holliman and
Etheldred Gray, Auditors.

Page 149a: BENJAMIN JUDKINS. Inventory. Date: 16 Apr. 1771. Rec.: 22
May 1771. John Davis, James Seward and John Cocks, Appraisers.

Page 150:   ANN COLLIER. Inventory. Date: 2 Aug. 1770. Rec.: 22 May
1771. John Watkins, John Bartle and Nicholas Cryer, Appraisers.

Page 151:   JOSEPH NEWSAM. Inventory. Date: ----. Rec.: 18 June 1771.
Jacob Faulcon and Randolph Price, Appraisers.

Page 153:   JOHN BARHAM of Southwark Parish, Surry. Will. Date: 29
Sept. 1770. Rec.: 16 July 1771. John and Joseph Barham,
Executors. Sons: Jesse, John, Joseph and Benjamin Barham.
Daughters: Mary Judkins, widow of Benjamin; Ann, Eliza-
beth and Martha Barham. Witnesses: Samuel Judkins, Sr. &
William Barham.

Page 155:   RANDOLPH HOLT. Inventory. Date: 21 Nov. 1770. Rec.: 20 Aug.
1771. William Drew, Robert Hunnicutt and William Holt, Appraisers.

Page 156:   THOMAS BARHAM. Account Current. Date: July 1765. Rec.:
20 Aug. 1771. John Pettway presents. Mentions payments to
widow, and orphan Elizabeth Barham. William Heath and John
Stewart, Auditors.

Page 157:   WILLIAM SEWARD of Southwark Parish, Surry. Will. Date: 1
June 1769. Rec.: 20 Aug. 1771. Sister: Ann Thomas. Nephews: William Caufield Seward, John, Edwin, Thomas Seward
and John Thomas. Brother-in-law: William Drew. Friends:
William Hart and Richard Baker. Neice: Mary Seward. Witnesses: John Salter, Harwood Coman, and Samuel Shacklet.
(William Drew and William Hart, Executors.).

Page 159:   Mrs. HANNAH BROWN. Inventory. Date: 18 June 1771. Rec.:
17 Sept. 1771. John Watkins, Phil West and John Collier,
Appraisers.

Page 162:   Cabin Point Tobacco Warehouse Inspection.

Page 163:   Gray's Creek Tobacco Warehouse Inspection.

Page 163:   WILLIAM EDWARDS of Southwark Parish, Surry, Gent. Will.
Date: 9 June 1771. Rec.: 19 Nov. 1771. Martha Edwards,
and Nicholas Faulcon, Jr., Executors. Wife: Martha. Nephews: William Edwards (not 21); William and James Walker;
Micajah, Richard and Benjamin Edwards (none 21). Neices:
Elizabeth Harriss; Mary Butts, wife of Thomas; Ann Edwards,
daughter of Micajah (not 21); Lucy, Elizabeth and Martha

(Page 163 - EDWARDS cont'd.): Edwards (not 21). Brother: Micajah, deceased. Witnesses: William Hay, John Faulcon and James Sterling; Will Ward.

Page 166: JOHN INMAN of Surry. Will. Date: 23 Dec. 1767. Rec.: 19 Nov. 1771. Samuel Warren, Executor. Wife: Ann. Sons: James (not of age), John, Isaam (not of age). Daughters: Elizabeth Long, Hannah Warren, Priscilla Wallis, and Mary Inman (not of age). Grandson: John Ogburn. Friend: Samuel Bailey. Witnesses: Michael Bailey, ---- Hamlin and Mark Nicolson.

Page 168: ELIZABETH EDWARDS of Southwark Parish, Surry. Will. Date: 21 Sept. 1771. Rec.: 19 Nov. 1771. Joel Thompson, Executor. Daughters: Mary Edmunds, wife of Nicholas; Mildred Williams, wife of Lewis. Sons: James Seward; Benjamin Edwards. Grandchildren: Jesse Barham and Fanny Clark. Fr.: James Price. Witnesses: Richard Rowell and Lewis Williams.

Page 170: THOMAS COLLIER of Surry. Will. Date: 26 Sept. 1771. Rec.: 19 Nov. 1771. Thomas Bailey, Executor. Daughters: Mary Bailey; Elizabeth and Sarah Collier. Son: Moody. Wife: Charity. Grandson: William Bailey. Mentions: Moody and Sarah not of age; land in Southampton County. Friend: Mr. John Collier. Witnesses: John Watkins and John Watkins, Jr.

Page 172: MARTHA JUDKINS of Southwark Parish, Surry. Will. Date: 19 Jan. 1767. Rec.: (page torn). Sons: Charles, Joseph, Samuel and Jesse. Daughters: Mary Barham; Sarah Barham; and Ann Mooring. Granddaughter: Patty Thompson. Witnesses: John Davis, Zechariah Madera and Nathan Davis.

Page 174: JORDAN CLARY of Surry. Will. Date: (torn). Rec.: 19 Nov. 1771. Charles Clary, Executor. Brothers: James; John and Barnes (not of age); William and Charles. Mother: (unnamed). Sister: Sucky Clary. Mentions: Hannah Jordan, daughter of Matthew. (Will torn). Witnesses: William Nelson, John Davis and Dempsey Marlow.

Page 176: ANSELM BAILEY of Surry. Will. Date: 6 Apr. 1770. Rec.: 21 Jan. 1772. Samuel and Anselm Bailey, Executors. Wife: Mary. Sons: Anselm, John, Michael, Lemuel, Samuel and Benjamin. Daughters: Ann Hunnicutt, and Mary Bailey. Son-in-law: Samuel Pretlow. Witnesses: Arthur, William and Robert Holliman.

Page 180: ANTHONY EVANS. Account Current. Date: ----. Rec.: 21 Jan. 1772. Benjamin Evans and Richard Wrenn, Administrators. Mentions payments to: Benjamin Evans, Joseph Bennit for wife, Sarah Magget, Henry Davis for wife, John Cooper for wife, Richard Wrenn for wife, and Anthony Evans. Samuel & Anselm Bailey, and Willis Wilson, Auditors.

Page 182: Dr. PATRICK ADAMS. Inventory. Date: 21 Feb. 1770. Rec.: 17 Mar. 1772. John Lucas and John Andrews, Appraisers.

Page 187: ARTHUR BARKER. Account Current. Date: ----. Rec.: 17 Mar. 1772. Charles Judkins, Sheriff presents. Richard Cocke and Henry Cocke, Auditors.

Page 187: BENJAMIN COLLIER. Account Current. Date: 1770. Rec.: 17 Mar. 1772. Ann Collier, Administratrix, dec'd.; Samuel Moody, Executor. Mentions: payments to John, Lucy and to Ann Collier. Wil Salter, Auditor.

Page 189: MARTHA JUDKINS. Inventory. Date: 4 Jan. 1772. Rec.: 17 Mar. 1772.

Page 189:   JOHN HEATH of Surry. Will. Date: 25 Mar. 1772. Rec.: 21
            Apr. 1772. Richard and Lemuel Cocke, Executors. Sisters:
            Betty Bilbro, Lucy Harrison and Martha Heath. Wife: Ann.
            Brother: William. Witnesses: James Jones, Thomas Peete
            and Mary Jones.

Page 191:   RICHARD COCKE of Southwark Parish, Surry. Will. Date: 13
            Sept. 1771. Rec.: 21 Apr. 1772. Hartwell and Richarc Cocke,
            Executors. Sons: Hartwell, John and Nathaniel. Brother:
            Benjamin. Nephew: Allen son of Benjamin. Daughters:
            Elizabeth Thornton, Rebekah Taliaferro, Ann Brown, and Lucy
            Ruffin. Sons-in-law: Richard Taliaferro, William Brown and
            William Ruffin. Mentions: land in Goochland, Lunenburg,
            Southampton and Halifax Counties. Witnesses: Will Hay ,
            Henry Davis and Jesse Judkins.

Page 198:   JACOB CORNWELL of Surry. Will. Date: 27 Sept. 1770. Rec:
            21 Apr. 1772. Elizabeth Cornwell, Executrix. Daughters:
            Mary White, Mourning Trueblood; Agatha Cornwell (not 18).
            Sons: John; Aaron, Moses and Joseph (not 21). Wife: Eliza-
            beth. Witnesses: Stephen Bell, Edward Brown, Thomas Gwalt-
            ney and Samson Clark.

Page 200:   BARNES CLARY. Inventory. Date: 17 Sept. 1771. Rec.: Apr.
            21, 1772. William Drew, Jeremiah Pierce and Joseph Willson,
            Appraisers.

Page 203:   JORDAN CLARY. Inventory. Date: 11 Dec. 1771. Rec.: 21
            Apr. 1772. James Taylor, Jeremiah Pierce and Josiah Will-
            son, Appraisers.

Page 206:   HENRY DAVIS of Surry. Will. Date: 17 Oct. 1771. Rec.: 21
            Apr. 1772. Amith Davis, William Crews, and John Hartwell
            Cocke, Executors. Wife: Amith. Son: William (not 16).
            Mentions: all my children. Child in esse. Witnesses:
            Owen Matthis, Jesse Judkins and Nathaniel Cocke.

Page 208:   WILLIAM TAYLOR. Account Current. Date: 1771. Rec.: 21
            Apr. 1772. James Taylor and Richard Scammel, Executors.
            Mentions: widow and children. William Ruffin and William
            Nelson, Auditors.

Page 210:   Allotment of dower to MARY TAYLOR, widow of WILLIAM TAYLOR.

Page 211:   JOHN DEBORIX. Inventory. Date: 12 Feb. 1772. Rec.: April
            21, 1772. William Simmons, William Pully, Sr. and John
            Lucas, Appraisers.

Page 212:   JOHN BARHAM. Inventory. Date: ----. Rec.: 19 May 1772.
            James Davis, Jr. , Edmund Waller and Eth'd Lane, Appraisers.

Page 213:   JETHRO BARKER. Inventory. Date: 6 May 1772. Rec.: 19 May
            1772. Moses Hill, John Barker and John Avoriss, Apprais-
            ers.

Page 214:   Capt. WILLIAM SEWARD. Inventory. Date: 30 Sept. 1771.

Page 216:   Capt. WILLIAM SEWARD. Inventory. (Scotland Neck). Date:
            20 Nov. 1771. Rec.: 19 May 1772. William Nelson, William
            Holt and Robert Hunnicut, Appraisers.

Page 218:   HENRY JOHNSON of Surry. Will. Date: 27 Feb. 1772. Rec.:
            19 May 1772. William Johnson, Executor. Sons: Landon,
            and Henry. Wife: Rebekah. Witnesses: Jonathan Ellis,
            Henry Duggar and David Flowers.

Page 219:   PHILIP BURT. Inventory. Date: 11 Feb. 1772. Rec.: 19 May
            1772. William Simmonds, Thomas Sorsby and Stephen Sorsby,
            Appraisers.

Page 221:   PHILIP KING. Inventory. Date: 21 Mar. 1769. Rec.: 19 May
             1772. John Watkins, Matthias Marriott and Drewry Warren, Ap-
             praisers.

Page 222:   PHILIP KING. Account Current. Date: 1769. Rec.: 19 May
             1772. James Baird, Administrator. Adam Flemming, Archi-
             bald Campbell and Robert Hunnicutt, Auditors.

Page 225:   WILLIAM COLWELL of Surry. Will. Date: 16 Apr. 1772. Rec.:
             23 June 1772. Adam Flemming, Executor. Daughter: Josheba
             Glass. Witnesses: Samuel Russell and Francis Moreland.

Page 226:   FRANCIS LITTLE. Will. Date: 14 Oct. 1771. Rec.: 23 June
             1772. Sons: John and James. Wife: Mary. Daughters:
             Pricilla, Elizabeth and Martha Little. Witnesses: Richard
             Scammell and James Taylor.

Page 228:   HENRY JOHNSON. Inventory. Date: 21 May 1772. Rec.: 23 Jun.
             1772. Jonathan Ellis, William Maget and James Gilchrist,
             Appraisers.

Page 230:   JOHN JUDKINS. (Slave Appraisal). Rec.: 23 June 1772.

Page 231:   JOHN INMAN. Inventory. Date: 17 Nov. 1772. Rec.: 28 Jul.
             1772. William Evans and Lewis Pully, Appraisers.

Page 233:   HENRY DAVIS. Inventory. Date: 28 July 1772. Rec.: 28 Jul.
             1772. Jesse Judkins and Philip West, Appraisers.

Page 235:   HARTWELL COCKE of Surry. Will. Date: 29 May 1772. Rec.:
             25 Aug. 1772. John Hartwell Cocke, Executor. Wife: Anne.
             Sons: John Hartwell Cocke (eldest), Richard; Hartwell, Rob-
             ert, and Benjamin (last three not of age). Daughters: Mary;
             Martha, Anne and Elizabeth Hartwell Cocke (last three not
             of age). Brother-in-law: Robert Ruffin. Mentions: land
             in Goochland, Southampton Counties. Witnesses: William
             Browne, David Donnon and Thomas Fenner.

Page 240:   JOHN INGRAM. Inventory. Date: 23 June 1772. Rec.: 25 Aug.
             1772. Richard Rowell, Lazarus Holloway and James Seward,
             Appraisers.

Page 243:   JOHN THOMPSON. Inventory. Date: ----. Rec.: 25 Aug. 1772.
             Thomas Pretlow, Administrator. George Kem, Thomas Fenner
             and Willis Wilson, Appraisers.

Page 245:   Cabin Point Tobacco Warehouse Inspection.

Page 246:   Gray's Creek Tobacco Warehouse Inspection.

Page 247:   BENJAMIN JUDKINS. Inventory. Date: ----. Rec.: 22 Sept.
             1772. John Judkins, Administrator.

Page 248:   BENJAMIN JUDKINS. Account Current. Date: ----. Rec.: 22
             Sept. 1772. John Judkins, Administrator.

Page 249:   SARAH PETTWAY of Southwark Parish, Surry. Will. Date: 10
             Sept. 1772. Rec.: 27 Oct. 1772. Edward Hart, Executor.
             Daughter: Lucy Hart. Grandchildren: Edward, Joseph, Sar-
             ah, Jesse and William Hart; Sally Pettway. Witnesses:
             Nicholas Faulcon, Jr. and John Petway.

Page 251:   WILLIAM NEWET EDWARDS. Account Current. Date: ----. Rec:
             27 Oct. 1772. Etheldred Edwards, Executor.

Page 252:   REBECCA PRETLOW of Surry. Will. Date: 6 Mar. 1772. Rec.:
             22 Dec. 1772. Samuel Pretlow, Executor. Granddaughter:
             Rebecca Pretlow, daughter of Joshua. Son: Samuel. Wit-
             nesses: Carter Crafford, Jr. and Thomas Newby.

Page 253: JAMES PRICE of Surry. Will. Date: 11 Dec. 1772. Rec.: 22 Dec. 1772. Randolph Price, Executor. Son: Randolph. Daus: Cilviah Bell; Rebekkah Holt; Martha Holt, wife of Thomas; and Hannah Copland Price. Granddaughter: Hannah Bamer Holt. Witnesses: Samuel Judkins, Sr. and John Judkins, Jr.

Page 256: WILLIAM CREWS of Surry. Will. Date: 8 Apr. 1772. Rec.:22 Dec. 1772. William Clinch, Jr., Executor. Sisters: Amith Davis; and Edith Boak. Nephew: Robert Davis, son of Amith. Neice: Jenny Davis, daughter of Amith. Witness: Jesse Judkins.

Page 258: WILLIAM BARHAM. Inventory. Date: 16 June 1772. Rec.: 22 Dec. 1772. John Cocke, Randolph Price and Edmund Waller, Appraisers.

Page 260: THOMAS WHITE. Inventory. Date: ----. Rec.: 22 Dec. 1772. James Taylor, Jeremiah Pierce and Etheldred Edwards, Appraisers.

Page 262: BENJAMIN HOLT. Account Current. Date: ----. Rec.: 22 Dec. 1772. Nicholas Faulcon, Administrator.

Page 264: Mrs. ELIZABETH EDWARDS. Inventory. Date: 28 Nov. 1771. Rec.: 22 Dec. 1772. Richard Rowel, John Cox and Etheldred Lane, Appraisers.

Page 267: JAMES CARRELL of Surry. Will. Date: 12 Dec. 1772. Rec.:26 Jan. 1773. William Ruffin, Executor. Daughters-in-law: Ann Snipe and Sarah Barrom. Mentions: Elizabeth Ruffin, daughter of friend, William Ruffin; neighbor Alice Drew;Ann Newsum, daughter of William Newsum of Surry; John, Lucy and Silvier Snipe, all of Surry; Betsy Barrom, daughter of Peter Barrom; Molly Waller of Surry. Witnesses: Alice Drew, William Newsum and Robert Ward.

Page 269: STEPHEN LUCAS of Surry. Will. Date: 21 Jan. 1772. Rec: 26 Jan. 1773. James Kee, Executor. Daughters: Rebekah Cook; Mary Cook; Ann, Elizabeth, Sally and Susannah Lucas. Sons: John and Stephen. Friends: Henry Cook and John Lucas. Witnesses: Stephen Sorsby, John Jarratt and Stephen Collier.

Page 272: THOMAS WHITE of Surry. Will. Date: 2 Apr. 1769. Rec.: 26 Jan. 1773. Benjamin White, Executor. Daughters: Martha Little, Ann Holleman, Avis Harris, Olive Clifton and Sarah Presson. Sons: John, William, James and Benjamin White. Witnesses: Lewis Pully, William Evans and William Clinch, Jr.

Page 273: THOMAS WHITE. Inventory. Date: ----. Rec.: 26 Jan. 1773. Benjamin White, Executor.

Page 274: WILLIAM MADDERA. Will. Date: 25 June 1772. Rec.: 23 Feb. 1773. Joel Maddera, Executor. Wife: Elizabeth. Children: Christopher (not 21), Samuel, Bob, James, Silviah, Lenor, Elizabeth and Lucretia. Brother: Joel. Friend: James Rae. Witnesses: William Clinch, Jr., Samuel Moody and William Hamlin.

Page 277: JOHN BILBRO of Surry. Will. Date: 5 Feb. 1773. Rec.: 23 Mar. 1773. Betty Bilbro, Executrix. Wife: Betty. Sons: Thomas (not 14); Benjamin, Berryman, Burwell and Barnett. Mentions: all my children. Friend: Drury Barker. Mentions land in Bute County, (North Carolina). Witnesses: Lewis Williamson, John Justice and Sarah Justice.

Page 279: BENJAMIN EDWARDS. Inventory. Rec.: 20 Mar. 1773. Etheldred Lane, John Cox and Richard Rowel, Appraisers.

Page 280:   THOMAS JONES of Surry. Will. Date: (undated). Rec.: 23 Mar. 1773. Jane Jones, Executrix. Wife: Jane. Son: Scarbrow. Daughters: Rebekah Barker, Lucy Jones and Sarah Jones. Friend: Benjamin Ellis. Witnesses: John Barker, William Justiss and Thomas Barker.

Page 281:   FRANCIS LITTLE. Inventory. Date: 19 Mar. 1773. Rec.: Mar. 23, 1773. Thomas Pierce, Jeremiah Pierce and Josiah Wilson, Appraisers.

Page 284:   NICHOLAS THOMPSON of Surry. Will. Date: 2 Nov. 1771. Rec: 23 Mar. 1773. Joel Thompson, Executor. Daughter: Lucy Holloway. Granddaughters: Lucy, Charity and Sally Thompson. Son: Joel. Friend: Samuel Warren. Witnesses: Lazarus Holloway, Jesse Holloway and Elizabeth Inman.

Page 286:   Col. RICHARD COCKE. Inventory. (Halifax County). Date: -- Rec.: 27 Apr. 1773. William Thompson, Armistead Washington and John Thompson, Appraisers.

Page 289:   CHARLES HOLT of Southwark Parish, Surry. Will. Date: 9 Oct. 1767. Rec.: 27 Apr. 1773. Johnathan Ellis, Executor. Sons: William, Charles, Samuel and Henry. Daughters: Lucy Wall, Ann, Hannah and Sarah Holt. Wife: Elizabeth, daughter of Richard Presson. Witnesses: Samuel Judkins, Richard Ellis and Aaron Wall.

Page 291:   ROGER DELK of Surry. Will. Date: 10 Feb. 1773. Rec.: 27 Apr. 1773. Richard Hardy, Executor. Sons: William; Rhodwell (Rhodewell) (not 21). Daughters: Mary Mavery, Ann Allen, Lucy Lancaster and Elvirie Delk. Grandchildren: Moreland Delk; Nancy Delk, daughter of William; ch. of Mary Mavery. Witnesses: Richard Hardy, Charles Clary and Nathaniel James.

Page 294:   HARDY HARGRAVE. Account Current. Date: 1772. Rec.: 27 Apr. 1773. Michael Bailey, Executor. Mentions: legacies to: Thomas, Augustine and Olive Hargrave.

Page 295:   NICHOLAS THOMPSON. Inventory. Date: 18 Apr. 1773. Rec.: 27 Apr. 1773. Joel Thompson, Executor.

Page 297:   DRURY WARREN of Surry. Will. Date: 21 Feb. 1771. Rec: 25 May 1773. Frederick Warren and Joseph Warren, Executors. Wife: Elizabeth. Friend: Thomas Davis. Mentions: children to be schooled. Witnesses: Richard Respiss and Philip Thompson.

Page 299:   WILLIAM DEWEL of Southwark Parish, Surry. Will. Date: 20 Jan. 1772. Rec.: 25 May 1773. Mary Dewel, Executrix. Wife: Mary. Sons: James, Beary, Drury, Jesse, Richard and William. Witnesses: Stephen Sorsby, Faith Ellis and James Jordan.

Page 301:   JAMES CARRELL. Inventory. Date: ----. Rec.: 26 May 1773. William Ruffin, Executor.

Page 302:   DRURY WARREN. Inventory. Date: 25 May 1773. Rec.: 22 June 1773. Matthias Marriott, Randolph Price and James Davis, Appraisers.

Page 303:   SAMUEL BENNET of Surry. Will. Date: 6 July 1773. Rec.: 24 Aug. 1773. Samuel Warren and Joel Thompson, Executors. Dau: Brambley Hart. Wife: Mary. Nephew: Jesse Bennet. Son-in-law: Thomas Hart. Grandsons: Lemuel and William Hart (not 21). Witnesses: Henry Mangum, Britain Mangum, Cheziah Clark and Samuel Warren.

Page 307:   WILLIAM CREWS. Inventory. Date: 26 Jan. 1773. Rec.: 24 Aug. 1773. Matthias Marriott, John Watkins, Jr., and John Collier, Appraisers.

Page 308:   HENRY DAVIS. Account Current. Date: 1772. Rec.: 24 August
             1773. John Hartwell Cocke, Executor. Mentions legacy to Amy
             Davis.

Page 310:   Cabin Point Tobacco Warehouse Inspection.

Page 310:   Gray's Creek Tobacco Warehouse Inspection.

Page 311:   PETER REDBOND. Account Current. Date: 1768. Rec.: 28 Sept.
             1773. John Gray, and Henry Howard, Auditors.

Page 312:   CHARLES HOLT. Inventory. Date: 27 Apr. 1773. Rec.: 28 Sept.
             1773. Joseph Judkins, William Evins and John Wilson, Ap-
             praisers.

Page 316:   ELIZABETH NERN of Surry. Will. Date: 12 Sept. 1772. Rec.:28
             Sept. 1773. Mary Bage, Executrix. Daughter: Mary Bage. Last
             husband: Robert Nern. Witnesses: John Warren and Zach'r Mad-
             dera.

Page 317:   LUCY GRAY of Surry. Will. Date: 30 Dec. 1772. Rec.: 28 Sept.
             1773. John Gray, Executor. Brothers: John Gray; and James
             Gray (not 21). Witnesses: Matthias Marriott, Thomas Wall
             and Elizabeth Marriott.

Page 320:   MARTHA EDWARDS of Southwark Parish, Surry. Will. Date: 12
             June 1773. Rec.: 23 Nov. 1773. Nicholas Faulcon, Jr., Exe-
             cutor. Mother: Sarah Epps. Brothers: Francis, Peter and Ham-
             lin Epps. Sisters: Betty Jones, Mary Branch, Rebecca Royal
             and Lucy Royal. Nephews: Frederick and Cadwallarder Jones;
             William Edwards; and William Walker. Neices: Sarah & Martha
             Epps, daughters of Hamlin; Frances Jones, daughter of Betty;
             Ann Jones, Martha Jones (not of age), Martha Epps, daughter
             of Francis (not of age), and Martha Epps, daughter of Peter
             (not of age). Friend: John Harris. Witnesses: John Wes-
             son, James Forester and Lucy Clark.

Page 327:   MARY SPRATLEY of Surry. Will. Date: 19 Mar. 1773. Rec.: 23
             Nov. 1773. William Spratley, Executor. Brother: William
             Hamlin. Daughter: Ann Spratley. Sons: William, John, Ben-
             jamin, Thomas and Walter (not 21). Witnesses: William Clinch
             and Jacob Faulcon.

Page 329:   ANN SNIPES. Inventory. Date: (ordered) Nov. 1773. Rec.:22
             Jan. 1774. James Davis, Robert Pyland and George Pyland,
             Appraisers.

Page 330:   HENRY GRAY of Surry. Will. Date: 10 Oct. 1773. Rec: 22 Jan.
             1774. Henry Gray, Executor. Sons: James, Joseph, Thomas,
             Henry, William and Jesse. Daughter: Martha Gray. Wife: Sar-
             ah. Witnesses: James Edwards, Mary Edwards and Josiah Wil-
             son.

Page 331:   WILLIAM BARHAM. Account Current. Date: 1774. Rec.: 22 Jan.
             1774. Joseph Holt, Administrator.

Page 333:   ROGER DELK. Inventory. Date: 1 May 1773. Rec.: 22 Jan. 1774.
             Will Cofield Seward, William Holt and James Taylor, Appr.

Page 336:   WILLIAM DEWELL. Inventory. Date: 10 Dec. 1773. Rec.: 22 Jan.
             1774. Jonathan Ellis, Stephen Sorsby and James Gilchrist,
             Appraisers.

Page 337:   ELIZABETH NERN. Inventory. Date: 30 Dec. 1773. Rec.: 22 Jan.
             1774. John Watkins, Jr., Matthias Marriott and John Warren,
             Sr., Appraisers.

Page 338:   Capt. WILSON. Inventory. Date: 13 Oct. 1773. Rec.: 22 Feb.
             1774. Joseph Holliman, Executor.

Page 340: JOHN INMAN. Account Current. Date: ----. Rec.: 22 Feb. 1774. Mentions legacies to: John Inman, Elizabeth Long, John Ogburn; Ann Inman her 1/3 part, Isham Inman his part, Mary Inman her part; part given my wife by will---Samuel Warren, Executor. Willis Wilson and Robert Hunnicutt, Auditors.

Page 342: SAMUEL BENNETT. Inventory. Date: 22 Feb. 1774. Rec.: 22 Feb. 1774. Samuel Warren and Joel Thompson, Executors.

Page 344: REBECCA PRETLOW. Inventory. Date: (ordered) 22 Dec. 1772. Rec.: 22 Mar. 1774. Carter Crafford, Robert Hunnicutt and Carter Crafford, Jr., Appraisers.

Page 345: RICHARD JONES of Southwark Parish, Surry. Will. Date: 14 Feb. 1774. Rec.: 22 Mar. 1774. Nathan Jones and Hamilton Jones, Executors. Wife: Ann. Sons: Nathan, Hamilton, James, Richard, John, Robert and William. Daughters: Susannah and Ann. Witnesses: Benjamin Bishop, Moses Hill and Sterling Hill.

Page 347: CHARLES HOLT. Account Current. Date: ----. Rec.: 22 March 1774. Willis Wilson and Thomas Howard, Appraisers.

Page 348: ANN JONES of Southwark Parish, Surry. Will. Date: 18 Feb. 1774. Rec.: 22 Mar. 1774. Nathan Jones and Hamilton Jones, Executors. Daughters: Susanna Cureton and Ann Eldridge. Sons: John, Robert, William, Nathan and Hamilton. Witnesses: William Thompson, Thomas Cureton, Moses Hill and Edmund Ogburn.

Page 350: WILLIAM MOORING. Will. Date: 21 Mar. 1774. Rec.: 22 March 1774. Son: John. Witnesses: Benjamin Mooring and William Braddon.

Page 351: WILLIAM RUFFIN of Surry. Will. Date: 1 May 1773. Rec.: 26 Apr. 1774. John Ruffin, Jr. and John Hartwell Cocke, Executors. Wife: Lucy. Son: Theoderick Bland Ruffin (not 21). Mentions: my wife's two children: Elizabeth and (unnamed in Will), not of age; Col. Theoderick Bland, father of my 1st wife. Brothers: John, and Thomas. Friends and relations: William Browne, Richard Taliaferro, Jr., John Hartwell Cocke, Thomas Ruffin, John Ruffin, Jr. Witnesses: Nicholas Faulcon, Jr., Edmund Ruffin, Jr., Edward Archer, Lewis Williams and Edmund Waller.

Page 356: Mrs. MARY SPRATLEY. Inventory. Date Ordered: 23 Nov. 1773. Rec.: 26 Apr. 1774. William Clinch, William Smith and James Smith, Appraisers.

Page 361: ELIZABETH STITH of Surry. Will. Date: 3 Nov. 1774. Rec: 22 Feb. 1774. (further proven 26 Apr. 1774). Arthur Smith was granted Administration. Daughter: Katherine Cocke. Grandchildren: Allen Cocke; Katherine Allen Bradby; and Rebekah Cocke. Son: James Allen. Legacies to: Thomas Smith (the old family seal ring); James Rodwell Bradby; Col. Joseph Bridger (tankard marked ASM); Col. Philip Johnson; Mrs. Elizabeth Johnson; James Allen Bridger; Mrs. Sarah Bridger, wife of Capt. James Bridger; Mrs. Delk; Mrs. Alyce Drew; Mrs. Holt, wife of Francis Holt. Pall bearers: John Cornwell, Francis Holt, Nathaniel Sebrell and James Holt. Mentions: ring marked AAE; ring with T. Bray on it; my father's picture; Allen Cocke's grandfather Allen's aunts picture; the property of Mr. Smith's Estate. Godchildren: Henry Baker, Charlotte Mackie, Elizabeth Browne; Martha, daughter of James and Rebecca Taylor. Mentions: bequests to Southwark Parish, Free School at Smithfield. Trustees: Richard Kello, Arthur Smith, Thomas Pierce, William Hodsden, Col. Bridger and Miles Cary. Witnesses: Richard Hardy, William Philip Edwards, Francis Holt and William Edwards. Codicil. Date:

(Page 361 - STITH cont'd.): 4 May 1769. Witnesses: Martha Edwards, Martha Holt. James Bridger, Gent. refuses Executorship.

Page 368:   Mrs. ELIZABETH STITH. Inventory. Date: 9 Mar. 1774. Rec: 26 Apr. 1774. Arthur Smith, Gent., Administrator. William Drew, William Nelson and William C. Seward, Appraisers.

Page 372:   WILLIAM MADDERA. Inventory. Date: Mar. 1773. Rec: 26 April 1774. James Rae and Joel Maddera, Executors. William Clinch, Jr., Samuel Moody and William Spratley, Jr., Appraisers.

Page 375:   ALEXANDER BOAKE. Inventory. Date: 29 May 1773. Rec: 27 Apr. 1774. Charles Judkins, Matthias Marriott and William Smith, Appraisers.

Page 379:   ZACHERIAH MADDERA. Inventory. Date: 26 Apr. 1774. Rec.: 28 June 1774. Thomas Davis, Administrator. Charles Judkins, William Smith and Thomas Warren, Appraisers.

Page 380:   MARY SLADE. Inventory. Date: 22 Mar. 1774. Rec.: 28 June 1774. James Davis, Samuel Judkins, Jr. and George Pyland Appraisers.

Page 381:   SARAH PETWAY. Inventory. Date: 23 Aug. 1774. Rec.: 23 Aug. 1774. William Pyland, George Pyland and Joseph Holt, Appraisers.

Page 383:   WILLIAM MARRIOTT. Account Current. Date: Jan. 1767. Rec.: 23 Aug. 1774. Mathias Marriott, Administrator. Mentions: legacies to Benjamin Marriott's orphans. John Stewart and Will Cocke, Auditors.

Page 385:   Cabin Point Tobacco Warehouse Inspection.

Page 386:   Gray's Creek Tobacco Warehouse Inspection.

Page 387:   THOMAS KING. Inventory. Date: 25 June 1773. Rec.: 25 Oct. 1774. William Clinch, James Gilchrist and Samuel Moody, Appraisers.

Page 389:   MATTHIAS MARRIOTT of Surry. Will. Date: 13 July 1774. Rec: 22 Nov. 1774. Elizabeth Marriott and John Watkins, Sr., Executors. Sons: William (not 18) and Thomas. Daughter: Sarah Marriott. Wife: Elizabeth. Mentions: children to be educated; (monies) to the poor of the Parish. Witnesses: George Pyland, Charles Hanson, Mary Bage and John Watkins.

Page 393:   JAMES CLEVELAND. Account Current. Date: 1765. Rec.: 24 Jan. 1775. William Collins, Administrator.

Page 394:   Capt. THOMAS HOLT. Inventory. Date: 15 Nov. 1774. Rec.: 28 Feb. 1775. (Dinwiddie County). Thomas Barrette, Abraham Smith and Daniel Spain, Appraisers.

Page 396:   Mrs. EDITH BOAKE. Dower Salves(Slaves? or Halves?) Alloted. Date: 24 Jan. 1775. Rec.: 28 Feb. 1775. Nicholas Faulcon and Jacob Faulcon divide.

Page 396:   JOYCE CLARK of Surry. Will. Date: 28 July 1773. Rec.: 28 Feb. 1775. James Davis, Executor. Sons: Samson and James. Grandsons: William Clark (not 21); James and Samson Clark. Granddaughter: Lucy Thompson. Daughters: Mary White and Elizabeth Gwaltney; Lucy Harriss, Martha Lancaster and Winnie Davis. Witnesses: Willis Wilson, John Slade and Sarah White.

Page 398:   JOYCE CLARK. Inventory. Date: 27 Feb.1775. Rec.: 28 Feb'y. 1775. James Clark, Executor.

Page 399: JOHN ANGUS. Inventory. Date: 28 June 1774. Rec.: 25 April 1774. Robert Andrews, James Davis and Stephen Sorsby, Appraisers.

Page 401: JOHN JUSTISS of Southwark Parish, Surry. Will. Date: 11 Apr. 1774. Rec.: 25 Apr. 1775. John and William Justiss, Executors. Sons: John and William. Daughter: Elizabeth Justiss. Mentions: all my children. Witnesses: Thomas Howard, Henry Howard and George Cooper.

Page 402: HOPKINS HARRISS of Surry. Will. Date: 21 Aug. 1774. Rec.: 25 Apr. 1775. Hartwell Harriss, Executor. Wife: (unnamed). Son: Hartwell. Mentions: eight (8) children. Friend: Michael Bailey. Witnesses: John Hancock, Nicholas Wilson and James Inman.

Page 404: THOMAS WRENN of Surry. Will. Date: 31 Mar. 1775. Rec.: 23 May 1775. Richard Wrenn, Executor. Wife: Elizabeth. Sons: Richard, John and Thomas. Daughters: Mary Clary, Rebecca Washington, Jane Hart, Lucy Hancock; Sarah, Millea and Silvia Wrenn. Witnesses: John Atkinson, James Atkinson and Hartwell Hargrave.

Page 405: WILLIAM WOLELING (WALING) of Surry. Will. Date: 8 Feb. 1775. Rec.: 27 June 1775. Executor refused; Sarah Waling granted Administration. Sons: William, Michael, Drury, and John. Wife: Sarah. Daughters: Priscilla and Elender. Friends: William Bailey, William Andrews and Stephen Sorsby. Witnesses: Mary Andrews, Sarah Bailey and Benjamin Putney.

Page 407: JOHN BILBRO. Inventory. Date: 2 Apr. 1773. Rec.: 22 August 1775. Betty Bilbro, Executrix. James Hee, her Attorney. John Aviss, Moses Hill and Nathan Jones.

Page 410: THOMAS HOLT. Inventory. (Surry Co.) Date: 1774. Rec.: 26 Sept. 1775. William Cocke, Francis Moreland and William Collins, Appraisers.

Page 415: NATHANIEL JAMES of Surry. Will. Date: 2 Nov. 1773. Rec.: 26 Sept. 1775. Jeremiah James, Executor. Wife: (unnamed). Sons: John (not 21) and Jeremiah. Daughters: Mildred Kea; Sally, Betty and Lucy. Friend: William Cox, Sr. Witnesses: William Nelson and James Edwards.

Page 417: Cabin Point Tobacco Warehouse Inspection,

Page 417: Gray's Creek Tobacco Warehouse Inspection.

Page 418: ANN CRYER of Surry. Will. Date: 4 Oct. 1771. Rec.: 26 Mar. 1776. Son: Nicholas (Executor). John Watkins and Lucy Watkins, Witnesses.

Page 419: DAVID DREW of Surry. Will. Date: 13 Nov. 1774. Rec.: 26 Mar. 1776. William Hart, Executor. Cousins: Edward Drew Hart, William Ruffin Hart, and Mary Ridley Hart, children of William Hart; William Hart, son of Robert Hart. Mentions: Mary Drew Judkins, daughter of Charles; Elizabeth Blow, the daughter of Michael; Elizabeth Gray, daughter of Etheldred; Coufield Seward, son of William C. Seward. Witnesses: Richard Loyd and William Kea.

Page 421: JOHN THOMPSON's Heirs. Claims and receipt from Thomas Pritlow, Administrator of John Thompson, the balance of Account Current. Date: July 1774. Rec.: 26 Mar. 1776. Mentions legacies/payments: to John Watkings, Jr., Executor of John Thompson, Jr. William Clinch, and William Clinch, Jr., Auditors.

Page 422: BRUTON KEA of Surry. Will. Date: 29 Sept. 1775. Rec: 26 Mar.

(Page 422 - KEA cont'd.): 1776. William Kea, Executor. Wife: Sarah. Daughters: Martha Edwards; and Mary Kea. Sons: William and Robert Kea. Mentions: my grandfather Bruton's estate. Witnesses: John Bailey and Jo. Holleman.

Page 423: JOSEPH HARGRAVE of Surry. Will. Date: 31 Oct. 1770. Rec: 26 Mar. 1776. Jesse Hargrave, Executor. Wife: Martha. Sons: Anselm, Joseph, Jesse and Robert. Daughters: Hannah Moore; Selah, Mary and Martha Hargrave. Mentions: Meeting House to be used by Samuel, Anselm, Benjamin, Michael Bailey and Heirs and all others of Society. Witnesses: Samuel Bailey, Thomas Hargrave and Benjamin Hargrave.

Page 427: TENHAM GEORGE of Surry. Will. Date: 13 Oct. 1775. Rec.: 26 Mar. 1776. William George, Executor. Father: (unnamed). Brothers: William and Frederick. Witnesses: William Browne, John Jarques and William Hamelton.

Page 428: JOSEPH HARGRAVE, JR. of Surry. Will. Date: 10 Aug. 1775.Rec: 26 Mar. 1776. Jesse and Robert Hargrave, Executors. Wife: Mary. Sons: Lemuel, Samuel and Richard. Daughter: Elizabeth Hargrave. Brothers: Jesse and Robert. Cousin: Anselm Bailey. Witnesses: Benjamin Bailey, John Bailey and Daniel Pond.

Page 430: MARY GLOVER of Surry. Will. Date: 19 Aug. 1773. Rec: 17 Aug. 1776. Henry Mangum, Executor. Daughters: Elizabeth Mangum, Sarah Mangum and Mary Glover. Son-in-law: Henry Mangum. Fr: Samuel Warren. Witnesses: Lazarus Hollaway, Jesse Hollaway and Samuel Warren.

Page 432: MARY ALLSTIN of Surry. Will. Date: 22 Mar. 1776. Rec: 22 Oct. 1776. William Cocke, Executor. Nephews: Lewis and William Collins. Mentions: William Weathers, son of John and Elizabeth. Witnesses: William Cocke, James Stewart, Lucy Roseman, Sarah Cocke and William Simmons. Codicil. Date: 24 Mar. 1776. Mentions: Susannah Baker, daughter of Martin and Ann. Witnesses: William Cocke, Thomas Peter and James Stewart.

Page 434: TENHAM GEORGE. Inventory. Date ordered: 26 Mar. 1776. Rec: 23 July 1776. John Lane, Jr., William Spratley, Jr., and Benjamin Evans, Sr., Appraisers.

Page 436: BRUTON KEA. Inventory. Date: 6 Aug. 1776. Rec.: 27 August 1776. Joseph Holleman, Joseph Judkins and Samuel Judkins,Jr. the Appraisers.

Page 438: THOMAS WRENN. Inventory. Date: 3 Nov. 1776. Rec.: 27 Aug. 1776. Isham Inman, John Atkinson and David Andrews, Appraisers.

Page 440: NATHANIEL JAMES. Inventory. Date: 10 Aug. 1776. Rec.: 27 Aug. 1776. James Smith, William Riggan and William Lane, Appraisers.

Page 442: HENRY DAVIS, SR. Account Current. Date: 1768. Rec.: 22 Oct. 1776. Etheldred Gray, Executor. Mentions payments to: Benjamin Ezell for wife; Benjamin Ezell, guardian of James Davis; James Taylor for wife; James Taylor, guardian of Elizabeth Davis; Ann Davis; Benjamin Davis; William Taylor for wife; William Taylor, guardian for Silvia Davis; Isham Davis; Randolph Davis; Matthias Marriott and Benjamin Davis for Henry Davis; Thomas Marriott, guardian of Marriott Davis; and William Davis. James Kee and Lemuel Cocke, Auditors.

Page 444: WILLIAM CREWS. Account Current. Date: 1773. Rec.: 22 Oct. 1776. William Clinch, Jr., Executor. William Cocke and Josiah Wilson, Auditors.

Page 446:   ELIZABETH EDWARDS. Account Current. Date: ----. Rec.: 22 Oct. 1776. Joel Thompson, Executor. Mentions: payments to Mary Edmunds' legacy; Lewis Williams; Benjamin Edwards' legacy; and James Seward. John Wesson and Goddrich Wilson, Auditors.

Page 448:   WILLIAM BURT of Surry. Will. Date: 3 Apr. 1776. Rec.: 26 Nov. 1776. John Cole and Henry Moring, Executors. Sons: Edward; and Harrod (not 21). Daughters: Marget Burt; Elizabeth Cole; and Anne Judkins Burt. Son: John Cole. Witnesses: Henry Moring, Rebekah Moring and Becky Thompson.

Page 449:   WILLIAM NEWSUM of Surry. Will. Date: 20 June 1775. Rec: 26 Nov. 1776. Carter Crafford, Sr., Executor. Daughters: Mary, Sarah and Ann Newsum. Sons: Thomas and Joel. Friend: Carter Crafford, Jr. Witnesses: Edmund Waller and Henry Crafford.

Page 450:   SAMUEL MOODY of Surry. Will. Date: 9 Apr. 1776. Rec.: 26 Nov. 1776. Henry Mooring and William Smith, Executors. Wife: Hannah. Son: Blanks. Daughters: Rebecca and Mary Moody (not of age). Friend: William Clinch, Jr. Witnesses: Elizabeth Madera, Rebecca Hamlin, William Clinch, Jr. and Benjamin Spratley.

Page 452:   THOMAS COLLIER. Inventory. Date: 24 Mar. 1772. Rec: 28 Jan. 1777. John Watkins, John Watkins, Jr. and John Bartle, Appraisers.

Page 454:   THOMAS COLLIER. Inventory (Southampton Co.) Date: 15 Dec. 1772. Rec.: 28 Jan. 1777. James Moore, Benjamin Clifton and John Meacum, Appraisers.

Page 455:   THOMAS BAILEY. Inventory. Date: 10 Feb. 1772. Rec: 28 Jan. 1777. John Watkings, William Clinch and John Lucas, Appraisers.

Page 457:   MICHAEL NICHOLSON of Surry. Will. Date: 6 Mar. 1775. Rec: 28 Jan. 1777. Harris and John Nicholson, Executors. Wife: (deceased). Sons: George (not 16); Robert, Michael and Chisman. Daughter: Mary Nicholson. Brothers: Harris, Mark and John. Witnesses: Thomas Cocke, Nathaniel Sebrell and Robert Lamb.

Page 458:   MICHAEL NICHOLSON. Inventory. Date: ----. Rec.: 28 January 1777. Harris and John Nicholson, Executors.

Page 459:   ADAM FLEMING. Will. Date: 19 Jan. 1777. Rec.: 25 Mar. 1777. James Willison, Executor. Sisters: Katherine and Williammina Fleming. Brother: Malcom. Mentions: James Willison; business of Mess'rs. Glasford, Gordon, Monbath & Co., Merchants of Glasgow. Friends: Benjamin Harrison, Jr. of Brandon, William Allen, Esq., and Archibald Dunlop, Esq. Witnesses: George Kerr, Susanna Buchanan, Mary J'Anson, Alexander Leslie and Archibald Dunlop.

Page 460:   WILLIAM PULLEY the elder, of Southwark Parish, Surry County. Will. Date: 29 Jan. 1777. Rec.: 25 Mar. 1777. Lewis Pulley, Executor. Daughters: Mary Fugler, Lucy Pulley and Ellinor McDaniel. Sons: Lewis and William. Grandson: Richard Fugler. Witnesses: William Collins and Thomas Sorsby.

Page 460:   THOMAS FISHER of Surry. Will. Date: 30 Jan. 1777. Rec: 25 Mar. 1777. Maj. Colin Campbell, Executor. Son: Edward (serving his country in the War). Grandchildren: five (5) unnamed children of Benjamin Ramsay and Anney, of James City. Friend: Randolph King. Witnesses: Thomas Barker, James Rae.

Page 461:   JOHN EDWARDS. Inventory. Date: 7 Oct. 1775. Rec.: 25 March

Page 461: WILLIAM THORP. Inventory. Date: 3 June 1775. Rec.: 27 May 1777. William Holt, William C. Seward and Samuel Bristow, Appraisers.

Page 462: HENRY COCKE of Southwark Parish, Surry. Will. Date: July 6, 1776. Rec.: 27 May 1777. Lemuel Cocke, Executor. Wife: Katherine. Sons: Lemuel; David, and Henry (last two not of age). Daughters: Elizabeth and Katharine. Mentions: tablespoons marked TH; part of Capt. Thomas Holt's estate that is my share. Friends: Lemuel Cocke, Augustine Willis, William Harris, Thomas Harris and Thomas Peete. Witnesses: John Cargill, James Larke, Thomas Peete and William Parker.

Page 463: JOHN BARKER of Surry. Will. Date: 30 Dec. 1775. Rec.: 27 May 1777. Lucy Barker, Executrix. Sons: John, Thomas and Ambrose. Daughters: Ann Barker, and Winney Jestis. Wife: Lucy. Mentions: my portion of negroes in the possession of Elizabeth Reeks given her for life by Thomas Reeks and others to descend to Sarah, Mary, Charles and Philip Reeks and myself. Friend: Philip Reeks. Witnesses: James Kee, Doiley Kee and Robert Lanier.

Page 464: GEORGE PYLAND. Inventory. Date: 28 Jan. 1777 (ordered). Rec.: 27 May 1777. Samuel Judkins, John Pettway and Randolph Price, Appraisers.

Page 465: JAMES ATKINSON. Inventory. Date: 10 Dec. 1776. Rec.: 27 May 1777. John Atkinson, Administrator. John Wrenn, Thomas Wrenn and William Evans, Appraisers.

Page 466: HOPKIN HARRIS. Inventory. Hartwell Harris, Administrator. Date: 14 Feb. 1777. Rec.: 27 May 1777. John Wilson, James Harris and William Evans, Appraisers.

Page 466: BENJAMIN HARRIS. Inventory. Date: 14 Feb. 1777. Rec.: 27 May 1777. Hartwell Harris, Administrator. John Wilson, William Evans and James Harris, Appraisers.

Page 466: SAMUEL MOODY. Inventory. Date: 14 Dec. 1776. Rec.: 22 Jul. 1777. William Clinch, Jr., John Batts and James Smith (now deceased), Appraisers.

Page 467: HENRY COLLIER of Southwark Parish, Surry. Will. Date: 30 May 1777. Rec.: 22 July 1777. Joseph Cheatham, Executor. Wife: Dinah. Daughters: Ann Marks, wife of John Marks of Henrico County; Lucy Baldwing; Martha Forster, wife of Arthur Forster of Southampton County; Sarah Bailey, wife of William Bailey of Surry; and Rebecca Cheatham, wife of Joseph Cheatham of Surry. Witnesses: William Simmons, Littleberry Dewell, John Collier and Faithy Dewell.

Page 468: THOMAS BADGETT of Surry. Will. Date: 5 June 1777. Rec.: 22 July 1777. Lewis Pulley, Executor. Son: John Badgett. Daughters: Elizabeth Badgett and Ann Partin. Wife: (not named). Witnesses: Jonathan Ellis, Elizabeth Pulley and Richard Ellis.

Page 469: WILLIAM PILAND of Southwark Parish, Surry. Will. Date: 8 Dec. 1776. Rec.: 22 July 1777. James Davis, Executor. Wife: (unnamed) Sons: William, John and Thomas. Daughters: Mary Piland and Lucy Slade. Witnesses: Etheldred Lane, Robert Pyland and James Davis.

Page 469: JAMES PRICE. Inventory. Date: 3 Jan. 1773. Rec.: 22 July 1777. Randolph Price, Executor. Thomas Davis, George Pyland and Frederick Warren, Appraisers.

Page 470:   THOMAS FISHER. Inventory. Date: 1 Apr. 1777. Rec.: 22 Jul. 1777. Amos Sledge, Thomas Bishop and Swan Lunsford, Appr.

Page 471:   JOHN WATKINS, SR. of Surry. Will. Date: 7 Apr. 1777. Rec.: 22 Jul. 1777. Robert Watkins, Executor. Sons: Robert, Nicolson; and John (not of age). Wife: Lucy. Daughters: Sarah, Dolly and Lilly. Mentions: when children come of age.Son-in-law: Richard Yarbrough. Witnesses: Archibald Campbell, Nicholas Faulcon, Jr., and Fanny Bailey.

Page 472:   JAMES SIMPSON of Southwark Parish, Surry. Will. Date: 21 Jan. 1777. Rec.: 26 Aug. 1777. Ann Simpson, Executrix.Wife: Ann. Witnesses: William Drew and William C. Seward.

Page 472:   CHRISTOPHER BURN of Surry. Will. Date: 7 May 1776. Rec: 26 Aug. 1777. Mother: (unnamed). Brother: Lewis. Friend: Lazarus Hollaway. Mentions: Elizabeth Hunecut. Witnesses: Jesse and Job Hollaway.

Page 473:   JOSEPH CARY. Inventory. Date: 14 Oct. 1775. Rec.: 26 Aug. 1777. Thomas Sorsbury, Thomas Grantham and Henry Cook, Appraisers.

Page 473:   WILLIAM SAVIDGE of Southwark Parish, Surry. Will. Date: 16 Jan. 1777. Rec.: 26 Aug. 1777. Sarah Savidge, Executrix. Sons: William, James, Willis, Hezekiah and Edwin. Daughter: Rebecca Savidge. Wife: Sarah. Friend: William Smith, Sr. Witnesses: Henry Moring and Hartwell Savidge.

Page 473:   Cabin Point Tobacco Warehouse Inspection.

Page 474:   PHILIP THOMPSON of Surry. Will. Date: 7 Sept. 1776. Rec.: 26 Aug. 1777. William Clinch, Jr., Executor. Mother: (unnamed). Brothers: Nathaniel and William. Sisters: Rebecca and Ann Thompson. Witnesses: William Smith, Jr., and John Judkins. (Mentions: schooling for brother William).

Page 474:   ANN BELL of Southwark Parish, Surry. Will. Date: 11 Nov'r 1776. Rec.: 23 Sept. 1777. Micajah and Benjamin Bell, Executors. Daughters: Lucy; and Martha, wife of Sampson Clark. Sons: Micajah and Benjamin. Witnesses: William Hart and William Pleasant.

Page 475:   THOMAS EMERY, SR. of Surry. Will. Date: 18 Jan. 1777. Rec: 23 Sept. 1777. John Emery and James Emery, Executors. Wife: Sarah. Sons: James, Thomas and Wyatt. Daughters: Elizabeth, Sarah, Katey and Jane Emery. Brother: John. Witnesses: John Emery, William Johnson and Mary Emery.

Page 475:   MATTHIAS MARRIOTT. Account Current. Date: ----. Rec.: 23 Sept. 1777. James Belsches and Archibald Campbell, Auditors.

Page 476:   LEVETER JOHNSON of Southwark Parish, Surry. Will. Date: 12 May 1777. Rec.: 23 Sept. 1777. Peter Johnson and Hardy Sheffill, Executors. Daughters: Sally Johnson and Lucy Hudgings. Son: Levie. Grandson: Thomas Hudgings. Mentions: Thomas Johnson Muslewhite (not 21); all my children. Witnesses: Peter and Mary Johnson.

Page 476:   MARY GLOVER. Inventory. Date: 6 Dec. 1776. Rec.: 23 Sept'r. 1777. Henry Mangum, Executor. Joel Thompson, Willis Wilson and Richard Rowell, Appraisers.

Page 477:   WILLIAM SMITH of Surry. Will. Date: Aug. 1777. Rec.: 23 Dec. 1777. Wife: Lucy. Sons: William, Nathaniel, Willis; James, and John (not 21). Daughters: Martha and Betty Smith (not of age). Witnesses: William Clinch, Jr., Thomas Warren and William Dicken.

Page 478:	MARY BAGE of Surry. Will. Date: 5 Aug. 1774. Rec.: 23 Dec. 1777. William Salter, Executor. Legatee: Elizabeth Yates, daughter of Daniel of North Carolina. Friends: John Weston and Thomas Davis. Witnesses: William Clinch and Mary Clinch.
Page 478:	Mr. JOHN WATKINS. Inventory. Date: 24 Oct. 1777. Rec.: 23 Dec. 1777. John Watkins, Will Browne, Jr. and Randolph Price, Appraisers.
Page 479:	JOHN LANE, SR. of Surry. Will. Date: 11 Nov. 1777. Rec.: 23 Dec. 1777. William Lane and John Lane, Jr., Executors.Sons: William, Benjamin, John, Jr., Frederick; and Micajah (not 21). Daughter-in-law: Rebecca Lane, wife of Joseph, dec'd. Daughters: Lucy Smith and Sarah Lane. Grandchildren: Martha and William Judkins. Mentions: ch. of Joseph Lane, deceased. Witnesses: Jesse Cocks, William Cocks, Jr. , and Henry Smith.
Page 480:	Mr. WILLIAM BURT. Inventory. Date: 7 Dec. 1776. Rec.: 23 Dec. 1777. William Smith, Charles Judkins and James Smith, Appraisers.
Page 481:	CHRISTOPHER THORP of Southwark Parish, Surry. Will. Date: 8 Sept. 1774. Rec.: 23 Dec. 1777. Maj. William Browne and Nicholas Faulcon, Jr., Executors. Mentions: Housekeeper-Mary Gray; Dize Maddra, daughter of John of Surry. Friend: John Watkins, Sr. Witnesses: Charles Judkins, Henry Moring and John Watkins.
Page 482:	JAMES SMITH. Inventory. Date: 20 Feb. 1777. Rec.: 23 Dec. 1777. Etheldred Gray, John Lane and William Spratley, Appraisers.
Page 482:	WALTER SPRATLEY of Surry. Will. Date: 10 Apr. 1776. Rec.: 23 Dec. 1777. William and Benjamin Spratley, Executors. Brothers: William, John, Benjamin and Thomas. Sister: Ann Faulcon. Witnesses: John Wesson and William Smith, Jr.
Page 483:	Capt. THOMAS HOLT. Inventory. Date: 18 Nov. 1777. Rec.: 24 Feb. 1778. James Belsches, Archibald Dunlop and Thomas Peter, Appraisers.
Page 483:	JOHN WATKINS. Inventory. Date: ----. Rec.: 24 Feb. 1778. James Boisseau, John Boisseau and Benjamin Boissear, Apprs.
Page 483:	THOMAS EMERY. Inventory. Date: 28 Sept. 1777. Rec.: 24 Feb. 1778. Stephen Jordan, Peter Johnson, Jr. and James Sheffill, Appraisers.
Page 484:	NICHOLAS PYLAND of Surry. Will. Date: 4 Apr. 1776. Rec.: 24 Feb. 1778. Mary Pyland, Executrix. Sisters: Mary and Martha Pyland. Cousin: Rebecca Judkins. Witnesses: Samuel Judkins, Sr. and William Judkins.
Page 484:	SAMPSON CLARK of Surry. Will. Date: 10 June 1776. Rec.: 24 Feb. 1778. Martha Clark, Executrix. Wife: Martha. Sons: William and James. Daughters: Mary, Sarah and Anne. Friend: Thomas Gwaltney. Witnesses: William White, Thomas White and Mary White.
Page 485:	THOMAS BURN. Inventory. Date: 23 Feb. 1778. Rec.: 24 Feb. 1778. Richard Rowell, Jesse Hollaway and Jobe Hollaway, Appraisers.
Page 485:	PHILIP THOMPSON. Inventory. Date: 20 Nov. 1777. Rec.: 24 Mar. 1778. Will Clinch, Jr., Executor. William Clinch, William Riggan and Benjamin Spratley, Appraisers.
Page 485:	JOSEPH CLARK. Inventory. Date: 24 Mar. 1778. Rec.: 26 May

(Page 485 - CLARK cont'd.): 1778. Richard Rowell, John Cocks and John Judkins, Jr., Appraisers.

Page 486: MARY BAGE. Account Current. Date: 1777. Rec.: 26 May 1778. Wil Salter, Executor. Mentions legacy to Mr. Daniel Yates, guardian to heir (of Onslow County, North Carolina).

Page 486: MARY BAGE. Inventory. Date: 26 Jan. 1778. Rec.: 26 May 1778. Wil Salter, Executor.

Page 487: LUCY COLLIER. Inventory. Date: 24 Mar. 1772. Rec.: 26 May 1778. John Watkins, John Watkins, Jr. and Nicholas Cryer, Appraisers.

Page 487: THOMAS BURN. Account Current. Date: 1778. Rec.: 26 May 1778. Lazarus Holloway, Administrator. William Smith and Thomas Davis, Auditors.

Page 488: ELIZABETH PRICE. Inventory. Date: ----. Rec.: 23 Jun. 1778. Arthur Exum, Administrator.

Page 488: ELIZABETH PRICE. Account Current. Date: 1774. Rec.: 23 Jun. 1778. Arthur Exum, Administrator. Samuel Kello and Samuel Pitman, Auditors.

Page 489: WILLIAM DREW of Southwark Parish, Surry. Will. Date: 19 Apr. 1778. Rec.: 23 June 1778. Michael Blow and Etheldred Gray, Executors. Daughters: Priscilla Blow, Martha Hart, Rebecca Drew and Sally Drew. Wife: Mary. Grandchildren: Cofield Seward, William Robert Gray, Charles Gray, Etheldred Gray, Elizabeth Gray and Ann Thomas. Witnesses: John Holt, John Bennett and Joseph Harding.

Page 490: ANN BELL. Account Current. Date: 1778. Rec.: 28 July 1778. Micajah and Benjamin Bell, Executors. Charles Judkins and Jesse Judkins, Auditors.

Page 490: JOSEPH LANE of Southwark Parish, Surry. Will. Date: 18 Sep. 1777. Rec.: 28 July 1778. Samuel Judkins, Executor. Wife: Rebecca. Sons: Joel, and John (not 19). Child in esse. Witnesses: James Davis, Jesse Bennett, Benjamin Bell and Samuel Judkins, Jr.

Page 491: ROBERT HUNNICUTT of Surry. Will. Date: 19 June 1778. Rec: 28 July 1778. John Hunnicutt, Executor. Sons: John and Robert. Daughters: Marget Hunnicutt; Fanny, wife of John Nasworthy; and Pennelope, wife of John Smally. Grandson: Davis Price (not 21). Witnesses: Samuel Pretlow and Thomas Pretlow, Jr.

Page 492: WILLIAM PHILLIPS of Southwark Parish, Surry. Will. Date: 23 Feb. 1778. Rec.: 28 July 1778. Henry Crafford and Richard Rowell, Executors. Wife: (unnamed). Sons: Zachariah, William and Robert. Daughters: Elizabeth and Salley Phillips. Mentions: Ch. not of age. Witnesses: Edward Wright, Rebecca Wright and Joseph Bishop.

Page 493: ANN BELL. Inventory. Date: 1777. Rec.: 28 July 1778. Willis Wilson, Robert Bell and Thomas Gwaltney, Appraisers.

Page 493: LEVETO JOHNSON. Inventory. Date: 15 Oct. 1777. Rec.: 28 July 1778. Thomas Bishop, Swan Lunsford and James Shiffill, Appraisers.

Page 494: NICHOLAS PYLAND. Inventory. Date: ----. Rec.: 25 Aug. 1778. Mary Pyland, Executrix.

Page 494: ARTHUR HOLLIMAN of Surry. Will. Date: 17 Dec. 1777. Rec.: 25 Aug. 1778. Micajah and Arthur Holliman, Executors. Sons:

(Page 494 - HOLLIMAN cont'd.): William, Robert, Micajah and Arthur. Daus: Elizabeth, Ann, Charity and Rebecca Holliman. Granddaughters: Sarah and Mary Warren. Witnesses: John Bailey, Benjamin White and Thomas Holleman.

Page 495: MARY KEA of Southwark Parish, Surry. Will. Date: 6 Oct.1775. Rec.: 27 Oct. 1778. John Briand and Elizabeth Kea, Executors. Daughters: Mary Briand and Elizabeth Kea. Witnesses: Samuel Judkins and Joseph Lane.

Page 496: JOSEPH LANE. Inventory. Date: 7 Aug. 1778. Rec.: 27 Oct'r. 1778. Samuel Judkins, Executor.

Page 496: WILLIAM SIMMONS of Southwark Parish, Surry. Will. Date: 3 June 1778. Rec.: 27 Oct. 1778. Rebekah Simmons, Executrix. Sons: William, James Mason, and Thomas (not 21). Daughters: Elizabeth Mansell Simmons, Mary, and Rebekah Simmons (not 18). Friends: Mr. William Collins and Mr. Edwin Gray. Mentions: dispute with estate of Capt. Thomas Holt (grandfather of Elizabeth Mansell Simmons); land in Granville Co., North Carolina; land in Southampton County, - see will of John Simmons the elder. Witnesses: John Bell, Thomas Sorsby and John Lucas.

Page 500: WILLIAM PHILIPS.. Inventory. Date: 18 Sept. 1778. Rec.: 27 Oct. 1778. Richard Rowell and Henry Crafford, Executors.

Page 501: Cabin Point Tobacco Warehouse Inspection.

Page 502: JAMES SMITH. Account Current. Date: 1778. Rec.: 27 Oct'r. 1778. William Smith and William Magget, Administrators. Mentions: payments to son, William Smith; Nathaniel Smith, the heir of Susanna Smith; and Henry Smith's part. Charles Judkins and Henry Crafford, Auditors.

Page 503: FREDERICK BRYAN of Southwark Parish, Surry. Will. Date: 6 Mar. 1778. Rec.: 24 Nov. 1778. Jesse Bryan, Executor. Bros: James, John and Jesse. Father: (unnamed). Witnesses: Charles Judkins, Elizabeth Judkins and Rebekah Bryan.

Page 504: MARY KEA. Inventory. Date: 21 Nov. 1778. Rec.: 24 November 1778. Jesse Cocks, Joseph Judkins and James Judkins, Appraisers.

Page 505: RANDOLPH PRICE of Surry. Will. Date: 18 Oct. 1778. Rec: 24 Nov. 1778. John Wesson, Executor. Wife: Lucy. Father: James Price, dec'd. Son: David (not 21). Child in esse. Mentions: Robert Hunnicutt, grandfather of son David Price; the poor of Southwark Parish. Witnesses: William Hamlin, Thomas Holt, Jane Waller and Mary Pyland.

Page 509: JOHN LANE. Date: 30 Dec. 1777. Rec.: 24 Nov. 1778. William Lane and John Lane, Executors. Etheldred Gray, William Spratley, Jr., and John Judkins, Appraisers.

Page 511: NATHANIEL BENNETT of Surry, now in camp at Portsmouth. Will. Date: 28 Sept. 1776. Rec.: 24 Nov. 1778. Thomas Davis, Executor. Brother: William. Sister: Elizabeth Bennett. Mother: Mildred Williams. Witnesses: John Watkins, Jr., John Davis and John Judkins, Jr.

Page 512: RICHARD PUTNEY the Elder of Southwark Parish, Surry County. Will. Date: 22 July 1773. Rec.: 22 Dec. 1778. William Collins, Executor. Sons: James, Ellis, Lewis, David, Richard and Benjamin. Daughter: Rebecca. Granddaughter: Rebecca Putney, daughter of Benjamin. Witnesses: Martha Cary, Mary Minningtree, William Simmons and Randolph King.

Page 513: JOHN JUSTICE. Inventory. Date: 1 Apr. 1775. Rec.: 26 Jan.

(Page 513 - JUSTICE cont'd.): 1779. John Justice, and William Justice, present.

Page 514:   JOHN BARKER. Inventory. Date: ----. Rec.: 23 Feb. 1779. James Rae, Amey Sledge and Lemuel Cocke, Appraisers.

Page 516:   RICHARD GRAY of Surry. Will. Date: 7 Apr. 1777. Rec.: 23 Feb. 1779. John Gray and Jacob Person, Executors. Sons: John, Samuel and Henry (youngest). Daughters: Hannah and Jean Gray; Mary Jones; and Martha Thomas. Wife: Martha. Legatee: Frederick Gray, son of Lucy Gray. Witnesses: Mason Braddy, Charles Goodrich, Josiah Mangum and Henry Gray. (Mentions land in Isle of Wight County).

Page 519:   JOSEPH JUDKINS of Southwark Parish, Surry. Will. Date: 3 Oct. 1778. Rec.: 23 Feb. 1779. James Judkins and John Lane Executors. Son: James. Daughter: Sally Lane. Grandson: Judkins Lane. Mentions: John Lane. Witnesses: William Evans, Jesse Cocks, Henry Smith and William Cocks, Jr.

Page 520:   JOHN LANE. Account Current. Date: 1777. Rec.: 23 Feb'y 1779. William and John Lane, Executors. Mentions: legacies paid to - John Lane, Jr.; William and Martha Judkins. John Watkins and William Edwards, Auditors.

Page 522:   REBEKAH HOLDSWORTH. Inventory. Date: 18 Nov. 1778. Rec.: 23 Feb. 1779. Robert Watkins, Will Browne, Jr. and John Bartle, Appraisers.

Page 522:   Mr. JOHN WATKINS. Account Current. Date: 1777. Rec.: 23 Feb. 1779. Robert Watkins, Executor. Thomas Howard and William Irby, Auditors.

Page 5:   DINAH COLLIER. Dower in the Estate of Henry Collier. Date:
               -----. Rec.: 24 Mar. 1778. William Simmons and Stephen
               Sorsby divide.

Page 13:   Mrs. CATHERINE COCKE. Dower in the Estate of Henry Cocke.
               Date: 21 July 1777. Rec.: 28 July 1778. James Belsches,
               William Short, William Harris and Archibald Dunlop divide.

Page 40:   REBEKAH KEE. Dower in the Estate of Doiley Kee of Surry.
               Date: 6 Mar. 1779. Rec.: 23 Mar. 1779. James Kee, heir
               at law. William Clinch, Jonathan Ellis and William Maget
               divide.

Page 60:   THOMAS BADGET. Account Current. Date: 21 June 1777. Rec:
               23 Feb. 1779. Lewis Pulley, Executor. Mentions: Elizabeth
               Badget. Thomas J'Anson and William Evans, Auditors.

Page 61:   WILLIAM SALTER of Surry. Will. Date: 17 Feb. 1777. Rec.:
               23 Mar. 1779. William Salter, Executor. Sons: William &
               John. Daughters: Sarah; and Mary, wife of Joseph Holt.
               Friend: Anselm Jones. Witnesses: Mary Bage, Nicholas
               Faulcon, Jr., Henry Crafford and Richard Rowell.

Page 63:   WILLIAM DAVIS. Inventory. Date: 1 Dec. 1778. Rec.: 23 Mar.
               1779. William Clinch, Jonathan Ellis and William Maget,
               Appraisers.

Page 64:   MARY ADAMS of Southwark Parish, Surry. Will. Date: 28 July
               1778. Rec.: 23 Mar. 1779. John Pettway, Executor. Daugh-
               ter-in-law: Mary Adams, widow. Granddaughter: Elizabeth
               Adams. Cousin: Stephen Bell. Witnesses: Samuel Judkins,
               Samuel Judkins, Jr. and Joseph Judkins.

Page 65:   JAMES ATKINSON. Account Current. Date: 1776. Rec.: 23 Mar.
               1779. John Atkinson, Administrator.

Page 67:   WILLIAM NEWSUM. Inventory. Date: 23 Mar. 1779. Rec: 23
               Mar. 1779. Carter Crafford, Sr., Executor.

Page 68:   WILLIAM DREW. Inventory. Date: 4 July 1778. Rec.: 22 June
               1779.

Page 69:   SARAH SIMMONS of Southwark Parish, Surry. Will. Date: 19 May
               1779. Rec.: 22 June 1779. James Belsches of Surry, Execu-
               tor. Nephews: James Mason Simmons, William Simmons and
               Thomas Simmons. Neices: Elizabeth Mansel Simmons, Mary &
               Rebecka Simmons. Witnesses: Will Cocke and Thomas Sorsbury.

Page 71:   RICHARD PUTNEY. Inventory. Date: 8 Jan. 1779. Rec.: 22
               June 1779. John Jarrat, Thomas Shrusbury and William Bail-
               ey, Appraisers.

Page 74:   Mr. ROBERT HUNNICUTT. Inventory. Date: ----. Rec.: 22 Jun.
               1779. Carter Crafford, Jr., Henry Crafford and Josiah Wil-
               son, Appraisers.

Page 78:   HANNAH PITTS of Southwark Parish, Surry. Will. Date: 5
               Jan. 1779. Rec.: 22 June 1779. William Pyland, Executor.
               Legatees: William Thorn, Samuel Judkins, Sr., William Py-
               land and Thomas Passfield Pyland. Witnesses: Samuel Jud-
               kins, Sr. and Samuel Judkins, Jr.

Page 79:   THOMAS BADGET. Inventory. Date: 21 Aug. 1777. Rec.: 22
               June 1779. Jonathan Ellis, William Maget and William Sprat-
               ley, Jr., Appraisers.

Page 80:   Capt. JOSEPH NEWSUM. Account Current. Date: 1770. Rec.:

(Page 80 - NEWSUM cont'd.): 22 June 1779. John Wesson, Executor of Mr. Randolph Price, Executor of Mr. James Price, Administrator of Capt. Joseph Newsum. Benjamin Bailey and James Willison, Auditors.

Page 82:   Mr. JAMES PRICE. Account Current. Date: 1772. Rec.: 22 Jun. 1779. John Wesson, Executor of Mr. Randolph Price, Executor of Mr. James Price. Benjamin Bailey and James Willison, Auditors.

Page 83:   NICHOLAS PYLAND. Account Current. Date: 1779. Rec.: 22 June 1779. Mary Pyland, Executrix. John Wesson and Thomas Davis, Auditors.

Page 84:   RICHARD GRAY. Inventory. Date: 27 Apr. 1779. Rec.: 24 Aug. 1779. Willis Wilson, Richard Rowell and John Thompson, Appraisers.

Page 87:   DOILEY KEE. Inventory. Date: 27 Feb. 1779. Rec.: 24 Aug. 1779. Rebecca Kee, Administratrix. Burwell Sharp, Thomas Howard and Jonathan Ellis, Appraisers.

Page 89:   JOHN DEGGE of Surry. Will. Date: 20 June 1769. Rec.: 24 Aug. 1779. Anthony Degge, Jr. granted administration. Father: (unnamed). Mother: (unnamed). Brother: (one - unnamed). Sisters: (unnamed). Brother: Allen Smith. Witnesses: John Presson, Joanner Degge, Averillah Smith and Anthony Degge.

Page 90:   MICAJAH BELL of Surry. Will. Date: 14 July 1779. Rec.: 24 Aug. 1779. Wife: (unnamed). Sons: James Price Bell, John Bell and Samuel Bell. Daughters: Nancy Champion Bell, Rebeckah Bell. Child in esse. Mentions: children to be educated. Brother: Benjamin. Witnesses: William Hart and William Pleasant.

Page 92:   WILLIAM PYLAND. Inventory. Date: 28 Sept. 1779. Rec.: 28 Sept. 1779. James Davis, Executor.

Page 93:   HANNAH PITTS. Inventory. Date: 28 Sept. 1779. Rec.: 28 Sep. 1779. John Warren, James Davis and Jesse Barham, Appraisers.

Page 94:   WILLIAM SALTER. Inventory. Date: ---. Rec.: 28 Sept. 1779. Wil Salter, Executor.

Page 95:   WILLIAM SALTER. Account Current. Date: 1779. Rec.: 28 Sept. 1779. Wil Salter, Executor. Mentions: legacies paid to William Salter; John Salter; Anselm Jones; and Joseph Holt. Jesse Cocks and John Hunnicutt, Auditors.

Page 102:   WILLIAM WILLIAMS of Southwark Parish, Surry. Will. Date: 7 Apr. 1779. Rec.: 26 Oct. 1779. Frances Williams granted the administration. Sons: William, Thomas, John, Jeremiah and Walter. Daughters: Bathsheba and Elenden. Wife: Frances. Friend: Col. Allen Cocke. Witnesses: William Holt and Jesse Bryant.

Page 103:   JOHN DEGGE. Inventory. Date: 2 Oct. 1779. Rec.: 26 October 1779. Henry Moring, Hartwell Long and Lucas Long, Appraisers.

Page 104:   JOHN DEGGE. Inventory. (Gloucester County). Date: 20 July 1779. Rec.: 26 Oct. 1779. Matthias James, Isaac Smith and Josiah Foster, Appraisers.

Page 116:   BENJAMIN BAILEY of Surry. Will. Date: 23 Feb. 1778. Rec: 23 Nov. 1779. Philip West granted administration. Brother: Edward (not in the North). Sisters: Sarah and Hannah. Fr.: Benjamin Putney. Witnesses: Rebeckah Putney, James Kee and Lewis Putney.

Page 118: JOSEPH LANE. Account Current. Date: 1778. Rec.: 23 Nov. 1779. Samuel Judkins, Executor. William Clinch, Jr. and Joel Thompson, Auditors.

Page 119: HANNAH PITTS. Inventory. Date: ----. Rec.: 23 Nov. 1779. William Pyland, Executor.

Page 121: GEORGE DAWSON of Surry. Will. Date: 1 Aug. 1779. Rec.: 28 Mar. 1780. Margaret Dawson, Executrix. Wife: Margaret. Sons: \ Lewis and Charles. Daughters: Mildred Bunkley; Fathy and Elsibet Dawson. Witnesses: Charity Andrews, Daniel Moring, James Kee and Philip West.

Page 123: ALLEN WARREN of Surry. Will. Date: 8 Feb. 1780. Rec.: 28 Mar. 1780. William and Jesse Warren, Executors. Sons: William, Arthur, John and Jesse. Wife: (unnamed). Daughters: Martha White and Mary Murfee. Granddaughter: Rebecca White. Witnesses: William Hart, Eldred Edwards, and Stephen Bell, Jr.

Page 134: WILLIAM DELK. Inventory. Date: ---. Rec.: 28 Mar. 1780.

Page 137: JOHN KENNON. Will. Date: -- 10, 1778. (Second River). Rec.: 25 Apr. 1780. Allen Cocke, Gent., granted administration. Mentions: devisor is Lt. 2nd Virginia Reg't.; legatees are Mr. William Randolph, and sisters (unnamed). Richard Kennon, and William Burton swear to handwriting.

Page 139 COLIN CAMPBELL, Major & Adjutant,of Surry Will. Date: 21 Feb. 1780. Rec.: 25 Apr. 1780. Capt. James Belsches, Mr. Hamilton Jones Executors. Sister: Jane Campbell of Borough of Southwark, London. Neice: Jane Coupland, widow. Son: Archibald. Grandson: Colin Campbell. Legatees: Mr. William Lymberry son of Mr. Armado Lymberry, ship carpenter; Lady Campbell; Susanna Wills, daughter of Thomas Wills of Warwick County (under age); Archibald and Colin Wills, the sons of Thomas Wills (under age); Miss Rebecca Aitcheson, daughter of Mr. William Aitcheson, Merchant, (once in Norfolk). Witnesses: Nathan Jones, William Wylie, and Amos Sledge. Codicil. Nathaniel Wills.

Page 148: RICHARD PUTNEY. Account Current. Date: 1779. Rec.: 23 May 1780. William Collier, Executor. Mentions: legacies in father's will paid to - James, Ellis, Lewis, David and Richard Putney; paid share of father's estate to - Benjamin, James, Ellis, Lewis, David and Richard Putney, and Frederick Holt. James Ramsay and Willis Wilson, Auditors.

Page 149: WILLIAM PULLY, SR. Account Current. Date: 1777. Rec.: 23 May 1780. Lewis Pully, Executor. Charles Judkins and Willis Wilson, Auditors.

Page 152: GEORGE PYLAND. Account Current. Date: 1777. Rec.: 23 May 1780. Robert Pyland, Administrator. James Kee and Archibald Dunlop, Auditors.

Page 153: WILLIAM MADDERA. Account Current. Date: 1773. Rec.: 23 May 1780. James Rae and Joel Maddera, Executors.

Page 155: GEORGE THOMAS WHITE. Account Current. Date: ---. Rec.: 27 June 1780. Ann White, now Ann Pierce, Administratrix. Allen Cocke and Josiah Wilson, Auditors.

Page 157: Mr. RANDOLPH PRICE. Inventory. Date: 1779. Rec.: 27 June 1780. John Wesson, Executor.

Page 162: MILDRED PHILLIPS. Account Current. Date: 1780. Rec.: June 27, 1780. Richard Rowell and Henry Crafford, Executors. John Watkins and Samuel Judkins, Jr., Auditors.

Page 164: GEORGE DAWSON. Inventory. Date: 10 Apr. 1780. Rec.: 25 Jul. 1780. Margaret Dawson returns.

Page 168: JESSE BARHAM. Inventory. Date: ----. Rec.: 28 Nov. 1780. Thomas Lane, James Davis and James Seward, Appraisers.

Page 169: AMOS SLEDGE of Surry. Will. Date: 2 Dec. 1780. Rec.: 26 Dec. 1780. Lemuel Cocke, Executor. Wife: Ann. Sons: Hubbard, Peyton, Hamlin (not of age, to be schooled); Lamuel Clary and Amos Sledge. Daughters: Martha Epps; Dolly Sledge; Elizabeth and Rebecca Sledge (to be schooled). Mentions: all children not 21, except Martha Epps and Dolly Sledge. Fr.: James Kee. Witnesses: William Justiss, Joshua Bishop, William Johnson and Lemuel Cocke.

Page 172: WILLIAM PHILLIPS. Account Current. Date: 1780. Rec.: 26 Dec. 1780. Richard Rowell and Henry Crafford, Executors. Mention of payments to: Robert, Zechariah and Sally Phillips. Wil Salter and Willis Wilson, Auditors.

Page 173: ALLEN WARREN. Inventory. Date: 30 Mar. 1780. Rec.: 26 Dec. 1780. Jesse Warren and William Warren, Executors.

Page 176: JOHN LANIER. Account Current. Date: 1767. Rec.: 27 Feb. 1781. James Belsches, Administrator. Mentions division between: Robert, Lucy and John Lanier. William Short and James Kee, Auditors.

Page 177: SARAH SLADE of Surry. Will. Date: 29 Jan. 1781. Rec.: 27 Feb. 1781. William Slade and John Slade, Executors. Sister: Joice Slade. Legatees: Sarah Harrison; Martha Slade, daughter of William; William Slade, Jr.; Clemmy Slade, son of John. Witnesses: Capt. John Davis and Obediah Pyland.

Page 180: MICHAEL CASELEY of Surry. Will. Date: 2 Mar. 1780. Rec.: 27 Feb. 1781. Michael Caseley, Executor. Sister: Martha Caseley. Sons: Michael, John, Edmond, Hartwell, Jesse & Austin. Daughters: Nancy, Anner, Peggy, Molly and Betsey. Witnesses: James Kee, Stephen Sorsby, John Andrews and Richard Ellis.

Page 182: ELIZABETH BADGETT of Surry. Will. Date: 4 Apr. 1781. Rec: 24 Apr. 1781. Mr. William Collins, Executor. Legatees: Patrick Henry Adams and James Gilchrist. Witnesses: Richard Ellis, John Ellis and Pamela Andrews.

Page 183: Col. ALLEN COCKE. Inventory. (Goochland County). Date: 9 Mar. 1781. Rec.: 26 June 1781.

Page 183: Col. ALLEN COCKE. Inventory. (Quarter on North River, Fluvanna County). Date: 10 Mar 1781. Rec.: 26 June 1781.

Page 184: Col. ALLEN COCKE. Inventory. (Upper quarter, Fluvanna Co.). Date: 12 Mar. 1781. Rec.: 26 June 1781. William Browne and Samuel Kello, Executors.

Page 184: EDWARD WRIGHT of Surry. Will. Date: 23 Apr. 1781. Rec.: 26 June 1781. John and William Wright, Executors. Wife: Rebecca Wright. Sons: Willis, William, John, Isham, Edward and James (not of age). Daughters: Elizabeth, and Rebecca (not of age). Witnesses: Wil Salter, Ann Hunnicutt and Hartwell Hunnicutt.

Page 187: JACOB TANN of Surry. Will. Date: 1 Dec. 1780. Rec.: 26 Jun. 1780. William Dunn, Executor. Sons: Thomas and Jacob (not of age) Daughter: Martha Tann (not of age) Wife: (unnamed) Friends: James Barlow and John Harrison. Witnesses: John Harrison, William Dunn and Nathaniel Thompson.

Page 188: HAMILTON JONES of Southwark Parish, Surry. Will. Date: 23

(Page 188 - JONES cont'd.): Oct. 1780. Rec.: 28 Aug. 1781. Nathan Jones, Executor. Wife: Jacobina. Brothers: William and Nathan. Mentions: all my children when of age; land devised me by John Hamilton, late of Prince George County, dec'd. Friend: Capt. Lemuel Cocke. Codicil. Date: 30 Mar. 1781. Witness: none. James Belsches, Thomas Peter and Archibald Campbell swear to handwriting.

Page 191:   JACOBINA JONES of Surry. Will. Date: 22 Apr. 1781. Rec.: 28 Aug. 1781. Nathan Jones, Executor. Aunt: Elizabeth Willie. Mentions: children when 21; estate due me from my uncle, William Willie, dec'd. Friend: Lemuel Cocke. Witnesses: Ann Cocke, Elizabeth Jones and Lemuel Cocke.

Page 192:   BENJAMIN HARGRAVE. Will. Date: 14 Oct. 1780. Rec.: 28 Aug. 1781. John Hargrave, Executor. Sons: John, Hinche and Benjamin. Wife: Lucy. Mentions: all my children. Witnesses: Daniel Pond, John Pond and Thomas Handcock.

Page 194:   SARAH COCKE of Surry. Will. Date: 17 July 1781. Rec.: 28 Aug. 1781. Thomas Peter, Executor. Aunt: Martha Reed. Brother: William Cocke. Legatees: Gwin Reed, son of aunt Martha; Susuanna Buchannan, Elizabeth Stewart and Patsy Cocke. Uncle: William Short. Friend: James Willison. Witnesses: Thomas Peter, John J'Anson and Martha Read.

Page 195:   MASON BISHOP of Southwark Parish, Surry. Will. Date: 11 Nov. 1780. Rec.: 28 Aug. 1781. Joshua Bishop, Executor. Wife: Ann. Sons: Henry; Mason (not 12); and William (not of age). Daughter: Rebekah Bishop. Brother: Joshua. Friend: Capt. Lemuel Cocke. Witnesses: Hamilton and Jacobina Jones (both now deceased), and Nathan Jones.

Page 197:   HENRY BEDINGFIELD of Surry. Will. Date: 20 Oct. 1775. Rec: 28 Aug. 1781. Ann Bedingfield, Executrix. Wife: Ann. Mentions: all my children. Friend: Jesse Barker. Witnesses: Jonathan Ellis, Hannah Ellis (now deceased) and Richard Ellis.

Page 198:   JOHN GEORGE WILLS of Surry. Will. Date: 29 Aug. 1779. Rec: 28 Aug. 1781. Carter Crafford, Jr. returned; Jesse Gray granted administration. Sister: Alice Goff Gray. Brother: William. Mother-in-law: Mary Wills. Legatees: Mary Crafford, daughter of John, dec'd.; Elizabeth Crafford, daughter of Carter, Sr.; John Wilson, son of Josiah of Surry. Witnesses: Martha Taylor and Mary Fiveash.

Page 201:   JESSE JUDKINS. Will. Date: 25 Oct. 1780. Rec.: 26 June 1781. Henry Moring, Executor. Wife: (deceased). Brothers: Charles, Samuel and John. Father: John. Sisters: Mary Barham, Sarah Barham and Ann Moring. Neices: Becky and Sally Moring. Legatees: Hannah Moody; Beckey Lane; James Judkins; Thomas and Mark Judkins; John Judkins, son of Nicholas; Sally Lane; Frederick Lane's wife, Becky; Patty Warren; Thomas, Jordan and Mark Judkins; Katey Simmons. Mentions: to be buried in yard of father and mother; money due my wife from the estate of Capt. Charles Simmons to be divided between Mr. Urquhart, Mr. Kirby and Katey Simmons. Witnesses: Carter Seward, Elizabeth Holloway. (Further proven 28 Aug. 1781).

Page 203:   ANTHONY ADKINS. Will. Date: 3 July 1781. Rec.: 28 Aug. 1781. Stephen Jordan, Executor. Sons: (3), James (youngest). Daughters: (5). Brother-in-law: Stephen Jordan. Brother: James. Friend: Frederick Cooper. Mentions: none of sons are 21. Witnesses: Thomas Howard, William Thompson and Benjamin Ellis.

Page 205:   CARTER CRAFFORD of Surry. Will. Date: 14 Aug. 1781. Rec:

(Page 205 - CRAFFORD cont'd.): 22 Jan. 1782. Henry Crafford, Executor. Wife: (unnamed). Son: Henry. Daughters: Leah Hilliard, Lucy Pitt, Elizabeth Crafford and Martha Crafford. Granddaughter: Elizabeth Hilliard. Witnesses: Arthur Sinclair, Susanna Sinclair and Carter Crafford, Jr.

Page 207: WILLIAM PYLAND of Surry, soldier in the Continental Service. Will. Date: 18 Sept. 1780. Rec.: 22 Jan. 1782. John Wesson, Executor. Brothers: Thomas and John. Sisters: Lucy Slade and Mary Judkins (and children). Mother: Mary. Friend: John Warren, son of Thomas. Brother-in-law: John Judkins. Witnesses: Charles Judkins, John Warren, Jr. and Benjamin Barham.

Page 208: EDWIN JAMES. Inventory. Date: 13 Oct. 1781. Rec.: 22 Jan. 1782. John Lane, John Judkins and William Lane, Appraisers.

Page 209: MICHAEL CASELEY. Inventory. Date: 21 Mar. 1781. Rec.: 22 Jan. 1782. Jesse Cocks, Henry Howard and John Tillot, Appraisers.

Page 210: ETHELDRED LANE of Surry. Will. Date: 19 May 1781. Rec.: 22 Jan. 1782. Lucy Lane, Executrix. Wife: Lucy. Mentions: all my children; child in esse. Witnesses: Jesse Cocks, Philip Thompson and Thomas Pyland.

Page 212: GILSON BERRIMAN of Southwark Parish, Surry. Will. Date: 27 Mar. 1778. Rec.: 22 Jan. 1782. Mary Berriman, Executrix. Daughter: Anna Berriman. Wife: Mary. Friend: Richard Rowell. Witnesses: Mary Rowell and John Cox (Cocks), now deceased.

Page 213: JOHN GEORGE WILLS of Southwark Parish, Surry. Will. Date: 22 Jan. 1781. Rec.: 23 Jan. 1782. Matthew Wills, Executor. Wife; Mary. Sons: William, Matthew and Langley. Friends: Carter Crafford, Jr., and Nicholas Faulcon, Jr. Mentions: land in Warwick County. Witnesses: Edmund Waller, Josiah Davis and Julia Cook.

Page 215: EDMUND WALLER of Surry. Will. Date: 28 Aug. 1781. Rec.: 23 Jan. 1782. Benjamin Waller, Executor. Sons: Benjamin; William and Thomas (not 21). Wife: Lucy. Daughters: Elizabeth, and Mary (not 18); unbaptized. Friend: William Salter. Witnesses: John G. Wills (dec'd), Wil Salter and Hannah Easley.

Page 217: ALLEN COCKE of Surry. Will. Date: 20 Nov. 1780. Rec.: 27 Mar. 1781. Col. William Browne, Executor. Sons: Benjamin Allen Cocke, Richard and Allen (not 21). Daughters: Ann Hunt Cocke (eldest), and Catharine (both under age). Sister: Eaton. Relation: Richard Cocke, Sr. Friends: Micajah Young, Mr. William Burton, Samuel Kello, and John Tyler. Witnesses: John Hutchings, J. M. Galt, Francis Ruffin and George Nicholas. (Further proven 26 Mar. 1782.) Mentions: land in Fluvanna and Goochland Counties.

Page 221: JOSEPH CHEATHAM. Will. Date: 20 May 1779. Rec.: 26 March 1782. Capt. James Belsches and Benjamin Moring, Executors. Wife: Rebecca. Daughter: Suky Duke Cheatham. Sister's children: John Simmons, Thomas Simmons, Wiant Moring, Nancy Moring, Suky Moring and Polly Moring. Mother: (unnamed). Friends: Col. Richard Kello and William Collins. Witness: none. James Belsches and Lewis Pully swear to handwriting.

Page 222: THOMAS BARKER of Surry. Will. Date: 28 Sept. 1781. Rec: 26 Mar. 1782. Thomas Howard and Elizabeth Barker, Executors. Wife: Elizabeth. Mentions: all my children; child in esse. Witnesses: Rhoda Justiss and Suky Adkins.

Page 223: EDWARD WRIGHT. Inventory. Date: 15 Jan. 1782. Rec.: 26 Mar.

114

(Page 223 - WRIGHT cont'd.): 1782. John Wright and William Wright, Executors.

Page 224: JESSE JUDKINS. Inventory. Date: 26 July 1781. Rec.: Mar. 26, 1782. Henry Moring, Executor. John Davis, Jr. and John Warrin, Jr., Appraisers.

Page 228: JAMES DAVIS. Will. Date: 5 Mar. 1781. Rec.: 26 Mar. 1782. Thomas Davis, Executor. Wife: Hannah. Sons: John, Thomas, James and Henry. Daughters: Mary, Lucy, Jane and Ann Davis. Brother: Thomas. Witnesses: Thomas Holt, John Pyland and John Davis.

Page 229: GEORGE COOPER of Surry. Will. Date: 14 Oct. ---. Rec.: 26 Mar. 1782. Frederick Cooper, Executor. Wife: Mary. Son: Frederick. Daughters: Emelia Collier; Jane and Agnes Cooper. Witnesses: Ira Ellis, Martha Sebrell and Thomas Howard.

Page 233: Mrs. HANNAH PITTS. Account Current. Date: 1779. Rec.: 26 Mar. 1782. John Wesson, Executor of William Pyland, who was Executor of Hannah Pitts. James Belsches and James Gilchrist, Auditors.

Page 233: CARTER CRAFFORD, SR. Inventory. Date: 1782. Rec.: 26 Mar. 1782. Henry Crafford, Executor.

Page 234: JOHN G. WILLS., JR. Inventory. Date: 3 Aug. 1781. Rec.: 26 Mar. 1782. Josiah Wilson, John Little and James Taylor, Appraisers.

Page 235: SAMUEL PRETLOW of Surry. Will. Date: 11th month 14th day of 1781. Rec.: 23 Apr. 1782. Thomas Pretlow and Anselm Bailey, Executors. Wife: Kezia. Sons: Samuel and Benjamin. Daughters: Ann, Mary, Jane and Rebecca. Friends and Relations: Thomas Pretlow, Anselm Bailey and Benjamin Johnson. Witnesses: Edward Stabler and Joseph G. Bailey. Mentions his wife's property in North Carolina.

Page 238: WILLIAM CAUFILL SEWARD of Southwark Parish, Surry. Will. Date: 5 Nov. 1780. Rec.: 26 Mar. 1782. (Further proven on 23 Apr. 1782). Nicholas Faulcon and Jacob Faulcon, Executors. Son: Caufill (not 21). Daughter: Martha Seward (not 21). Aunt: Elizabeth Hamlin. Sister: Polly Harris. Brother: Edwin. Witnesses: Michael Blow, Joel Wall and H. Blunt.

Page 244: WILLIAM NELSON. Inventory. Date: 22 Apr. 1782. Rec.: 23 Apr. 1782. Anthony Degge, Rodwell Delk and Jeremiah Pierce, Appraisers.

Page 246: JAMES HOLT of Surry. Will. Date: 18 Sept. 1781. Rec.: 23 Apr. 1782. Elizabeth Holt and Archibald Holt, Executors. Son: Archibald. Daughters: Betty Drew Holt; Molly & Dolly (not of age). Wife: Elizabeth. Legatees: Martha and John Drew. Witnesses: Richard Rowell, Nathaniel Berriman and Nicholas Faulcon, Jr.

Page 248: WILLIAM PYLAND. Inventory. Date: 1782. Rec.: 23 Apr. 1782. John Wesson, Executor.

Page 251: HENRY BEDINGFIELD. Inventory. Date: 25 Feb. 1782. Rec.: 23 Apr. 1782. James Gilchrist, William Maget and Henry Gilbert, Appraisers.

Page 252: RANDOLPH PRICE. Account Current. Date: 1778. Rec.: 23 Apr. 1782. John Wesson, Executor. Mentions: Mrs. Price. Richard Cocke and Thomas J'Anson, Auditors.

Page 255: JACOB TANN. Inventory. Date: 1781. Rec.: 2̲4̲ Apr. 1782. William Dunn, Executor.

115

Page 256:   CHRISTOPHER MADDERA. Will. Date: 5 Sept. 1779. Rec.: 24 Apr.
             1782. Joel Maddera, Executor. Sisters: Silviah Scammell &
             Elizabeth Maddera. Uncle: Joel Maddera. Witnesses: Ann C.
             Thompson, John Collier and Will Savidge.

Page 257:   ABRAHAM MITCHELL of Southwark Parish, Surry. Will. Date:
             11 May 1768. Rec.: 28 May 1782. John Mitchell, Executor.
             Sons: John, Abraham, William and Thomas. Daughters: Rebec-
             ca Thompson and Martha Mitchell. Wife: (unnamed). Witnes-
             ses: William Drew (dec'd.) and James Putney.

Page 258:   JOHN COCKS of Southwark Parish, Surry. Will. Date: 13 Sep.
             1773. Rec.: 28 May 1782. Mary Cocks, Executrix. Wife: Mary.
             Sons: Benjamin, John, Thomas and James. Daughter: Ann Hol-
             leway. Friend: Thomas Lane. Witnesses: Etheldred Lane,
             Thomas Lane and Joseph Barham.

Page 260:   ETHELDRED LANE. Inventory. Date: ----. Rec.: 28 May 1782.
             Lucy Lane, Executrix.

Page 261:   WILLIAM DOWDEN of Surry. Will. Date: 18 Mar. 1781. Rec.:
             28 May 1782. John Avriss, Executor. Sons: Thomas (in the
             Army), John (in the Army), and George. Daughter: Elizabeth
             Dowden (not of age). Grandsons: James Dowden, son of John
             and James Bagley Dowden (not of age). Friend: Lemuel Cocke.
             Witness: Lemuel Cocke.

Page 266:   JOSEPH CHEATHAM. Inventory. Date: 25 Apr. 1782 (ordered).
             Rec.: 25 June 1782. Benjamin Moring returns. Stephen Sors-
             by, Stephen Collier and John Stewart, Appraisers.

Page 268:   EDWARD HART of Southwark Parish, Surry. Will. Date: 7 Jan.
             1782. Rec.: 25 June 1782. Ann Hart, Executrix. Wife: Ann.
             Son: John (not 21). Daughters: Elizabeth Pettway Hart; Pat-
             sy and Annliley Hart. Brother-in-law: John Watkins. Friend:
             James Judkins. Witnesses: Lewis Pully, John Judkins and
             Joseph Hart.

Page 269:   ETHELDRED EDWARDS. Will. Date: 17 Apr. 1781. Rec.: 25 Jun.
             1782. Jane Edwards sues for administration. Wife: Jane.
             Mentions: all my children. Witnesses: George Mallicoat and
             William Heath.

Page 270:   SAMUEL PRETLOW. Inventory. Date: 7 May 1782. Rec.: 25 Jun.
             1782. Thomas Pretlow and Anselm Bailey, Executors. Nicholas
             Faulcon, Jr., Carter Crafford and Henry Crafford, Apprais-
             ers.

Page 276:   SAMUEL JUDKINS. Will. Date: 1 Feb. 1782. Rec.: 23 Jul. 1782.
             William Judkins, Executor. Sons: William, Samuel; Joseph
             and John (not 21). Daughter: Rebekkah Judkins. Grand-daugh-
             ter: Martha Wilkins Judkins. Wife: Martha. Witnesses:
             Lucy Price, William Adams and James Adams.

Page 281:   MARTHA CLEAVELAND. Inventory. Date: 25 Aug. 1782. Rec.: 27
             Aug. 1782. James Belsches, W. Cocke and Thomas Peter, Ap-
             praisers.

Page 282:   FRANCIS MORELAND. Inventory. Date: 22 Aug. 1782. Rec.: 27
             Aug. 1782. James Belsches, Thomas Peter and Andrew Nimmo,
             Appraisers.

Page 294:   JOHN MADDERA of Surry. Will. Date: 10 July 1782. Rec.: 27
             Aug. 1782. James Kee and William Clinch, Jr., Executors.
             Sons: Micajah; John, and Thomas (not of age). Daughters:
             Rebekah, Nancy, Martha Maddera; Diecey and Priscilla Mad-
             dera (not of age). Wife: (unnamed). Witnesses: William
             Hamlin, William Dicken and Elizabeth Maddera.

Page 296:   JOHN JOHNSON of Southwark Parish, Surry. Will. Date: 18
             July 1782. Rec.: 27 Aug. 1782. Joshua Bishop, Executor.
             Wife: Mary. Legatees: Henry Johnson, son of Thomas of Sur-
             ry County; Moses Bishop, son of Thomas of Surry. Friend:
             Lemuel Cocke. Witnesses: Archibald Campbell, David Bishop
             and Benjamin Ellis.

Page 298:   PHILIP THOMPSON. Inventory. Date: 25 Nov. 1777. Rec.: 27
             Aug. 1782. William Clinch, Jr., Executor.

Page 298:   SHAROD CHARITY. Inventory. Date: 10 Aug. 1782. Rec.: 24
             Sept. 1782. Sarah Charity returns. Stephen Sorsby, John
             Burgess and Benjamin Ellis, Appraisers.

Page 302:   WILLIAM NELSON of Surry. Will. Date: 28 Mar. 1781. Rec: 26
             Mar. 1782. (Further proven 24 Sept. 1782). Ann Nelson, Wil-
             liam Nelson and Laurence Baker, Executors. Wife: Ann. Sons:
             William, John and Thomas. Daughters: Mary, wife of John
             Goodrich; Ann, Sarah, Hepsiba, Elizabeth and Catharine Nel-
             son. Witnesses: Richard Hardy, Francis Young and John Hun-
             nicutt.

Page 305:   MOSES HILL of Southwark Parish, Surry. Will. Date: 21 Jan.
             1782. Rec.: 24 Sept. 1782. Sterling Hill, Executor. Wife:
             Mary. Sons: Benjamin (dec'd).; Lewis, and Sterling. Grand-
             children: children of Benjamin. Witnesses: Nathan Jones,
             Robert Eldridge and John Carseley.

Page 319:   MICAJAH BELL. Inventory. Date: 3 Sept. 1779. Rec.: 22 Oct.
             1782. Benjamin Bell, Executor. James Davis, Thomas Gwalt-
             ney and Edward Brown, Appraisers.

Page 324:   JOHN COCKES. Inventory. Date: ----. Rec.: 24 Dec. 1782.
             Mary Cocks presents.

Page 325:   WILLIAM GREEN of Surry. Will. Date: 3 Oct. 1777. Rec.: 24
             Dec. 1782. Lazarus Holloway, Executor. Daughter: Sally
             Green (not 18). Friend: William Hart. Legatee: Mary Mid-
             calf. Witnesses: William Hart, Milley Holloway and Mima
             Holloway.

Page 326:   WILLIAM SHORT of Surry. Will. Date: 14 Sept. 1781. Rec.:
             24 Dec. 1782. William Short and Peyton Short, Executors.
             Sons: William and Peyton. Daughters: Martha, Eliza, Sarah
             and Jane Short. Legatee: Elizabeth Campbell (unmarried).
             Witnesses: none. John Cocke and James Belsches swear to
             handwriting. Mentions: land in North Carolina.

Page 330:   SAMUEL WARREN of Surry. Will. Date: 15 Sept. 1778. Rec.:
             28 Jan. 1783. Isham Inman, Executor. Wife: Hannah. Sons:
             John, Samuel. Daughters: Sarah, Elizabeth and Peggy Warren.
             Friend: Anselm Bailey. Mentions: all children are under
             age; division to be made by Quakers at Blackwater Monthly
             Meeting. Witnesses: Mary Wall, Elizabeth Inman and Jonathan
             Wall.

Page 332:   WILLIAM MORING. Inventory. Date: 24 Nov. 1774. Rec.: 28
             Jan. 1783. William Bailey, Thomas Sorsby and Maj. William
             Simmons (dec'd.).

Page 334:   AARON (ARON) WALL of Surry. Will. Date: 15 Nov. 1781. Rec:
             28 Jan. 1783. James Wall, Executor. Wife: Elizabeth. Daus:
             Elizabeth Wall; and Mary Wren. Sons: Joel, James, Jonathan
             and Thomas. Witnesses: Jo. Holleman, Jr., Jesse Brown, Jo-
             seph Holleman and Wilson Holleman.

Page 336:   MICAJAH BELL. Account Current. Date: 1780. Rec.: 28 Jan.
             1783. Benjamin Bell, Executor. Mentions legacies to the
             orphans: James Price Bell, Samuel Bell, Ann Bell, Rebecca

(Page 336 - BELL cont'd.): Bell and Elizabeth Bell. William Browne, Jr. and Thomas Cocke, Auditors.

Page 337:   JOHN HOLT of Surry. Will. Date: 6 Feb. 1782. Rec.: 28 Jan. 1783. Nicholas Faulcon, Jr. and William Clinch, Jr., Executors. Wife: unnamed. Daughters: 3 unnamed (not of age). Sons: John and Rowland. Brother: Josiah. Friends: Jacob Faulcon and Christopher Clinch. Witnesses: William Spratley, William Boyce, Carter Crafford, William Clinch and Michael Blow.

Page 339:   JACOB TANN. Account Current. Date: 1780. Rec.: 28 January 1783. William Dun, Administrator. Carter Crafford and Samuel Judkins, Auditors.

Page 340:   GEORGE COOPER. Inventory. Date: 22 Feb. 1783. Rec.: 25 Feb. 1783. Thomas Howard, Henry Howard and Michael Caseley, Appraisers.

Page 344:   THOMAS COCKE of Surry. Will. Date: 28 Mar. 1781. Rec.: 25 Feb. 1783. Susanna Cocke, Executrix. Sons: Acrill; Archibald, William, and Benjamin (not of age). Daughters: Lucy, and Nancy (not of age). Ch.: Acrill and Lucy's uncle: William Acrill. Wife: Susanna. Witnesses: Jesse Cocks, William Spratley and John Spratley.

Page 346:   Capt. WILLIAM COFIELD SEWARD. Inventory. Date: 22 April 1782. Rec.: 25 Feb. 1783. Nicholas Faulcon, Jr., Executor. John Wesson, John Pettway and Robert Pyland, Appraisers.

Page 348:   DANIEL POND of Surry. Will. Date: 28 July 1782. Rec.: 25 Feb. 1783. Harris Nicholson and Lemuel Bailey, Executors. Sons: Matthew, John and Daniel. Wife: Mary. Daughter: Hannah. Witnesses: John Hargrave, Hinchy Hargrave and Isham Inman.

Page 356:   WILLIAM EMERY. Inventory. Date: 15 Feb. 1782. Rec.: 25 Feb. 1783. Ruth Emery, Administratrix. Benjamin Waller, Phillip Thompson and William Ward, Appraisers.

Page 359:   WILLIAM GREEN. Inventory. Date: 2 Jan. 1783. Rec.: 25 Feb. 1783. Lazarus Holloway, Executor. Joel Thompson, James Bryant and Jesse Hollaway, Appraisers.

Page 360:   JACOB PERSONS. Inventory. Date: 10 Apr. 1782. Rec.: 25 Feb. 1783. James Davis, Joel Thompson and Thomas White, Appraisers.

Page 362:   WILLIAM WALDWIN, SR. Inventory. Date: 10 July 1775. Rec.: 25 Feb. 1783. John Jarratt, William Bailey, Sr. and William Andrews, Appraisers.

Page 364:   ELIZABETH MADDERA. Will. Date: 14 Aug. 1774. Rec.: 25 Mar. 1783. John Davis, Executor. Legatees: Mary Cariel; John Davis, son of Nathan, dec'd., (not 21), and his brother & sister; Nathaniel, Sarah, William and Elizabeth Davis, children of Nathan, dec'd.; John Davis, Sr. Witnesses: John Warren and William Pyland (dec'd).

Page 365:   SARAH SLADE. Inventory. Date: 24 Mar. 1783. Rec.: 25 Mar. 1783. Henry Moring, Capt. John Davis, Obediah Pyland and William Slade, Appraisers.

Page 366:   Mr. DAVID HUNTER. Inventory. Date: 3 Feb. 1783. Rec.: 25 Mar. 1783. James Belsches, Sr., Thomas Peter and Archibald Dunlop, Appraisers.

Page 371:   WILLIAM BURT. Account Current. Date: 1777. Rec.: 25 March 1783. Henry Moring and John Cole, Executors. Mentions pay-

118

(Page 371 - BURT cont'd.): ments to: Edward and Margaret Birt.   John
          Presson and William Maget, Auditors.

Page 373:   HARTWELL LONG of Surry. Will. Date: 25 Nov. 1782. Rec.: 28
             Mar. 1783. Joel Thompson and David Long, Executors. Wife:
             unnamed. Daughter: Rebecca. Sons: William and Hartwell.
             Mentions: all my children. Brother: David. Witnesses: Jo-
             seph Holleman, Jr., Wilson Holleman and Benjamin Briggs.

Page 380:   ELIZABETH MADDERA. Inventory. Date: 4 Apr. 1783. Rec.: 22
             Apr. 1783. John Davis, Executor.

Page 382:   WILLIAM PYLAND. Account Current. Date: 1782. Rec.: 23 Apr.
             1783. John Wesson, Executor. Mentions payments to: Thomas
             Pyland, John Pyland, John Slade, John Judkins and John Wes-
             son. James Belsches and James Gilchrist, Auditors.

Page 383:   Mr. THOMAS COCKE. Inventory. Date: Mar. 1783. Rec.: 27 May
             1783. Susanna Cocke presents.

Page 384:   WILLIAM THORP. Account Current. Date: 1783. Rec.: 27 May
             1783. Etheldred Gray, Administrator. Charles Judkins and
             Jesse Cocks, Auditors.

Page 385:   HARTWELL LONG. Inventory. Date: 17 Apr. 1783. Rec.: 27 May
             1783. Joel Thompson and David Long, Executors. Lazarus Hol-
             loway, Jesse Hollaway and William Slade, Appraisers.

Page 388:   BENJAMIN PHILLIPS. Account Current. Date: 1767. Rec.: 27
             May 1783. Carter Crafford, Sheriff, presents.

Page 388:   EDWARD BAILEY, JR. Account Current. Date: 1763. Rec.: 27
             May 1783. Mary Bailey, Administratrix of Thomas Bailey,
             Administrator of Edward Bailey. Mentions: part of father,
             Edward Bailey's estate by will (1768); part of Zechariah
             Madera's estate received of Edward Marks (1769).   James
             Belsches and Thomas Peter, Auditors.

Page 1:   ROBERT WARD. Inventory. Date: 3 July 1781. Rec.: 24 June
             1783. Benjamin Waller, Administrator. Joseph Holt and Rob-
             ert McIntosh, Appraisers.

Page 2:   JAMES RODWELL BRADBY. Account Current. Date: Sept. 1772-
             Apr. 1783. Rec.: 22 July 1783. William Hay, Administrator.
             Mentions: sales in Surry, Amelia and Cumberland Counties.
             James A. Bradby, Mrs. Catharine Allen Bradby (afterwards
             Mrs. Haynes.)

Page 6:   ALEXANDER BOAKE. Account Current. Date: June 1773-April
             1783. Rec.: 22 July 1783. William Hay, Administrator. Men-
             tions Mrs. Edith Boake.

Page 9:   HANNAH PHILLIPS. Inventory. Date: 20 May 1783. Rec.: 22 Jul.
             1783. John Wesson, Thomas Davis and John Ellis, Appraisers.

Page 11:   JOSEPH CARY. Account Current. Date: Oct. 1775-Sept. 1783.
             Rec.: 23 Sept. 1783. Randolph King, Administrator.

Page 11:   WILLIAM PHILLIPS. Additional Account Current. Date: 1781-
             1783. Rec.: 23 Sept. 1783. Richard Rowell and Henry Craff-
             ord, Executors. Mentions: hire of slave division to - Wil-
             liam Phillips guardian, Zechariah Phillips guardian, Rob-
             ert Phillips part, Sally Phillips part, and Elizabeth Phil-
             lips part.

Page 12:   BENJAMIN PHILLIPS. Account Current. Date: June 1765-Oct.
             1779. Rec.: 23 Sept. 1783. Francis Phillips, Administra-
             tor of Hannah Phillips. Mentions: coffin for Thomas Phil-
             lips (Feb. 1769), William Phillips estate, A. Phillips'
             widow's third. John Wesson and Thomas Davis, Examiners.

Page 14:   JESSE JUDKINS of Surry. Will. Date: 28 Apr. 1781. Rec.: 28
             Oct. 1783. Henry Moring, Executor. Sister: Ann Moring.
             Brother-in-law: Henry Moring. Witnesses: Charles Duncan,
             John Cook and Frederick Taylor.

Page 15:   WILLIAM WARD of Southwark Parish, Surry. Will. Date: 26
             July 1783. Rec.: 28 Oct. 1783. Nicholas Faulcon, Executor.
             Wife: Faithy. Son: Freeman. Granddaughter: Molly Brown.
             Nephew: Thomas Savidge. Friend: William Wilkinson. Wit-
             nesses: Mike Holt and Benjamin Waller.

Page 16:   DANIEL POND. Inventory. Date: 18 Mar. 1783. Rec.: 25 Nov.
             1783. Harris Nicholson and Lemuel Bailey, Executors. Isham
             Inman, Lewis Pulley and James Harris, Appraisers.

Page 17:   NICHOLAS FAULCON, SR. of Southwark Parish, Surry. Will.
             Date: 6 Jan. 1781. Rec.: 23 Dec. 1783. Nicholas Faulcon &
             Jacob Faulcon, Executors. Sons: Nicholas, Jacob and John.
             Daughters: Elizabeth Sebrell (wife of Nathaniel), Martha,
             Jane; Ann Spratley; Rebecca Hamlin. Grandsons: Nicholas
             Faulcon and Edward Faulcon. Granddaughter: Martha Seward
             (under age). Witnesses: John Petway, Robert Mackintosh &
             Joseph Judkins.

Page 19:   ELIZABETH BINNS of Southwark Parish, Surry. Will. Date: 5
             Feb. 1784. Rec.: 24 Feb. 1784. Nicholas Faulcon, Executor.
             Daughters:Priscilla; Elizabeth Hunnicutt; Martha. Sister:
             Hannah Crawley. Son-in-law: Robert Hunnicutt. Witnesses:
             James A. Bradby and Nathaniel Adams.

Page 20:   JAMES DAVIS of Surry. Will. Date: 9 Dec. 1783. Rec.: 24 Feb.
             1784. Stephen Sorsby, Executor. Sons: John and Samuel. Son-
             in-law: Stephen Sorsby. Daughters: Mary Atkinson, Susanna
             Kilby. Daughter-in-law: Martha Davis, and children of dec'd

(Page 20 - DAVIS cont'd.): son, William Davis. Grandchildren: Penelope
Davis, daughter of John; Nat'l. Davis, son of William, de-
cesead; Archibald, Nathaniel and William Davis; William,
Jane, Fanny and Mary Davis, children of Henry, dec'd.;
Martha Sorsby (one seventh of remaining estate). Witness-
es: Richard Ellis, Thomas Ellis and William Ellis.

Page 23: SUSANNA COCKE. Will. Date: 6 Dec. 1783. Rec.: 24 Feb. 1784.
Archibald Cocke, Executor. Sons: Archibald, William and
Benjamin Cocke. Mentions: deceased husband's will. Wit-
nesses: Thomas Howard, Elizabeth Sebrell and Rebecca Cocks.

Page 23: BUFORD PLEASANT of Surry. Will. Date: 13 Jan. 1781. Rec:
24 Feb. 1784. William Pleasant, Executor. Sons: William,
George and Thomas. Daughter: Abigail Pleasant. Grandsons:
Buford Pleasant, Burwell Pleasant, Thomas Pleasant and William Pleasant. Witnesses: Lemuel Bailey, Charles Holdsworth and James Holloway.

Page 24: Mrs. ELIZABETH BINNS. Inventory. Date: 5 Mar. 1784. Rec.:
23 Mar. 1784. Nicholas Faulcon, Executor. William Edwards,
Robert McIntosh and Benjamin Waller, Appraisers.

Page 25: ANN JARRATT of Southwark Parish, Surry. Will. Date: 8 May
1782. Rec.: 27 Apr. 1784. Benjamin Collier, Executor. Legatee: Martha Collier. Witnesses: John Watkins and Susanna
Cryer.

Page 26: LEWIS LONG of Surry. Will. Date: 12 Apr. 1783. Rec.: 27 Apr.
1784. David Long, Executor. Wife: Hannah. Sons: Hartwell
(dec'd.), and David. Grandchildren: Charlotte Long, Becca,
William and Hartwell Long (children of Hartwell); Charlotte,
Willis and Nancy Long (children of David). Friend: Joel
Thompson. Mentions: son Hartwell Long's widow. Witnesses:
Richard Rowell, Hartwell Hunnicutt and Isham Wright.

Page 28: SUSANNA COCKE. Inventory. Date: 8 June 1784. Rec.: 23 June
1784. Thomas J'Anson, Executor. James Kee, Thomas Peter &
Archibald Dunlop, Appraisers.

Page 30: FRANCIS MORELAND. Inventory. Date: 25 Mar. 1784. Rec.: 22
July 1784. Archibald Dunlop, Administrator. Thomas Peter,
James Willison and Archibald Campbell, Appraisers.

Page 31: PEGGY CLEVELAND. Inventory. Date: 29 May 1783. Rec.: 22 Jul.
1784. Archibald Dunlop, Administrator. Thomas Peter, Andrew Nimmo and James Belsches, Appraisers.

Page 32: ROBERT HARGRAVE of Surry. Will. Date: 14 May 1784. Rec.:22
July 1784. Jesse Hargrave and Harris Nicholson, Executors.
Brothers and Sisters: Anselm, Jesse, Celia, Mary, Martha
Hargrave; and Hannah Moor. Mentions: children of deceased
brother Joseph. Witnesses: Anselm Bailey, Lemuel Bailey &
Marriott Davis.

Page 33: LEWIS LONG. Inventory. Date: 19 June 1784. Rec.: 22 July
1784. Joel Thompson and David Long, Executors. Lazarus Holloway, Job Holloway and Jesse Moore, Appraisers.

Page 34: WILLIAM WILLIAMS. Inventory. Date: 10 Mar. 1784. Rec: 24
Aug. 1784. Jesse Cocks, Burwell Sharp and William Rose, Appraisers.

Page 35: WILLIAM HUNTER. Inventory. Date: 8 Mar. 1784. Rec.: 28 Sep.
1784. Thomas Peter and Archibald Dunlop, Appraisers.

Page 37: JOHN LITTLE of Southwark Parish, Surry. Will. Date: 20 May
1783. Rec.: 28 Sept. 1784. Jesse Little and James Brown,
Executors. Wife: Martha. Grandson: John Little. Granddaugh-

(Page 37 - LITTLE cont'd.): ters: Mary Savedge and Anne Kea. Daughter: Sarah Brown. Grandchildren: Sarah, Samuel, Jesse and Elizabeth Little. Son: Jesse. Son-in-law: James Brown. Mentions: Randolph Fitchett. Witnesses: Samuel Judkins, John Evans Judkins and James Judkins.

Page 38:   SAMUEL MAGGET JUDKINS. Inventory. Date: (none). Rec: 28 Sept. 1784. Samuel Judkins, Administrator. James Judkins, William Lane and Frederick Lane, Appraisers.

Page 39:   WILLIAM JUDKINS of Southwark Parish, Surry. Will. Date: 16 Sept. 1784. Rec.: 26 Oct. 1784. Samuel Judkins, Executor. Mother: Martha Judkins. Brothers: Samuel, Joseph & John. Sister: Rebekah Judkins. Witnesses: William Boyce, William Adams and John Pettway.

Page 41:   BENJAMIN HARGRAVE. Inventory. Date: 6 Dec. 1782. Rec.: 26 Oct. 1784. Isham Inman and Lewis Pulley, Appraisers.

Page 42:   JAMES DAVIS. Inventory. Date: 14 Feb. 1784. Rec.: 23 Nov. 1784. Stephen Sorsby, Executor.

Page 43:   BURWELL PETTWAY. Will. Date: 30 July 1780. Rec.: 23 Nov. 1784. Anthony Calthorp, Executor. Nephews: Charles and Edwin Calthorp. Brother-in-law: Anthony Calthorp. Witnesses: Joel Briggs, Thomas Broadrib and Etheldred Gray.

Page 44:   EDMOND WALLER. Inventory. Date: 20 May 1782. Rec.: 23 Nov. 1784. Benjamin Waller, Executor.

Page 45:   SILVYA BELL of Surry. Will. Date: 9 Oct. 1782. Rec.: 23 Nov. 1784. Benjamin Bell, Executor. Son: Samuel. Daughters: Nancy Champion Bell, Rebekah Bell and Betsy Bell. Friend: Benjamin Bell. Mentions: all my children. Witnesses: William Hart and Thomas Cofer.

Page 46:   MARTHA WARREN of Surry. Will. Date: 28 Oct. 1784. Rec.: 23 Nov. 1784. William Riggan, Executor. Sisters: Sarah Riggan and Lucy Gardner. Mother: Mary Warren. Brother-in-law: William Riggan. Witnesses: Will Clinch, Jr. and Benjamin Riggan.

Page 47:   ELIZABETH KEA of Southwark Parish, Surry. Will. Date: May 7, 1784. Rec.: Nov. 23, 1784. William Kea and Jesse Bryant, Executors. Brothers: Bruton Kea (and children), John Kea (and children). Sister: Mary Bryant (and children). Witnesses: Samuel Judkins, James Judkins and Rebecca Harden.

Page 48:   MARTHA ADAMS. Inventory. Date: (none). Rec.: 23 Nov. 1784. John Pettway, Robert McIntosh and Samuel Judkins.

Page 49:   WILLIAM DREW. Account Current. Date: 1780. Rec.: 23 Nov. 1784. Mentions payments to: Will Cofield Seward (his sons legacy), Michael Blow (his wife's part), Will Hart (his wife's part), Will Evans (his wife's part), Will Cofield Seward (his wife's part), Etheldred Gray (his children's part), Michael Blow, guardian to Nanny Thomas. John Wesson, William Edwards, Auditors.

Page 50:   JOHN LUCAS of Surry. Will. Date: _ Sept. 1784. Rec.: 25 Jan. 1785. John Lucas (minor) and Christopher Lucas (refused), Executors. Daughter: Mary Lucas. Son: Christopher Lucas. Wife: Sarah. Friends: Stephen Sorsby, Benjamin Collier and James Kee. Codicil. Sons: John and James. Witnesses: Thomas Sorsby, William Simmons and Benjamin Collier.

Page 54:   EDWIN JAMES. Account Current. Date: 1784. Rec.: 25 Jan. 1785. Enos James, Administrator. Mentions payments to: John Gardner, John James, John Gardner, Jr., Susanna James, self

(Page 54 - JAMES cont'd.): (E. James, and Emanuel James.

Page 55:   HANNAH WHITE. Nunc. Will. Date: 4 Jan. 1785. Rec.: 25 Jan.
             1785. Dep. of Sarah Savidge. Legatees: Sally White, daugh-
             ter of Henry; her daughter, Mary Maddera; and Henry White.

Page 56:   MARTHA WARREN. Inventory. Date: (none). Rec.: 22 February
             1785. William Riggan, Executor. Benjamin Spratley, William
             Lane and Frederick Lane, Appraisers.

Page 56:   JOHN LITTLE. Inventory. Date: 29 Sept. 1784. Rec.: 22 Feb.
             1785. Jesse Little and James Brown, Executors.

Page 58:   BENJAMIN BAILEY, JR. of Surry. Will. Date: 24 July 1782.
             Rec.: 22 Mar. 1785. Lemuel Bailey and William Bailey, Ex-
             ecutors. Wife: Elizabeth. Sons: Benjamin (not 21), Will-
             iam and Edward. Brothers: Anselm, Michael and Lemuel Bail-
             ey. Mentions: land bought of father, land held jointly
             with Samuel Bailey. Witnesses: William Browne, William
             Browne, Jr., Richard Kello and Benjamin Browne.

Page 62:   THOMAS ADAMS. Account Current. Date: 1770-1774. Rec.: 22
             Mar. 1785. Nicholas Faulcon, Executor. Mentions: payments
             to Elizabeth and Mary Adams, Mrs. Martha Adams; Mrs. Adams
             childs part, William Boyce (wife's part), Thomas Wall (his
             wife's part), William Adams part, Nathaniel Adams part,
             James Adams part, Miss Anne Adams part by N. Adams, guard-
             ian.

Page 66:   CHARITY PENELUNA COLLIER of Surry. Will. Date: 17 April
             1784. Rec.: 22 Mar. 1785. Henry Moring, Executor. Sons:
             John, Henry and Nicholas Smith. Daughters: Mary Moring,
             and Sarah Collier. Last children: Moody and Sarah Collier.
             Witnesses: John Watkins and John Watkins, Jr.

Page 68:   BRUTON KEA. Inventory. Date: 3 May 1784. Rec.: 26 Apr.
             1785. William Kea, Executor.

Page 70:   JOHN BATTS of Southwark Parish, Surry. Will. Date: 14 Mar.
             1785. Rec.: 26 Apr. 1785. Jesse Cocks, Executor. Wife:
             Mary. Sons: Benjamin (not 12), John, Frederick, and Henry.
             Daughters: Betsy, Patty and Sally Batts. Friends: Jesse
             Cocks and Richard Rowell, Sr. Witnesses: Elizabeth Savidge,
             Joel Savidge and Robert Rowell.

Page 72:   NICHOLAS SMITH. Will. Date: 19 Nov. 1784. Rec.: 26 April
             1785. John Warren and Charity Smith, Executors. Wife:
             Charity. Children: Mirandy and Susanna. Witnesses: John
             Lane, Dorothy Coman and Susanna Bridges.

Page 73:   ELIZABETH KEA. Inventory. Date: 5 Nov. 1784. Rec.: 24 May
             1785. William Kea and Jesse Bryant, Executors.

Page 74:   WILLIAM WARREN. Inventory. Date: 11 Apr. 1785. Rec.: May
             24, 1785. John Andrews, Administrator. Stephen Sorsby,
             Drewry Duell and Jonathan Ellis, Appraisers.

Page 75:   WILLIAM JUDKINS. Inventory. Date: 22 Mar. 1785. Rec: 25 May
             1785. John Pettway, William Adams and Robert McIntosh, Ap-
             praisers.

Page 76:   ISHAM INMAN of Surry. Will. Date: 7 May 1785. Rec.: 26 Jul.
             1785. Mary Inman and Joseph Holleman, Jr., Executors. Wife:
             Mary. Natural Son: Isham Gibbons (not 21). Daughter: Sarah
             Dawson. Friend: Jonathan Wall. Mentions: Child in esse.
             Land father, John Inman, bought. Witnesses: John White,Jr.
             and Joel Wall.

Page 78:   CHARITY COLLIER. Inventory. Date: 1 Apr. 1785. Rec: 26 Jul.

(Page 78 - COLLIER cont'd.): 1785. John Bartle, Sr., John Watkins and
Thomas Spratley, Appraisers.

Page 79: NICHOLAS SMITH. Inventory. Date: 26 May 1785. Rec: 26 Jul.
1785. John Lane, Willis Smith and Joseph Warren, Appraisers.

Page 81: HENRY WATKINS. Account Current. Date: 1770-1772. Rec.: 28
Sept. 1785. Jonathan Ellis, Executor. Mentions payments
to: Edward Hart (his wife's part), John Watkins part, Henry Watkins part, Elizabeth Watkins part; coffin for Rebecca Watkins; schooling for Mary Watkins. Thomas Spratley
and Thomas Bartle.

Page 82: THOMAS EDWARDS of Surry. Will. Date: 12 Sept. 1782. Rec.:
22 Nov. 1785. J'Anson Edwards and Richard Edwards, Executors. Wife: Unity. Sons: Lewis, J'Anson, Michael, Richard
and Newet. Daughter: Nancy. Witnesses: Richard Hardy,
William Hardy and William Edwards. Codicil. Date: 15 Nov.
1782. Witnesses: Richard Hardy, William Edwards and John
Harrison.

Page 86: LUCY WARREN. Will. Date: 29 Mar. 1783. Rec.: 22 Nov. 1785.
John Warren, Executor. Daughters: Mary Bates, Rebeckah Dav-
is and Charity Smith. Sons: Thomas and John. Son-in-law:
Richard Rowell. Witnesses: Joseph Warren and John Carrell.

Page 87: THOMAS KING. Account Current. Date: (none). Rec.: 22 Nov.
1785. Mary King, Administratrix. Mentions payments to:
Jesse King (his part of his father's estate); Edward King
(ditto); Thomas King (ditto), and Phillip King (ditto).

Page 88: JOHN BATTS. Inventory. Date: 9 May 1785. Rec.: 2 Dec. 1785.
Joel Savidge, William Riggan and John Lane, Appraisers.

Page 89: THOMAS DAVIS of Surry. Will. Date: 3 June 1784. Rec.: 27
July 1784. (Further proven 24 Jan. 1786.) John Warren and
Jacob Faulcon, Executors. Wife: Rebecca. Sons: Littleberry
(minor), and Lemuel. Daughters: Pamilea, Rebecca, Miranda
and Dolly. Brother-in-law: John Warren. Witnesses: Hannah
Davis and Thomas Holt.

Page 91: ETHELDRED EDWARDS of Surry. Will. Date: 15 May 1784. Rec.:
24 Jan. 1786. Mary Edwards and James Davis, Executors.
Wife: Mary. Sons: Thomas, John and James. Daughters: Sarah,
Mary, Martha and Elizabeth. Witnesses: Joseph Davis, Jo.
Holleman, Jr., and John Warren.

Page 93: Capt. WILLIAM SEWARD. Account Current. Date: 1772. Rec.:
24 Jan. 1786. William Drew, and William Hart, Executors.
Robert Hunnicutt and Samuel Pretlow, Auditors.

Page 95: WILLIAM BROWNE of Surry. Date: (none). Rec.: 25 Jan. 1786.
Benjamin E. Browne and William Browne, Jr., Executors.
Wife: (unnamed). Son: William Taylor Browne. Daughter:
Ann Browne. Brother: Benjamin E. Browne. Friend: Henry
Browne. Witness: (none).

Page 97: HENRY BEDINGFIELD. Inventory. Date: 26 Nov. 1785. Rec.:
28 Mar. 1786. John Andrews, Administrator. Jonathan Ellis,
Richard Ellis and William Maget, Appraisers.

Page 98: WILLIAM CLINCH of Surry. Will. Date: 6 Nov. 1783. Rec: 28
Mar. 1786. William Clinch, Jr., Executor. Wife: (unnamed).
Son: William. Daughter: Mary. Witnesses: William Clinch,Jr.,
William Hamlin and Archibald Davis.

Page 100: JOSEPH HOLLEMAN of Surry. Will. Date: 17 Nov. 1785. Rec.:
27 June 1786. Joseph Holleman, Executor. Wife: Elizabeth.
Sons: Thomas, Joseph, Wilson, Edmund, John and James. Daus:

124

(Page 100 - HOLLEMAN cont'd:) Sarah Gwaltney, Unity Delk; Elizabeth,
          Mary and Lucy Holleman. Grandson: Jordan Gwaltney. Men-
          tions: money due from Sharp Reynold's estate; his interest
          in the estate of Thomas Wilson and Whitfield Wilson's in-
          terest in his father's estate, which he has purchased. Wit-
          nesses: James Wall, Jesse Bryant, John White and Robert
          Kea.

Page 104:   BENJAMIN COLLIER. Inventory. Date: 25 Nov. 1785. Rec.:
             27 June 1786. B. E. Browne, Thomas Spratley and Henry Mor-
             ing, Jr., Appraisers.

Page 105:   PHILLIP WEST. Inventory. Date: 28 Apr. 1784. Rec.: 27
             June 1786. Thomas Spratley, Administrator. Benjamin Ed-
             wards Browne, Thomas Bage, Jr. and James Clarke, Appraisers.

Page 107:   AARON WALL. Inventory. Date: (Court ordered) June 1783.
             Rec.: 27 June 1786. Joseph Holleman, Jr. and Charles Cham-
             pion, Appraisers.

Page 108:   JOHN BAILEY of Surry. Will. Date: 14 Apr. 1786. Rec.: 27
             June 1786. Lemuel Bailey and William Clinch, Executors.
             Son: Robert (to learn cabinet-making as apprentice to Sam-
             uel Cornwell.) Daughters: Jane and Elizabeth Bailey (min-
             ors). Brothers: Lemuel and Anselm. Sister: Ann Hunni-
             cutt. Friend: William Clinch, son of James Clinch. Men-
             tions: brother Anselm to assist Joseph Scott and Thomas
             Pretlow respecting his right in estate of William and Eliza-
             beth Scott. Witnesses: Harris Nicholson, Samuel Bailey &
             Benjamin White.

Page 111:   JOHN STEWART of Southwark Parish, Surry. Will. Date: 1785.
             Rec.: 27 June 1786. William Cocke, Executor. Wife: Eliza-
             beth. Daughter: Sarah (not 18). Son: James (not 21).
             Friend: Lemuel Cocke. Mentions: money in Scotland left
             him by father, entered in William Stewart and Co.; land in
             Argileshire called "Ackinskee".

Page 114:   THOMAS DAVIS. Inventory. Date: 31 Dec. 1785. Rec.: 27 Jun.
             1786. John Warren, Jr. and Jacob Faulcon, Executors.

Page 115:   WILLIAM BROWNE of Surry. Will. Date: 19 June 1783. Rec.:27
             June 1786. William Browne and Benjamin Browne, Executors.
             Sons: William, Benjamin, George, Richard and John (last 3
             sons not 21). Daughter: Mary. Friends: Richard Nathan-
             iel and John Cocke. Nephews: William and Henry Browne.
             Mentions: land in Brunswick and Sussex Counties; son, Wil-
             liam to make good a title of land sold to John Watkins, son
             being entitled to land as heir of his mother. Witnesses:
             Thomas Bage, William Clinch, Jr., Thomas Spratley and Henry
             Credeel. Codicil. Date: 27 Mar. 1786. Sons: George and
             Richard, both deceased. Wife: Dolly, daughter of Josiah
             Jordan and widow of John Hay. Wife's daughter: Peggy Hay.
             Friend: John Hartwell Cocke. Mentions: land in So'n (?)
             bought of Henry Browne. Witnesses: R. Kello, Susanna Sin-
             clair, Benjamin Parker and Wyatt Moring.

Page 122:   JAMES BISHOP of Surry. Will. Date: 6 Mar. 1786. Rec.: 25
             July 1786. Joshua Bishop, Executor. Sons: Joshua, John
             and James. Daughters: Faithy Gresham and Lucy Dun. Grand-
             children: James (son of Joshua Bishop), Mason (son of son
             Mason Bishop); James and Mary (children of Joshua Bishop).
             Witnesses: Joseph Ellis, Scarbrough Jones and Benjamin
             Emery.

Page 123:   ETHELDRED EDWARDS. Inventory. Date: 23 Jan. 1786. Rec.: 25
             July 1786. William Warren, Benjamin Bell and Thomas Cofer,
             Appraisers.

Page 124:   JESSE COCKS of Surry. Will. Date: 4 Oct. 1784. Rec.: 26 Sep.

(Page 124 - COCKS cont'd.): 1786. Rebecca Cocks, Executrix. Wife: Rebecca. Children: (unnamed). Brother: William Cocks. Witnesses: (none). James Kee and John Judkins swear to handwriting.

Page 125:   Mrs. MARTHA EDWARDS. Inventory. Date: Dec. 1773. Rec: 26 Sept. 1786. Nicholas Faulcon, Jr., Executor.

Page 126:   RANDOLPH KING of Surry. Will. Date: 22 Apr. 1786. Rec.: 26 Sept. 1786. Richard Putney, Executor. Wife: (unnamed). Son: James. Daughters: Lucy and Betsey. Witnesses: Joseph Ellis, Martha Cary and Andrew Kelsy.

Page 127:   WILLIAM BRIDGES. Account Current. Date: 1784-1786. Rec: 26 Sept. 1786. Archibald Davis, Administrator. Mentions payments to: Samuel Carrell, Isaac Bridges and Eliza Bridges. Nathan Jones and James Belsches, Auditors.

Page 128:   WILLIAM EDWARDS. Account Current. Date: 1773. Date: Sept. 26, 1786. Nicholas Faulcon, Executor. Mentions legacy paid to John Harris; Martha Edwards, Executrix. Will Salter & John Hunnicutt, Auditors.

Page 130:   Mrs. MARTHA EDWARDS. Account Current. Date: 1773. Rec: 26 Sept. 1786. Nicholas Faulcon, Executor. Mentions payments to William Edwards(legacy from uncle William Edwards), Frederick Jones (legacy), Miss Patsy Jones (legacy), Benjamin Branch (wife's legacy), executor (legacy from Mrs. Martha Edwards), Charles Irby (wife's legacy); uncollectable open account with Micajah Edwards in So'n. Will Salter and John Hunnicutt, Auditors.

Page 134:   LUCY WARREN. Inventory. Date: 2 Feb. 1786. Rec.: 26 Sept. 1786. John Warren, Jr., Executor.

Page 135:   SILVIAH BELL. Inventory. Date: 13 Nov. 1784 (Court order). Rec.: 24 Oct. 1786. Tomer Presson, James Davis and Robert Bell, Appraisers.

Page 137:   Mr. JACOB PATE. Inventory. Date: 20 Oct. 1786 (Williamsburg, York County). Rec.: 24 Oct. 1786. Robert Nicolson, James Galt and Benjamin Bucktrout, Appraisers.

Page 137:   SILVIAH BELL. Account Current. Date: May 1785. Rec.: 24 Oct. 1786. Benjamin Bell, Executor. Joseph Holleman and Lemuel Bailey, Auditors.

Page 138:   STEPHEN LUCAS. Account Current. Date: 1773. Rec.: 24 Oct. 1786. James Kee, Executor. Mentions payments to: Charles Lucas (his guardian account in full); Henry Cook for Betsy Lucas, orphan of Stephen; Betty Cook (in full); James Kee, guardian of Ann, Sarah, Susan, Eliza and John Lucas. John Watkins, Archibald Cocke and Stephen Sorsby, Auditors.

Page 142:   JAMES TAYLOR of Surry. Will. Date: 20 Nov. 1783. Rec.: 26 Dec. 1786. Francis Taylor, Executor. Wife: Rebecca. Sons: Francis, and James. Daughter: Martha White. Witnesses: Josiah Wilson and Richard Scammell.

Page 143:   JOHN LUCAS. Inventory. Date: 26 Feb. 1785. Rec.: 23 Jan. 1787. Sarah Lucas, Administratrix. Thomas Sorsby, Stephen Sorsby and William Bailey, Appraisers.

Page 146:   JESSE COCKS. Inventory. Date: 13 Dec. 1786. Rec.: 23 Jan. 1787. Rebecca Cocks, Executrix. Nathaniel Sebrell, Jonathan Ellis and Stephen Sorsby, Appraisers.

Page 147:   JOHN MADDERA. Inventory. Date: 28 Apr. 1783. Rec.: 23 Jan. 1787. James Kee and William Clinch, Executors. William Clinch the younger and William Hamlin, Appraisers. (cont'd)

(Page 147 - MADDERA cont'd): John Batts, the other appraiser, is dead.

Page 148: HENRY MORING. Inventory. Date: 6 Nov. 1786. Rec.: 27 Feb. 1787. William Bailey, Christopher Lucas and William Andrews, Appraisers.

Page 150: FAITH BARKER of Surry. Will. Date: 30 Oct. 1783. Rec.: 26 June 1787. Randolph King, deceased - Elizabeth Barker was granted administration. Neice: Anny King. Nephew: John Barker, son of brother John. Cousins: Susan Barker, dau. of Thomas Barker, deceased (not 16); Lucy Barker, daughter of Samuel(?) Barker. Witnesses: Eliza Barker and A. Barker.

Page 151: JOHN BAILEY. Inventory. Date: 23 May 1787. Rec.: June 26, 1787. William Andrews and Nathaniel Andrews, Appraisers.

Page 151: NICHOLAS CRYER. Inventory. Date: (none). Rec.: 26 June 1787.

Page 153: JAMES WILLISON of Surry. Will. Date: 22 June 1787. Rec.: 24 July 1787. Mary Willison, Carter Bassett Harrison and Thomas J'Anson, Executors. Father: John Willison (of Port Glasgow). Mother: Margaret Willison. Son: John (not 25). Wife: Mary. Children: (unnamed). Child in esse. Friend: Thomas Peter. Mentions: mercantile concern with both John Stewart and William Cocke. Codicil. Sister: Janet Willison (next passage to Britain). Witnesses: James Belsches, Sr., Archibald Dunlop, William Laughton and James Gilchrist.

Page 156: BENJAMIN MORING. Inventory. Date: 28 Feb. 1785. Rec.: 24 July 1787. Henry Moring, Administrator. Thomas Sorsby, James Belsches, Sr. and William Bailey, Appraisers.

Page 158: ISAAC ELLIS of Surry. Will. Date: 12 June 1787. Rec.: Sept. 25, 1787. William Nicholson, Executor. Wife: Cherry Ellis. Children: (unnamed). Child in esse. Witnesses: William Ellis, Nathaniel Sebrell and Frederick Cooper.

Page 159: JOHN ANDREWS, SR. of Surry. Will. Date: 4 May 1787. Rec.: 25 Sept. 1787. Nathaniel Andrews and James Kee, Executors. Son: Nathaniel. Wife: Mary. Daughters: Nancy Andrews, Martha Rae, Hannah Rae, and Priscilla Brit. Grandchildren: Samuel and John Andrews, sons of Nathaniel. Codicil. Dau.: Martha Rae is dead. Her part to her children: John and William Rae. Witnesses: Thomas Rose, John Sebrell and Jesse Carseley.

Page 160: JOHN BARHAM. Will. Date: 20 Dec. 1785. Rec.: 23 Oct.1787. Sarah Barham, Executrix. Wife: Sarah. Children: (unnamed). Friend: Benjamin Waller. Witnesses: Benjamin Waller and Mary Waller.

Page 161: ABRAHAM MITCHELL. Inventory. Date: 9 May 1786. Rec.: 23 Oct. 1787. John Mitchell, Executor. Widow: Mary Mitchell, deceased.

Page 163: WILLIS SMITH of Surry. Will. Date: 1 Aug. 1787. Rec.: 23 Oct. 1787. John Moring, Executor. Wife: Rebecca. Daughter: Lucy (not of age). Son: Henry (not 21). Friend: William Dicken. Brothers: James Smith and John Moring. Mentions land left him by father. Witnesses: Henry Moring, Ann Moring and John Warren, Jr.

Page 165: FRANCES MORELAND. Account Current. Rec.: 23 Oct. 1787. Archibald Dunlop, Administrator. Thomas Fletcher, Thomas Bartle and Thomas Forsyth, Auditors.

Page 167: WILLIAM WHITE. Inventory. Rec.: 23 Oct. 1787. Thos. White.

127

Page 168:   JOSEPH CHEATHAM. Account Current. Date: 1781. Rec.: 23
              Oct. 1787. Benjamin Moring, Executor. Mentions his part
              of his mother's estate after her death (1782). James Bel-
              sches, Sr. and Thomas Peter, Auditors.

Page 170:   JONATHAN ELLIS of Surry. Will. Date: 5 Jan. 1787. Rec.: 22
              Jan. 1788. Richard Ellis and Thomas Ellis, Executors.
              Sons: Richard, John, Thomas and William. Daughter: Eliza-
              beth Presson. Witnesses: William Clinch, Jr., Archibald
              Davis and William Warren.

Page 172:   WILLIAM WHITE. Inventory. Date: Jan. 1782. Rec.: 22 Jan.
              1788. James Davis, Toomer Presson and Willis Wilson, Ap-
              praisers.

Page 174:   THOMAS SORSBY of Surry. Will. Date: 11 Nov. 1787. Rec.:
              22 Jan. 1788. Lucy Sorsby and John Southall, Executors.
              Wife: Lucy. Daughter: Sarah. Son-in-law: John Southall.
              Grandson: Francis Walker Southall (not 21). Sister: Eli-
              zabeth White. Friend: James Kee. Mentions: Thomas Sors-
              by, son of Stephen Sorsby; negro at Henry White's to his
              sister Elizabeth at mother's death. Witnesses: Christo-
              pher Lucas, Stephen Sorsby and Richard Fugler.

Page 177:   WILLIAM MORING. Account Current. Date: 1772. Rec.: 22
              Jan. 1788. John Moring, James Belsches, Sr. and Thomas
              Peter, Auditors.

Page 178:   BENJAMIN WALLER. Inventory. Date: _____ Rec.: 26 Feb. 1788.
              James Andrews, Philip Thompson and Joseph Barham, Apprais-
              ers.

Page 179:   ISAAC ELLIS. Inventory. Date: 25 Oct. 1787. Rec.: 26 Feb.
              1788. William Nicholson, Executor. Nathaniel Sebrell, Fred-
              erick Cowper and William Justiss, Appraisers.

Page 181:   JOHN WHITE of Surry. Will. Date: 10 Nov. 1787. Rec.: 26 Feb.
              1788. John White and Henry Crafford, Executors. Daughters:
              Mary White and Jane Crafford. Son: John. Wife: Jane. Son-
              in-law: Henry Crafford. Witnesses: James Kee, William
              Clinch, John Judkins and John Spratley.

Page 183:   WILLIS SMITH. Inventory. Date: _____. Rec.: 26 Feb. 1788.
              John Moring, Executor.

Page 183:   JOHN BARHAM. Inventory. Date: 14 Dec. 1787. Rec.: 26 Feb.
              1788. Nathaniel Berriman, Thomas Pyland and Robert Pyland,
              Appraisers.

Page 184:   JOHN BAILEY. Inventory. Date: 8 July 1786. Rec.: 22 April
              1788. Lemuel Bailey and Will Clinch, Executors. John Pres-
              son, Joseph G. Bailey and Joseph Holleman, Appraisers.

Page 187:   JONATHAN ELLIS. Inventory. Date: _____ Rec.: 22 April 1788.
              William Maget, Joseph Hill and John Pettway, Appraisers.

Page 189:   JAMES GRAY of Surry. Will. Date: 9 Feb. 1788. Rec.: 24 Jun.
              1788. Josiah Gray and James Gray, Executors. Wife: Sarah.
              Sons: Josiah, James and Nathaniel (the last a minor). ...
              Daughters: Sarah, wife of Richard Rowell; Mary Davis; Ann,
              Elizabeth and Susanna Gray, minors. Witnesses: Jacob Faul-
              con, Nathaniel Berriman and Thomas Cocks.

Page 193:   JOHN ANDREWS. Inventory. Date: _____. Rec.: 22 July 1788.
              William Bailey, John Marks and John Jarratt, Appraisers.

Page 195:   JAMES WILLISON. Inventory. Date: 5 Oct. 1787. Rec.: 23 Sep.
              1788. Archibald Dunlop, William Cocke and William Calder,
              Appraisers.

Page 201:   ANNE KING of Surry. Will. Date: 23 Oct. 1787. Rec.: Sept. 23, 1788. Starling Hill, Executor. Son: James. Daughters: Lucy and Betsey. Brother: Ambrous Barker. Friend: Starling Hill. Mentions: James Bishop in Granville County, North Carolina to raise her son. Witnesses: Abigail Johnson and Elizabeth Barker.

Page 203:   THOMAS COCKE. Account Current. Date: 1784. Rec.: 23 Sept. 1788. Thomas J'Anson, Executor. Mentions payments to: Archibald Cocke (one third); Acrill Cocke, guardian for Benjamin (one third); Thomas J'Anson, guardian for William Cocke (one third). Lemuel Bailey and Archibald Davis, Aud.

Page 204:   HENRY HOWARD. Will. Date: 20 Feb. 1786. Rec.: 27 Jan. 1789. Henry Howard, Executor. Sons: Thomas and Henry. Daughter: Anner. Grandson: Patrick Henry Adams. Mentions: Elizabeth Watkins; Littleberry Newsum's children by my daughter (unnamed). Witnesses: Edmund Caseley, Joshua Williams, Polly Bedingfield and William Ellis.

Page 206:   JOHN CHEATHAM of Surry. Will. Date: 30 Mar. 1788. Rec.: 27 Jan. 1789. James Cheatham, Executor. Wife: Martha. Sons: James and Stephen. Daughters: Nancy, Betsey and Sally. Mentions: children. Witnesses: J. Kee, Frederick Cooper and Archer Moody.

Page 208:   JAMES GRAY. Inventory. Date: 8 Oct. 1788. Rec.: 27 January 1789. Josiah Gray and James Gray, Executors. Robert Pyland, Samuel Judkins and James Adams, Appraisers.

Page 211:   WILLIAM NEWSUM. Account Current. Date: 1777. Rec.: 29 Apr. 1789. Henry Crafford, Executor. Mentions: John Daniel (paid legacy); Simon Barnes (paid legacy); son Joel; Reuben ---- (illegible, paid legacy). Nicholas Faulcon, Jr. and John Judkins, Auditors.

Page 212:   JOHN STEWART. Inventory. Date: 13 Apr. 1787. Rec.: 30 Apr. 1789. Thomas Peter and James Belsches, Sr., Appraisers.

Page 215:   DAVID ANDREWS of Surry. Will. Date: Jan. 12, 1789. Rec.: June 23, 1789. Joseph Hart and John Hart, Executors. Sons: Henry, Richard and William. Grandson: David Anthony Andrews. Daughters: Faith and Olive Andrews. Wife: Jane. Children: Henry, Mary, Richard, Sary, Mildred, Jane, Faith, William, Olive and Elizabeth. Mentions: Joseph Hart; daughter Elizabeth's part to Jesse Hart to divide equally between her children. Witnesses: John Atkinson, Samuel Atkinson and Joseph Hart.

Page 217:   HENRY HOWARD of Southwark Parish, Surry. Will. Date: 3 Jan. 1789. Rec.: 27 Jan. 1789 (further proven: 23 June 1789). Samuel Jones, Executor. Wife: Sarah. Sons: John Heath Howard (not 21), Nicholas, James and Henry Jones Howard. Dau: Patsey Howard. Mentions: all my children; James Boysseau Jones. Friends: Nathan Jones and Benjamin Bilbro. Witnesses: John Baldwin, William Baldwin, Betty Howard and Samuel Barker. (Also mentions part that came with Sarah Bilbro; part that came to him at the death of Betty Howard).

Page 219:   BENJAMIN RHOADS. Will. Date: 24 Mar. 1789. Rec.: 23 June 1789. Joseph Davis, Executor. Wife: (unnamed). Son: John. Witness: Joel Thompson.

Page 220:   ROBERT WARD. Account Current. Date: 1781-1789. Rec.: 23 Jun. 1789. Mary Waller, Administratrix of Benjamin Waller, administrator of Richard Ward. John Southall and Benjamin Bilbro, Auditors.

Page 221:   JOHN GRAY. Inventory. Date: 29 Jun. 1789. Rec.: 28 July 1789. William Salter, Sheriff. John Thompson, William Mit-

129

(Page 221 - GRAY cont'd): chell and Hartwell Hunnicutt, Appraisers.

Page 223:   JOHN GRAY. Account Current. Date: ---- Rec.: 28 Jul. 1789.
               William Salter, Sheriff.

Page 224:   RICHARD JONES. Inventory. Date: May 1774. Rec.: 28 Jul.1789.
               Nathan Jones, Executor. Lemuel Cocke, Moses Hill and Henry
               Cocke, Appraisers.

Page 229:   ANN JONES. Inventory. Date: May 1774. Rec.: 28 July 1789.
               Nathan Jones, Executor. Lemuel Cocke, Moses Hill and Henry
               Cocke, Appraisers.

Page 234:   HAMILTON JONES. Inventory. Date: 10 Dec. 1781. Rec.: 28 Jul.
               1789. Nathan Jones, Executor. Sterling Hill and William Jus-
               tiss, Appraisers.

Page 239:   ROBERT PETER, late of Cabin Point, Virginia, now of Chamber
               St., Goodmans Fields, County Middlesex - Merchant. Will.
               Date: 8 July 1788. Rec.: 28 July 1789. Daughter: Clermont
               Peter (a minor). Brother: Thomas Peter of Cabin Point, mer-
               chant. Brother-in-law: James Holt of Norfolk County, Va.
               Witnesses: Charles Taylor of Chamber St., Samuel Smith of
               Chamber St., and James Morgan of Great Prescot.

Page 241:   JONATHAN WALL of Southampton. Will. Date: 22 Oct. 1788.
               Rec.: 22 Sept. 1789. Mary Wall, Executrix. Wife: Mary Wall.
               Mentions: 6 children and child in esse; land in Surry Co.
               Witnesses: Joseph Holleman, Joel Wall and James Lancaster.

Page 242:   JOHN PRESSON of Southwark Parish, Surry. Will. Date: 10
               May 1788. Rec.: 22 Sept. 1789. Samuel Judkins, Executor.
               Wife: Lucy. Daughters: Hanner Judkins, Mary Judkins; Anne,
               Betsey and Lucy Presson. Son: John. Grandchildren: Dan-
               iel Presson Judkins and Nancy Lamb Judkins. Son-in-law:
               Samuel Judkins. Witnesses: John Judkins, John White and
               Randolph Harriss.

Page 244:   DAVID HOLLOWAY. Will. Date: 17 July 1789. Rec.: 22 Sept.
               1789. Jesse Holloway, Executor. Sons: Lazarus, Jesse and
               Job. Children: (unnamed). Witnesses: Joel Thompson and
               William Slade, Jr.

Page 246:   JAMES STEWART. Will. Date: 4 July 1789. Rec.: 22 Sep. 1789.
               Nathaniel Harrison, Christopher Lucas and John Southall,
               Appraisers.

Page 248:   Dr. PATRICK ADAMS. Account Current. Date: 1771-1778. Rec:
               22 Sept. 1789. James Belsches, Sr., Administrator. Joseph
               Holleman, William Cocke and William Boyce, Auditors.

Page 251:   WILLIAM CALDER. Inventory. Date: 10 Nov. 1788. Rec.: 27
               Oct. 1789. Archibald Dunlap, Administrator. Thomas Peter,
               James Belsches, Sr., William Cocke, William Laughton, Gent.,
               Appraisers.

Page 256:   LEMUEL BARKER of Surry. Will. Date: 2 May 1789. Rec.: 27
               Oct. 1789. Sterling Hill, Executor. Son: Benjamin. Daugh-
               ters: Lucy and Elizabeth. Friend: Lemuel Cocke. Witnesses:
               Henry Bishop, Mary Bishop and Bernard Bilbro.

Page 258:   Capt. WILLIAM LAUGHTON. Nunc. Will. Date: 30 Nov. 1789 -
               (Cabin Point, Surry). Rec: 22 Dec. 1789. Wife: Elianor.
               Children: William and Jennett. Witnesses: Thomas Peter,
               Lyon Powell, John Gains Atkins and Andrew Nimmo.

Page 259:   GEORGE PYLAND. Account Current. Date: ____. Rec.: 22 Dec.
               1789. Robert Pyland, Administrator. Mentions: Mary Pyland,
               Administratrix of William Pyland. Joseph Holleman and Jes-
               se Warren, Auditors.

Page 260:   MARY EDWARDS of Surry. Will. Date: 4 Dec. 1789. Rec.: 26
             Jan. 1790. James Davis and Joseph Holleman, Executors.
             Daughters: Elizabeth, Mary, Sarah and Martha. Sons: Thomas,
             and John. Brother: James Davis. Witnesses: Thomas Davis,
             Martha Millington and Martha Davis.

Page 262:   REBECCA HOLDSWORTH of Southwark Parish, Surry. Will. Date:
             19 Apr. 1789. Rec.: 28 July 1789. (Further proven 26 Jan.
             1790). Thomas Spratley, Executor. Grand-daughters: Eliza-
             beth (Betsey) Gray and Sarah West. Daughters: Betsey Mere-
             dith, Sally Washington and Anne Spratley. Friends: Lewis
             Meredith and Nicholson Washington. Mentions: account with
             Philip West estate for board of grand-daughters. Witnesses:
             John Hartwell Cocke and John Watkins, Jr.

Page 264:   ISAAC ELLIS. Account Current. Date: 1787. Rec.: 26 January
             1790. William Nicholson, Executor. Mentions: Benjamin and
             Thomas Ellis; Richard Ellis estate.

Page 266:   DAVID HOLLOWAY. Inventory. Date: ---. Rec.: 26 Jan. 1790.
             Jesse Holloway, Executor.

Page 267:   JOHN WARREN of Surry. Will. Date: 31 Dec. 1788. Rec.:   27
             Apr. 1790. John Wesson and John Pettway, Executors. Wife:
             Elizabeth. Legatees: John Pettway, John and Elizabeth Wes-
             son, John Warren son of Samuel, and Thomas Rispess. Friend:
             John Warren son of Thomas. Witnesses: John Lane, Michael
             Smith and Thomas Holt.

Page 268:   ROBERT PETER. Inventory. Date: 8 Feb. 1790. Rec.: 27 Apr.
             1790. Thomas Peter (requests inventory). James Belsches,Sr.,
             William Cocke and Thomas J'Anson, Appraisers. John Southall,
             P. Jemm and John Lucas, Auditors.

Page 270:   ROBERT PETER. Sale. Date: ----. Rec.: 27 Apr. 1790. Thomas
             Peter, purchaser. James Gilchrist, Andrew Nimmo, Thomas
             Bartle and James Baird, Witnesses.

Page 274:   CHRISTOPHER MORING. Inventory. Date: 12 Feb. 1790. Rec.: 27
             Apr. 1790. William Moring, deceased. Christopher Lucas,
             William Bailey and William Collins, Appraisers.

Page 275:   ISAAC ELLIS. Account Current. Date: 26 Jan. 1790. Rec.: 22
             June 1790. William Nicholson, Executor. Henry Marks and
             William Clinch, Auditors.

Page 276:   DAVID ANDREWS. Inventory. Date: 31 July 1789. Rec.: 22 Jun.
             1790. John Hart and Joseph Hart, Executors. Robert Atkinson,
             John Atkinson and Thomas Clary, Appraisers.

Page 278:   RANDOLPH PRICE. Account Current. Date: 1782. Rec.: 27 July
             1790. John Wesson, Executor. Mentions: debts greater than
             balance; orphans: David Price and Randolph Price; John El-
             lis married the widow. Nicholson Watkins and William Bailey,
             Auditors.

Page 280:   JAMES HOLT. Inventory. Date: 6 Jan. 1790. Rec.: 28 Septem-
             ber 1790. Rodwell Delk, Richard Scammell and James Simpson,
             Appraisers.

Page 282:   BENJAMIN COLLIER. Account Current. Date: 1786-1790. Rec.:
             28 Sept. 1790. Samuel Carrel and wife; and William Bailey,
             Administrators. Mentions: Martha Carrel, widow, formerly
             Collier - her dower thirds. Thomas J'Anson, Henry Moring
             and Archibald Dunlop, Auditors.

Page 284:   JOHN BARHAM. Account Current. Date: Feb. 1787. Rec.: 26 Oct.
             1790. Sarah Barham, Executrix. John Lucas and Nathan Jones,
             Auditors.

Page 285:   JOHN PRESSON. Inventory. Date: Sept. 1789. Rec.: 28 Dec.
             1790. Joseph Holleman, Benjamin White and Arthur Holleman,
             Appraisers.

Page 287:   SAMUEL PRETLOW of Southwark Parish, Surry. Will. Date: Feb.
             1, 1790. Rec.: Dec. 28, 1790. Daughter: Charlotte. Brother:
             Benjamin. Sisters: Ann Bendford, Rebecca and Jane Pritlow.
             Friends: Lemuel Bailey, William Bailey and Thomas Pretlow.
             Witnesses: (none). Langley C. Wills, and Sim Thompson do
             swear to the handwriting.

Page 288:   ELIZABETH WESSON of Southwark Parish, Surry. Will. Date:
             29 Aug. 1789. Rec.: 28 Sept. 1790. John Wesson, Executor.
             Son: John. Witnesses: Joseph Warren, William Warren and
             Benjamin Warren. (Further proven on 25 Jan. 1791.)

Page 289:   JOHN HARTWELL COCKE of Southwark Parish, Surry. Will. Date:
             29 Jan. 1791. Rec.: 22 Feb. 1791. William Mackenzie and
             Richard Cocke, Jr., Executors. Wife: Elizabeth. Daughters:
             Sally, Ann H., Elizabeth, Mary Kennon and Martha Ruffin
             Cocke (not 21). Son: John Hartwell Cocke (not 21). Brother:
             Richard Cocke, Jr. and Benjamin Cocke. Friends: Francis Ruf-
             fin and Samuel Kello. Mentions: land in Kentucky, Brunswick
             County, Halifax County and Buckingham County. Witnesses:
             Benjamin Parker, Benjamin A. Cocke, Richard Cocke, Jr. and
             Ns. Faulson, Jr.

Page 292:   ELIZABETH WESSON. Inventory. Date: July 1790. Rec.: 22 Feb.
             1791. John Wesson, Executor.

Page 293:   Mr. JOHN WARREN. Inventory. Date: 8 Feb. 1790. Rec.: 22 Feb.
             1791. John Wesson and John Pettway, Executors.

Page 295:   LUCY COLLIER of Southwark Parish, Surry. Will. Date: 6 Dec.
             1790. Rec.: 22 Feb. 1791. John Watkins, Sr., Executor.
             Daughters: Lucy Collier and Mary Collier (both deceased).
             Son: Benjamin. Grandchildren: Lucy, Emelia, Benjamin, John
             and George Collier. Witnesses: William Cryer and Moody
             Collier.

Page 296:   AMOS SLEDGE. Inventory. Date: 28 Feb. 1781. Rec.: 26 Apr.
             1791. Lemuel Cocke, Executor. William Justiss and Joshua
             Bishop, Appraisers.

Page 298:   JOHN JUDKINS. Inventory. Date: 6 Jan. 1791. Rec.: 28 June
             1791.'Jacob Judkins, Administrator. Hartwell Hart, William
             Maget and John Spratley, Appraisers.

Page 300:   ETHELDRED EDWARDS. Account Current. Date: 1789-1791. Rec.:
             28 June 1791. William Bailey, Administrator. Mentions:
             Benjamin Edwards in Georgia. Richard H. Cocke and Benjamin
             Cocke, Auditors.

Page 301:   SAMUEL BIDGOOD. Will. Date: 10 Mar. 1791. Rec.: 27 Sep.1791.
             John Murry, Executor. Daughter: Polly Wren Bidgood. Lega-
             tees: Nathaniel Dews Bidgood (not of age); Elizabeth Gray
             Lupo. Friend: Joseph Bidgood. Witnesses: Elizabeth Harri-
             son and John J. Wheadon.

Page 302:   THOMAS GRANTHAM of Surry. Will. Date: 12 Nov. 1790. Rec.:
             27 Sept. 1791. James Grantham and Sampson Grantham, Execu-
             tors. Sons: James and Sampson. Daughters: Joice Tillott,
             Sarah Boykin, Lucy Brock, Rebecca Turner and Martha Smith.
             Grandchildren: Thomas Grantham Tillott, Mary Tillott, Sarah
             Smith, and Lucy Smith. Sons-in-law: John Tillott and Fran-
             cis Smith. Witnesses: Thomas Bailey, Ann Bailey, Henry
             Bailey and Benjamin Putney.

Page 305:   JOHN CHEATHAM. Inventory. Date: 8 Jan. 1790. Rec.: 27 Sept.
             1791. James Cheatham, Executor. John Burgess, Stephen

(Page 305 - CHEATHAM cont'd.): Sorsby and Archer Moody, Appraisers.

Page 307:   LUCY COLLIER. Incentory. Date: 2 Mar. 1791. Rec.: 27 Sept. 1791. Mildred Collier, Administratrix. John Bartle, Moody Collier and William Cryer, Appraisers.

Page 308:   HENRY HOWARD, SR. Inventory. Date: 6 Oct. 1790. Rec.: 27 Sept. 1791. John Watkins, Administrator. John Watkins, Jr., John Tillot, and William Justiss, Appraisers.

Page 310:   SWAN LUNSFORD of Surry. Will. Date: 13 June 1790. Rec.: 27 Sept. 1791. (Further proven on 25 Oct. 1791). Lemuel Cocke, Executor. Sons: Swan, John, Jesse and Thadeus. Daughters: Susannah (not 21), and Nancy Holdsworth. Witnesses: John Wagoner and William Justiss.

Page 312:   JOHN WARREN. Account Current. Date: Dec. 1784. Rec.: 25 Oct. 1791. Ann Warren, Administratrix. Mentions: widow's third and expenses of 7 children (not named).

Page 313:   JOHN WARREN. Account Current. Date: 1791. Rec.: 25 October 1791. John Wesson and John Pettway, Executors. Mentions: Mrs. Warren's funeral sermon and grave. Benjamin Bilbro & Robert Pyland, Auditors.

Page 316:   ELIZABETH WESSON. Account Current. Date: July 1790. Rec.: 25 Oct. 1791. John Wesson, Executor. Benjamin Bilbro and Robert Pyland, Auditors.

Page 316:   Mrs. LUCY WALLER. Inventory. Date: 8 Jan. 1791. Rec.: 25 Oct. 1791. Joel Thompson, Administrator. John Warren, Sr., James Smith and William Lane, Appraisers.

Page 318:   BENJAMIN SPRATLEY of Surry. Will. Date: 30 Jan. 1789. Rec.: 28 Feb. 1792. Susanna Spratley and Thomas Spratley petition for administration. Wife: Susanna. Children: Polly, Walter, Henry and Benjamin. Child in esse. Witnesses: Richard Rowell, Jr. and John Cocks.

Page 319:   JAMES GILCHRIST of Surry. Will. Date: 15 May 1789. Rec.:28 Feb. 1792. Thomas Peter and Walter Johnston, Executors. Sister: Isabel, of New Castle, England. Legatees: my boy Billy Buck, the white son of my servant Fanny, to have his freedom and an education; Dew Graham; Mrs. Thomas Peter; Fanny's children: Nancy, Glasgow, Jenny and Charlotte to have their freedom at age of 21. Friend: Andrew Nimmo. Witnesses: Archerbald Dunlop, James Belsches, Sr., Peter Jemm, William Cocke, Sr., William Cocke, Jr., James Kee and Richard Ellis.

Page 324:   AUGUSTINE HUNNICUTT of Surry. Will. Date: 3 Dec. 1787. Rec: 28 Feb. 1792. Hartwell Hunnicutt, Executor. Son: Hartwell. Daughters: Ann Wright, Elizabeth Williams and Lucy Pettway. Wife: (unnamed). Friend: Sterling Pettway. Witnesses: William Wills, William Phillips and Will Salter.

Page 325:   Mr. CHARLES HOLDSWORTH. Inventory. Date: 19 Nov. 1789. Rec: 28 Feb. 1792. Thomas Spratley, Administrator. J. Watkins, Jr., B. E. Browne, James Clark and M. Collier, Appraisers.

Page 326:   Mrs. REBECCA HOLDSWORTH. Inventory. Date: 5 Aug. 1789. Rec.: 28 Feb. 1792. Thomas Spratley, Executor. J. Watkins, Jr., Moody Collier, B. E. Browne and James Clarke, Appraisers.

Page 328:   ARTHUR SINCLAIR of Surry, Town of Cobham. Will. Date: 31 Oct. 1791. Rec.: 28 Feb. 1792. John Pettway and Jacob Faulcon, Executors. Wife: Susanna. Son: Arthur (not 21). Frs.: Overton Cosby, Capt. William Edwards and Nicholas Faulcon, Jr. Witnesses: John Holt, Samuel Ellis, Hugh Hopkins and

(Page 328 - SINCLAIR cont'd.): Josiah Savidge.

Page 330:   GEORGE GARDNER of Southwark Parish, Surry. Will. Date: 19
             Oct. 1790. Rec.: 28 Feb. 1792. Lucy Gardner, Executrix.
             Wife: Lucy. Daughters: Sarah, Elizabeth, and Ann Jones.
             Grandchildren: Frances Ward, Dawson Ward, Ann Ward, and
             Elizabeth Ward. Friends: Joseph Warren and John Warren, son
             of Thomas. Witnesses: B. E. Browne, Robert McIntosh and Na-
             thaniel Adams.

Page 332:   THOMAS GRANTHAM. Inventory. Date: 28 Sept. 1791. Rec.: 26
             June 1792. Thomas Bailey, William Bailey, William Andrews
             and Henry Bailey, Appraisers.

Page 334:   JOSEPH CLARKE. Account Current. Date: 1778. Rec.: 26 June
             1792. John Judkins, Jr., Administrator. Mentions: Mary,
             Lucy, Sarah, Benjamin, Ann, and Martha Clarke. Lemuel Bail-
             ey, Robert McIntosh and James Wall, Auditors.

Page 335:   REBECCA SIMMONS. Inventory. Date: 2 June 1792. Rec.: 24 Jul.
             1792. Christopher Lucas, Thomas Lucas and Samuel Lucas, Ap-
             praisers.

Page 336:   WILLIAM COCKE. Inventory. Date: 29 Jan. 1791. Rec.: 24 Jul.
             1792. John Lucas, James Belsches, Sr., and William Simmons,
             Appraisers.

Page 339:   THOMAS J'ANSON. Inventory. Date: 11 May 1791. Rec.: 24 Jul.
             1792. John Lucas, B. Major, and William Simmons, Appraisers.

Page 343:   STEPHEN BELL of Surry. Will. Date: 26 Apr. 1789. Rec.: 22
             Dec. 1789. Robert Bell, Executor. Sons: Robert, Stephen &
             Benjamin. Daughters: Ann, Jane and Selah. Grandson: James,
             son of Robert. Friend: William Hart. Witnesses: Jesse War-
             ren, James Wright and William Hart.

Page 1:   MARTHA DREW of Surry. Will. Date: 12 Mar. 1792. Rec.: 25
Sept. 1792. Archer Holt, Executor. Son: John (not 21). Witnesses: William Phillips, Mary Holt and Elizabeth Holt.

Page 2:   ELIZABETH STEWART. Inventory. Date: 8 Dec. 1790. Rec.: 25
Sept. 1792. William Cocke, Administrator. Richard Blunt,
Sterling Hill and Lemuel Cocke, Appraisers.

Page 3:   CHARLES HOLDSWORTH. Account Current. Date: ---. Rec.: 25
Sept. 1792. Thomas Spratley, Administrator. William Maget
and John Pettway, Auditors.

Page 4:   REBECCA HOLDSWORTH. Account Current. Date: 1789. Rec.: 25
Sept. 1792. Thomas Spratley, Executor. William Maget and
John Pettway, Auditors.

Page 6:   JOHN STEWARD of Surry. Will. Date: 8 Dec. 1786. Rec.: 24
July 1792. Wife: Mary. Sons: Stephen; William, Jesse, Nathaniel (not of age); and Hubbard. Daughters: Hannah, Elizabeth and Susannah. Friends: Stephen Sorsby, James Kee, William Collins, Richard Ellis and Archerbald Davis. Witnesses
were John Collier, Jesse Dewell and William C. Partin. Codicil. Date: 7 Mar. 1792. Witnesses: Duncan McGuriman, Jesse
Dewell and William C. Partin.

Page 8:   THOMAS MALLICOTE of Southwark Parish, Surry. Will. Date:
1 Dec. 1790. Rec.: 28 Dec. 1790. (Further proven on Sept.
25, 1792.) Robert McIntosh and William Boyce, Executors.
Wife: Mildred. Brother and sister: (unnamed). Friend and
Kinsman: Robert McIntosh and William Boyce. Witnesses: Archer Holt, William Wills and John Williams.

Page 10:   STEPHEN BELL. Inventory. Date: Jan. 1790. Rec.: 23 October
1792. Jesse Warren, Joseph Holleman and David Long, Appr's.

Page 12:   STEPHEN BELL. Account Current. Date: 1789. Rec.: 23 Oct'r.
1792. Benjamin Bell, Administrator. Mentions: Stephen Bell,
Robert Bell; Benjamin Bell's legacy; Ann Bell's portion;
Jane Bell's portion; Selah Steward's portion. John Warren,
and Joseph Holleman, Auditors.

Page 13:   PETER VALENTINE of Surry. Will. Date: 21 Dec. 1785. Rec.:
23 Oct. 1792. Priscilla Valentine, deceased; Peter Smith,
Executors. Wife: Priscilla. Sons: James and Frederick.
Daughters: Mary, Mason, Mildred, Charlott, Sarah and Hannah.
Witnesses: Stephen Sorsby, Edward Porter and William Dewel.

Page 14:   ANN THOMPSON of Surry. Will. Date: 15 Sept. 1792. Rec.: 23
Oct. 1792. Thomas Spratley, Executor. Daughters: Ann Cocke
Maddera; Rebecca Clinch. Sons: Nathaniel Thompson and Wil-
liam Edlow Thompson. Son-in-law: William Clinch. Witnesses:
Henry Moring and William Collier.

Page 16:   JOSEPH THORP. Inventory. Date: ---. Rec.: 23 Oct. 1792. Nathaniel Andrews presents. William Bailey, Will Clinch and
J. King, Appraisers.

Page 17:   NICOLSON WATKINS of Southwark Parish, Surry. Will. Date: 14
Dec. 1790. Rec.: 22 Jan. 1793. Robert Watkins, Executor.
Brother: Robert. Mentions: land in Petersburg. Witnesses:
James Clarke, Mich'l. Smith and Sarah Yarbrough.

Page 18:   BURWELL BILBRO of Southwark Parish, Surry. Will. Date: 19
Mar. 1789. Rec.: 25 Aug. 1790. (Further proven 22 Jan. 1793)
Benjamin Bilbro, Executor. Mother: Betty Howard. Brothers:
Thomas, Benjamin, Bernard and Berriman Bilbro. Sister: Sa-
rah Howard. Brothers: John Heath Howard, Nicholas Howard &

(Page 18 - BILBRO cont'd.): Patsey Howard. Mentions: land in North Carolina (to be divided according to father's will.) Witnesses: John Avriss, Henry Bishop and John Carseley.

Page 20:   BLACKBURN ANDREWS of Surry. Will. Date: 22 Feb. 1792. Rec.: 22 Jan. 1793. Benjamin Andrews, Executor. Wife: Elizabeth. Daughter: Polly Blackburn Andrews. Brother: Benjamin. Witnesses: Henry Bishop and Lemuel Cocke.

Page 21:   DOLLY PARKER of Surry. Will. Date: 25 Dec. 1790. Rec.: 22 Jan. 1793. Daughter: Peggy Hay. Son: John (deceased). Former husband: John Hay. Husband: Benjamin Parker. Mentions: negro Betty Jones given to me by my father. Witnesses: (none). Carter Bassett Harrison, John Lucas, William Browne and Jacob Faulcon swear to handwriting.

Page 22:   HENRY BEDINGFIELD. Account Current. Date: ---. Rec.: 22 Jan. 1793. John Andrews, Administrator of Ann Bedingfield, Executrix of Henry Bedingfield, presents. Mentions: Thomas Bedingfield.

Page 24:   ANN THOMPSON. Inventory. Date: 19 Nov. 1792. Rec.: 22 Jan. 1793. William Maget, John Pettway and Thomas Ellis, Appr.

Page 25:   ELIZABETH ANDREWS. Renunciation of husband's Will. Date: 14 Apr. 1792. Rec.: 22 Jan. 1793. Witnesses: William Bailey and John H. Parker.

Page 26:   Mr. NICOLSON WATKINS. Inventory. Date: 5 Feb. 1793. Rec.: 26 Feb. 1793. Robert Watkins, Executor. Mich'l. Smith, William Cryer and James Clarke, Appraisers.

Page 27:   MARY REVELY of Surry. Will. Date: 31 Jan. 1793. Rec.: 26 Feb. 1793. Father: John. Mentions: amount due me from the estate of Col. John H. Cocke to be put in the hands of Mr. Craughton, Merchant in Fredericksburg; Mrs. Ann Newell in Faulmouth; Ann Morland. Witnesses: Richard Cocke, Jr. and Ann H. Cocke.

Page 28:   BENJAMIN COLLIER. Additional Account Current. Date: ----. Rec.: 26 Feb. 1793. Samuel Carrell and William Bailey, Administrators. Robert Cocker and Robert Watkins, Auditors.

Page 29:   PETER VALENTINE. Inventory. Date: 2 Nov. 1792. Rec.: 23 Apr. 1793. John Andrews, Administrator. Stephen Sorsby, Edward Porter and William Dewell, Appraisers.

Page 30:   SAMUEL BEDGOOD. Inventory. Date: 5 May 1791. Rec.: 23 Apr. 1793. J'Anson Edwards, Shelley White and James Barlow, Appraisers.

Page 33:   JOHN DAVIS, SR. of Surry. Will. Date: 22 June 1792. Rec.: 25 June 1793. John Davis and Nathaniel Davis, Executors. Daughter: Mary Carrell. Grandchildren: John Davis, son of James; John, Nathaniel, William, Elizabeth Davis and Sarah Cocks, children of Nathan; Thomas, Elizabeth, Polly, Sally Davis and Martha Gray, children of John. Son: John. Mentions: Selah Davis, widow of Nathan. Witnesses: John Pyland, Burwell Barham and Thomas Davis.

Page 35:   ARCHIBALD DUNLOP of Surry. Will. Date: 2 Apr. 1793. Rec.: 25 June 1793. Susanna Dunlop, Executrix. Wife: Susanna. Sisters: Agnes and Christian Dunlop. Legatees: Harwood Charity (not 25); Queen Charlotte Charity. Friends: Dr. John J'Anson, Thomas Peter, John Southall, Peter Jemm and Walter Johnston. Witnesses: William Cocke, William Anthony, Edward Avery, Edward Maynard, Thomas Grantham and Andrew Nimmo.

Page 37:   JAMES TAYLOR. Account Current. Date: Jan. 1788. Rec.: July

(Page 37 - TAYLOR cont'd.): 23, 1793. Thomas Taylor, Executor. Mentions: Thomas, William, Frederick, and Mary Taylor. Lemuel Bailey, W. Nicholson and James Belsches, Sr., Auditors.

Page 38:   DREWRY WARREN. Account Current. Date: 1773. Rec.: 23 July 1793. Joseph Warren, Executor. William Hamlin, Langley C. Wills and John Wesson, Auditors.

Page 40:   JOHN DAVIS. Inventory. Date: 15 July 1793. Rec.: 23 July 1793. John Warren, Sr., Burwell Barham and John Pyland, Appraisers. John Davis and Nathaniel, Executors.

Page 41:   SARAH WEST of Surry. Will. Date: 15 May 1793. Rec.: 23 Jul. 1793. Brother-in-law: Josiah Gray. Aunt: Anne Spratley. Uncle: Thomas Spratley. Witnesses: William Spratley, William E. Thompson and William Spratley, Jr.

Page 42:   JEREMIAH PIERCE of Surry. Will. Date: 29 July 1793. Rec.: 24 Sept. 1793. Richard Pierce, Executor. Sons: John, Richard and Jeremiah. Daughter: Frances Pierce. Witnesses: Abel James,John Nelson and Martha Dobbs.

Page 44:   WILLIAM SIMMONS. Inventory. Date: 16 May 1792. Rec.: Sept. 24, 1793. John J'Anson, Samuel Lucas and B. Major, Jr., Appraisers. Inventory of negroes. John J'Anson, Christopher Lucas and Samuel Lucas, Appraisers.

Page 46:   NICHOLAS FAULCON, SR. of Southampton. Will. Date: 28 July 1792. Rec.: 24 Sept. 1793. Nicholas Faulcon and Edward Faulcon, Executors. Wife: Elizabeth. Sons: Nicholas, Edward; William (not 21). Brother: Jacob. Daughters: Elizabeth Alston; Jenny (not 21). Overseer: Jesse Bryant. Witnesses: Robert Goodwyn, James Sebrell and Jesse Bryant.

Page 49:   WILLIAM ALLEN of Surry. Will. Date: 4 Sept. 1789. Rec.: 24 Sept. 1793. William Allen, Executor. Wife: Mary, deceased. (Will dated 8 Apr. 1788). Sons: William and John. Daughters: Patcy; Ann Armstead Allen (not 21); Martha Bland Allen (not 21). Grandson: William Allen Harrison (not 21) and his mother. Tutoress: Miss Garrett. Mentions: land in New Kent, James City, Southampton, Nansemond, Surry, Sussex Counties; land in Mehurin, Christiana Fort. Witnesses: (none).

Page 52:   SAMUEL JUDKINS of Southwark Parish, Surry. Will. Date: 3 Jan. 1793. Rec.: 24 Sept. 1793. John Judkins, Executor. Wife: Hannah. Son: Robert. Brothers and Sister: only John named. Cousin: Martha Wilkins Judkins. Witnesses: James Adams, Robert Pyland and Richard Pyland.

Page 54:   BENJAMIN SPRATLEY. Inventory. Date: ----. Rec.: 22 October 1793. John Pettway, William Maget and Henry Lane, Appr's.

Page 55:   JOHN JUDKINS, SR. of Surry. Will. Date: 21 Aug. 1790. Rec: 28 Jan. 1794. Jesse Judkins, Executor. Sons: John and Jesse. Grandsons: John Hartwell Judkins and Hartwell Edwards. Daughters: Mary; Selah Davis; Faithy Barham; Sarah Slade; and Silvia. Friend: Henry Moring. Witnesses: John Wesson, Thomas Cocks and James Cocks. Codicil. Date: 25 May 1793. Grandson: William Judkins, son of Benjamin.

Page 58:   JOHN BADGETT. Inventory. Date: 7 Oct. 1793. Rec.: 28 Jan. 1794. Richard Ellis, William Milby and Joseph Holt, Appr.

Page 59:   JAMES STEWART. Account Current. Date: 1789. Rec.: 28 Jan. 1794. William Collins, Administrator (deceased). Mentions: orphans - Elsey, Sally, Thomas and James Stewart. W. Nicholson and John Lucas, Auditors.

Page 61:   SAMUEL JUDKINS. Inventory. Date: ---. Rec.: 28 Jan. 1794. William Adams, Robert Pyland, John Ellis, Appraisers.

Page 63:   JONATHAN ELLIS. Account Current. Date: 1788. Rec.: 28 Jan.
             1794. Richard and Thomas Ellis, Executors. Mentions: John
             Ellis legacy; William Ellis legacy; John Ellis' portion;
             Tomer Presson portion; Thomas Ellis portion; Richard Ellis,
             administrator of William Ellis' portion. James Belsches,Sr.
             and John Pettway, Auditors.

Page 64:   JOHN WARREN - Hatter. Inventory. Date: 11 Feb. 1794. Rec:
             22 Apr. 1794. Robert Watkins, William Cryer and Samuel Car-
             rell, Appraisers.

Page 66:   NICHOLAS CRYER. Account Current. Date: 1786. Rec.: 23 Apr.
             1794. William Cryer and John Bartle, Administrators. John
             Pettway and Thomas Spratley, Auditors.

Page 68:   BENJAMIN COCKE of Surry. Will. Date: 8 June 1794. Rec.: 22
             July 1794. Robert Cocke, Executor. Brothers: Robert and
             Richard. Sister: Mary Archer, deceased, and children. Moth-
             er: Ann Cocke. Friends: William Urquhart, Samuel Kello of
             Southampton, Joseph Ruffin and Thomas Fearn of Isle of
             Wight. Mentions: land in Southampton County. Witnesses:
             Carter Nicholas, Sim Thompson and Will Ruffin. Codicil.
             Date: 14 June 1794. Mentions: William Ruffin. Witnesses:
             Robert Watkins and Sim Thompson.

Page 70:   WILLIAM ANTHONY. Inventory. Date: 12 Feb. 1794. Rec.: 22
             July 1794. Thomas Bartle, Richard Shackleford and Sampson
             Grantham, Appraisers.

Page 71:   DRURY DEWELL. Inventory. Date: 7 Feb. 1794. Rec.: 22 July
             1794. Richard Ellis, John Andrews and Thomas Ellis, Appr.

Page 71:   JOHN LITTLE of Surry. Will. Date: 31 Oct. 1793. Rec.: 22
             July 1794. Mary Little, Executrix. Daughter: Charlotte.
             Wife: Polly. Brother: James. Witnesses: Josiah Wilson and
             Thomas Wrenn.

Page 73:   MARY CARRELL of Southwark Parish, Surry. Will. Date: Dec.
             14, 1793. Rec.: Oct. 28, 1794. Samuel Carrell and William
             Frazier, Executors. Daughters: Mary, Priscilla; and Sally
             Frazer. Sons: John and Samuel. Witnesses: John Warren, Sr.,
             Philip King and Martha Pyland.

Page 74:   BLACKBURN ANDREWS. Inventory. Date: 1 Apr. 1792. Rec.: 28
             Oct. 1794. Will Bailey, Sampson Grantham and John Jarratt,
             Appraisers.

Page 75:   MARTHA JUDKINS of Southwark Parish, Surry. Will. Date: 11
             Mar. 1794. Rec.: 28 Oct. 1794. John Judkins, Executor.
             Sons: Joseph and John. Daughter: Rebecca. Grandchildren:
             Martha Wilkins Judkins; Robert, John and Ann Lamb Judkins.
             Witnesses: Nathaniel Adams, William Adams and John Lane.

Page 77:   SAMUEL BIDGOOD. Account Current. Date: 1791. Rec.: 28 Oct.
             1794. John Murray presents. Mentions: wife's portion of Mr.
             Carrell's estate. David Cocke and Henry Crafford, Auditors.

Page 78:   THOMAS MARRIOTT. Inventory. Date: 3 Dec. 1794. Rec.: 27 Jan.
             1795. Ro. Watkins, William Hamlin and Langley C. Wills, Ap-
             praisers.

Page 81:   LUCY PRESSON of Surry. Will. Date: 12 Nov. 1794. Rec.: 27
             Jan. 1795. John White, Executor. Son: John. Daughters: Ann,
             Elizabeth and Lucy. Friend: John White. Witnesses: Joseph
             Holleman, John Holleman and Benjamin White.

Page 82:   SAMUEL BIDGOOD. Account Current. Rec.: 27 Jan. 1795. John
             Murry, Executor. John Wesson, David Cocke and John Holleman,
             Auditors.

Page 83:   ELIZABETH KEA. Account Current. Date: ---. Rec.: 27 Jan.
            1795. William Kea, Executor. James Sebrell, J. Bartle, Jr.,
            Auditors.

Page 84:   BRUTON KEA. Account Current. Date: ---. Rec.: 27 Jan. 1795.
            William Kea, Executor. James Sebrell, J. Bartle, Jr., Aud.

Page 85:   THOMAS FORSYTH. Inventory. Date: 3 June 1790. Rec.: 24 Feb.
            1795. James Anderson presents. Arthur Sinclair, Nicholas
            Faulcon and Richard Edwards, Appraisers.

Page 86:   WILLIAM ANDREWS of Surry. Will. Date: 17 July 1793. Rec.:
            24 Feb. 1795. Benjamin Andrews and Thomas Bailey, Executors.
            Son: Benjamin. Daughters: Parmelia Brit; Sarah and Ann An-
            drews; Mary Rae; Faithy and Elizabeth Andrews. Grand-daugh-
            ter: Mary Blackburn Andrews. Witnesses: Nathaniel Andrews,
            Patty Larter Andrews and Sarah Bailey.

Page 87:   BETTY HOWARD of Southwark Parish, Surry. Will. Date: 20 Dec.
            1794. Rec.: 24 Feb. 1795. Thomas Bilbro, Executor. Sons:
            Benjamin, Thomas, Berriman and Bernerd Bilbro. Daughter:
            Sarah Moyler. Grandson: John Heath Howard. Witnesses: Hen-
            ry Bishop and Lucy Austin.

Page 90:   RICHARD FOSTER of Surry. Will. Date: 26 Nov. 1794. Rec.: 24
            Feb. 1795. Ransom Foster and Peter Foster, Executors. Sons:
            Ransom and Peter. Grandchildren: John Foster; Susanna R.
            Clark (not 21). Witnesses: John Gwaltney, Tomer Presson and
            James Clark.

Page 91:   WILLIAM STEWARD. Inventory. Date: 22 Dec. 1794. Rec.: 24
            Feb. 1795. James Holt, Stephen Sorsby and Richard Ellis,
            Appraisers.

Page 92:   JOHN COLLIER. Inventory. Date: 8 Feb. 1791. Rec.: 28 Apr.
            1795. Emelia Collier, Administratrix. John Burgess, Edmund
            Carseley and Michael Carseley, Appraisers.

Page 95:   JEREMIAH PIERCE. Inventory. Date: 21 Dec. 1793. Rec.: 28
            Apr. 1795. Rodwell Delk, James Edwards and Henry Marks, Ap-
            praisers.

Page 97:   MARTHA EDWARDS. Will. Date: 8 Mar. 1795. Rec.: 28 Apr. 1795.
            Daughters: Rebecca and Cherry. Son: Joel. Witnesses: Will-
            iam Warren and William Kee.

Page 97:   ROBERT COLLINS of Surry. Will. Date: 20 Feb. 1795. Rec.:28
            Apr. 1795. Legatees: Mrs. Sarah Moring; Nancy Bailey Moring
            and Mary Moring, daughters of John and Sarah. Witnesses:
            Thomas Bailey, Henry Lucas, Pleasant Harrison and Jinny Har-
            rison.

Page 99:   JOHN SAVIDGE of Surry. Will. Date: 3 Feb. 1795. Rec.: 28
            Apr. 1795. David Savidge, Executor. Son: David. Daughter:
            Selah Slade. Mentions: all my children. Witnesses: Joel
            Savidge, William E. Batts and James Savidge.

Page 100:   JOHN STEWART. Inventory. Date: 5 Mar. 1795. Rec.: 29 Apr.
            1795. J. Kee, Executor. Stephen Sorsby, John Tillott and
            Edmund Carseley, Appraisers.

Page 102:   WILLIAM ELLIS. Inventory. Date: ---. Rec.: 29 Apr. 1795.
            William Maget, John Pettway and Jos'h Holt, Appraisers.

Page 103:   LEMUEL COCKE, JR. of Surry. Will. Date: 11 Apr. 1795. Rec:
            26 May 1795. Uncle: Lemuel Cocke. Sister: Catharine Cocke.
            Codicil. Brother: Henry Cocke. Mentions: deceased father's
            estate. Witnesses: (none). Nathan Jones, and John Lucas
            swear to handwriting.

Page 105:   JOHN SAVIDGE. Inventory. Date: 28 Apr. 1795. Rec.: 23 June 1795. David Savidge, Executor. Joel Savidge, Benjamin Riggan and William E. Thompson, Appraisers.

Page 106:   WILLIAM ANDREWS. Inventory. Date: 23 Mar. 1795. Rec.: 23 June 1795. William Bailey, Henry Bailey and Sampson Grantham, Appraisers.

Page 107:   NAT ROBERTS of Southwark Parish, Surry. Will. Date: 21 Apr. 1795. Rec.: 23 June 1795. John Holleman, Executor. Wife: Hannah. Grandsons: Nat and Mike (Roberts). Mentions: Hannah Green. Witness: John Presson.

Page 109:   REBECCA EVANS of Surry. Will. Date: 5 Sept. 1793. Rec.: 23 June 1795. Caufield Seward and William R. Hart, Executors. Daughters: Dolly (not 21); and Sally Drew Evans. Son: William (not 21). Deceased Husband: William Evans. Nephews: William R. Hart, and Caufield Seward. Witnesses: James Hancock and Joanna Rogers.

Page 110:   PRISCILLA CARRELL of Surry. Will. Date: 26 Oct. 1792. Rec: 23 June 1795. John Carrell and William Epps Frazier, Executors. Brother: John Carrell. Mentions: Polly Watkins Frazier; Ann Carrell; Polly Carrell, daughter of John (none 18) and Thomas Carrell Frazier; James Davis Frazier. Witnesses: James Clarke and John Davis.

Page 111:   WILLIAM HART. Account Current. Date: ---. Rec.: 23 Jun.1795. Edwin D. Hart, Administrator. Mentions: legacies from David Drew with 15 years interest to: Caufield Seward, Elizabeth Gray and Elizabeth Blow; balance due from William Drew division in 1779 to: Caufield Seward, and Rebecca Drew; due Edwin Seward legatee of Capt. William Seward, from William Hart, Executor. Willis Wilson and Henry Crafford, Auditors.

Page 113:   WILLIAM MAHONE of Surry. Will. Date: 4 Feb. 1795. Rec.: 23 June 1795. James Mahone and William Mahone, Executors. Sons: James, and William (not 21). Wife: Susanna. Daughters: Nancy, Sally, Patsey and Lucy. Witnesses: John Holt, James Simpson and Albridgton Seward.

Page 115:   JOHN THOMPSON. Account Current. Date: 1773. Rec.: 28 July 1795. Thomas Pretlow, Administrator. Richard Edwards, Henry Marks and Richard Shackleford, Auditors.

Page 116:   JOSEPH JUDKINS of Southwark Parish, Surry. Will. Date: 22 Mar. 1795. Rec.: 28 July 1795. Mary Judkins, Executrix. Wife: Mary. Son: John Wilkins Judkins (not 18). Daughter: Ann Lamb Judkins. Mentions: land left me by my father and by my brother, William. Witnesses: Henry Gilbert, John Ellis and Richard Pyland.

Page 118:   THOMAS FORSYTHE. Account Current. Date: 1791. Rec.: 28 Jul. 1795. James Anderson, Administration. Thomas Pretlow, Benjamin Bilbro and Joseph Mason, Auditors.

Page 119:   WILLIAM EMERY. Account Current. Date: 1772. Rec.: 22 Sept. 1795. Ruth Emery, Administratrix. Mentions: payment to William Boyce, ward of William Emery. John Wesson, John Pettway and Henry Crafford, Auditors.

Page 121:   PRISCILLA CARRELL. Inventory. Date: 18 Jul. 1795. Rec.: 22 Sept. 1795. John Carrell and William E. Frazier, Executors. Henry Moring, William Lane and James Smith, Appraisers.

Page 122:   THOMAS J'ANSON. Account Current. Date: 1791. Rec.: 22 Jul. 1795. John Southall, Administrator. John Lucas, Thomas Peter and Peter Jemm, Auditors.

Page 125:   JOHN COOPER of Surry. Will. Date: 25 Sept. 1795. Rec.: 27

140

(Page 125 - COOPER cont'd.): Oct. 1795. James Kee, Executor. Son: Coleman. Daughters: Charlotte and Permelia. Witnesses: Edmund Carseley, John Justiss, Frederick Cooper and Joseph Ellis.

Page 126:   WILLIAM WHITE. Account Current. Date: 1781. Rec.: 27 Oct. 1795. Thomas White, Administrator. Benjamin and Thomas White mentioned; paid sheriffs of Surry and Isle of Wight Counties. Willis Wilson and John Warren, Jr., Auditors.

Page 129:   EDWARD BROWN of Surry. Will. Date: 30 July 1795. Rec.: 26 Jan. 1796. Jesse Turner, Executor. Daughters: Martha Battin and Ann Turner. Grandchildren: Ann Cornwell, Ann Long, Willis Long and David Long. Friend: James Davis. Son-in-law: Jesse Turner. Witnesses: John Gwaltney, William Cornwell and William Bennett.

Page 131:   ANN THOMPSON, Account Current. Date: 1792. Rec.: 13 Feb. 1796. Thomas Spratley, Executor. Mentions judgement vs. William Edloe Thompson. John Pettway, Thomas Ellis and Archibald Davis, Auditors.

Page 132:   RICHARD D. BROWN. Account Current. Date: 1793. Rec.: 23 Feb. 1796. Dixon Brown, Administrator. Mentions: payments for the board of: Martha, Jean, Frances and Molly Brown; payments to sheriffs of Surry, York and Warwick Counties. Will Boyce and Robert Hunnicutt, Auditors.

Page 134:   MARY LANE of Surry. Will. Date: 27 Apr. 1794. Rec.: 23 Feb. 1796. Thomas Lane, Executor. Son: Thomas. Daughter: Sally Barham. Grandchildren: Elizabeth Whitaker Lane; Mary Haynes Rogers; Sally Lane; Mary Ann Barham; Thomas Lane; Peggy Lane; Martha Lane, and Lucy Lane. Daughter-in-law: Lucy Lane. Witnesses: Wil Salter and Henry Crafford.

Page 136:   ANN SIMPSON of Surry. Will. Date: 24 Oct. 1793. Rec.: 22 Mar. 1796. James Simpson, Executor. Sons: James and Thomas. Daughter: Deborah. Friend: James A. Bradby. Witnesses: Rodwell Delk and Richard Scammell.

Page 138:   JOHN SPRATLEY. Inventory. Date: 14 Nov. 1793. Rec.: 26 Apr. 1796. William Maget, Thomas Ellis and Richard Ellis, Apprs.

Page 141:   ROBERT PYLAND of Surry. Will. Date: 23 Nov. 1795. Rec.: 26 Apr. 1796. Sally Pyland and Benjamin Pyland, Executors. Wife: Sally. Sons: Benjamin; Robert and Thomas (not of age) Daughters: all (none named). Friends: John Pyland and John Wesson. Witnesses: William Davis, John H. Judkins and Amos Judkins.

Page 143:   HARTWELL HARGRAVE of Surry. Will. Date: 10 Sept. 1794. Rec: 28 Apr. 1796. Herman and James Hargrave, Executors. Sons: Herman and James. Daughters: Sarah Ellisson, wife of Robert Ellisson; Milly. Grandchildren: Joshua, John and Sarah Hargrave. Witnesses: Lemuel Bailey, Lemuel Atkinson and Patience Bailey.

Page 145:   JOHN BURGESS of Surry. Will. Date: 30 Mar. 1796. Rec.: 26 Apr. 1796. Miles Burgess, Executor. Wife: Mary. Son: Miles. Daughters: Alice Carseley, and Rebecca (Burgess). Mentions all of my children. Witnesses: Faith Dewell, J. Kee and Susan D. Cheatham.

Page 147:   HENRY COCKE. Inventory. Date: 11 Dec. 1777. Rec.: 26 April 1796. Lemuel Cocke presents. James Belsches, Sr., Nathan Jones and Hamilton Jones (deceased).

Page 151:   JOHN ATKINSON of Surry. Will. Date: 23 Feb. 1796. Rec.: 26 1796. John Atkinson and Samuel Atkinson, Executors. Sons: Oney, William, John and Samuel. Daughters: Nancy Hart;

(Page 151 - ATKINSON cont'd.): Elizabeth; Martha Oney, and Lucy. Witnesses: Joshua Bailey, Robert Atkinson and Lemuel Atkinson.

Page 154: SAMUEL PRETLOW. Inventory. Date: 3 Jan. 1791. Rec.: 26 Apr. 1796. Samuel Blow, Richard Edwards, John Hunnicutt and Robert Hunnicutt, Appraisers.

Page 157: LEWIS GRANTHAM of Southwark Parish, Surry. Will. Date: 4 Mar. 1791. Rec.: 28 June 1796. Thomas Grantham, Executor. Wife: (unnamed). Father: Stephen. Brother: Thomas. Witnesses: John Avriss, William Averiss and Agnes Austin.

Page 158: WILLIAM MILBY. Inventory. Date: 5 June 1795. Rec.: 28 June 1796. John Lucas, William Simmons and Henry Dewell, Apprs.

Page 160: WILLIAM COLLINS. Inventory. Date: 24 Jan. 1794. Rec.: 28 June 1796. John Lucas, William Simmons and Christopher Lucas (deceased), Appraisers.

Page 163: JOHN SOUTHALL. Inventory. Date: 13 Dec. 1794. Rec.: 28 Jun. 1796. John Lucas, William Simmons and Christopher Lucas, (deceased), Appraisers.

Page 167: THOMAS BAGE of Southwark Parish, Surry. Will. Date: 9 Feb. 1792. Rec.: 26 May 1795. (Further proven 28 June 1796.) Son: Thomas. Friend: John Watkins, Jr. Witnesses: Will Browne, Robert Cocke and J. Watkins, Jr.

Page 169: SAMUEL BAILEY of Surry. Will. Date: 3rd mo. 22, 1796. Rec.: 27 Sept. 1796. Joseph G. Bailey and Samuel Cornwell, Executors. Daughters: Margaret Bailey, Sarah Cornwell and Ann Pretlow. Son: Joseph G. Bailey. Sons-in-law: Samuel Cornwell, Thomas Pretlow. Witnesses: Wyke Hunnicutt, Mary Hunnicutt, Ann Hunnicutt, William Carrell, Isham Inman and Anselm Hargrave.

Page 172: ROBERT BELL of Surry. Will. Date: 14 July 1796. Rec.: 27 Sept. 1796. John H. Bell and James Bell, Executors. Wife: Ann. Sons: Micajah, Thomas A., James, John H. Bell. Daughters: Lucy C. Bell; Martha Delk. Witnesses: Drewry P. Warren, Benjamin Bell and James H. Warren.

Page 175: LUCY COLLIER. Account Current. Date: 1791. Rec.: 27 Sept. 1796. Emelia Collier, Administratrix. John Watkins, Archibald Cocke and Archibald Davis, Auditors.

Page 176: JOHN COLLIER. Account Current. Date: 1791. Rec.: 27 Sept. 1796. Emelia Collier, Administratrix. Mentions: boarding for John, George, Lucy and Benjamin. John Watkins, Archibald Cocke and Archibald Davis, Auditors.

Page 178: JOSEPH JUDKINS. Inventory. Date: Dec. 1795. Rec.: 27 Sept. 1796. Mary Judkins, Executrix.

Page 179: NATHANIEL SAVIDGE of Surry. Will. Date: 31 Mar. 1796. Rec: 27 Sept. 1796. Susanna Savidge rel. (releases?) rt.(right?) to provision in will. Wife: Susanna. Son: Robert (not of age). Daughters: Cherry Cocks Savidge; Susanna Savidge; Hannah Bruton Savidge. Friend: William Clinch, Jr. Witnesses: Thomas Spratley, John Lane and Benjamin Cocks.

Page 181: JAMES COLLIER. Inventory. Date: 1 Feb. 1796. Rec.: 27 Sep. 1796. Sampson Grantham, Jesse Dewell and James Cheatham, Appraisers.

Page 182: JOHN BARHAM. Add. Account Current. Date: ---. Rec.: 27 Sep. 1796. Sarah Barham, Executrix.

Page 182: MARY LANE. Inventory. Date: 25 Mar. 1796. Rec.: 25 Oct. 1796. Thomas Lane, Executor.

Page 183:   WILLIAM CYPRESS of Surry. Will. Date: 18 Jan. 1796. Rec.:
              25 Oct. 1796. Howell Debereaux, Executor. Wife: (unnamed).
              Children: (unnamed). Friend: Howell Debereaux. Witnesses:
              J. Kee and Joseph Holt.

Page 184:   JOHN DAVIS. Account Current. Date: 1793. Rec.: 25 Oct. 1796.
              John and Nathaniel Davis, Executors. Mentions legacies to:
              John Davis, son of James; Selah Davis; Archer Davis; Will-
              iam Davis; James Crocker (for wife); Thomas Davis; Jesse
              Gray (for wife); Betsey Davis; Polly Davis, Elizabeth Dav-
              is; John Davis, son of Nathan; Nathaniel Davis; and Sally
              Davis (a minor). Thomas Spratley and Thomas Bailey, Aud.

Page 186:   MARTHA R. COCKE, widow of Robert Cocke, late of Surry, de-
              ceased. Releases right of administration of husband's es-
              tate. Date: 22 Oct. 1796. Rec.: 25 Oct. 1796. John Newsum
              and Francis Ruffin, Witnesses:

Page 186:   MARY ANDREWS of Surry. Will. Date: 3 Sept. 1796. Rec.: 25
              Oct. 1796. James Rae, Executor. Legatees: Rhoda Justiss,
              Howell Deberix and James Rae. Witnesses: Jesse King, Thom-
              as Bailey, Jr., and Thomas Bailey, Sr.

Page 187:   HANNAH TUCKER. Will. Date: 12 Feb. 1796. Rec.: 27 Sept.
              1796. (Further proven 25 Oct. 1796.). Lemuel Cocke, Execu-
              tor. Sister: Sarah. Witnesses: Benjamin Bilbro, Henry Bis-
              hop, Winne Bell and Bernard Bilbro.

Page 188:   MARY SPRATLEY. Account Current. Date: 1778. Rec.: 25 Oct.
              1796. William Spratley, Executor. Mentions: William Sprat-
              ley's part; John Spratley's part; Benjamin Spratley's part;
              Jacob Faulcon's part; Walter Spratley's part to his distri-
              butees (each claimants part = 1/6). Edward Faulcon, Will-
              iam Simmons and Nicholas Sebrell, Auditors.

Page 190:   CHRISTOPHER THORP. Account Current. Date: ---. Rec.: 25 Oct.
              1796. Nicholas and Edward Faulcon, Executors of Nicholas
              Faulcon, Executors with William Browne of Christopher Thorp.

Page 191:   JOHN BADGELL. Account Current. Date: 1793. Rec.: 24 Jan'y.
              1797. William C. Partin, Administrator. Mentions: Elizabeth
              Badgell's part. Freeman Ward and Samuel Ellis, Auditors.

Page 192:   WILLIAM COLLIER of Surry. Will. Date: 16 Aug. 1796. Rec.:
              24 Jan. 1797. Howell Collier, Executor. Brothers: Howell &
              Stephen. Sisters: Patsy & Dolly Collier. Father: Stephen,
              deceased. Witnesses: William C. Partin, Faithy Dewell and
              Wyatt Dewell.

Page 194:   SAMUEL LUCAS. Inventory. Date: 4 Mar. 1795. Rec.: 24 Jan.
              1797. John Lucas, Henry Dewell and Sampson Grantham, Appr.

Page 196:   HENRY WHITE of Surry (aged). Will. Date: 23 Sept. 1791.
              Rec.: 28 Feb. 1797. Elizabeth White granted administration.
              Sons: James, Samuel, Charles, and Walter. Daughters: Sarah,
              and Elizabeth. Grandson: Henry White Carrell. Wife: Eliza-
              beth. Friend: James Kee. Mentions: land which descended to
              my wife Elizabeth from her father, Thomas Sorsby. (Deed of
              Gift: Date: 19 June 1753). Witnesses: N. Barker, Henry John-
              son and Richard Barker.

Page 198:   JOHN ATKINSON. Inventory. Date: 15 Mar. 1796. Rec.: 28 Feb.
              1797. John and Samuel Atkinson, Executors. Thomas Clary,
              Robert Atkinson and Thomas Wren, Appraisers.

Page 200:   JOHN COOPER. Inventory. Date: 26 Nov. 1795. Rec.: 28 Feb.
              1797. James Kee, Executor. Edmund Carseley and William Jus-
              tiss, Appraisers.

Page 202:   BENJAMIN WOOD of Surry. Will. Date: 14 Nov. 1796. Rec.: 28

(Page 202 - WOOD cont'd.): Feb. 1797. Lemuel Bailey and Isham Inman, Executors. Daughter: Elizabeth Phillip S. Wood (not of age).
Nephews and Neices: John, Sarah, Nancy, Joshua, and Edmund
Wood, children of Joel. Brother(s) and Sister(s): only Joel
named. Mother: (unnamed). Mentions: father's estate. Witnesses: Thomas Riggan, Samuel Ellis and James Holleway.

Page 204:   MARY BATTS. Inventory. Date: 30 Jan. 1796. Rec.: 28 Feb.
1797. John Warren, Administrator. Benjamin Cocks, Joel Savidge and James Smith, Appraisers.

Page 205:   ROBERT PYLAND. Inventory. Date: 10 May 1796. Rec.: 28 Mar.
1797. William Bennett, William Adams, and James Adams, Appraisers.

Page 208:   THOMAS MALLECOTE. Account Current. Date: 1791. Rec.: 25 Apr.
1797. Robert McIntosh and William Boyce, Executors.

Page 209:   WILLIAM EDWARDS of Southwark Parish, Surry. Will. Date: 2
Sept. 1791. Rec.: 25 Apr. 1797. Richard Edwards, Executor.
Wife: Susannah. Sons: William, Thomas, and Richard Henry.
Daughter: Ann. Child in esse. Brother: Richard. Mentions:
land in Surry and Southampton Counties; land given me by
father and uncle, William Edwards. Witnesses: (none). Nicholas Faulcon, Richard Cocke, and John Wesson swear to the
handwriting.

Page 212:   ROBERT COCKE. Inventory. Date: 12 Nov. 1796. Rec.: 25 Apr.
1797. (Estate in Southampton County). Jacob Turner, William
Urquhart and John Taylor, Appraisers.

Page 214:   ROBERT COCKE. Inventory. (Town of Petersburg.) Date: 19 Nov.
1796. Rec.: 25 Apr. 1797. James Durell, Erasmus Gill and
William Durell, Appraisers.

Page 215:   ROBERT COCKE. Inventory. (Surry County). Date: 3 Dec. 1796.
Rec.: 25 Apr. 1797. B. E. Browne, James Clarke and Sim
Thompson, Appraisers.

Page 217:   ROBERT COCKE. Inventory. (Property not previously appr'd).
Date: ---. Rec.: 25 Apr. 1797. John Newsum, Administrator.

Page 220:   JAMES ALEXANDER. Inventory. Date: 6 June 1797. Rec.: 27 Jun.
1797. Henry Crafford, William Phillips and James Jones, Appraisers.

Page 222:   HENRY WHITE. Inventory. Date: 17 June 1797. Rec.: 27 June
1797. Elizabeth White, Executrix. Charles Judkins, William
Spratley and Frederick Lane, Appraisers.

Page 223:   JOHN JUDKINS. Account Current. Date: 1791. Rec.: 25 July
1797. Jacob Judkins, Administrator. Mentions: John Judkins,
deceased guardian of Ann Judkins Burt; Jacob Judkins part
of Nicholas Judkins' estate; Wilmot Egerton's part of the
Nicholas Judkins' estate; Wilmot Egerton, Executor of James
Egerton's estate. Auditors: William Cocke, B. Major and Walter Johnston.

Page 225:   JOHN LUCAS. Account Current. Date: 1785. Rec.: 25 July 1797.
Sarah Lucas, Administratrix. Mentions: payments to Stephen
Lucas estate; Sarah Lucas, widow, her thirds; Christopher
and Sarah Lucas for keeping slaves; received from Samuel
Lucas estate. Thomas Peter, Walter Johnston and John J'An-
son, Auditors.

Page 231:   WILLIAM EDWARDS. Inventory. Date: 16 May 1797. Rec.: 26 Sep.
1797. (Southampton County, where Amos Stephens lives). John
T. Blow, Richard Blow and Thomas Vaughan, Appraisers.

Page 232:   WILLIAM EDWARDS. Inventory. Date: ---. Rec.: 26 Sept. 1797.

144

(Page 232 - EDWARDS cont'd.): (Southampton County, where Edward Shelvay
lives). John T. Blow, Sr., John Underwood, Richard Blow,
Appraisers. Richard Edwards, Executor.

Page 233:   WILLIAM EDWARDS. Inventory. Date: 16 June 1797. Rec.:   26
Sept. 1797. (Surry County). Richard Edwards, Executor. John
Hunnicutt, Henry Gilbert and N. Faulcon, Appraisers.

Page 237:   LEMUEL ATKINSON of Surry. Will. Date: 11 Sept. 1797. Rec.:
24 Sept. 1797. Mark Carrell, Executor. Wife: Patty. Sons:
James and Thomas. Daughter: Becky. Friend: William Atkinson
of Southampton. Witnesses: Thomas Wrenn, Elizabeth Atkinson and Lucy Atkinson.

Page 239:   ARCHER HOLT of Surry. Will. Date: 24 Mar. 1797. Rec.: Sept.
24, 1797. Mary Holt, Executrix. Wife: Mary. Sons: James,
John and Drew. Daughters: Elizabeth Warren, and Mary Holt.
Mother: (unnamed). Friend: William Boyce. Mentions schooling for: Elizabeth Warren, Mary and Drew. Witnesses: William E. Thompson, Maget Smith and William Wright.

Page 240:   ANSELM HARGRAVE of Surry. Will. Date: 7th mo. 8, 1797. Rec:
24 Sept. 1797. Joshua Bailey, Executor. Wife: Hannah. Sons:
Jordan, Anselm and Lemuel. Daughters: Peggy, Sally, Nancy
and Hannah. Sister: Martha Hargrave (her bequests to my
children). Witnesses: William Trotter, Herbert Sledge and
Martha Sledge.

Page 242:   WILLIAM ROSE of Surry. Will. Date: 16 Mar. 1785. Rec.: 24
Oct. 1797. James Kee, Executor. Sons: John, Benjamin and
Samuel. Wife: (unnamed). Wife's daughter: Susanna Harrison.
Mentions: all my children. Witnesses: Nathaniel Sebrell,
Burwell Sharp and John Stiles.

Page 243:   JOHN WATKINS, JR. of Surry. Will. Date: 15 Aug. 1796. Rec.:
24 Oct. 1797. Robert Watkins, Executor. Sisters:Sarah Yarbrough, Elizabeth L. Waddill and Dolly Watkins. Brothers:
Nicholas (deceased), and Robert. Neice: Lucy G. Waddill.
Nephew: John Waddill. Friend: Noel Waddill. Mentions: Elizabeth L. Waddill's other children; land in Kentucky. Witnesses: (none). John Bartle, Jr., William Nicholson and William Cryer swear to handwriting.

Page 245:   EDWARD BROWN. Inventory. Date: 18 Jan. 1796. Rec.: 24 Oct.
1797. Jesse Turner, Executor. James Davis, Thomas Cofer &
Joseph Davis, Appraisers.

Page 246:   WILLIAM HARRISS of Surry. Will. Date: 29 Mar. 1796. Rec.:
28 Nov. 1797. Hamlin Harriss, Executor. Son: Hamlin. Daughter: Elizabeth Campbell. Son-in-law: Francis Ruffin (and
wife). Mentions: all my children; land in Nottoway, Dinwiddie and Curry Counties. Witnesses: (none). Thomas Harriss, James Belsches, Sr., William Simmons and David Cocke
swear to handwriting.

Page 248:   JOHN COCKE of Surry. Will. Date: 1 Apr. 1795. Rec.: 23 Jan.
1798. Walter Cocke, Executor. Daughters: Mary Stark Harrison; Ann Cocke; and Rebecca Cocke. Son: Walter. Friend: Henry Harrison. Witnesses: Travis Harris, John Newsum and Hamlin Harris.

Page 249:   SAMUEL LUCAS. Account Current. Date: 5 Mar. 1795. Rec.: 23
Jan. 1798. Mary Lucas, Executrix. Carter Nicholas, John
Bartle, Jr. and Lemuel Bailey, Appraisers.

Page 250:   THOMAS GWALTNEY of Surry. Will. Date: 25 Nov. 1797. Rec.:
23 Jan. 1798. Sarah Gwaltney, Executrix. Son-in-law: Benjamin Bell. Grandson: Benjamin C. Bell. Daughters: Sarah Holleman; Rebecca Phillips; Martha Cofer; Ann Cofer; Polly
Gwaltney; and Nancy Gwaltney. Son-in-law: Benjamin Shelly.

145

(Page 250 - GWALTNEY cont'd.): Sons: Thomas P. and Ludwell. Wife: Sarah.
Witnesses: John Gwaltney, Joseph Davis and William White.

Page 253:   ARTHUR WARREN of Surry. Will. Date: 1 May 1797. Rec.: 23
Jan. 1798. Drewry P. Warren and Mark Holleway, Executors.
Wife: Ann. Sons: Drewry P., Judkins; and Lemuel (not 21).
Daughters: Lucy, Sarah and Nancy. Son-in-law: Mark Holleway.
Witnesses: John D. Warren, Thomas Warren, Joel Holleway &
William Warren.

Page 254:   PERRY JORDAN. Inventory. Date: 15 July 1797. Rec.: 27 Feb.
1798. Bathshaba Jordan presents. Michael Carseley, Edmund
Carseley and John Stiles, Appraisers.

Page 255:   SAMUEL WARREN. Inventory. Date: 29 Jan. 1798. Rec.: 27 Feb.
1798. William Adams, John Judkins and John Ellis, Appraisers.

Page 256:   JOHN LITTLE. Inventory. Date: 20 Nov. 1797. Rec.: 27 Feb.
1798. R'd. Pierce, Samuel Wilson and Jeremiah Pierce, Appraisers.

Page 257:   Mrs. REBECCA EVANS. Inventory. Date: ---. Rec.: 27 Feb.
1798. James Wall, William Holt and Joel Wall, Appraisers.

Page 258:   REBECCA JUDKINS of Southwark Parish, Surry. Will. Date: 5
Jan. 1798. Rec.: 27 Feb. 1798. John Judkins, Executor.Bro:
John Judkins. Neice: Martha Wilkins Judkins. Witnesses: Hen-
ry Gilbert and Binns Gilbert.

Page 259:   WILLIAM CYPRESS. Inventory. Date: 11 Nov. 1796. Rec.: 27
Feb. 1798. John Andrews, Richard Ellis and John Pettway,
Appraisers.

Page 260:   Mr. JOHN WATKINS, JR. Inventory. Date: 13 Nov. 1797. Rec.:
27 Feb. 1798. John Bartle, Jr., William Cryer and James
Clarke, Appraisers.

Page 262:   JOHN MARSTON of Surry. Will. Date: 25 Oct. 1797. Rec.: 27
Mar. 1798. Susanna Marston, Executrix. Wife: Susanna. Witnesses: James Belsches, Jr., William Cocke and James Stewart.

Page 263:   WILLIAM HART of Surry. Will. Date: 26 Feb. 1798. Rec.: 24
Apr. 1798. William Ingram and Joel Thompson, Executor. Wife:
Sarah. Sons: Robert, William and Edward. Daughters: Polly,
and Sally. Witnesses: Benjamin Bell and David Long.

Page 264:   CHRISTOPHER LUCAS. Inventory. Date: 5 Dec. 1796. Rec.: 24
Apr. 1798. Thomas Bailey, William Bailey, Sampson Grantham
and William Simmons, Appraisers.

Page 266:   STEPHEN COLLIER. Inventory. Date: 29 Jan. 1796. Rec.: 24
Apr. 1798. Sampson Grantham, James Cheatham and Thomas Bailey, Appraisers.

Page 267:   MARY ANDREWS. Inventory. Date: 28 Oct. 1796. Rec.: 24 Apr.
1798. William Bailey, Thomas Bailey and Henry Bailey, Appraisers.

Page 268:   WILLIAM COLLIER. Inventory. Date: 29 Dec. 1796. Rec.: 24
Apr. 1798. Thomas Bailey, Sampson Grantham and Jesse Dewell,
Appraisers.

Page 269:   SAMUEL WARREN. Account Current. Date: ---. Rec.: 26 June
1798. William Boyce, Administrator.

Page 269:   RANDOLPH PRICE. Account Current. Date: 1780. Rec.: 26 June
1798. John Wesson, Executor. Mentions: payments to Mrs.
Price; Randolph Price, (orphan); David Price, (orphan); Lu-

(Page 269 - PRICE cont'd.): cy Ellis (her portion); John Ellis (his wife's portion). Edward Faulcon, Will Scammell, Langley C. Wills, and Pe. Hamlin, Auditors.

Page 277: JOHN WAGONER. Inventory. Date: 1 Feb. 1798. Rec.: 26 June 1798. Samuel Carrell, William M. Davis and William Cryer, Appraisers.

Page 278: MARGARET HARRISON of Southwark Parish, Surry. Will. Date: 12 Jan. 1779. Rec.: 24 July 1798. Elizabeth Ogburn granted administration. (She was Elizabeth Massenburg.) Sister: Martha Rives and her two sons: Charles Binns and Anthony (not 21). Brother: Timothy Rives. Witnesses: Elizabeth Rives, Elizabeth Massenburg and George Rives.

Page 280: LEMUEL ATKINSON. Inventory. Date: 29 Dec. 1797. Rec.: 24 July 1798. Mark Carrell, Executor. Robert Atkinson, Herman Hargrave and William Carrell, Appraisers.

Page 281: WILLIAM ROSE. Inventory. Date: 28 Oct. 1798. Rec.: 24 July 1798. James Kee, Executor. Edmund Carseley, John Stiles & John Tillott, Appraisers.

Page 282: BENJAMIN SPRATLEY. Account Current. Date: 1792. Rec.: 24 July 1798. Thomas Spratley, Administrator. Mentions: Board of Mary, Walter, Henry, Benjamin, Elizabeth,and Nathaniel Spratley, orphans; coffins for Benjamin and Susanna Spratley. William Clinch, John Pettway, and James S. Lane, Aud.

Page 285: RICHARD SHELL. Account Current. Date: 1794. Rec.: 24 July 1798. Benjamin Barker, Administrator. John Hunnicutt, W. Clinch, Jr., and John Moring, Jr., Auditors.

Page 286: RANDOLPH PRICE. Supp'l. Account Current. Date: ---. Rec.: 31 Aug. 1798. John Wesson, Executor.

Page 287: WILLIAM COCKS of Southwark Parish, Surry. Will. Date: 15 July 1793. Rec.: 25 Sept. 1798. William Cocks and Benjamin Cocks, Executors. Daughters: Sarah Champion and Charity Cocks. Sons: William, Benjamin, John and Thomas. Son-in-law: Charles Champion. Grandchildren: Nathaniel and Jesse Cocks. Wife: Elizabeth. Witnesses: Samuel Judkins, Sr., Charles Robert Judkins, Patty Judkins and Charity Judkins.

Page 289: LUCY SMITH of Surry. Will. Date: 13 June 1798. Rec.: 25 Sept. 1798. James Smith, Executor. Sons: James, William and John. Daughter: Betsy Moring. Grandson: William Anderson. Witnesses: Batts Lane and John Lane.

Page 290: BENJAMIN MORING. Account Current. Date: 1785. Rec.: 25 Sep. 1798. Henry Moring, Administrator. Mentions: John Moring. Thomas Spratley and W. Clinch, Jr., Auditors.

Page 292: JACOB JUDKINS of Surry. Will. Date: 7 July 1798. Rec.: 23 Oct. 1798. Edward Burt, Executor. Sons: John C., Nicholas H., Jacob and William G. Judkins. Daughters: Elizabeth Burt; Lucy, Susanna and Mary Judkins. Wife: Sarah. Friends: Edward Burt and John Burt. Witnesses: James S. Lane, Edmund Wood and George Judkins.

Page 294: JOHN DARDEN WARREN of Surry. Will. Date: 1 Oct. 1798. Rec: 23 Oct. 1798. Drewry P. Warren, Executor. Wife: Cherry. Son: John Judkins Warren (not 21). Friend: Joel Lane. Witnesses: William Warren and Ann Riggan.

Page 295: MARTHA DREW. Account Current. Date: 1792. Rec.: 23 October 1798. Langley C. Wills, Administrator. Benjamin Bilbro and Henry Crafford, Auditors.

Page 296: MARTHA FAULCON of Surry. Will. Date: 4 Dec. 1793. Rec.: 23

(Page 296 - FAULCON cont'd.): Oct. 1798. Jacob Faulcon, Executor. Neice: Martha Seward. Brothers: Nicholas Faulcon (deceased), and Jacob Faulcon. Sister: Jane Faulcon. Mentions: Ann, Walter, Mary Ann; John, and Jacob (not 21) - children of brother, Jacob; Lucy, daughter of brother, Nicholas; money due me from the estate of father. Witnesses: Samuel Rowell and Joseph Berriman.

Page 298:   MARTHA DREW. Inventory. Date: 3 Nov. 1792. Rec.: 23 October 1798. Langley C. Wills, Administrator.

Page 298:   JOHN BISHOP of Surry. Will. Date: 3 May 1796. Rec.: 23 Oct. 1798. James Bishop, Executor. Sons: James, William, Isham. Daughters: Lucy Anthony; Esther and Mary Bishop. Grandson: John Bishop, son of William. Friend: Richard Fletcher. Mentions: land in Prince George County where son James lives. Witnesses: James Williamson, Walter Warthen and Peter Shuffield.

Page 300:   ANTHONY ATKINS. Account Current. Date: 1792. Rec.: 23 Oct. 1798. William Thompson, Administrator. Mentions payments to Joseph Ellis, Hannah Atkins, Mary Atkins, Rebecca Atkins & William Atkins. Thom. Kee and John Ellis, Auditors.

Page 300:   RICHARD SCAMMELL of Surry. Will. Date: 21 May 1798. Rec.: 22 Jan. 1799. William and James Scammell, Executors. Sons: James, John and William. Daughter: Mary Scammell. Neice: Mary Scammell. Witnesses: Thomas Scammell and James Simpson.

Page 302:   ELIZABETH JUSTICE of Southwark Parish, Surry. Will. Date: 2 June 1791. Rec.: 22 Jan. 1799. Rhoda Justice, Executrix. Daughter: Rhoda Justice. Witnesses: John Watkins, Elizabeth Watkins and Patrick H. Adams.

Page 303:   RICHARD EDWARDS of Surry. Will. Date: 14 Dec. 1798. Rec: 22 Jan. 1799. Benjamin Blunt, Executor. Nephews: Richard Henry Edwards and Richard Edmunds. Sisters: Ann Blunt and Mary Butts. Neice: Ann Ruffin. Daughter: Elizabeth. Neighbour: John Hunnicutt. Mentions: children of deceased brother William; i.e. - Ann Ruffin; William, Thomas, Richard H., Rebecca Browne Edwards, and Charlotte Bolling Edwards. Children of sister Elizabeth Edmunds: Polly and Richard. Children of sister Ann Blunt: John, Elizabeth and Benjamin Edwards Blunt. Witnesses: John Bartle, Jr., John Judkins, Blanks Moody, Newett Edwards and Catharine Hutchings. (Mentions land in So'n. County.)

Page 304:   JOHN MORING of Surry. Will. Date: 26 Sept. 1798. Rec.: 26 Feb. 1799. Sarah Moring, Executrix. Son: William. Daughters: Sarah, Susanna; and Elizabeth King. Grandson: William King. Wife: Sarah. Witnesses: Thomas Bailey, John Putney and John Avery.

Page 306:   JOHN MOORE. Inventory. Date: 31 Jan. 1798. Rec.: 26 Feb'y. 1799. Robert Hunnicutt, William Mitchell and Jessee Moore, Appraisers.

Page 307:   Mr, JOHN STEWART. Account Current. Date: 1791. Rec.: 26 Feb. 1799. Lemuel Cocke, Executor. Mentions: Sarah Stewart, Melvill Stewart, Mr. James Stewart, and John Melvill Stewart. Thomas Peter, Walter Johnston and John Newsum, Auditors.

Page 312:   Mrs. ELIZABETH STEWART. Account Current. Date: ---. Rec.: 26 Feb. 1799. Lemuel Cocke, Administrator. Thomas Peter, Walter Johnston and John Newsum, Auditors.

Page 314:   THOMAS MALLICOAT. Inventory. Date: 4 Jan. 1791. Rec.: Feb. 26, 1799. William Boyce, Executor. Robert Hunnicutt, Appr.

Page 315:   EDWARD BROWNE. Account Current. Date: 1796. Rec.: 26 Feb.

(Page 315 - BROWNE cont'd.): 1799. Jesse Turner, Executor. Mentions: family. Willis Wilson and William Wilson, Auditors.

Page 317: WILLIAM LANE, SR. of Surry. Will. Date: 26 May 1798. Rec: 26 Feb. 1799. Henry and Batts Lane, Executors. Sons: Henry, Batts and John. Wife: Elizabeth. Daughters: Elizabeth, Sarah and Rebecca Lane; Mary Judkins and Lucy Judkins. Granddaughter: Clotilda Moring. Mentions: John Moring, who married my daughter Martha. Witnesses: John Smith, James Smith and William Smith.

Page 319: JOSEPH HOLT of Southwark Parish, Surry. Will. Date: 2 Oct. 1798. Rec.: 23 Apr. 1799. Edward S. Holt, Executor. Wife: (unnamed). Sons: Edward S. and Phillip. Daughter: Mary S. Holt. Witnesses: John Pettway, Thomas Ellis and Richard Ellis.

Page 321: RICHARD BARKER of Surry. Will. Date: 13 Mar. 1799. Rec.: 23 Apr. 1799. Nancy Barker, Executrix. Wife: Nancy. Son: Jehu Nicholas Barker. Witnesses: David Sebrell, Stephen Andrews and William Maget.

Page 322: PHILLIP THOMPSON. Will. Date: 8 Sept. 1792. Rec.: 23 April 1799. William E. Thompson, Executor. Wife: (unnamed). Son: William E. Children: (unnamed). Friends: Jesse Warren and Freeman Ward (both deceased at time of recording). Witnesses: Joseph Barham and Thomas Lane.

Page 323: JOHN STEWART. Account Current. Date: 1795. Rec.: 23 April 1799. James Kee, Executor. Mentions: payments of full portion of estate to: Jessee Stewart, Nathaniel Stewart, Hubbard Stewart, Stephen Stewart, Elizabeth Stewart, Hannah Dewel and Susanna Stewart. Langley C. Wills and Thomas Bailley, Sr., Auditors.

Page 324: LEMUEL BARKER. Inventory. Date: 9 Dec. 1789. Rec.: 25 June 1799. Henry Bishop, Lemuel Cocke and Richard Blunt, Appr's.

Page 325: RICHARD BARKER. Inventory. Date: 27 Apr. 1799. Rec.: 25 June 1799. David Sebrell, Robert Ellis and Nathaniel Sebrell, Appraisers.

Page 327: LEMUEL BARKER. Account Current. Date: 1789. Rec.: 25 June 1799. Sterling Hill, Executor. Mentions: Benjamin Barker. John Pettway and John Peter, Auditors.

Page 328: JOHN COMAN. Account Current. Date: 1797. Rec.: 25 Jun. 1799. Jesse Dewell, Administrator. Thomas Ellis and Benjamin Cocke are Auditors.

Page 329: RICHARD EDWARDS. Inventory. (Southampton County). Date: 31 Jan. 1799. Rec.: 24 July 1799. Edward Bailey, Harmon Harris and Thomas Pretlow, Appraisers.

Page 331: PHILLIP THOMPSON. Inventory. Date: 24 June 1799. Rec.: 24 Sept. 1799. James Adams, John Mallicote and Joseph Barham, Appraisers.

Page 332: BENJAMIN ALLEN COCKE of Surry. Will. Date: 20 July 1799. Rec.: 24 Sept. 1799. John Hunnicutt, Executor. Wife: Susannah. Brother: Allen. Neighbours: Henry Crafford, Robert Hunnicutt, John Hunnicutt and Sally Norsworthy. Friend: William Edwards, son of Phillip. Witnesses: Rowland Holt, James Simpson and Thomas Seward. Mentions: land in Goochland Co.

Page 334: SAMUEL BLOW of Surry. Will. Date: 19 Apr. 1796. Rec.: 27 Sept. 1796. Micajah Blow and Thomas Ridley Blow, Executors. Wife: Mary Ridley. Son: Robert Ridley Blow (not 21). Daughter: Lucy Blow. Child in esse. Brothers: Micajah and Thomas Ridley Blow. Friend: William Ruffin Hart. Witnesses:

149

(Page 334 - BLOW cont'd.): James Simpson, Thomas Walke and Richard Scammell.

Page 336:   ELIZABETH WARD of Surry. Will. Date: 9 May 1799. Rec.: 22
              Oct. 1799. Josiah Savidge, Executor. Legatee: Josiah Sav-
              idge. Witnesses: William Coman, William Newsum and John
              Wesson.

Page 337:   RICHARD EDWARDS. Inventory. (Surry County). Date: 23-25
              Jan. 1799. Rec.: 22 Oct. 1799. James Adams, John Mallicote
              and Newet Edwards, Appraisers.

Page 341:   HENRY MORING of Surry. Will. Date: 21 Mar. 1796. Rec.: 22
              Oct. 1799. John Moring and William Cocks, Executors. Sons:
              John and Christopher S. Daughters: Rebecca Carrel, Sarah
              Cocks and Elizabeth E. Cocks. Witnesses: William Warren, Jr.,
              John Spratley and Hartwell Savidge.

Page 343:   ARCHIBALD DUNLOP. Account Current. Date: 1793. Rec.: 22 Oct.
              1799. Susanna Marston, Executrix. John Newsum and John J'-
              Anson, Auditors.

Page 346:   PLEASANT HARRISON of Surry. Will. Date: 26 Aug. 1799. Rec:
              22 Oct. 1799. Bernard Major, Executor. Wife: (unnamed).
              Sons: Christopher Lucas, James and Walter Harrison. Friend:
              Peter Jemm. Witnesses: William Aldridge, James Dowden and
              Randolph Harrison.

Page 346:   REBECCA JUDKINS. Inventory. Date: ---. Rec.: 22 Oct. 1799.
              Henry Gilbert, William Adams and Richard Pyland, Appraisers.
              Ex. to qualify at a future date.

Page 347:   CHARITY COCKS of Surry. Will. Date: 9 Apr. 1799. Rec.: 22
              Oct. 1799. Thomas Cockes, Executor. Brother: Thomas Cockes.
              Sister: Champion. Legatees: Sally Judkins, daughter of
              James; Patsy Cocks, daughter of William. Mentions: father's
              estate. Witnesses: James Judkins, Sr., Samuel Judkins and
              Littleberry Davis.

Page 349:   JACOB TANN. Add. Account Current. Date: ---. Rec.: 22 Oct.
              1799. William Dunn, Executor. Langley C. Wills and William
              Cocks, Auditors.

Page 350:   BURWELL SHARP of Surry. Will. Date: 18 Aug. 1799. Rec.: 22
              Oct. 1799. James Kee, Executor. Wife: Sarah. Sons: Thomas,
              John Gibbons and Wyatt Sharp. Mentions: all my children;
              ch. by wife Sarah, underage. Friends: Archibald Cocke,
              James S. Lane, Archibald Davis and David Sebrell. Witness-
              es: Thomas Clary, James White and Elizabeth White.

Page 352:   BLACKBURN ANDREWS. Account Current. Date: 1792. Rec.: 22
              Oct. 1799. Benjamin Andrews, Executor.

Page 353:   JOHN MORING. Inventory. Date: 11 Mar. 1799. Rec.: 22 Oct.
              1799. Thomas Bailey, Sr., Henry Bailey and William Bailey,
              Appraisers.

Page 354:   JOHN PETTWAY of Surry. Will. Date: 29 Sept. 1791. Rec.: 27
              Nov. 1799. Eliza Pettway, Executrix. Wife: Eliza. Daughters
              are: Sarah (provided she not marry William Hopkins), Nancy
              and Mary. Friends: Henry Crafford, Joseph Holt, and William
              Clinch, Jr. Witnesses: Archibald Davis, James White and
              Sarah Clinch. Codicil. Revokes provision about Sarah's mar-
              riage. Witnesses: Thomas Spratley, James White and Thomas
              Ellis.

Page 356:   HENRY MARKS. Inventory. Date: 29 May 1798. Rec.: 24 Dec.
              1799. Thomas Bailey, William Bailey, Thomas Bilbro and John
              Bartle, Jr., Appraisers.

Page 358:	WILLIAM SALTER of Surry. Will. Date: 26 Jan. 1798. Rec.: 24 Dec. 1799. Mary Salter, James Jones and Henry Crafford, Executors. Wife: Mary. Daughters: Mary; and Betsey Jones, the wife of James Jones. Friend: William Wilkinson. Witnesses: Henry Crafford and Margaret Albridgeton.
Page 361:	WILLIAM BROWNE of Southwark Parish, Surry. Will. Date: 14 Nov. 1799. Rec.: 24 Dec. 1799. William Ruffin, Nicholas Faulcon and Edward Faulcon, Executors. Daughter: Sally (not 21). Legatees: William F. R., Jane Ruffin, children of Theoderick B. Ruffin; Dr. Stephen Hopkins, Jr.; William Cocke, son of Col. Richard Cocke of Isle of Wight County, (not 21); William Browne, son of Henry Browne of Norfolk, deceased; children of Benjamin Edwards Browne of Surry; children of William Taylor Browne; Nancy Browne (last three are children of William Browne of "Pipsico"); children of Henry Browne of Norfolk, deceased; children of Thomas Eaton of North Carolina. Wife: (deceased). Friends: William Ruffin, Nicholas Faulcon and Edward Faulcon. Mentions land in Sussex, and Brunswick Counties; my right in land in Southampton County where Thomas Gray lives (his wife's dower). Witnesses: Jacob Faulcon, James A. Bradby, Samuel Butler and B. E. Browne. Codicil. Jane, sister of Nicholas Faulcon; Mrs. S. Ruffin, wife of Theoderick B. Ruffin and her children: William F. Robert and Jane Bland (neither 15). Mentions: "Four Mile Tree", home of William Browne.
Page 366:	JAMES BARLOW of Surry. Will. Date: 10 Aug. 1798. Rec.: 28 Jan. 1800. Samuel Wilson and Richard Pierce, Executors. Daughters: Patsey, Nancy; and Priscilla Goodson. Grandchildren: Rosey and Becky Pettit; Becky Barlow, daughter of George, deceased; Nancy Barlow, daughter of Benjamin; Patsy and Becky Goodson, daughters of Priscilla. Legatee: James Barlow, son of Benjamin, deceased. Witnesses: Shelly White, Shadrach Goodrich, John Shelly and Samuel Wilson.
Page 367:	RICHARD BLUNT of Surry. Will. Date: 27 July 1796. Rec.: 28 Jan. 1800. Thomas Blunt, executor. Brothers: Thomas and Colin Blunt. Sister: Dolly Graves. Friend: Samuel Blunt. Witnesses: (none). James Oney, Hartwell Caseley, Jesse Caseley and Beverly Boothe swear to handwriting.
Page 369:	THOMAS DAVIS of Surry. Will. Date: 6 Oct. 1799. Rec.: 28 Jan. 1800. Joseph Davis and James P. Bell, Executors. Sons: Edwin and Littleberry. Wife: Martha. Witnesses: James Gwaltney, Polly Gwaltney and Mary Edwards.
Page 371:	Miss DOROTHY WATKINS. Inventory. Date: 28 Jan. 1800. Rec: 28 Jan. 1800. Robert Watkins presents. Symme Thompson, Samuel Carrell and James Edwards, Appraisers.
Page 372:	MARY KING of Surry. Will. Date: 1 Nov. 1799. Rec.: 28 Jan. 1800. Jesse King, Executor. Sons: Jesse, Edward, Thomas & Phillip. Grandchildren: Sarah, Hannah, Sally, William and Mary Bailey King. Witnesses: Will Clinch and Dicy Madera.
Page 373:	BETTY (ELIZABETH) HOWARD. Inventory. Date: 7 Mar. 1795.Rec: 28 Jan. 1800. Beverly Boothe and Henry Bishop, Appraisers.
Page 375:	JOSEPH HOLT. Inventory. Date: 24 Aug. 1799. Rec.: 28 Jan. 1800. Edward S. Holt, Executor.
Page 376:	STEPHEN SORSBY. Inventory. Date: 27 Jan. 1796. Rec.: 25 Feb. 1800. Richard Ellis, and Thomas Ellis, Appraisers.
Page 377:	THOMAS SPRATLEY. Inventory. Date: 10 Apr. 1798. Rec.: 25 Feb. 1800. Archibald Davis and Thomas Ellis, Appraisers.
Page 379:	JOHN H. COCKE. Account Current. Date: 1791. Rec.: 25 Feb. 1800. Richard Cocke, Jr., Executor. Mentions: Sally Cocke,

(Page 379 - COCKE cont'd.): (married 13 Apr. 1793), John H. Cocke, Nancy H. Cocke, Robert Cocke, Jack Cocke, Polly Cocke, Patsy Cocke, Eliza Cocke and Mrs. Ann Cocke; suit vs. Allen Cocke's ex.; Benjamin Cocke's estate; payments to Carter Nicholas (wife's legacy); Nicholas Faulcon (wife's legacy). Coffin for Patsy Cocke; "Bremo". Ro. Watkins, James S. Lane and Caufield Seward, Auditors.

Page 415: BENJAMIN A. COCKE. Inventory. Date: 15 Feb. 1800. Rec.: 25 Feb. 1800. Allen Cocke, Administrator. John Hunnicutt, Robert Hunnicutt and Henry Crafford, Appraisers.

Page 417: HENRY MORING. Account Current. Date: 1786. Rec.: 25 Feb'y. 1800. Thomas Peter and John Jarrett, Administrators. John Newsum and John J'Anson, Auditors.

Page 418: JAMES WILISON. Account Current. Date: 1785. Rec.: 25 Feb. 1800. C. B. Harrison, Acting Executor. Mentions: Miss Jane Willison, John Willison. Walter Cocke and Thomas Peter, Auditors.

Page 421: JAMES DREWRY. Inventory. Date: 5 Nov. 1799. Rec.: 25 Feb. 1800. Richard Drewry, Administrator. Frederick Lane, Hartwell Hart and Henry Lane, Appraisers.

Page 422: CHARITY COCKS. Inventory. Date: 23 Nov. 1799. Rec.: 25 Feb. 1800. Thomas Cocks, Executor. Frederick Lane, Hartwell Hart and Henry Lane, Appraisers.

Page 423: WILLIAM BISHOP. Account Current. Date: 7 Oct. 1799. Rec.: 25 Feb. 1800. Will Boyce, Sheriff, presents.

Page 424: THOMAS GRANTHAM. Account Current. Date: 1792. Rec.: 25 Feb. 1800. James and Sampson Grantham, Executors. Mentions payments to Thomas Smith, his wife's legacy; John Tillott's legacy. Thomas Bailey and William Simmons, Auditors.

Page 425: JAMES GILCHRIST. Account Current. Date: 1792. Rec.: 25 Feb. 1800. Thomas Peter, Executor. Mentions payments to Fanny Gilchrist. John Newsum and John J'Anson, Auditors.

Page 430: WILLIAM WILLS. Account Current. Date: 1790. Rec.: 25 Feb. 1800. John Wesson, Robert McIntosh and William Scammell, Auditors.

Page 431: BENJAMIN WHITE of Surry. Will. Date: 9 May 1789. Rec.: 22 Apr. 1800. Randolph Fitchet, Executor. Natural son: Randolph Fitchet. Friend: Sally James. Legatees: Elizabeth James; John White, son of John, deceased. Friend: Joseph Holleman. Witnesses: John Holleman, John Presson, Jr. and Randolph Harris. Codicil. Date: 30 May 1789. Mentions: Richard Presson, son of Thomas, deceased; my brothers and sisters children. Witnesses: same as to will.

Page 434: BENJAMIN WARREN of Surry. Will. Date: Aug. 1799. Rec.: 22 Apr. 1800. Sarah Warren, Executrix. Sister: Sarah Warren. Witnesses: (none). William Bennett, Sr., Elizabeth Warren, Joseph Warren swear to handwriting.

Page 435: JOHN AVRISS of Southwark Parish, Surry. Will. Date: 17 Feb. 1800. Rec.: 22 Apr. 1800. William Avriss, Executor. Wife: Patty. Son: William. Daughters: Nancy Avriss; Mason Avriss; Lucy Carseley; Rebecca Dewell. Friend: Willie Jones. Mentions: one quarter of estate to each: Nancy Avriss, Mason Avriss, John Carseley's children; William Dewell's children. Witnesses: Nathan Jones, Glaister Hunnicutt, Henry Bishop and Benjamin Barker.

Page 437: WILLIAM STEWART of Surry. Will. Date: 26 Aug. 1799. Rec.: 24 June 1800. Thomas Kee, Executor. Brother: James Stewart.

(Page 437 - STEWART cont'd.): Sister: Sarah. Witnesses: James Kee, John Blasengam and Thomas Kee.

Page 438: HENRY BISHOP of Southwark Parish, Surry. Will. Date: 4 Mar. 1800. Rec.: 24 June 1800. David Bishop, Executor. Wife: Susan(na). Son: Braxton. Friend: David Bishop. Witnesses: Thomas Lucas, William Bishop, Elijah Brockwell and Nathan Jones.

Page 439: WILLIAM RAE. Inventory. Date: 13 Jan. 1797. Rec.: 24 June 1800. Beverly Booth and William Thompson, Appraisers.

Page 440: RICHARD BLUNT. Inventory. Date: 11 Feb. 1800. Rec.: 24 Jun. 1800. Beverly Booth, Hartwell Carseley and Robert Booth, Appraisers.

Page 442: ELIZABETH BADGETT of Southwark Parish, Surry. Will. Date: 18 Aug. 1795. Rec.: 24 June 1800. Richard Ellis refuses to qualify. Natural son: Richard Badgett. Brother: John. Fr.: Richard Ellis. Witnesses: Edward Porter, Elizabeth Porter and Celia Walden.

Page 444: JOHN MOORE. Account Current. Date: 1798. Rec.: 24 Jun. 1800. William Boyce, Administrator. Langley C. Wills and Thomas Kee, Auditors.

Page 445: LEWIS EDWARDS. Account Current. Date: 1798. Rec.: 24 June 1800. Newett Edwards, Administrator. Mentions: Coffin for child, and widow's dower. John Wesson and John Holt, Aud.

Page 446: JOHN WOODCOCK. Inventory. Date: 24 June 1800. Rec.: 22 Jul. 1800. William Rae, Administrator. Josiah Savidge, John Wesson and Edward King, Appraisers.

Page 447: MARY ALEXANDER of Surry. Will. Date: 10 Jan. 1797. Rec.: 26 Aug. 1800. Hartwell Hunnicutt, James Edwards and John Williams, Executors. Sister: Mourning Edwards. Neices and Nephewa: Sally Edwards; James Edwards; Hartwell Hunnicutt; Anne Wright, wife of John Wright; Elizabeth Williams, wife of John Williams. Mentions: Rebecca, Samuel, Sally and Henry Clarke, children of Jesse Clarke(?). Friends: Henry Crafford and William Salter. Witnesses: Will Boyce, Henry Crafford and Margaret Moore.

Page 450: WILLIAM EDWARDS. Account Current. Date: 1797. Rec.: 23 Sep. 1800. Richard Edwards, Executor. Mentions: Benjamin Edwards; Mrs. Susanna Edwards (for use of family); R. H. Edwards (at school); and Susanna Edwards, guardian of William Edwards. Edward Faulcon and John Faulcon, Jr., Auditors.

Page 455: JAMES BARLOW. Will. Date: 8 Feb. 1796. Rec.: 23 Sept. 1800. Mary Barlow, Executrix. Daughters: Elizabeth Price; Mary & Lucy Barlow. Witnesses: John Williams and Willis Thompson.

Page 456: JONATHAN WALL. Inventory. Date: 11 Mar. 1800. Rec.: 29 Oct. 1800. Jesse Browne, Administrator. Joseph Holleman, Robert Kea and William T. Judkins, Appraisers.

Page 457: MARY BATTS. Inventory. Date: 5 Jan. 1796. Rec.: 23 Dec.1800. John Warren, Administrator. James Smith, Benjamin Cocks and Joel Savidge, Appraisers.

Page 458: HELENIA READ LAUGHTON of Cabin Point, Surry. Will. Date: 4 Nov. 1800. Rec.: 23 Dec. 1800. Thomas Peter, Executor. Mother: Jennett Nimmo. Father: Andrew Nimmo, deceased. Son: William Laughton. Daughter: Jennett Laughton. Husband: (unnamed; deceased). Mentions: neither child of age. Witnesses: Travis Purkinson, James Nimmo and Thomas Peter.

BAILEY/BALEY/BAYLEY, cont'd.
Benjamin 44,70,77,92,101,
110,123
Benjamin, Jr. 44,70,75,
123
Edward 2,6,8,16,17,19,
20,21,25,27,28,39,43,53,
54,57,58,68,75,78,110,
119,123,149
Edward, Jr. 16,75,78,119
Elijah 70,71
Elizabeth 16,123,125
Faith 16
Fanny 104
Hanah/Hannah 16,110
Henry 75,132,134,140,
146,150
Jane 16,125
John 75,82,90,92,101,107,
125,127,128
Joseph 70
Joseph G. 115,128,142
Joshua 142,145
Lemuel 92,118,120,121,
123,125,126,128,129,132,
134,137,141,144,145
Lucy 75
Margaret 142
Martha 70
Mary 16,62,75,92,119
Michael 90,92,96,100,101,
123
Patience 141
Philip 5
Robert 125
Samuel 70,71,92,101,123,
125,142
Sarah 16,75,100,103,110,
139
Thomas 16,17,20,23,62,
75,79,80,81,82,84,86,87,
88,90,92,102,119,132,134,
139,143,146,148,149,150
152
Thomas, Jr. 74,76,78,143
Tryal 70
Will/William 75,80,90,
92,100,103,109,117,118,
123,126,127,128,131,132,
134,135,136,138,140,146,
150
BAIRD, Benjamin 33,53,60,63,
67
Eaph'r/Ephraim 56,68,71
James 86,88,94,131
Reuben 57
Thomas 43
BAKER, Ann 101
Benjamin 71
Henry 98
James 10,26,29,31,32,41,
59
Laurence 117
Martin 83,101
Richard 87,91
Susannah 101
BALDWIN, John 129
William 6,129
BALDWING, Lucy 103
BALFLOUR, James 33,34
BALLARD, Faith 59
BAMAR, Ann/Anne 4
Hannah 4,16
John 4,35,56
Mary 4,16
William 4
BANKS, Benjamin 79
Mary 79
BARD, Sarah 33
BARHAM, Ann 91
Benjamin 91,114
Burwell 136,137
Charles 3,71
Elizabeth 74,89,91

BARHAM, cont'd:
Faithy 137
Jesse 91,92,110,112
John 89,91,93,127,128,
131,142
Joseph 91,116,128,149
Lewis 33
Lucy 89
Martha 91
Mary 71,92,113
Mary Ann 141
Robert 71,89
Sally 141
Sarah 71,92,113,127,131,
142
Thomas 35,84,91
William 89,91,95,97
BARKER, A. 127
Agnes/Agness 22,34,40
Alce 62
Ambrose/Ambrous 103,129
Ann 75,103
Arthur 72,90,92
Benjamin 130,147,149,152
Christopher 29
Drewry/Drury 68,95
Eliza 127
Elizabeth 40,45,62,68,
70,90,114,127,129,130
Faith/Fathy 12,13,26,45,
72,73,127
George 34,40
Grace 45,73
Henry 40,50,53
Howell 70,71
Jane 40
Jehu/Jehur 40,41,53
Jehu Nicholas 149
Jesse 113
Jethreu/Jethro 40,41,49,
62,63,68,93
Joel 2,45
John 26,29,30,40,44,45,
50,62,64,68,69,72,73,93,
96,103,108,127
Jos'h 10
Joshua 45,67,74,84
Josiah 26,30,45,72,73
Josiah, Jr. 10
Josias 39
Lamuel/Lemuel 72,90,130,
149
Lucy 103,127,130
Marry/Mary 22,29,40,45
Maryanna 90
May 45
N. 143
Nancy 149
Priselah 24
Rebecca/Rebekah 41,90,
96
Richard 10,45,59,60,143,
149
Samuel 127,129
Sarah 40,62,90
Susan 127
Thomas 68,96,102,103,
114,127
Tiver 72,73
William 45,73,86
BARLOW, Becky 151
Benjamin 151
George 151
James 112,136,151,153
John 20
Lucy 153
Mary 153
Nancy 151
Patsey 151
William 32
BARNES/BARNS, Benjamin 67,
71
Elizabeth 71
Henry 67,68,71,72,77

BARNES/BARNS, cont'd:
John 5,66,67,71,76
Lucy 67
Naomy/Neomy 71,77
Samuel 67
Sarah 76,86
Simon 129
William 67,71
BARRADELL, Robert 85
BARRETT/BARRETTE, Elizabeth
89
Thomas 99
BARRICK, George 35,72
Priscilla 72
BARROM, Betsy 95
Peter 95
Sarah 95
BARROW, Sarah 16,18
BARTEN, Ann 24
William 10
BARTLE, J., Jr. 139
John 89,91,102,108,124,
133,138
John, Jr. 145,146,148,
150
Mary 89
Thomas 124,127,131,138
BATES, Mary 124
BATT, William 9
BATTEL/BATTLE, Charls 43
John, Jr. 58
BATTIN, Martha 141
BATTS, Benjamin 123
Betsy 123
Elizabeth 30,32
Frederick 123
Henry 123
John 30,32,86,103,123,
124,127
John, Jr. 123
Martha 30
Mary 30,32,123,144,153
Mrs. 30
Patty 123
Sally 123
Sarah 7,32
William 7,28,30,32,44,
56
William E. 139
BEDGOOD (see BIDGOOD)
BEARD, Thomas 43
BEDDINGFIELD/BEDINGFIELD/
BEDINGFELD/BEDINGFILD,
Ann 113,136
Henry 24,40,113,115,124,
136
Isabel 40
Mary 24
Nathaniel 40
Polly 129
Thomas 25,26,30,34,39,
40,49,51,53,55,63,64,
67,69,136
BELCHES/BELSCHES, Alexander
71
James 67,71,75,77,80,81,
83,84,104,105,109,111,
112,113,114,115,116,117,
118,119,121,126,127,128,
129,130,131,133,134,137,
138,141,145
James, Jr. 146
BELL, Amy 11
Ann 15,38,50,53,89,104,
106,117,134,135,142
Balaam 38
Benjamin 11,14,29,38,40,
50,53,104,106,110,117,
122,125,126,134,135,142,
145,146
Benjamin C. 145
Betsy 122
Borrel/Burrell 8,38
Elizabeth 11,118

COCK/COCKE, Lemuel cont'd:
133,135,136,139,141,143,
148,149
Lemuel, Jr. 139
Lucy 118
Martha 41,77,94
Martha R. 143
Martha Ruffin 132
Mary 94
Mary Kennon 132
Nancy 118
Nancy H. 152
Nathaniel 93
Nicholas 3,10,16,29,31,
41,42
Patsy 113,152
Polly 152
Rebecca/Rebekah 77,98,
145
Richard 11,12,24,33,37,
39,40,64,66,77,88,90,
92,93,94,96,114,115,138,
144,151
Richard, Jr. 132,136,151
Richard H. 132
Robert 94,138,142,143,
144,152
Sally 64,132,151
Sarah 64,77,101,113
Susan 77
Susanna/Susannah 41,64,
118,119,121,149
Thomas 3,16,22,23,31,41,
47,48,54,56,57,61,62,64,
71,81,88,90,102,117,118,
119,129
W. 70,116
Walter 22,23,31,145,152
Will/William 6,30,41-43,
62,64-66,69,77,80,99,
100,109,113,118,125,127-
131,133-136,144,146,151
William, Jr. 77,133
COCKER, Robert 136
COCKES/COCKS, Benjamin 116,
142,144,147,153
Champion 150
Charity 147,150,152
Elizabeth 147
Elizabeth E. 150
James 116,137
Jesse 105,107,108,110,
114,118,119,121,123,125,
126,147
John 65,91,106,116,117,
133,136,147
Mary 78,116,117
Nathan 136
Nathaniel 136,147
Patsy 150
Rebecca 121,126
Sarah 136,150
Thomas 116,128,137,147,
150,152
William 69,72,73,87,126,
136,147,150
William, Jr. 105,108
COFER, Ann 145
Martha 145
Thomas 122,125,145
COGGIN/COGGING/COGING/COG-
INGS, Elizabeth 18
Micajah 89
Thomas 18,23,66,77
Will/William 3,4
COKER, John 32
COLE, Elizabeth 102
John 102,118
COLLIER/COLLYER/COLYER,
Ann/Anne 62,89,91,92
Benjamin 6,15,85,90,92,
121,122,125,131,132,136,
142
Charity 89,92,123

COLLIER/COLLYER/COLYER,
cont'd:
Charity Peneluna 123
Charles 6
Dinah 103,109
Dolly 143
Elezabeth/Elizabeth 15,
35,62,92
Emelia 132,139,142
George 132,142
Grace 6
Henery/Henry 6,39,60,
64,68,70,103
Howell 143
James 142
Jane 58
Jean 60
John 2,6,7,15,18,28,29,
39,45,47,52,54,62,63,
66,67,76,79,85,90,91,
92,96,103,116,132,135,
139,142
Lucy 58,60,90,92,106,
132,133,142
Martha 121
Mary 6,132
Mildred 133
Moody 92,123,132,133
Patsy 143
Sampson/Samson 62,63,68
Sarah 18,92,123
Stephen 62,63,68,72,90,
95,116,143,146
Thomas 2,6,7,18,28,29,
42,47,48,58,60,66,76,92,
102
William 6,35,111,135,
143,146
COLLINS, Ann 14
John 9,47
Lewis 101
Robert 139
William 75,81,82,84,85,
87,90,99,100,101,102,
107,112,114,131,135,137,
142
COLWELL, William 94
COMAN, Dorothy 123
Harwood 91
John 149
William 150
COOK/COOKE, Amy 26
Elizabeth 26
Hannah 26
Henry 95,104,126
James 26,27,67,78
John 120
Julia 114
Mary 26,95
Rebeccah/Rebekah 26,95
Rubin 21,26
Sarah 26
Susana 26
William 17,26,27,30,50,
59,67
COOPER, Agnes 115
Alic 86
Benjamin 29
Cannan 29
Charlotte 141
Coleman 141
Elizabeth 10,11,18,21,
70
Emelia 115
Frederick 113,115,127,
129,141
George 70,100,115,118
Hannah 70
James 10,11,21
Jane 115
Johana 10
John 10,27,51,70,74,86,
87,88,92,140,143
John, Jr. 86

COOPER, cont'd:
Martha 10
Mary 70,74,86,115
Permelia 141
Phebe 57
Richard 74,86
Sarah 70
Thomas 10,27,61
William 10,25,51,70
CORLISLY, Richard 67
CORNWALL, Jacob 35
John 35
CORNWEL/CORNWELL, ___ 61
Aaron 93
Agatha 93
Ann 141
Elizabeth 93
Isaac 12
Jacob 4,42,93
John 93,98
Joseph 93
Mary 69
Moses 93
Samuel 4,125,142
Samuel, Jr. 4
Sarah 142
William 41,42,63,69,141
COSBY, Overton 133
COTTON, John 67
Lucy 67
Richard 49,52
COUPLAND, Jane 111
COWPER, Frederick 128
COX, John 95,114
William, Sr. 100
CRAFFORD, Ann 68
Carter/Ctr. 9,13,14,33,
36,40,42,44,50,55,57,63,
66.68,69,70,71,74,75,78,
80,82,84,86,98,102,109,
113,115,118,119
Carter, Jr. 13,94,98,102,
109,113,114
Constant 33
Elizabeth 113,114
Faith 33
Henry 102,106,107,109,
111,112,114,115,120,128,
129,138,140,141,144,147,
149,150,151,152,153
Jane 128
John 23,33,36,40,41,50,
63,68,73,113
Martha 114
Marry/Mary 13,68,113
Robert 13,14
CRAUGHTON, ___ 136
CRAWLEY, Hannah 120
CREDEEL, Henry 125
CREW/CREWS, Margaret 51
William 44,51,74,93,95,
96,101
CRIPPS/CRIPS, Elizabeth
44.56
John 44
Mariott 22
Mary 44,56
William 22,44,47,56
CROCKER, James 143
CROSLE, Jean 58
CRUSE, William 6
CRUTCHFIELD, John 73
CRYER, Ann/Anne 60,75,76,
82,86,88,100
Elizabeth 75,87
George 18,44,56,58,60,
61,73,75,76,86,87
Mary 60,61
Nicholas 58,60,85,87,91,
100,106,127,138
Patty 85
Samuel 60
Susanna 85,121
William 60,85,89,132,133,

DUNLOP, cont'd:
Christian 136
Susanna 136
DUN/DUNN, Joel 69
John 21
Lucy 125
Thomas 21
William 112,115,118,150
DURELL, James 144
William 144

EACOLLS, Robert 45
EASLEY, Hannah 114
EATON, Mary 40
Thomas 151
William 33
ECHOLS, Edward 52
ECKLES, Edward 45
Robert 45
EDLOE, Henry 11,40
Jane 40
John 40
Mary 40
Philip 40
Rebecca 11,40
William 40
EDMONDS/EDMUNDS, Anne 1,14,
17
Christian 25,59
David 25
Elizabeth 1,25,59,148
Faith 25,59
Fillis/Phillis 25,59
Howell 1,2,41
Mr. J. 9,79
John 49,52,56,59,68,76,
81,88
John Edmongray 25
Mary 18,25,26,59,92,102
Nicholas 1,19,24,26,39,
41,79,92
Polly 148
Richard 148
Sarah 25
Susannah 25
Thomas 1,2,3,7,10,11,12,
14,17,18,32
William 25,26
EDWARDS, ___ 61
Ann 91,144
Arthur 66
B. 35
Benjamin 10,35,46,61,76,
91,92,95,102,132,153
Charlotte Bolling 148
Cherry 139
Eldred 111
Elizabeth 34,36,51,58,
59,74,91,92,95,102,124,
131,148
Theldred 74,76,94,95,
116,124,125,132
Hannah 36
Hartwell 137
James 63,97,100,124,139,
151,153
Jane 34,116
J'Anson 124,136
Joel 139
John 42,66,102,124,131
Joseph 42,124
Lewis 124,153
Lucy 74,91
Martha 80,91,97,99,101,
124,126,131,139
Mary 36,61,66,71,97,124,
131,151
Micajah 41,91,92,126
Michael 124
Mourning 66,153
Nancy 124
Newet/Newett/Newit/New-
itt 4,18,26,30,44,74,75,
124,148,150,153

EDWARDS, cont'd:
Phillip 149
Rebecca 36,139
Rebecca Browne 148
R. H. 153
Richard 91,124,139,140,
142,144,145,148,149,150,
153
Richard H. 148
Richard Henry 144,148
Sally 153
Sarah 36,74,124,131
Susannah 144,153
Thomas 5,14,34,51,55,58,
74,76,124,131,144,148
Unity 124
W. 34,36,53,63,65,69,
70,73,74,86,87
Will/William 4,6,14,18,
19,26,27,30,36,67,68,74,
76,77,83,91,97,98,108,
121,122,124,126,133,144,
145,148,149,153
William, Jr. 46,59,68,
144
William Newet 94
William Phillip 66,98
EECKLE, Robert 45
EELBECK, Henry 11,54
Rev. 11
EGERTON, James 144
Wilmot 144
ELDRIDGE, Ann 27
Eliza 54
Elizabeth 27,49,58
Jane 27
Judith 27
Martha 27
Mary 27
Richard 27
Robert 117
Thomas 17,27,28,34,44,
49,50,58
Thomas, Jr. 12,17
William 27,90
ELEXANDER, David 66
ELLESS, Jeremyah 20
ELLIS, Amelia 74
Benjamin 33,35,38,39,40,
41,44,74,86,96,113,117,
131
Caleb 30,59,67,70,73,74,
80
Caleb, Jr. 64,67,74
Cherry 127
Dann 74
Edward 60
Elizabeth 20,42,60
Faith/Fathy 73,96
Hannah 78,113
Ira 115
Isaac 127,128,131
Jeremiah 10,20
Jeremiah, Jr. 3
John 24,25,112,120,128,
131,137,138,140,146,147,
148
Johnathon/Jonathan 51,
53,66,68,73,78,83,85,88,
90,93,94,96,97,103,109,
110,113,123,124,126,128,
138
Joseph 55,62,125,126,
141,148
Joshua 39
Lucy 146,147
Mary 22,24,25,60,73,74
Meley 22
Mildred 24
Richard 22,74,86,96,103,
112,113,121,124,128,131,
133,135,137,138,139,141,
146,149,151,153
Robert 149

ELLIS, cont'd:
Samuel 133,143,144
Sarah 60,73
Stephen 74
Thomas 121,128,131,136,
138,141,149,150,151
William 121,127,128,129,
138,139
ELLISSON, Robert 141
ELLISON, Sarah 141
EMERY, Benjamin 10,125
Elizabeth 104
Green 10
James 104
Jane 104
John 10,104
Katey 104
Mary 104
Ruth 118,140
Sarah 104
Susanna/Susannah 10,11
Thomas 10,104,105
William 118,140
Wyatt 104
EMREY/EMRY, Benjamin 73
Fathia 73
Thomas 11
EPES/EPPES/EPPS/EPS, Daniel
10,34,50,57
Daniel, Jr. 9,19
Edward 50,53,57
Elizabeth 57
Francis 34,97
Hamlin 97
Martha 97,112
Mary 9,52,57
Peter 97
Rebecca 37
Richard 34
Sarah 34,97
Susanna/Susanno 27,34
Thomas 10
William 20,30,34
EVANS/EVENS/EVINS, Anne 13
Anthony 13,56,70,87,92
Anthony, Jr. 80
Benjamin 92,101
Cilia 56
Dolly 140
Elizabeth 13,14
John 8,13,34
Martha 13
Mary 13
Priscilla 56
Rebecca 140,146
Sally Drew 140
Will/William 13,14,24,
31,38,56,57,72,89,90,94,
95,97,103,108,109,122,
140
EWART, James 12
EXUM, Arthur 106
Micajah 74
EZEL/EZELL, Agnes 42
Benjamin 101
Edmond 3
George 3,52
Hannah 75
John 3,91
Joseph 52
Martha 42
Mary 3
Rebeccah/Rebecher/Re-
becka 3,10
Timothy 32
William 3,38,52,75

FANN, James 71
William 71
FARRINGTON, Edward 5,31
Mary 49
Robert 31,37,39,45,47,
51,66
FATHERBE, Anne 13

161

GOODWIN, John 4
GOODWYN, Francis 4
  John 4,5,32,33,36,41,59
  Mary 4
  Pennellopy 4
  Robert 137
  Thomas 4,9
  William 4
GOODWYNE, Thomas 5
GOODWYNN, William 56
GORDON, ___ 102
GRAHAM, Dew 133
GRANTHAM, James 132,152
  John 24,25
  Lewis 142
  Mary 60
  Sampson 132,138,140,142,
  143,146,152
  Sarah 24,25
  Stephen/Steven 24,71,142
  Thomas 24,25,60,70,72,
  104,132,134,136,142,152
GRAVES, Dolly 151
  John, Jr. 25
GRAY, Ann 128
  Benjamin 44,81
  Charles 106
  Edmund 15,35,66
  Edwin 107
  Elizabeth 61,100,106,
  128,140
  Elizabeth (Betsey) 131
  Etheldred 72,73,77,80,
  83,85,87,88,91,100,101,
  105,106,107,119,122
  Frederick 108
  Gilbert 15,25,33,38,40,
  48,53,61,79
  Hannah 108
  Henry 10,97,108
  J. 79
  James 15,35,51,66,70,79,
  84,86,97,128,129
  Jean 108
  Jesse 97,143
  John 79,84,97,108,129,
  130
  Joseph 15,19,35,61,66,
  79,82,97
  Josiah 128,129,137
  Lucy 15,40,66,79,84,97,
  108
  Margaret 79,82,84,86
  Margret 61
  Martha 97,108,136
  Mary 65,67,79,105
  Nathaniel 128
  Richard 66,86,108,110
  Robert 5,12,15,19,20,21,
  22,24,25,28,33,34,35,36,
  54,56,57,66,79,81
  Samuel 108
  Sarah 79,97,128
  Susanna/Susannah 66,128
  Thomas 15,19,20,29,31,
  35,36,49,53,56,58,66,97,
  151
  William 4,15,19,35,61,66,
  97
  William Robert 106
GREEN, Ann 9,31
  Benjamin 45
  Burrell 9,45,47
  Burwell 31
  Elizabeth 37,45
  Frederick 37
  Hannah 140
  Jane 37
  Mary 37,39,45
  Mildend 37
  Nathaniel 37,66
  Nathaniel, Sr. 47
  Olive 37

GREEN, cont'd:
  Peter 2,13,25,37,39,49
  Robert 5,7,46,47
  Sally 117
  William 13,39,45,46,66,
  117,118
  William, Jr. 39
  William, Sr. 45
GRESHAM, Faithy 125
GRESSWITT, Marmaduke 30
GRESWITT, Ann 30
  Marmaduke 30
  Mary 30
GRIFFIN, Elizabeth 70
  James 46
  John 70,73
  Thomas 73
GRIFFIS, Ann 47
  Edith 67
  Edward 67
  John 67
  Luccey 67
  Sarah 78
  Thomas 67,78
GRIFFITH, John 11,17,18,26
GRIMER, Robert 18,30
GRIMES, William 82
GRIMMER, Robert 18
  Sarah 14
GRISSWITT, Ann 30
GROVES, John 25,33,44
GRUSWITT, George 30
  Thomas 30
  Walter 30
GUALTNEY, Martha 8
GUILLAM, Thomas 12
GUTTRE, Daniel 30
GWALTNEY, Benjamin 46,48,
  56
  Elizabeth 56,99
  James 46,48,56,151
  Jean 44
  John 7,40,48,56,139,141,
  146
  John, Jr. 42
  Jordan 125
  Joseph 46,48
  Ludwell 146
  Mar_ 7
  Martha 46,48,50,56
  Marthew 7
  Mary 7,8,42,56
  Nancy 145
  Polly 145,151
  Ruth 7
  Sarah 125,145,146
  Thomas 6,7,8,46,48,50,
  56,57,93,105,106,117,145
  Thomas P. 146
  William 7,46,48,56,57

HAGOOD, Francis 22
HALEY, James 78
  Sarah 78
HALFORD, Stephen 53
HALL, George 2
  Isaac 2
  Judith 2
  Lewis 2
  Thomas 15
  William 2
HALLEMAN, Henery 16
  John 16
  Josias John 16
  Martha 16
  Mary 16
  Matthew 16
  Robbert 16 (Robert)
  Thomas 7
HALLY, John 5
HAMELTON, William 101
HAMILTON, George 48
  John 113
HAMLIN, ___ 92

HAMLIN, cont'd:
  Ann 11
  Anne 22,24
  Elizabeth 72,115
  John 71
  Pe. 147
  R. 24
  Rebecca 102,120
  Richard 34,35,72
  Richard, Jr. 76
  Stephen 30,44,54
  Thomas 14,18,19,26,48
  William 95,97,107,116,
  124,126,137,138
HAMMERSLEY, John 3
HANCEL, Elizabeth 61
HANCOCK, Clement 50
  Duejates 5,11
  Elizabeth 5,11
  Fanny 46
  Henry 46
  James 46,140
  Jane 5,11,12
  Jean 5,6
  Jimmy 65
  John 5,6,11,13,37,38,46,
  100
  Joseph 5,11,12,15,26,30,
  31,40,46
  Martha 5,11
  Mary 11
  Sauanna 46
  Sus./Susannah 30,50,65
  William 11,46,47,65
HANDCOCK, Joseph 46
  Thomas 113
HANSFORD, Martha 3,16
  Mary 3
  William 3,16
HANSON, Charles 99
HARDIN, Benjamin 10
  Martha 10
  Rebecca 122
  Sarah 10
HARDING, Joseph 106
HARDY, Richard 51,52,96,98,
  117,124
  Sally 51
  William 124
HARGRAVE, Anselm 101,121,
  142,145
  Augustin/Augustine 8,
  13,38,75,77,87,89,96
  Benjamin 30,75,90,101,
  113,122
  Bray 19
  Celia 121
  Elizabeth 101
  Hannah 70,145
  Hardy 77,87,89,90,96
  Hartwell 75,77,100,141
  Herman 141,147
  Hinche/Hinchy 113,118
  James 141
  Jesse 30,42,54,59,69,
  75,101,121
  John 113,118,141
  Jordan 145
  Joseph 30,70,101,121
  Joseph, Jr. 101
  Josiah 75
  Joshua 141
  Katharine 77
  Lemuel 30,101,145
  Lucy 89,113
  Martha 70,101,121,145
  Mary 19,75,87,101,121
  Milly 141
  Mourning 75
  Nancy 145
  Olive 77,87,89,96
  Peggy 145
  Richard 101
  Robert 101,121

164

HOLLEMAN, cont'd:
Thomas 107,124
Wilson 117,119,124
HOLLEWAY, Ann 116
David 78
James 144
Joel 146
Mark 146
HOLLIMAN, Ann 107
Arthur 63,92,106,107
Charity 107
Elizabeth 107
John 20
Joseph 6,91,97
Josiah John 16,20
Mary 20
Micajah 106,107
Rebecca 107
Robert 93,107
Unity 6
William 92,107
HOLLOMAN, John 16
HOLLOWAY, David 130,131
Elizabeth 113
James 67,121
Jesse 96,101,130,131
Job 121,130
John, Sr. 67
Lazarus 94,96,101,106,
117,118,119,121,130
Lucy 96
Milley 117
Mima 117
HOLLOWMAN, Mary 16
HOLSWORTH, Charles 38,39,58
Mary 39
HOLT, Ann 64,96
Anna 79,89
Anne 18
Archer 135,145
Archibald 115
Benjamin 34,59,89,90,95
Betty Drew 115
Charles 11,18,19,26,35,
40,56,64,71,72,96,97,98
Dolly 115
Drew 145
Edward S. 149,151
Elizabeth 3,17,18,19,96,
115,135
Elvira 79
Francis 59,83,84,88,98
Mrs. Francis 98
Frederick 111
Hannah 59,64,96
Hannah Bamer 95
Henry 3,30,64,96
James 3,59,84,88,98,130,
131,139,145
John 18,24,44,79,80,81,
87,106,118,140,145,153
Joseph 89,97,99,109,110,
120,137,143,149,150,151
Josiah 79,89,118
Katherine 3
Kezia 79
Lucy 3,16,26,64,71,96
Martha 59,95
Mary 3,4,5,16,18,51,59,
79,89,109,135,145
Mary S. 149
Michael 89
Mike 120
Philip 89,149
Randolph 79,80,89,91
Rebekkah 95
Rowland 118,149
Samuel 64,96
Sarah 26,64,96
Tapphenas 18
Thomas 3,4,5,16,24,47,
58,60,63,77,83,95,99,
100,103,105,107,115,124,
131

HOLT, cont'd:
Thomas, Jr. 79
William 36,37,51,59,64,
91,93,96,97,103,110,146
HOOD, Thomas 9
HOPKINS, Hugh 133
Stephen, Jr. 151
William 150
HOTT, William 15
HOUSE, Charles 1
Lawrence 1
Isaac 1
HOUSMAN, Stephen 26
HOWARD, Anner 129
Betty 129,135,139,151
Elizabeth 151
Henry 80,88,97,100,114.
118,129,133
Henry Jones 129
James 129
John Heath 129,135,139
Nicholas 129,135
Patsey 129,136
Sarah 129,135
Thomas 98,100,108,110,
113,114,115,118,121,129
HOWELL, Ann 29
Edmund 5,40
Elizabeth 5,28
Joanna 28
Joannah 5
John 29
Mary 5,6,28,29
Nathaniel 20,29,31
Olive 40
Susanna/Susannah 29,32
Thomas 29
William 5,6,28,29
HOWSE, Sarah 35
HUBERD, Mathew 20
HUDGENS, Sarah 45
Thomas 45
HUDGINGS, Lucy 104
Thomas 104
HUDSON, Daniel 33,73
HULME, William 5
HUNECUT/HUNNICUT/HUNNICUTT,
Ann 92,112,125,142
Augustin/Augustine 9,32,
34,62,66,73,77,133
Austin 103
Benjamin 74
Elizabeth 104,120
Faithy 74,75
Glaister 152
Hartwell 112,121,130,
133,153
John 32,34,63,75,76,106,
110,117,126,142,145,147,
148,149,152
Marget 106
Martha 32,75
Mary 75,80,142
Robert 32,34,62,65,66,
73,75,78,80,83,84,86,
91,93,94,98,106,107,109,
120,124,141,142,148,149,
152
Sarah 75
Wyke 35,142
HUNNIFORD, Hugh 39
Jane 39,65
HUNNYCUTT, John 62
HUNT, Benjamin 47
Elizabeth 45
Faith 47
John 26
John, Jr. 47
William 47,48
HUNTER, David 59,60,118
William 49,121
HURDLE, Christian 40
Elizabeth 40
Joanna 40

HUSE, Ann 82
HUSKEY, Thomas 25,29
HUTCHINGS, Catharine 148
John 114
John, Jr. 76
HUTCHINS, Francis 12
Jane 12
HUX, Elesbath 20
William 6
HYDE, Benjamin 60

INGRAM, John 41,66,94
William 146
INMAN, Ann 92,98
Elizabeth 96,117
Isaam 92
Isham 98,101,117,118,
120,122,123,142
James 92,100
John 89,92,94,98,123
John, Jr. 92
Mary 92,98,123
IRBY, Charles 126
John 39,41,51,55,62
Mary 39
William 108
IVEY, Hugh 37,47
Thomas 47
IVIE, Amy 57
Christian 57
Hugh 40
John 57,58
Thomas 57
William 57
IVY, Thomas 58

JACKSON, Ambrose 43
Amey 43
John 2,8,20,45
Robert 45
Thomas, Jr. 47
JAMES, Abel 137
Betty 100
Edwin 114,122
Elizabeth 152
Enos 122
Emanuel 122
Jeremiah 100
John 100,122
Lucy 100
Matthias 110
Nathaniel 96,100,101
Sally 100,152
Susanna 122
J'ANSON, John 55,57,64,65,
67,81,113,136,137,144,
150,152
Lucy 67
Mary 67,102
Thomas 67,109,115,121,
127,129,131,134,140
JARQUES, John 101
JARRAD, John 24
Nicholas 9
JARRAT/JARRATT/JARRET/JAR-
RETT/JARROTT,
Ann/Anne 35,85,121
Jane 67
John 5,11,35,39,48,53,
58,67,69,85,95,109,118,
128,138,152
John, Jr. 82
Nathaniel 85
Nicholas 9,67
JEFFERSS, John 38
JEFFRES/JEFFRYS, John 37,
54,56
John, Jr. 37
Joseph 37
Lucy 37
Martha 54,56
Mary 54
Rebecca 37
Richard 37

KELLO, Samuel 106,112,114,
132,138
KELO, R. 79
KELSY, Andrew 126
KEM, George 94
KENNON, John 111
Richard 111
KERR, G. 81
George 90
Hugh 91
John 90,91
Margaret 90
Robert 90
Samuel 90,91
KERSEY, Hannah 73,76,81
Mary 75
William 74,75,76
KEY, Ann 51
Dile 51
James 51
KILBY, Susanna 120
KILLEBREW, Sarah 53
KING, Anne/Anny 127,129
Benjamin 6,28,36
Betsey 126,129
Comfort 24
Deborah 6,16,36
Edward 124,151,153
Elizabeth 6,73,148
Faith 25
Faitha 19
Hannah 151
Henry 15
James 6,70,73,126,129
Jane 6
Jesse 124,143,151
John 6,19
Joseph 6
Lucy 126,129
Mary 6,124,151
Mary Bailey 151
Philip/Phillip 84,94,
124,138,151
Randolph 102,107,120,
126,127
Sally 151
Sarah 151
Thomas 6,50,99,124,151
William 6,148,151
KIRBY, ___ 113
KNIGHT, Daniel 45
Elizabeth 57
William 53,58
KNOT, Mary 14,30
KNOTT, Christian 28
KUR, George 73

LAIN, William 30
LAMB, Robert 102
William 75
LANCASTER, Elizabeth 72,85
James 130
Laurence 48
Lawrence 36,54
Lucy 96
Martha 99
Mary 27,36,54
Robert 6,15,23
Samuel 15,23,35,72
Samuel, Jr. 13
Silvia/Silviah 72,85
William 27
LANCASTOR, Anne 22
Elizabeth 22
Joseph 22
Mary 22
Robert 22
Samuel 22
William 22
LANCESTER, Sammuel 16
LAND, Curtis 1,2
John 1
Mary 1,2
Rebeckah 1

LAND, cont'd:
Robert 1
Thomas 1
William 1
LANDCASTOR, Robert 22
LANDS, Sarah 43
LANE, Batts 147,149
Beckey 113
Benjamin 105
Elizabeth 149
Elizabeth Whitaker 141
Eth'd/Etheldred 90,93,
95,103,114,116
Frederick 105,113,122,
123,144,152
Henry 137,149,152
James S. 147,150,152
Joel 106,147
John 10,82,90,105,106,
107,108,114,123,124,131,
138,147,149
John, Jr. 101,105,108
Joseph 10,105,106,107,
111
Judkins 108
Lucy 114,116,141
Martha 32,141
Mary 10,90,141,142
Micajah 105
Peggy 141
Rebecca 105,106,149
Sally 90,108,113,141
Sarah 105,149
Thomas 10,19,32,55,62,
65,76,77,82,90,112,116,
141,142,149
William 78,82,101,105,
107,108,114,122,123,133,
140,149
LANEER, Sampson 22
LANIER, Elizabeth 12,13
John 70,73,80,81,112
Lucy 80,112
Nicholas 45,53
Priscilla 80
Prissilah 12
Richard 51
Robert 13,34,45,47,52,
63,65,70,80,103,112
Sampson 4
Thomas 10,13,26
William 52
LARKE, James 103
LASHLEY, John 75
Walter 61
William 75
LASHLY, Hannah 49
Joel 49
John 49
Patrick 49
Thomas 49,50
Walter 49,50
William 49
LASLEY, Thomas 61
LATHER, Jane 28
LAUGHTON, Elianor 130
Helenia Read 153
Jennett 130,153
William 127,130,153
William, Jr. 130
LAURENCE, John 85
LAWRENCE, Elizabeath 1
John 1
Thomas 1
LAYLAND, Robert 87,89
LEATH, Elizabeth 20
John 20
Peter 20
Sarah 20
LEDBETTER, Richard 38
Richard, Jr. 38
LEE, Ann 52
Fdward 47,52
Henry 52,53,54

LEE, cont'd:
John 52
LESLIE, Alexander 102
LESLY, Elizabeth 75
LESTER, Andrew 19,21,24,25
LEVERSEDGE, Ann 59
LEWIS, Miles 12
Richard 2,3,12,14,32,52
LIGHTFOOT, Phillip, Jr. 58
William 58
LITEL, William 27
LITLE, Francis 10
LITTEL, Benjamin 27
William 27
LITTELL, John 22
LITTLE, ___ 6
Ann/Anne 22,31,33
Benjamin 27
Boaz 47
Booz 31,33
Catherine 27
Charlotte 138
Elizabeth 94,122
Francis 4,10,46,47,74,
75,89,94,96
Jacob 50
James 94,138
Jane 50
Jesse 121,122,123
John 22,27,42,43,56,66,
73,94,115,121,123,138,
146
Latherine (Catherine?)
27
Martha 94,95,121
Mary 94,138
Patience 27
Polly 138
Pricilla 94
Robert 10,46,47
Samuel 122
Sarah 47,122
William 17,27,40,42,43,
48
LITTELLBOY, Elizabeth 6
LITTLEBOY, Elizabeth 2
Robert 2
LOFTIN, Clee 15
Cornelius 15
Cornelus 15
Elizabeth 15
Mary 15
Rebeckah 15
Sarah 15
William 15
LOFTING, Cornelius 50
William 50
LONG, Ann 59,61,141
Becca 121
Charlotte 121
David 61,119,121,135,
141,146
Edward 43,44
Elizabeth 92
Frances 43
George 29,43
Hannah 55,60,121
Hartwell 110,119,121
Jesse 121
Lewis 43,121
Lucas 110
Marget 29
Mary 29,43,61
Mary Ann 43
Mercy 43
Nancy 121
Rebecca 119
Robert 55,60
Thomas 43
William 43,59,61,119,121
Willis 121,141
LONGBOTTOM, James 8
Jean 8,9
John 8,12

LONGBOTTOM, cont'd:
Samuel 8
Tommos 8
William 8,9,12
LOYD, Richard 100
LUCAS, Ann 95,126
Betsy 126
Charles 3,6,12,15,17,24,
31,45,46,47,52,55,56,58,
63,68,70,88,91,126
Christopher 122,127,128,
130,131,134,137,142,144,
146
Eliza 126
Elizabeth 88,95
Henry 139
James 122
John 68,79,80,83,85,88,
92,93,95,102,107,122,
126,131,134,136,137,139,
140,142,143,144
Mary 68,79,83,88,122,
145
Rebecca/Rebekah 68,91
Sally 88,95
Samuel 68,79,88,134,137,
143,144,145
Sarah 122,126,144
Stephen 58,64,68,69,70,
74,79,81,84,88,91,95,
126,144
Susan 126
Susannah 95
Thomas 88,134,153
William 68,79,88
LUNSFORD, Jesse 133
John 133
Swan 104,106,133
Susannah 133
Thadeus 133
LUPO, Elizabeth Gray 132
LYMBERRY, Armado 111
William 111

MC DANIEL, Ellinor 102
MC DONNAE, Henry 13,14
MC GUREMAN/MC GURIMAN/ MC
GURRIMAN, Duncan 68,86,135
MC INNISH, Donald 55,70
MC INTOSH, Robert 120,121,
122,123,134,135,144,152
MC KENZIE, Ken 68
Kenneth 84
Kennith 24
MC RAE, Christopher 90
Pamelia 90

MABREY/MABRY, Charles 40,
43,57
Cilia 56
Elizabeth 43,58
Francis 14,19,32
Mary 19
Rebecca/Rebeccah 43,57,
58
William 45,52,58
MABURY, Eleanor 29
Francis 29
MACKENZIE, William 132
MACKIE, Charlotte 98
MACKINTOSH, Robert 120
MACLIN, Amy 26
James 5,74
John 5,26,66,74
Mary 74
Sarah 74 (Sary)
William 4,74,76
MACSHODEN, Anne 18
MAC'THOMPSON, Stephen 70
MADDARRA/MADDERA/MADERA/
MA/MADDERRA/MADDERNA/MADRA/
MADDRA/MADRAY,
Ann 52
Ann Cocke 135

MADDERA/MADDERRA, etc.
cont'd from last column:
Bob 95
Christopher 95,116
Diecey/Dicy/Dize 105,
116,151
Elizabeth 52,95,102,116,
118,119
James 37,52,95
Joel 52,95,99,111,116
Joanna/Johanna 40,52
John 40,52,73,105,116,
126
Lenor 95
Lucretia 95
Lucy 52
Martha 52,116
Mary 123
Micajah 90,116
Nancy 116
Priscilla 52,82,116
Rebekah 116
Samuel 95
Sarah 52,83
Silviah 95
Thomas 116
Will/William 40,52,72,
73,74,86,88,95,99,111
Zachariah/Zacharias/
Zach'r/Zecha./Zechariah
Zacha's, 19,40,44,51,52,
92,97,99,119
MAGARRITY, Mary 60
MAGEE, Robert 3
MAGET/MAGETT/MAGGET/MAG-
GETT/MAGIT/MAGOT/MAGGOTT,
Ann 36,38,57,61
Fortune 36
Jane 36
John 75
N. 73
Nicholas 8,11,12,16,18,
28,36,38,61
Nicholas, Jr. 57
Samuel 9,12,17,18,22,24,
25,27,31,35,36,37,38,40,
44,53,54,56,57,60,67
Sarah 92
W. 79
William 66,69,73,78,83,
85,94,107,109,115,119,
124,128,132,135,136,137,
139,141,149
MAHONE, James 140
Lucy 140
Nancy 140
Patsey 140
Sally 140
Susanna 140
William 140
MAITHES, Edward 6
MAJOR, B. 144
B., Jr. 137
Bernard 150
MALLECOTE/MALLICOAT/MALLI-
COTE, George 116
John 149,150
Mildred 135
Thomas 135,144,148
MALLONE, Amey 7
Daniell 7
Drury 7
Nathaniel 7,8
Thomas 7
MALONE, Agnes 37
Amey 37
Anne 37
Elizabeth 37
Hannah 37
John 37
Milley 37
Nathaniel 8
Sarah 37
William 37

MANGUM, Britain 96
Elizabeth 73,101
Henry 96,101,104
John 35
Joseph 66,73
Josiah 108
Martha 73
Nicholas 66
Olive 35,40
Sarah 101
William 40
MARKS, Ann 103
Edward 119
John 79,103,128
Henry 131,139,140,150
MARLOW, Dempsey 92
James 63
William 88
MARRABLE, Hartwell 39
MARRIOT/MARRIOTT, Benjamin
63,82,84,99
Elizabeth 79,97,99
John 82
Mat./Matt. 62,63,71
Matthias 63,65,78,79,81,
82,84,94,96,97,99,101,
104
Mourning 84
Sarah 99
Thomas 82,83,99,101,138
William 4,12,37,41,73,
82,84,89,99
William, Jr. 41,55,60,
61,63
William, Sr. 63
MARSENGILL, James 44
MARSTON, John 146
Susanna 146,150
MARTIN, Mary 6
Sarah 17,19
William 4,17,19
MASON, Elizabeth 10
James 32,50,56,62
John 7,11,32
John, Jr. 25,29,31,39,
47,51,52
Joseph 23,38,45,56,140
Mary 56
Mrs. 16
Phebe 45
MASSENBURG, Elizabeth 147
Lucy 58
N's 52
Nicholas 57,58,59,60,61,
69
MASSEY, John 47
MASSINGELL, James 6
MATHESON, John 70
MATHIAS, Thomas 28
MATTHEWS, Ann 5
Edward 2
MATTHEWSON, John 79
MATTHIS, Owen 93
MATTRIS, John 53
MAVERY, Mary 96
MAYBRY, Charles 43
Cornelieus 43
Ebill 43
Elizabeth 43
Emidie 43
Francis 43
Mary 43
Rebeccah 43
William 43
MAYBURY, Eleanor 14
MAYNARD, Edward 136
MEACHUM, Harry 50
Henry 52
MEACUM, John 102
MEAD, Jane 85
John 85
MEARNS, William 29
MECHUM, Henry 8
MEED, Jane 82

168

PITT, cont'd:
  Lucy 46,114
  Milia 46
PLEASANT, Abigail 121
  Buford 65,121
  Burwell 121
  George 121
  Thomas 121
  William 104,110,121
POLLARD, Arthur 30
POND, Daniel 101,113,118,
  120
  Hannah 118
  John 113,118
  Mary 118
  Matthew 118
PORCH, Henry 7,8,12,52
  James 7,8,12
  Margery 7
PORTCH, James 8
PORTER, Edward 135,136,153
  Elizabeth 153
POWELL, John 49
  Lyon 130
  Mary 54
POYTHRESS, _____ 61
  Eliza 64
  Joshua 64
  Mary 64
  Peter 45
  William 64,76
PRESCOTT, Ann 42
  Rachell 42
PRESSON, Ann/Anne 130,138
  Betsey 130
  Elizabeth 96,128,138
  John 83,90,110,119,128,
  130,132,138,140
  John, Jr. 89,130,152
  Lucy 130,138
  Richard 65,66,78,83,96,
  152
  Sarah 95
  Thomas 65,152
  Tomar/Tomer/Toomer 126,
  128,138,139
PRETLOW, Ann 61,115,142
  Benjamin 115,132
  Charlotte 132
  Jane 115,132
  John 61
  Joseph 30
  Joshua 61,94
  Kezia 115
  Mary 115
  Rebecca/Rebekah 61,62,
  94,98,115,132
  Samuel 61,92,94,106,115,
  124,132
  Thomas 61,62,94,115,125,
  132,140,142,149
  Thomas, Jr. 27,106
  William 61,76
PRICE, David 107,131,146
  Davis 106
  Elizabeth 106,153
  Francis 31,40
  Hannah Copland 84,86,95
  James 83,84,92,95,103,
  107,110
  John 5,41,44
  Lucy 107,116
  Martha 27,83,84,86
  Randolph 84,90,91,95,96,
  103,105,107,110,111,115,
  131,146,147
  Rebecah/Rebekah 84,86
  Richard 7,14
  Samuel 84,85,86
  Silvere 84
  Silviah 86
PRINCE, Betty 67
  Edward 8
  Edward, Jr. 8

PRINCE, cont'd:
  Henry 67
  Nathan 67
  Nicholas 67
PRITCHARD, Casey 42
  Elizabeth 42,43
  John 42
  Morris 42,43
  Richard 42
PRICHETT, Morris 24
PRITLOW, Sarah 63
  Thomas 100
  Thomas, Jr. 42
  William 63,83
PROCTOR, Joshua 35,41,54
  Mary 35
  Richard 41
PROTER, Nicholas 4
PULLEY, Elizabeth 103
  Lewis 78,89,90,102,103,
  109,111,120,122
  Lucy 102
  Robert 79
  William 65,75,102,111
  William, Jr. 59,60
  William, Sr. 81,82
PULLY, Hanah 20
  John 15
  Lewis 94,95,114,115
  Marther 20
  Mary 20
  William 20,67,69,93
  William, Jr. 46
  William, Sr. 20
PURKINSON, Travis 153
PUTNEY, Benjamin 100,107,
  110,111,132
  David 90,107,111
  Ellis 107,111
  James 107,111,116
  John 148
  Lewis 107,110,111
  Rebecca/Rebeckah 107,110
  Richard 68,88,107,109,
  111,126
PUTTNEY, Benjamin 60
  James 60
  Richard 60
  Sarah 60

RACHEL, John 50
  Sarah 88
RACKLY, Anthony 20
RAE, Elizabeth 88
  Francis 88
  Hannah 127
  James 41,88,95,99,102,
  108,111,143
  John 127
  Lucy 88
  Martha 127
  Mary 88
  Robert 71,88
  William 127,153
RAIN, Duejates 11
  William 11
RAINES, _____ 4
  Hannah 5
  John 5
  Nathaniel 5
  Richard 5
RALSTON, David 70,74
RALTSTON, David 71
RAMSEY, Anney 102
  Benjamin 102
  James 111
RANDALL, George 31,34
  Mary 31,34,45
  Peter 28
RANDOL, Mary 28
  Peter 28
RANDOLPH, William 111
RANEY, William 31
RANSOM, Catherine 26

RANSOM, cont'd:
  Elizabeth 26
  Grisell 31
  Grissell 26
  Gwathmy 26
  James 5,10,26,31
  Mary 26
  Richard 19,20,25
RASCOW, Mary 29
  Mrs. 29
  William 29
RAWLINGS, Gregory 3,8,9,28,
  43
  William 20,25,60
RAWSER, Elizabeth 45
  Susanna 45
RAY, Affiah 25
  Francis 25
  John 52
  Lenard 15
  Martha 15,16,29
  Marthay 15
  William 4,15,16,25
READ, Clement 41
READE, Given 64
  Martha 64,113
  Robert 64
REDBOND, Peter 97
REDBURN, Peter 86,89
REECKS, Benjamin 61
REED, Gwin 113
  Martha 113
REEKES, Benjamin 22
  Jane 11
  Philip 73
  Thomas 11
REEKS, Benjamin 12,25,43,61
  Charles 89,103
  Elizabeth 35,103
  Faith 35
  Mary 35,103
  Philip 103
  Sarah 35,103
  Thomas 35,60,103
REEX, Thomas 36
REGAN, John 69
  Mary 6
REIGNS, John 3
REIVES, Timothy 53
REN/RENN, Joseph 47
  Sarah 31
  Thomas 59
  William 1,31
RESPESS/RESPISS/RISPES/
RISPESS/RISPIS/RISPUS,
  Ann/Anne 66,69
  Christopher 66
  Mary 66
  Richard 66,84,90,96
  Robert 66
  Thomas 66,67,131
REVELY, John 136
  Mary 136
REYNOLDS, Sharp 125
RHOADS, Benjamin 129
  John 129
RICHARDSON, Arthur 37,38,
  53,56
  Betty 39
  Elizabeth 40
  Hardy 40
  Hopkin 40
  John 40
  Joseph 39
  Martha 39
  Mary 39
  Patty 39
  Susanna 39
  William 3,39,51
RICHESSON, William 2
RICKS, Benjamin 59
  Charles 59,89
  Elizabeth 59
  Mary 59

RICKS, cont'd:
  Philemon 59
  Roberts 10
  Sarah 59
  Thomas 59
RIDLEY, James 41
  Mary 149
RIGGAN, Ann 147
  Benjamin 82,83,86,122,
   140
  Jane 6
  Jesse 82
  John 82,83
  Mary 82
  Sarah 122
  Thomas 144
  William 82,83,86,101,
   105,122,123,124
RIVERS, Hones 80
  John 80
RIVES, Anthony 147
  Charles Binns 147
  Christopher 38
  Elizabeth 147
  Frances 38,39
  Francis 53
  George 34,38,39,147
  John 38,45,53
  Judith 38
  Martha 147
  Richard 24,25,34,36
  Sarah 45
  Timothy 38,147
  William 38
ROBARDS, Elizabeth 27
  John 27
  Nazereth 27
ROBBERTSON, Christopher 13
ROBERSON, Mary 3
ROBERTS, Elizabeth 29
  Faith 25
  Frederick 44
  Hannah 140
  Mike 140
  Nat/Nathaniel 29,140
  Willat 51
  Williart, Jr. 51
  Willott 41
  Willut 25
ROBERTSON, Drury 13
  Elizabeth 13,51,52,71
  George 39,50
  Nathanell/Nathaniel 13
  William 52,71
ROBINS, Peter 15
ROBINSON, Elizabeth 71
  William 71
ROGERS, Benjamin 35
  Joanna 140
  Mary Haynes 141
  William 11,28,49
ROOKING, Ellen 65
ROOKINGS, Elizabeth 20,26
  Ellen 46,61
  Ellin 19,58
  James 14,20,23,28,34,42,
   43,47
  W. 11
  William 3,8,9,20,22,23,
   26,28,30,34,42,43,45,58,
   61
ROSE, Benjamin 145
  Elizabeth 16,64,66,81,
   82
  Frances 2
  Hannah 16,23
  Jane 16,17
  John 145
  Mary 20
  Richard 16,17,23
  Samuel 145
  Thomas 16,127
  W./William 2,13,27,38,51,
   53,81,82,121,145,147

ROSEMAN, Lucy 101
ROSSER, John 24
ROTTENBERRY, John 54,55
  Susanna 55
ROTTENBURY, Elizabeth 49
  John 5,16,19,45,49
  Lucy 49
  Mary 49
  Rachel 49
  Susanna 5,16,49
  Susannah 19,49
ROWELL, Mary 38,114
  Richard 17,18,38,65,70,
   73,76,83,92,94,95,103,
   104,105,106,107,109,
   110,111,112,114,115,
   120,121,123,124,128
  Richard, Jr. 133
  Robert 38,55,57,123
  Samuel 148
  Sarah 128
ROWLAND, Elizabeth 54
  John 54
  Joshua 54
  Simon 13
  William 54
ROYAL, Lucy 97
  Rebecca 97
ROYALL, William 83
RUFFIN, Ann 32,148
  Benjamin 59,61,62,65,
   74,79
  Capt. 19
  Edmond/Edmund 25,26,32,
   41,51,55
  Edmund, Jr. 98
  Elizabeth 95
  Francis 114,132,143,145
  Jane 151
  John 10,15,23,26,29,31,
   33,35,41,47,51,54,56,59,
   61,63,69,73,74,76,98
  John, Jr. 98
  Joseph 138
  Lucy 93,98
  Martha 15,73
  Robert 51,56,94
  Mrs. S. 151
  Theoderick B./Bland 98,
   151
  Thomas 98
  Will/William 56,73,75,
   77,84,89,93,95,96,98,
   138,151
  William F. R./Robert
   151
RUNN, James 49
RUSSEL/RUSSELL, Philleman
  61
  Samuel 94

SAFFOLD, Elizabeth 22
SAFFORD, William 59,61
ST. GEORGE, Hamilton Usher
  88
SALTER, John 91,109,110
  Mary 151
  Sarah 109
  Wil/Will/William 62,66,
   68,76,77,78,82,86,92,
   105,106,109,110,112,114,
   126,129,130,133,141,151,
   153
  Wil, Jr. 82
SANDS, ___ 9
  Samuel 15,19
SAUNDERS, John 61
  William 7,10
SAVAGE, Henry 28,59
  Lovelace 28
  Mary 28
  William 59
SAVIDGE, Andrew 86
  Benjamin 86,87

SAVIDGE, cont'd:
  Cherry Cocks 142
  David 139,140
  Edwin 104
  Elizabeth 86,87,123
  Hannah Bruton 142
  Hartwell 104,150
  Henry 43,52
  Hezekiah 104
  James 104,139
  Jane 79
  Joel 86,123,124,139,140,
   144,153
  John 86,139,140
  Josiah 134,150,153
  Mary 30,74,79
  May 86
  Nathaniel 142
  Rebecca 104
  Robert 142
  Sarah 104,123
  Susanna 142
  Thomas 120
  Will/William 104,116
  Willis 104
SAWREY, Henry 30
SCAMMEL/SCAMMELL, James 148
  John 148
  Mary 148
  Richard 88,93,94,126,
   131,141,148,150
  Silviah 116
  Thomas 148
  Will/William 147,148,
   152
SCARBRO/SCARBROUGH/SCARBROW,
  Edward 32
  Frederick 75,91
  Joanna/Joannah 28,67,74
  William 29,63,64,68,75,
   88,91
SCOGGEN, William 7
SCOTT, Adam 10
  Comfort 10
  David 77,79,81
  Elizabeth 125
  John 31
  Joseph 125
  William 125
SEAT, Bilusson 20
  James 20
  Joseph 19,21,27
  Mable 20
  Marchell 19
  Marshall 27
  Mary 20
  Thomas 19
SEBRELL, Benjamin 42,54,
   59,69
  Daniel 41,42,54,59,69
  David 30,31,149,150
  Elizabeth 42,54,59,120,
   121
  James 137,139
  John 127
  Joseph 42,54,59,69,71
  Lidia 42
  Martha 115
  Mary 42,46
  Moses 42,54,59,60
  Naomi 42
  Nathaniel 30,46,82,83,
   88,98,102,120,126,127,
   128,145,149
  Nicholas 142
  Samuel 4,42,54,59,69
  Sarah 30,54
  Susannah 30
SERGENTON, William 25
SEWARD, Albridgton 140
  Ann 72
  Carter 113
  Caufield/Caufill/Cofield/
   Coufield 100,106,115,140

www.ingramcontent.com/pod-product-compliance
Lightning Source LLC
Chambersburg PA
CBHW021828020426
42334CB00014B/528